RELIGION AND THE MAKING OF
NAT TURNER'S VIRGINIA

THE AMERICAN SOUTH SERIES
Edward L. Ayers, Editor

RELIGION

and the Making of

NAT TURNER'S VIRGINIA

Baptist Community and Conflict,
1740–1840

Randolph Ferguson Scully

University of Virginia Press   *Charlottesville and London*

University of Virginia Press
© 2008 by the Rector and Visitors of the University of Virginia
All rights reserved
Printed in the United States of America on acid-free paper

First published 2008

9 8 7 6 5 4 3 2 1

LIBRARY OF CONGRESS CATALOGING-IN-PUBLICATION DATA

Scully, Randolph Ferguson, 1970–
  Religion and the making of Nat Turner's Virginia : Baptist community and
conflict, 1740–1840 / Randolph Ferguson Scully.
    p. cm. — (The American South series)
  Includes bibliographical references and index.
  ISBN 978-0-8139-2738-1 (alk. paper)
  1. Baptists—Virginia—Southampton County—History—18th century.
  2. Baptists—Virginia—Southampton County—History—19th century.
  3. Turner, Nat, 1800?–1831—Influence. 4. Southampton Insurrection, 1831–
  5. Southampton County (Va.)—Church history—18th century. 6. Southampton
County (Va.)—Church history—19th century. I. Title.
  BX6248.V8S38 2008
  286'.175555209033—dc22

2008000077

For Joan, Naomi, and Marta

CONTENTS

TABLES

ACKNOWLEDGMENTS

LIKE ALL BOOKS, this one would not exist without the liberal and varied support offered by countless people and institutions. And as with most first books, the debts of gratitude have accumulated in multiple layers as both the project itself and the academic career with which it is entwined have evolved over the years.

Some of the earliest and most fundamental debts are to the exceptional teachers who inspired and nurtured my emerging love for the study of history. At Williams College, Robert Dalzell, Charles Dew, Shanti Singham, and especially Patricia Tracy introduced me to both subject matter and analytical approaches that have remained at the center of my interests. At the University of Pennsylvania, Richard Dunn, Richard Beeman, Drew Faust, Michael Zuckerman, Kathleen Brown, and Lynn Hunt expertly facilitated my initiation into the deeper mysteries of historiography and historical thinking.

Drew Faust supervised the dissertation on which this book is based, and her dedication, brilliance, and generosity are so well and widely known that it is hard to add anything except to say that her reputation does not do her justice. I cannot imagine a better mentor or role model. Richard Dunn and Michael Zuckerman introduced me to the graduate study of early American history, and both helped oversee this project from its very earliest stages. Kathy Brown provided invaluable insights, advice, and assistance when the project was only slightly further along and continued to do so as it grew and evolved. I am deeply grateful to all of them for their example, guidance, and feedback.

As the project progressed, I was extremely fortunate to find a supportive home at the McNeil (née Philadelphia) Center for Early American Studies. As directors of the center, Richard Dunn and Daniel Richter have done a tremendous service to early American history in developing the MCEAS into the diverse and intellectually vibrant institution that it is today. I thank them both for those efforts and for their personal kindness and support. Through the MCEAS I met a number of people who have influenced my work and made the process of research and writing more enjoyable and fruitful in countless ways: Amy Baxter-Bellamy, Krista Camenzind, Seth Cotlar, Konstantin Dierks, Carolyn Eastman, Rodney Hessinger, Brooke Hunter, Ann Kirshner, Albrecht Koschnik, Brendan McConville, Roderick McDonald, John Murrin, John Wood Sweet, and Colleen Terrell, as well as many others.

My fellow students of early America at Penn also provided support and stimulation over the entire course of my graduate career. Ed Baptist, John Bezis-Selfa, Niki Eustace, Sarah Knott, Ann Little, Liam Riordan, John Smolenski, Karim Tiro, and Kirsten Wood influenced this project in both small and large ways. I am also grateful to friends at Penn whose influence on this book was perhaps less direct but no less important. Bruce Lenthall, Calista Cleary, Mark Wilkens, Mark Santow, Bob Kane, Michael Kahan, Beth Clement, Kathryn Johnson, Adam Shear, Amy Smith, Leslie Patton, and Beth Hillman all helped make graduate school not just endurable but often actually fun.

Since returning to Virginia, I have continued to benefit from a supportive community of friends and scholars. As I was finishing my dissertation, Sue Fernsebner, René Hayden, and Jen Neighbors provided essential feedback and motivation, as well as the occasional diversion. At George Mason University my colleagues in the Department of History and Art History have been unfailingly helpful and generous. It would be impractical to list them all, but special mention goes to Michael Chang, Robert DeCaroli, Jack Censer, Jane T. Censer, Alison Landsberg, Matt Karush, Shaul Bakhash, Rosemarie Zagarri, Ben Carton, Paula Petrik, and the much-missed Larry Levine.

I would also like to thank the various organizations that provided essential funding for the book. The University of Pennsylvania and the Mellon Foundation funded my years of graduate study, including several years of dissertation research and writing. The Pew Program in Religion and American History and the MCEAS both provided one-year dissertation fellowships. I also benefited from short-term fellowships at the David Library of the American Revolution and the Virginia Historical Society. More recently, George Mason University has generously supported several rounds of new research and extensive revision with a Junior Faculty Study Leave and a Mathy Junior Faculty Award.

The staff of the Virginia Baptist Historical Society, most notably Darlene Slater Herod, research assistant, and Fred Anderson, executive director, have seen this project grow from its infancy, and it could never have been completed without their good-natured and extremely knowledgeable advice and assistance. Similar thanks are due to the staff of the Library of Virginia, whose remarkable expertise and efficiency have been equally essential to the book. The bulk of my research was conducted at these two archives, but I also received valuable help from the staffs of the Van Pelt Library at the University of Pennsylvania, the Virginia Historical Society, the David Library of the American Revolution, the Filson Historical Society, the University of Kentucky Library, and the Kentucky Historical Society.

I am extremely grateful to those scholars beyond those already named who read and commented on various stages of this book. Many thanks to Dee Andrews, Richard Blackett, Jon Butler, Dan Crofts, Douglas Egerton, Peter Kolchin, Janet Lindman, Donald Mathews, Roderick McDonald, John McKivigan, Alison Olsen, John Howard Smith, Harry Stout, and Christopher Waldrep. The attendees at the MCEAS seminar at which I presented an early version of this work provided me with months' worth of useful responses. A presentation at the George Mason University Department of History and Art History's Lawrence Levine Faculty Colloquium helped me as I worked through the revision process. Finally, anonymous reviewers for the *Journal of Southern History,* the *Journal of the Early Republic,* and the University of Virginia Press made cogent and detailed critiques that helped me sharpen the book's argument and analysis.

An early version of some of the material in this book appeared in *Explorations in Early American Culture* 5 (2001). Portions of chapters 4 and 5 appeared in the *Journal of the Early Republic* 27 (Winter 2007). My thanks to the publishers of these journals for permission to reprint that material.

Finally, and most importantly, I must thank my family for their support throughout the multiple stages of this project. My parents, Jane and Malcolm Scully, both editors, early on encouraged a love of writing and thinking and an appreciation of the relationship between the two. They read multiple versions and sections of this book and provided useful feedback and commentary, but more important than that has been their unfailing faith and love, which has seen me through far more than this project. My brother, Allen, watched this project evolve over the years and shared the frustrations and the successes with equal good humor and perspective. My in-laws, Naomi and Bill Bristol, also provided love, support, and encouragement, and I consider myself greatly blessed to have had Bill and still to have Naomi in my life.

This book is dedicated to Joan Bristol and to our daughters, Naomi and Marta, for everything.

RELIGION AND THE MAKING OF
NAT TURNER'S VIRGINIA

INTRODUCTION

Nat Turner's Virginia

In late August 1831, in Southampton County, Virginia, the enslaved preacher and prophet Nat Turner led one of the largest and most significant slave rebellions in the history of the United States. In less than a day and a half, beginning in the early morning of August 22, Turner and scores of fellow rebels killed approximately sixty whites, including many women and children. One commentator on the scene described "whole families, father, mother, daughters, sons, sucking babes, and school children, butchered, thrown into heaps, and left to be devoured by hogs and dogs, or to putrify on the spot."[1] An unknown number, probably hundreds, of black men and women also lost their lives, mostly in the days following the uprising, as angry and fearful whites took indiscriminate revenge on southeastern Virginia's black population. *"Many negroes are killed every day,"* wrote one correspondent, "the exact number will never be ascertained."[2] In several instances, the severed heads of suspected rebels were mounted on poles and displayed across the countryside, a practice that gave one Southampton crossroad the grisly, cautionary name Blackhead Signpost. The suddenness and brutal violence of the uprising and its aftermath sent shock waves across the nation and provoked a period of deep introspection and debate among Virginians, both black and white.

As it turned out, the physical suppression of the rebellion was only the beginning of a much wider battle to interpret and control its meaning and significance. The Southampton revolt momentarily exposed the racial and gendered fictions on which antebellum Virginia's social order rested. It shattered the comforting white illusions of reciprocity, respect, and affection between slave and master, and it dramatically demonstrated the inability of white men to protect their households, families, and dependents. These intertwined dimensions of white masculinity and patriarchal authority collapsed in the face of the rebels' determined violence. In response, white Virginians constructed a variety of explanations of the rebellion that preserved or reconstructed their sense of patriarchal order, familial security, and white superiority. Many quickly blamed northern abolitionists for encouraging rebelliousness among slaves, arguing that outsiders' reckless interference in Virginia's domestic institutions jeopardized white lives. Others looked inward, blaming white Virginians' own permissiveness toward slaves and free blacks and calling for a renewed, manly commitment to policing the state's African American population. Still others wondered whether slavery itself might be an intrinsic threat to white security, asking whether white households could ever be safe when "a Nat Turner might be in every family . . . [and] the same bloody deed could be acted over at any time in any place."[3] Such concerns even led the Virginia General Assembly to consider (though eventually reject) a proposal for gradual emancipation promoted by delegates from the western portion of the state.[4]

Like their white counterparts, black Virginians responded to the challenges of the rebellion and its aftermath in a variety of ways. After his capture at the end of October 1831, Turner himself intervened in the ongoing debate by relating his biography and account of the uprising to the white lawyer Thomas R. Gray. First published by Gray in late November, *The Confessions of Nat Turner* gained a wide readership, and the rebel slave's measured voice and disconcerting vision shone through in the text despite Gray's efforts to control and shape the story.[5] The *Confessions* attributed responsibility for the revolt, not to specific white failings, but rather to Turner's own lifelong sense of special purpose and the supernatural visions of bloody conflict and impending judgment that spurred him to gather his accomplices and lead them in a war of retribution against Virginia's white population. Turner's personal agency and leadership took center stage in this narrative, a focus that served both Gray's and Turner's purposes: Gray sought to support the case that Turner was insane, while Turner took the opportunity Gray provided to tell his own story and bring his detailed vision of the divinely inspired, violent overthrow of slavery to a larger audience.

Other black men and women had the double-edged opportunity to tell their own stories of the rebellion when they served as witnesses or defendants in the wave of trials after the uprising. Enslaved Virginians sometimes alleged a more extensive conspiracy or claimed to have heard rumors circulating beforehand, but most denied any foreknowledge of the uprising and presented it as an unexpected and upsetting intrusion into their daily routine: the rebels appeared and killed the white people; some joined them, most did not.[6] Painfully aware of the white backlash and their own vulnerability in the wake of the rebellion, these men and women had to confront and interpret, both for themselves and for a suspicious and shaken white audience, an event that must have expressed dimensions of their own anger and desire for freedom but had rebounded on them and their communities in devastating ways. Ironically, in many cases the surest protection for individuals and communities lay precisely in the reconstruction of the white patriarchy and self-interest that the rebellion had undermined, as slaves and free blacks relied on white masters, employers, or neighbors to vouch for their character and assure other whites of their future good behavior. In public and in private, from the halls of the legislature to county courthouses to rural churches, farms, and quarters, Virginians of both races strove to understand and to assert their own interpretations of why the rebellion had occurred, what it meant, and how they should respond.

As they sought to answer such questions, Virginians returned repeatedly to the theme of religion. Indeed, religion, and in particular the evangelical varieties of Christianity that had come to dominate Virginia's religious landscape in the nineteenth century, became central to the battle to understand, define, and control the Nat Turner revolt. Even before accurate details about Turner and his religious vision emerged, white Virginians assumed that the rebellion had religious roots. One account written on August 23 attributed the uprising to "about 250 negroes from a Camp Meeting about the Dismal Swamp."[7] Another reported on August 24 that "the prevalent belief is, that on Sunday week last at Barnes's [Methodist] Church in the neighborhood of the Cross Keys, the negroes who were observed to be disorderly, took offence at something . . . [and] that the plan of insurrection was then and there conceived."[8] In their rush to judge and to explain the revolt, these white commentators revealed deep underlying anxieties about the place of evangelical beliefs and institutions in Virginia society, despite their pervasiveness.

As more complete and reliable information about the revolt and Nat

Turner's prophetic leadership came to light, religious issues became the subject of intense debates about the uprising's underlying extent and nature. Some whites, including Virginia governor John Floyd, believed that Turner represented a broad network of insurrectionary black evangelical preachers who had planned a much more extensive conspiracy.[9] Others, like Gray, argued that Turner's apocalyptic vision marked him as a crazed fanatic who had only mustered a few gullible or bloodthirsty followers.[10] In this more limited construction of the rebellion, enthusiastic religion was a dangerous delusion that could mislead susceptible individuals, but it was not the larger, potentially revolutionary force envisioned by Floyd.[11] Turner's own account in the *Confessions* suggested a very different model. When questioned by Gray, he denied the existence of a wider network beyond his own followers, but he also implied that his inspiration was not merely individual but universal, contained in the dictates of Christianity and prophetic revelation. "Can you not think," he asked Gray, "the same ideas, and strange appearances about this time in the heaven's might prompt others, as well as myself, to this undertaking?"[12] From a variety of perspectives, both white and black, interpreting and framing the rebellion's religious content became a crucial part of assessing the revolt's size, significance, and larger implications.

White religion as well as black fell under suspicion. Some commentators suggested that white evangelicals had inadvertently contributed to the revolt by spreading their "ranting cant about equality," encouraging the "heated imaginations" of black fanatics.[13] But others defended evangelicalism from such criticisms, arguing that "true religion" would have restrained the "horrid, natural passions" on display in the revolt.[14] One insisted on a strictly institutional definition of religion, complaining that "this fellow [Turner] is very improperly represented to be a Baptist preacher. . . . He never was a member of the Baptist, or any other Church; he assumed that character of his own accord . . . and [was] never countenanced except by a very few of his deluded black associates."[15] White evangelicals themselves were not always so confident, however. Churches across the region reported a "painful dissatisfaction" with their black members and "an entire loss of confidence in their religious feeling." Black church members expressed their own confusion and suspicion of white motives in the wake of the rebellion, reportedly becoming "exceedingly refractory and ungovernable, refusing . . . the rule of the Church, and disobeying the injunctions of the Gospel."[16] When one church voted to retain its black members despite these tensions, a group of white members withdrew and refused to return for over a year because they "do not fellowship the Colured members of this Church."[17]

The debate about the Turner rebellion and its meaning had become a wide-ranging and multifaceted argument about religion. As advocates of different understandings of the revolt built their competing interpretations, it was impossible to discuss the uprising and its implications without addressing issues of religious authority, religious authenticity, religious legitimacy, and religious community. This book explores why and how this was so by reconstructing a vital segment of the contentious, biracial religious history that shaped the cultural and social world of Nat Turner's Virginia. Focusing on the remarkable and complex history of the Baptist denomination, it traces the rise and evolution of evangelical Christianity in southeastern Virginia from the mid-eighteenth to the mid-nineteenth century. By the time Turner led his fellow slaves on their deadly march across the fields and swamps of Southampton County, Virginia's religious landscape had been molded by more than eighty years of conflict about the implications of evangelical faith for the evolving, interrelated ideas about race, slavery, household, family, and patriarchy that underlay the state's social order. As the largest evangelical group among both blacks and whites in Virginia, the Baptists were at the heart of this process. The detailed records kept by Baptist churches provide unique insight into the ways the rapid growth of evangelicalism in the Old Dominion reshaped the patterns of thought and community that underlay the colonial order and brought Africans and African Americans into dialogue with their white neighbors in powerfully charged new ways. This relationship continued to evolve through the years of the American Revolution and into the nineteenth century as both black and white Virginians sought to elaborate evangelicalism's implications for their conceptualization of their relationship to God and to one another. The religious tensions and disagreements apparent in the rebellion and its aftermath were both a product and a continuation of this much longer history.

In taking up this longer history I pursue two complementary lines of analysis. First, I seek to enrich our understanding of the Turner revolt by tracing out in detail the complexities of its religious content and context. This context illuminates the rebellion's roots in racial and theological tensions within the religious culture of early nineteenth-century

Virginia, and these tensions in turn shed light on the nature of the threat the uprising presented to the state's social order and on the character of the debate that emerged in the months that followed. Second, and more fundamentally, I use the Turner uprising itself to shed new light on the religious history of Revolutionary and early national Virginia. The rebellion and its aftermath revealed a degree of diversity and disagreement about evangelicalism's meanings—both between and among black and white believers—that is often overlooked or minimized in the story of evangelicalism's successful conquest of the American South. Incorporating the Turner rebellion into the narrative of evangelicalism's rise in Virginia requires a reconceptualization of that narrative. By moving the multivalence of the movement's theology, language, and practice and the diversity of its adherents to the center of the story, I seek to provide a more complex and complete vision of this process. From this perspective, the Turner rebellion is as important for what it reveals about this larger story as it is in its own right.

Ultimately, then, this book is not primarily about slavery, slave community, or even slave rebellion, although it addresses all of those topics. Instead, it is most fundamentally a cultural and social history of an evolving religious movement that was embraced by both black and white Virginians, albeit often in different ways and for different purposes. It is a study of how religious issues of authority, authenticity, legitimacy, and community intersected with Virginians' ideas and practices of slavery, race, gender, and household and, more particularly, the ways in which specifically Baptist beliefs, discourses, and institutions mediated interactions between black and white Virginians from the mid-eighteenth to the mid-nineteenth century. These issues pervaded the Turner rebellion and its aftermath, but they also had deep roots in Virginia's history. By tracing those roots, I seek to illuminate not simply the rebellion itself but the creation and elaboration of the religious world in which the rebellion took shape—the making of Nat Turner's Virginia.

In Virginia, as in much of the rest of the nation, the dramatic expansion of evangelical religion was among the most significant cultural transformations of the Revolutionary era. Between about 1750 and 1830 the dominant modes of religious adherence and expression in Virginia were completely remade as evangelical groups like the New Side Presbyteri-

ans, the Baptists, and the Methodists challenged and eventually over-
threw Virginia's Anglican establishment. Like other eighteenth-century
revivalists, proponents of these movements preached the necessity of a
profound, inward conversion and deeply felt, "experimental" religion.
This inner change and emotional experience of faith represented the vital essence of Christianity for revivalists; without it the outward forms
and intellectual doctrines of religion were meaningless. In public and in
private, evangelical spokesmen railed against spiritual complacency and
the worldly forces that held back "true" religion's advance. In this vein,
some white evangelicals also made a point of reaching out to Virginia's
enslaved population, arguing that the establishment and its supporters
had shamefully neglected their duty to Christianize and instruct those
over whom they claimed oversight. For their own part, early black converts found a number of attractions in evangelicalism, in combinations
that undoubtedly varied according to person, time, and place. The broad
emotional and expressive range of evangelical worship could allow selective incorporation of (or offer parallels to) African and Afro-Virginian
spiritual and expressive practices. Some white evangelicals provided
interested blacks instruction in reading and writing, and evangelical
practices and institutions sometimes offered support for black family
and community life. Moreover, evangelicals' conversion-centered theology of liberation and transcendence resonated with slaves' own desires
for personal and communal freedom, whether in literal or metaphorical
terms, and their emphasis on lay spiritual authority sometimes opened
positions of leadership to black men who could serve as preachers or
exhorters.

For these very reasons, many—probably most—white eighteenth-
century Virginians perceived evangelical groups as a threat to the proper
ordering of society. Evangelicals' seemingly unrestrained emotionalism,
their disruptive rejection of established authorities and withdrawal from
the state church, and their self-conscious appeal to subordinate groups
like women, young people, slaves, free blacks, and poor whites marked
them as careless of time-honored social restraints at best and willfully
subversive at worst. The relative success of emerging evangelical denominations among many of these groups served to reinforce these anxieties.
Such concerns intensified in the years surrounding the American Revolution as a small but prominent minority of white southern evangelicals vocally supported the abolition of slavery. This only confirmed other

white Virginians' fears that evangelicals' rejection of traditional authority led them to reckless and destructive extremes. Even as evangelical denominations gained adherents at all levels of society, many white Virginians felt that these new religious movements undermined essential relationships of race, family, gender, household, and community.

In the decades following the American Revolution, influential white evangelical leaders sought to assuage these concerns. They worked to reshape their denominations to contain the aspects of their faith that produced the most resistance. By 1800 the vast majority of white leaders definitively rejected anti-slavery activism as counterproductive and divisive and branded the few remaining holdouts as either misguided idealists or self-aggrandizing troublemakers. Black men and women joined evangelical churches in increasing numbers in the early nineteenth century, but a host of small changes in rules of order and church practices tightened white male control of formal evangelical institutional life, and new regional and national organizations allowed ministers and prominent laymen to set and police the boundaries of denominational orthodoxy more effectively. More diffuse but equally important was a wide-ranging rhetorical effort to make evangelicalism central to the very relationships that its colonial opponents accused it of threatening. White evangelical leaders argued that true conversion made subordinates more obedient and more dutiful and superiors more kind and more just. By imbuing household relationships with Christian fellowship, they argued, evangelicalism would help ensure the stability and security of those relationships and of the white household itself. This newly articulated vision inverted earlier critiques of evangelicalism by claiming that it did not subvert existing social relations but in fact preserved and even improved them. By the 1820s evangelical denominations dominated Virginia's religious market, and white evangelical spokesmen were doing their best to help Virginians forget their movements' controversial history.

Nat Turner's Southampton revolt exposed the explosive tensions and contradictions of that history once again. Evangelicalism reemerged in public debate as a contested, problematic, and, most importantly, biracial force, undermining spokesmen's attempts to link it to the health and improvement of the white household. The uprising and subsequent debate indicated that white leaders' vision of evangelical religion was only one of many that held sway in different sections of Virginia society and demonstrated that those leaders' ability to impose their vision on others had very real limits. Both the content and the form of Turner's prophetic leadership highlighted the revolutionary potential of black interpretations of evangelical principles, and as a consequence black men and women found that the religious communities they had created in the interstices of white-controlled institutions had become objects of intense scrutiny and suspicion. White leaders who had sought to minimize the extent and independence of black religious activity found themselves confronted with distressing evidence to the contrary and faced renewed criticism from white opponents of evangelicalism. By bringing to light these subterranean currents of diversity and conflict in Virginia's religious order, the Turner rebellion revealed a world of evangelical belief and practice that was much larger and messier than most white Virginians, at least, wished to acknowledge.

The dimensions of the religious world revealed by the Turner uprising provide a new perspective on the central paradox in the history of southern evangelicalism: the contrast between its radical, seemingly proto-democratic tendencies in the eighteenth century and its central place in the conservative, proslavery ideologies of the white South in the decades preceding the Civil War.[18] The question of how a marginal dissenting movement that rejected the hierarchical, gentry-dominated values and practices of colonial Virginia became a powerful cultural and social support for the white South's particularistic defense of slavery and patriarchy in the antebellum era dominates historians' analysis of the movement. The most common explanation of this transformation is a narrative of declension in which white evangelicals gradually compromised and contained the most radical and egalitarian elements of their faith, particularly any anti-slavery tendencies, in exchange for more white converts and greater worldly influence.[19] In this view, nineteenth-century white evangelicals' use of their religious authority to support a paternalist justification of slavery and deference represented a nearly complete reversal of evangelicalism's eighteenth-century moral skepticism about worldly hierarchies: "the radicals had become the guardians" of a proslavery social and cultural order.[20]

More recently, some historians have reconsidered the extent of evangelical radicalism in the eighteenth century. These historians outline the ways in which white evangelicals' own ideas about and practices of race, family, household, and gender facilitated the compromises that brought their style of faith into the mainstream of southern culture and eventually into the service of proslavery conservatism and southern sectionalism.[21] Despite differences on issues of timing and other details, these accounts collectively highlight the point that conservatism, particularly with regard to gender and race, was a powerful force from a very early period in evangelicalism's development in the South, and they argue that these conservative dimensions were at least as responsible for its rise in the eighteenth century as any tentative radical implications. In this view, evangelicalism did not simply accommodate itself to white southern paternalism in the nineteenth century; it was a vital constitutive element of that paternalism.

The unruly history of Nat Turner's Virginia, however, serves as a powerful reminder that the triumph of a white, paternalist vision of evangelicalism was neither inevitable nor complete. The contentiousness and biracial complexity of the religious world of southeastern Virginia lead us away from large-scale judgments about radicalism or conservatism to a more specific examination of how the diverse black and white constituencies of evangelicalism in Virginia understood the implications of their faith and how they pursued those implications in dialogue with one another. The language, rituals, and institutions of that faith provided a common discourse of spiritual and moral significance that appealed to some Virginians at every level of society, but even those within the churches never fully agreed on the worldly import of these powerful spiritual imperatives. Through its emphasis on divine power, human humility, personal piety, and Christian fellowship, evangelicalism created a framework of authority, justice, and meaning that did not map directly onto worldly relationships. Deciding how to apply these principles in practice constituted much of the day-to-day business of evangelical communities, and disagreements and inconsistencies abounded. By moving this process to the foreground and making it the center of analysis, this book recast the evolution of evangelicalism as an ongoing process of interpretation and contestation rather than a one-way shift from radicalism to conservatism. The development and increasing power of a white paternalist vision of evangelicalism was undeniably real, and it remains a central part of the story, but situating this vision within the broader evangelical world revealed by the Turner rebellion emphasizes the contingency of both its rise and its dominance.

My focus on contingency and diversity reflects an underlying conceptual and theoretical orientation shaped by current trends in cultural history. In an important recent article, William H. Sewell Jr. describes cultural theorists' gradual move away from conceptions of culture that emphasize the systematic, coherent, highly integrated, and clearly bounded nature of cultural systems and communities toward a more historicist vision that treats culture "as a sphere of practical activity shot through by willful action, power relations, struggle, contradiction, and change." In this view, cultural meanings are not simply the product of a shared system of symbolic relationships but are constantly contested and reshaped through the deployment of symbols in practice. This process requires only the most minimal agreement among the participants about the nature and meaning of the symbols they use; they may constitute a "semiotic community" that recognizes the same general set of symbols, but that does not mean that they will use or value the symbols in similar ways or that they will "form a community in any fuller sense." Rather than being inherent aspects of symbolic systems, coherence, boundedness, and integration "must result from the way [a system's] semiotic structures are interlocked in practice with other structures—economic, political, social, spatial, and so on."[22] Culture cannot be reduced to these other structures, nor can it be fully understood independently of them. This conception of the way culture works is extraordinarily valuable for historians because it accords with their concern for conflict, context, and change over time while also providing a way of understanding how culture shapes actions and opportunities in ways that may run counter to or mitigate the impact of social, political, or economic forces.

Applying this approach to the religious evolution of Revolutionary and early nineteenth-century Virginia is not to deny the real impact of increasing white, male control or the conservative force of white evangelicalism. Instead, it allows us to understand those realities in a more complete and productive way, as part of an ongoing struggle to impose coherence and boundaries on a complex, overlapping, and mutually implicating compound of religious ideas, institutions, and practices. The model described by Sewell encourages us to see this struggle as a contradictory, decentralized process rather than a straightforward application of power or social control. In some instances, of course, there was an intentional and systematic effort on the part of white denominational

leaders to impose specific ideological orthodoxies or institutional practices, but in large part coherence evolved as an unintentional by-product
of decisions and compromises made by a variety of actors, black and
white, for a variety of reasons.

As Virginians of different sorts joined together in evangelical fellowship, they gradually developed working understandings of the meaning
of that fellowship and the range of acceptable interpretation of common
symbols and concepts. The white men who controlled the institutional
church exercised disproportionate power in these implicit negotiations,
but even they did not always or necessarily present a united front in promoting particular interpretations of evangelicalism's meaning. In many
cases, conflicts and other difficult issues were deferred or ignored for
as long as possible, leaving substantial room for varying interpretations
as long as those interpretations did not directly challenge the larger
community. What this meant was that the kind and degree of coherence
evangelicalism attained in the early nineteenth century were shaped not
only by white men's reflexive desire to protect their own privilege but
also by the individual and collective actions and beliefs of the movement's increasingly diverse constituency. Through their very participation in rituals of community, discipline, and authority, black men and
women influenced the shape of evangelical life in profound ways. Under
these circumstances, the coherence that evolved over time was fragile,
dependent on a delicate balance of forces and vulnerable to disruption
from any number of directions.

The social, cultural, and political ferment of the late eighteenth
and early nineteenth centuries further complicated attempts to maintain clear boundaries and unitary meanings in evangelicalism. Sewell
points out that the transfer of meanings from one context to another
is a crucial element of cultural practice, allowing for a significant degree
of agency and change within cultural systems as "actors . . . play on the
multiple meanings of symbols—thereby redefining situations in ways
that they believe will favor their purposes."[23] During and after the American Revolution, evangelicals of all sorts engaged in such transpositions
with particular enthusiasm. One of the most significant of these was the
cross-fertilization between Christian concepts of liberty and liberation
(which had their own complex and sometimes controversial history),
political battles for religious liberty, and debates about slavery and the
racial order of the new nation.

As denominational leaders appropriated the language of republicanism to argue for evangelicalism's central place in the cultural and moral life of the new nation, some activists argued that republican principles, along with Christian ones, required that the churches purge themselves and the nation of the sin of slavery. Their opponents in turn built on the same ideas to very different ends, claiming that such activism violated property rights and represented a form of extreme intolerance that usurped others' freedom of conscience and undermined unity among Christians. Revolutionary and evangelical concepts could be combined in many ways, and the interplay between them provided additional dimensions of creativity, dynamism, and conflict to the religious world of early national Virginia. Nat Turner himself built on these same themes in inspired and unexpected ways, and it was white Virginians' belated recognition of this fact that caused the religious crisis of confidence in the wake of the uprising.

Conceptualizing this complex history as a story of "Nat Turner's Virginia" accomplishes several important goals. As James Sidbury suggests in his evocation of Gabriel's Virginia as an alternative to Jefferson's Virginia, this sort of reframing broadens our vision and allows us to grapple with the "divergent meanings of Revolutionary Virginia's history for those who lived in it and for those who have been influenced by it."[24] More specifically, the idea of Nat Turner's Virginia brings together the history of the evolving, multifaceted debate about religion, race, and social order and the history of the communities in southeastern Virginia that constituted the geographic and social center of Nat Turner's world. Turner was born in Southampton County in 1800, into a community of small and medium farms in which black men and women constituted a slight majority of the population but tended to live in small groups, in close proximity to their white masters and neighbors. Nat Turner's Virginia was thus not merely a discursive or thematic construct; it was also a place where people—white and black, free and enslaved, men and women—lived, worked, worshipped, preached, and played. Highlighting this dimension of Nat Turner's Virginia facilitates a practice-oriented approach to larger cultural processes by focusing our attention on the dynamics of local communities and the ways in which groups and individuals experienced, reacted to, and in turn shaped the ambiguities and tensions in evangelical discourses and institutions.

As a history of Nat Turner's Virginia in all of these senses, this book combines a broad cultural analysis of evangelicalism's rise in Virginia with a close-grained study of Baptist communities in Southampton and neighboring Isle of Wight and Sussex counties. Other denominations, particularly the Methodists, were also active in these counties, but the detailed records of church business and discipline kept by Baptist churches provide unique insight into the daily operation of evangelical communities and the activities of church members, from the most routine matters to the most spectacular conflicts. Reconstructing the history of these churches and their congregations over the course of the Revolutionary era allows us to trace the growth and evolution of evangelicalism while also examining how this process was interpreted, promoted, and resisted at the local level. These communities, shaped by the distinctive social geography and history of southeastern Virginia, provided the most immediately relevant context in which black and white residents negotiated the meanings and implications of evangelical fellowship and shaped their reactions to the violent revolt that made the region the focus of national attention.

Isle of Wight, Southampton, and Sussex counties form a squat "V" in southeastern Virginia between the James River and the North Carolina border. Isle of Wight, the easternmost of the counties, touches the James River at its northeastern end and runs south and west to the Blackwater River, which forms the border with Southampton County. Southampton, formed from Isle of Wight in 1749, continues south and west to the North Carolina border, and Sussex County sits along Southampton's northwest border. In the late eighteenth and nineteenth centuries these counties constituted a rural borderland between southern Virginia's developing commercial and cultural centers of Portsmouth and Norfolk to the east and Richmond and Petersburg to the northwest. Aside from the small strip of Isle of Wight County along the James, these counties were neither fully part of the eighteenth-century Tidewater nor the nineteenth-century Southside. Their rivers, the Blackwater and the Nottoway, ran south toward the Chowan River and Albemarle Sound of North Carolina rather than north toward the James, and were only marginally navigable in any case, making transportation too inconvenient and costly for the development of a large-scale plantation economy. Instead, the counties were dotted with small farms and modest plantations producing hogs, corn, sweet potatoes, peas, a regionally renowned apple brandy, and, in lower Southampton in the nineteenth century, a small amount of cotton for market.[25]

Beginning in the seventeenth century, Quakers, Baptists, and other Protestant nonconformists found shelter in this backwater region, but it was not until the decade before the Revolution that a full-fledged evangelical revival took hold in southeastern Virginia. As both Baptists and Methodists gained converts and expanded their institutional reach, the region played an important role in the debates that shaped evangelical doctrine and practice across the Upper South. These included institutional milestones such as Methodists' decision to split from the Anglican church to organize their own denomination and Baptists' efforts to reconcile the "Separate" and "Regular" traditions in the state, but even more notable were the controversies over slavery that shook both evangelical groups in the closing decades of the eighteenth century. The Southampton County Baptist minister David Barrow and a handful of white church members helped make southeastern Virginia one of the most important centers of post-Revolutionary Baptist anti-slavery activity. The influential southern Virginia Methodist minister James O'Kelly's anti-slavery beliefs were part of his more general break with his denomination's leadership as he hoped to form "a republican, no slavery, glorious Church!"[26] Combined with the continuing influence of Quakers in the region, these leaders and their followers helped make opposition to slavery a significant minority opinion among southeastern Virginia's white population.

Given these distinctive circumstances, Southampton, Sussex, and Isle of Wight do not necessarily stand as representative of all of Virginia. Like the Turner rebellion itself, the history of these counties is valuable not for its typicality but for what it reveals about the larger forces at work in the region and the nation. These counties' very particularity provides unique insights into the social and cultural processes of evangelicalism's rise and its interaction with Virginians' conceptions of order and authority. The existence of relatively strong anti-slavery sentiment and the absence of a powerful, unified white planter class in Isle of Wight, Southampton, and Sussex counties allowed a wide range of interpretations of the meanings of evangelical practice to persist in the region for decades. Competing ideas of evangelical fellowship among both blacks and whites responded to a complex combination of local circumstances and broad ideological developments in the new nation without being overwhelmed by any single set of influences. In this context, the triumph of proslavery evangelicalism in the region was more remarkable, although less complete, than in planter- and plantation-dominated areas in Virginia or the rest of the South.[27] While not necessarily typical in its details, the story of southeastern Virginia's development across the Revolutionary era and into the nineteenth century illustrates tensions that pervaded the Upper South in this period and provides a specific example of how men and women reacted to and shaped these tensions and the social and cultural forces around them.

In order to capture this ongoing interaction between local practice and larger cultural developments, this book interweaves a narrative of evangelicalism's rise in Virginia with the specific history of the Baptist movement in Isle of Wight, Southampton, and Sussex counties. I pay careful attention to both the languages of evangelical faith and the specific practices that instantiated that faith in the world. Indeed, I frequently quote not only the most exalted rhetoric of evangelical ministers and controversialists but also the formulaic language of church minutes and associational reports in order to convey the ways in which these repetitive formulas themselves served as an interpretable discourse of meaning and community. Taking these multiple dimensions of evangelicalism seriously, in all their contradiction and ambiguity, allows us to paint a richer and more complex picture of the ways both black and white Virginians experienced and shaped the religious and social world in which Nat Turner's rebellion took shape.

This book is structured both thematically and chronologically. Each chapter examines a set of ideological and institutional developments that provide context and precedent for what follows, and each subsequent chapter provides an example of the elaboration and often reinterpretation of ideas, institutions, and practices in earlier chapters. Chapter 1 provides a baseline for the larger story of the emergence and shifting meanings of evangelicalism by exploring the development of Virginians' ideas about the relationship between religion and social order in the first half of the eighteenth century. The first stirrings of evangelical awakening in the 1740s gave older conceptions of the nature and meaning of religious dissent new implications and new significance as opponents accused evangelicals of fomenting racial unrest along with other kinds of social disorder. Chapter 2 carries this story further, tracing the rise of the Baptists in southeastern Virginia and the multivalent discourse of personal and social transformation through which Baptist spokesmen articulated their religious vision. Confronted by rhetorical and legal hostility—and even physical violence—in the 1760s and 1770s, Baptists became more aggressive and defiant in their rhetoric. In this context, biblical metaphors of upheaval and liberation sometimes took on literal significance for Baptists, who felt that worldly forces were conspiring against the advance of true Christianity. In chapter 3 I consider the continued elaboration of these ideas among Virginia Baptists of both races during and after the American Revolution as divergent beliefs about the implications of evangelical community for slavery complicated attempts to claim a central place for evangelicalism in the republican cultural and political order of the new nation.

Chapter 4 focuses directly on the dynamics of Baptist communities in Isle of Wight, Southampton, and Sussex from the aftermath of the Revolution to the eve of the Turner revolt itself. It outlines the changing profile of church membership over this period, the experiences of men and women of different races within the church, and the implications of increasing white male control over church government for the practices of evangelical fellowship. It also traces a set of evolving tensions between black and white men within the churches over access to religious authority, particularly in the form of license to preach. By exploring the growing divergence between black and white practices and interpretations of evangelicalism, this chapter sets the stage for a discussion of the Turner rebellion and its implications for evangelical fellowship in southeastern Virginia. The Turner rebellion reflected many of the evolving tensions within evangelical communities in the region, and the anger and distrust in its aftermath threatened to burst those communities apart. Chapter 5 considers both the rebellion itself and the ways in which evangelical community was reconstructed in its wake. Finally, in the epilogue I briefly suggest some of the long-term implications of the compromises created in the rebellion's aftermath for evangelicalism's place in Virginia's cultural order and for the religious interactions between black and white Virginians that it had sustained.

Ultimately, the story of Nat Turner's Virginia is part of a much larger story about how the southern colonies became "the South" of the antebellum era, and this book is one small piece in the larger puzzle of the emergence of the American South in the Revolutionary era. Many of the social and economic changes that shaped this transformation are well known, particularly the rapid movement of the population to the south and west, the decline of eastern tobacco-growing regions, the advent of cotton as a cash crop, and the resulting shift in the geographic center of plantation agriculture and slaveholding. But the ideological and cultural changes are much less completely understood and remain matters of deep disagreement among historians. Virginia and other southern states retained an ideological devotion to white supremacy and black subordination and to a gender system that valorized the patriarchal household and aggressive, competitive masculinity. Those searching for a revolutionary change in the hierarchical, frequently oppressive nature of the social and cultural systems of the southern colonies are hard pressed to find one. Nonetheless, changes did occur, and the rise of evangelicalism was among the most important. Understanding how these changes shaped the discourses of morality, identity, and authority, as well as social practices and institutional life, helps us craft a more nuanced and inclusive vision of the making of the American South and what that process meant for southerners of all races and both sexes.

CHARMING LIBERTY

*Discourses of Establishment and Dissent in
Eighteenth-Century Virginia*

In the spring of 1752 a heated debate about religious diversity and toleration erupted in the pages of the *Virginia Gazette,* the colony's only newspaper. On March 5 a writer calling himself "Philo-Virginia" published a call to exempt Presbyterian immigrants along the frontier from the parish levies that supported the established Anglican church. Pointing to the prosperity enjoyed by Pennsylvania, which he attributed to its growing population of industrious Scots-Irish and German settlers, he asked, "What but Liberty, charming Liberty, is the resistless magnet that attracts so many different Nations into that flourishing Colony?" If Virginia pursued a similarly liberal policy of religious toleration, he argued, it could benefit from a comparable stream of migration, which would settle and develop the colony's frontier. Later that month, on the twentieth, a response appeared from someone who chose the name "Philo-Bombastia" in mock tribute to the earlier author. Philo-Bombastia lived up to his name by aggressively satirizing Philo-Virginia's argument and rhetoric, taking both to unintended and inappropriate extremes. Toleration, he asserted, was such an unmitigated good that it should be expanded to include not just Presbyterians but "Roman Catholicks" and "Free-Thinkers, Infidels, Jacobites, and Convicts, who are *State Dissenters.*" He also lampooned his predecessor's rhapsodic invocations of the benefits of liberty. Tongue firmly in cheek, he claimed that the "*extensive* Toleration" he proposed would "make *England* a Land of Slavery in Comparison of *Virginia* for Liberty. —Liberty! —O charming Liberty!

Sing *lo Triumph* to Liberty." Through such pointed mockery, Philo-Bombastia implied that the liberty extolled by Philo-Virginia was not true liberty but reckless license, threatening the foundations of true religion, good government, and social order in the colony.

Philo-Bombastia did not leave the matter there. "And that you may be true Worshippers of Liberty," he continued, "make your Negroes as free as yourselves." Indeed, he asked, would it not meet exactly the purposes Philo-Virginia proposed *"to admit all Persons of all Nations and Opinions, from all Parts of the World, to be naturalized and tolerated, and to enjoy any Office in Church, or State, throughout the Colony of* Virginia, *and to set all Slaves free in this Country of Liberty"*? Philo-Virginia had made no mention of slavery, but by linking the cause of religious toleration to racial disorder Philo-Bombastia sought to transform the nature of the debate. His satire changed the subject from a relatively limited proposal for toleration of a specific group to a sweeping, intertwined series of potential threats to Virginia's social order. Other commentators consciously or unconsciously accepted this construction. In the April 10 *Gazette,* for instance, the pseudonymous "Peter Limits" worried that "sectaries" and slaves, both dangerous to society on their own, "together would invigorate, and complete the Malignity of the other," although he never said exactly how this would occur. Philo-Bombastia's objections to toleration had many sources, ethnic and political as well as racial, but he understood that one of the most rhetorically powerful condemnations he could make was to suggest that religious toleration constituted a threat to slavery, and he made this connection by playing on the language of liberty and liberation originally invoked by his antagonist.

The effectiveness of this tactic, as well as the intensity of the rancor behind it, derived not so much from concerns about the settlement of Virginia's frontier but rather from wide-ranging religious transformations in the colony in the middle decades of the eighteenth century. In the 1740s the first of a series of evangelical Awakenings took root in Virginia and was organized as an offshoot of revivalist Presbyterian organizations in the Middle Colonies. Critical of the established Church of England and its personnel in Virginia, these first evangelical "New Lights" provoked deep anxiety among those who saw the establishment as an essential buttress of social order and community. Moreover, because evangelicals reached out to Virginia's enslaved population outside of the orderly structures of the establishment, and because some slaves themselves took hold of this opportunity to transform their identities and relationships, they added a new layer of complexity to the colony's ongoing contests over the relationship between religious identity, race, and freedom. The tensions provoked by this confrontation made religious toleration a political issue on a scale that had not been seen in the colony since the Restoration. Because the Awakening took shape under Presbyterian auspices, that denomination was a particularly charged subject in public debate. By 1752, calling for the toleration of Presbyterians was anything but an uncontroversial act.

The debate and conflict surrounding this first wave of evangelical revival reshaped the languages of establishment and dissent in Virginia and set the pattern for subsequent controversies as other evangelical groups entered the colony in the second half of the eighteenth century. Concerns about religion and social order dated back to the colony's founding, but in the middle of the eighteenth century the rise of evangelicalism intersected with the Enlightenment- and Awakening-influenced language of liberty and the demographic transition that turned Virginia into a slave society to add new dimensions to these concerns. Philo-Bombastia's satire was built upon all of these developments, and it provides a valuable glimpse into the construction of the discursive landscape of what would become Nat Turner's Virginia. The links between liberty, religion, and race that were forged in the initial confrontation between eighteenth-century evangelicals and the Virginia establishment became central to the dynamic of religious conflict in the colony. Throughout the Revolutionary era and into the nineteenth century, these concepts and the relationship between them were interpreted, argued over, and reshaped by a variety of historical actors. This chapter traces the initial process by which these concepts became so deeply intertwined, examining both the background of the Anglican establishment in Virginia and the ways in which Presbyterian revivalists, enslaved men and women, and defenders of religious establishment such as Philo-Bombastia took hold of evolving ideas about social order and religious dissent in Virginia and wove them together in new and unexpected ways.

The complexity and explosiveness of the collision between evangelical and established religious values in eighteenth-century Virginia derived in part from the vitality of the Anglican church in the colony and its long history of confronting and containing religious dissent. For many years, historians sympathetic to evangelicalism or schooled in a New England–dominated historiographical tradition dismissed Virginia's religious establishment as hopelessly corrupt and spiritually inert. In this view, first propounded by evangelicals themselves, evangelicalism was an almost inevitable response to the failure of the establishment to provide spiritually hungry Virginians with a meaningful and heartfelt experience of true Christianity.[1] Other historians have taken the establishment more seriously but de-emphasize its spiritual role and focus on its functional significance as an element of the gentry's social, political, and cultural dominance in the colony.[2] Recently, however, historians have begun to reassess the Anglican establishment in Virginia in ways that emphasize its spiritual dynamism and broad relevance in daily life as well as its social and political importance to the colony. By taking Anglicanism seriously on its own terms, this approach overturns the stereotypes of complacency and coldness and considerably complicates our understanding of the dynamics of religious conflict in Virginia.[3] Evangelicals encountered, not a corrupt and crumbling relic of the past, but a dynamic and inclusive set of religious ideas and institutions that reflected powerful trends in the colony's social and cultural development in the eighteenth century.

The success of Anglicanism in Virginia was not inevitable. Virginia's religious establishment originated as part of early colonial leaders' more general and only partially successful struggle to bring English social, cultural, and governmental forms to the colony. As in England, in Virginia the Anglican church was supported by taxes and served a number of official, public functions, including keeping records of all marriages, christenings, and burials. All settlers technically fell under the church's jurisdiction, and regular attendance (which by the eighteenth century usually meant monthly) at services was required by law. Despite this powerful legal framework, however, the growth and influence of Anglicanism in Virginia was limited for much of the colonial period by an ongoing shortage of ministers and the geographic dispersal of the population, both of which prevented the replication of English patterns of faith and practice. These conditions were exacerbated by the lack of any powerful religious officials within the colony. There was no Anglican bishop in Virginia or any of the colonies to ordain ministers, induct them into parsonages, or preside over the confirmation of young adults in the faith. Instead, the Bishop of London oversaw the Church of England in America from a distance, and the colonies occupied a marginal place in the overall concerns of the church hierarchy in England during the seventeenth century.

Under these circumstances, Virginia's religious establishment developed an improvised degree of local independence and lay control not found in England. Congregants in large, undermanned parishes relied on lay readers to conduct services from the Book of Common Prayer, with only periodic visits from ordained ministers. Even for those with a settled minister, the large size of many parishes and the scattered population meant that parishioners relied heavily on local satellite churches, or "chapels of ease," which the minister visited in rotation, rather than attending a single parish church. County courts took over the functions of moral oversight that ecclesiastical courts performed in England. Parish vestries, usually drawn from the same group of local gentlemen who made up the county courts, gained the right to choose their ministers and present them to the governor for formal induction into their posts, a process that was controlled by individual patrons and bishops in England. In practice, the vestries often dispensed with the final step of induction, retaining the ability to dismiss ministers who displeased them for any reason and limiting ministers' control of church-owned property.[4] The vestries' authority in such matters became an ongoing point of contention in the eighteenth century as ministers complained to both the General Assembly and the church hierarchy in England about "the Precariousness in their Livings."[5]

Given this distinctive evolution, it is easy to see why historians so often focus on the Virginia establishment's role as an adjunct of gentry domination in the colony: each step toward local control took power out of the hands of church officials and put it in the hands of the Virginia elite. The colony's increasing wealth and population in the late seventeenth and eighteenth centuries mitigated some of the problems of personnel and geography the Anglicans had faced in earlier years, but the pattern set in the seventeenth century had indelibly marked the nature of Virginia's religious establishment. Local communities, and particularly the most prominent members of those communities, had come to view their influence over their parish as a permanent right rather than a temporary expedient. In 1689 the Bishop of London appointed James Blair, a talented Scottish minister, as his commissary to represent the Church of England in the colony. Despite his mandate to reassert regular order in Virginia's churches, Blair recognized the deeply entrenched nature of lay control in Virginia and "quickly realized that any effort to strengthen the church required the cooperation of the planter aristocracy."[6] Rather than attempting to remake Virginia's establishment along English lines, Blair came to focus on winning over the Virginia gentry to facilitate more achievable goals, most prominently the founding of the College of William and Mary to educate future ministers for the colony.

Blair's cooperative, accommodating approach proved effective. In the eighteenth century the Anglican church and the Virginia gentry prospered in tandem and both benefited from their relationship. The wealth and aspirations to refinement of the eighteenth-century planter class manifested themselves not only in genteel manor houses and stylish furnishings but also in a wave of new church building. In the period 1700–1776 Virginians funded and built at least 166 new churches and made significant additions to 46 existing churches.[7] These churches helped the establishment reach a greater proportion of the colony's growing population and indicated the increasing status of the Church of England in the colony. Just as manor houses demonstrated the wealth and power of the gentry, new churches proclaimed the importance and centrality of the Church of England to Virginians' collective spiritual, social, and political life. At the same time, however, they also served as symbolic and social expressions of the gentry's social dominance. Not only were the materials, decorative styles, and furnishings of the churches often paid for by wealthy parishioners but they echoed the materials, styles, and furnishings of gentry homes, creating a powerful ideological link between the two types of buildings. As the architectural historian Dell Upton puts it, "The house of God was not a slave's house or a common planter's house: it was a gentleman's house."[8]

Social practices associated with churchgoing reinforced this message. The elite occupied the most desirable and expensive seats in church and sometimes even negotiated the right to build their own private pews or galleries in exchange for donations or services to the parish.[9] On Sundays, churches also provided the opportunity for members of the gentry to display their wealth, taste, and authority through their clothing, horses, carriages, and personal bearing. In an oft-quoted journal entry, the New Jersey–born tutor Philip Vickers Fithian described how the Virginia gentry combined business, hospitality, and worship in ways that reaffirmed social solidarity and class privilege:

I observe it is a general custom on Sundays here, with Gentlemen to invite one another home to dine after Church; and to consult about, determine their common business, either before or after Service— It is not the Custom for Gentlemen to go into Church til Service is beginning, when they enter in a Body, in the same manner as they come out; I have known the Clerk to come out and call them in to prayers.—They stay also after the Service is over, usually as long, sometimes longer, than the Parson was preaching.[10]

By entering "in a Body" at the beginning of services, gentlemen demonstrated their precedence and ensured their visibility to the rest of the community. Such activities blended the spiritual and worldly dimensions of religious practice in ways that inscribed elite dominance in Virginians' essential rituals of community and communion.

The establishment's social and cultural connection to gentry power was thus quite real, but this reality did not prevent Anglican faith, theology, and practice from being deeply meaningful for Virginians of different classes and social backgrounds. The late seventeenth- and early eighteenth-century expansion of the establishment brought the regular rhythms and rituals of Anglican parish life to a greater number of Virginia's settlers in the eighteenth century, and for most of these men and women the establishment brought order and stability, in both practical and symbolic terms. On an institutional level, the establishment served as a way of organizing territory and enhancing community life. Parish development, for instance, often served as a precursor to the establishment of counties. In southeastern Virginia, Southampton County was formed from Isle of Wight County in 1749 out of the territory covered by Nottoway Parish, and Sussex County was similarly formed from Surry County out of most of Albemarle Parish in 1753.[11] Parishes and their vestries also performed a number of functions crucial to the smooth operation of Virginia's legal and governmental systems. Parishes provided relief to the poor, shared responsibility with the county courts for the upkeep of roads and ferries, and conducted the quadrennial "processions" that reaffirmed and clarified property boundaries and served as neighborhood social events as well.[12] Moreover, in a society with dispersed settlements, few towns, and limited opportunities for socializing, churchgoing provided weekly opportunities to gossip, flirt, and talk business, as well as participate in worship. If the established church served to reinforce the gentry's visibility and solidarity, it served similarly useful functions for those further down on the social scale.

To observers and historians steeped in an evangelical tradition, this mingling of secular and sacred functions (as they perceived it) exemplified the worldliness and corruption of the Virginia establishment. Fithian approvingly contrasted Presbyterian services near his home in New Jersey with his experiences in Virginia: "no rings of Beaux chatting before & after Sermon on Gallantry; no assembling in crowds after Service to dine & bargain; no cool, spiritless harangue from the Pulpit; Minister & people here seem in some small measure to reverence the Day, there [in Virginia] neither do the one or the other."[13] This perspective also cast the establishment's ritualism, reliance on the formulas of the Book of Common Prayer, and measured, rationalist style of preaching as coldness and spiritual indifference. Well into the twentieth century, many historians echoed the Presbyterian revivalist Samuel Davies's judgment that the "languid harangues on morality or insipid speculations" of Virginia's Anglican parsons were "not likely to do much service to the souls of men."[14]

Despite its persistence, this outsiders' view uncritically reflects evangelicals' critiques of the established church and misses crucial aspects of the purpose and nature of the establishment in Virginia. For the majority of Virginia's white residents, the links between the church, the authority of the gentry, and the convivial socializing of community gatherings were not defects in the colony's religious order; they were part of its purpose. The establishment brought the community together and helped legitimize the power of the gentry while encouraging both elites and common folk to work toward their own salvation and a more orderly, Christian society. At least in theory, the weekly practices of churchgoing made concrete the establishment's larger, more abstract goals of Christian unity and order. The repetition and formulaic nature of Anglican liturgy also served these purposes. Rather than promoting a sudden, dramatic conversion experience in the evangelical style, the Book of Common Prayer and the service it prescribed were "intended to work a gradual transformation in the lives of the faithful" through the repetition of words and themes. And rather than considering only the converted to be "true" Christians, mainstream Anglicanism included the entire community, "a people thought to be Christian by virtue of their membership in the English commonwealth."[15]

The vision of the church, the polity, and the English nation intertwined helped provide colonists with a sense of identity, purpose, and meaning as participants in sacred traditions with deep historical roots, traditions that they believed represented the best spiritual, social, and political systems that the world had to offer. John Wesley himself expressed this pride in Anglican traditions when he claimed that "there is no Liturgy in the world . . . which breaths more of a solid scriptural, rational piety, than the Common Prayer of the Church of England. And although the main of it was compiled more than two hundred years ago, yet is the language of it not only pure, but strong and elegant in the highest degree."[16] Participation in the established church confirmed and reinforced this sense of connectedness, rationality, elegance, and purity for many Virginians, and their participation often extended beyond simply attending church. The Book of Common Prayer was the second most commonly found work in Virginians' libraries, trailing only the Bible.[17] Together, formal Anglican ritual and private devotions promoted a "'reasonable' faith, moral conduct, benevolence, acceptance of the social order and one's attendant duties, and obedience to all in authority."[18] The vision of the Anglican establishment was orderly, hierarchical, and integrative. From the perspective of the establishment, the demands of the world and those of true religion were not only compatible but complementary.

Religious dissent fit uneasily into this idealized world. Because of the close link between the establishment and the social order, breaking with the established church was not merely a matter of private conscience or theological particulars. From the establishment's point of view, dissenters compounded their religious errors by separating themselves from the larger social body and disrupting the harmonious, orderly operation of communities and families. Nonetheless, religious diversity and dissent were nothing new to Virginia by the eighteenth century. Indeed, the establishment's attitudes were shaped in part in response to a series of challenges that prompted leaders to clarify and define the boundary between acceptable and unacceptable forms of religious expression in the colony.

In the early seventeenth century, settlers with puritan leanings found a foothold in the settlements south of the James River. The unsettled and usually local nature of religious life in the colony in this early period, as well as ongoing debates within the early seventeenth-century Church of England, meant that puritans operated within the malleable framework of the colony's nascent establishment rather than against it. After 1640, amidst the growing conflict of the English Civil War, Virginia's Royalist government began to police the boundaries of Anglican orthodoxy more zealously, requiring the use of the Book of Common Prayer in services and expelling several Massachusetts ministers who had been invited to the colony by the puritan congregations south of the James. By the late 1640s many of the puritans in southeastern Virginia had emigrated to Maryland, and puritanism ceased to be a major influence in the colony.[19]

Another product of the religious ferment of the English Civil War era had a much greater long-term influence on Virginians' conceptions of the dangers of religious dissent and the purpose and limits of religious toleration. Members of the radical sect known as the Quakers began arriving in the colony in the second half of the 1650s, and their reputation for confrontational religious performance and willful disobedience to civil authority preceded them. By elevating a divine "inner light" present in every individual to an equal status with the Bible as a source of Christian truth, Quakers shocked and outraged more orthodox Protestants, who thought that this idea undermined the very foundations of proper religious and social order. Stories of strange behavior, such as "going naked for a sign," and the prominence of female preachers and missionaries in the Quaker movement seemed to confirm these disorderly effects for many observers. Throughout the Anglo-American world, Quakers were viewed as disruptive and dangerous to society, and they came to represent a kind of boundary case for religious toleration. In Massachusetts Bay, four persistent Quaker missionaries were executed in the years 1659–61. Virginia's government did not go so far, but it passed a series of restrictive laws against Quakers, instituting steep fines for their nonattendance at the established church, their refusal to have children baptized, and their assembling together for worship or any other purpose. Other fines were levied on those bringing Quakers into the colony or permitting Quakers to hold meetings on their property.[20]

The language of the statutes reveals the nature of Virginia magistrates' hostility. A 1659 act declared that Quakers were an "unreasonable and turbulent sort of people" who held "unlawful assemblies and congregations of people, teaching and publishing lies, miracles, false visions, prophecies and doctrines, which have influence upon the communities of men both ecclesiastical and civil . . . attempting thereby to destroy religion, lawes, comunities and all bonds of civil societie, leaving arbitrarie to everie vaine and vicious person whether men shall be safe, lawes established, offenders punished, and governours rule." A law passed in 1663 claimed that Quakers held "sundry dangerous opinions and tenets, and—under pretence of religious worship, doe often assemble themselves in great numbers,—separating and dividing themselves from the rest of his Majesties good and loyall subjects."[21] In the eyes of Virginia's legislators, Quakers epitomized the dangers of dissent, threatening the real and necessary links between religious orthodoxy, good government, and social order. This threat came not only from their "lies" and "false visions, prophecies and doctrines" but also from their "separating and dividing themselves" from the rest of the community. These themes of deceit, error, order, and divisiveness would crop up again and again when issues of religious dissent and toleration arose in the colony, even as the setting and the main players in the drama changed.

Another lasting effect of these seventeenth-century controversies was the association of sectarian religion with gender disorder.[22] This rhetorical strategy built on strong European foundations but also resonated with the concerns and insecurities of Virginia's emerging colonial social and political order. The fragile patriarchal authority of the colony's government and its elite planters had been shaken by the English Civil War and continued to face attacks from political and religious foes, as well as more casual assaults from settlers, who felt free to challenge the legitimacy—often in a literal, genealogical sense—of the government and its officials whenever conflicts occurred. In this environment, feminizing religious dissent became a powerful and attractive way of marginalizing and delegitimizing it while emphasizing by contrast the patriarchal orderliness of the government and the establishment. Many seventeenth-century dissenting groups, especially the Quakers, sometimes featured women as preachers and missionaries, making them even more obvious targets for gendered criticism. But ultimately it was as much dissenters' refusal to yield to the patriarchal authority of local officials and ministers as it was their specific gender practices that marked them as disorderly. The idea of self-appointed preachers of either sex holding private, unregulated meetings where women and even slaves could attend and hear messages critical of the establishment (and thus the government and even the crown, in some views) made the defenders of Virginia's political and religious orthodoxy uneasy. And when these men and women seemed to seek out confrontation and boldly defied the magistrates who sought to enforce order, these suspicions of sedition were, in many minds, confirmed.

Enforcement of anti-Quaker laws became somewhat more sporadic after the mid-1660s owing to the shifting religious politics of Restoration England, local circumstances in Virginia, and Quakers' own official adoption of pacifism as a core belief. In 1689, in the wake of the Glorious Revolution, the English Parliament passed the Toleration Act, which established a broad formal framework that legitimized most activities of Protestant dissenters in England. The act required dissenters to take the oaths of allegiance and supremacy (Quakers, who opposed oath-taking, were allowed simply to declare their fidelity to the government) and obtain legal license for their ministers and meetinghouses, and it exempted them from the penalties for nonattendance at their Anglican parish church.[23] News of the Toleration Act helped create a less hostile climate for Quakers in Virginia, and in 1699 its provisions were incorporated into Virginia's legal code, largely due to Quaker efforts to test its limits and claim its protection.[24] The Toleration Act sought to contain the social and political disruption caused by dissent, making it more orderly and subjecting it to oversight by established authorities through the licensing requirements.

But if legal toleration allowed Quakers who accepted this framework to avoid the kind of harassment they faced in the seventeenth century, eighteenth-century Anglicans in both England and the colonies continued to make Quakers a target of criticism for their allegedly pernicious religious and social influence.[25] In Virginia, James Blair contrasted the orderly way in which Anglicans "submit ourselves to such Rulers, Pastors, and Teachers as *Christ* hath appointed in his Church" with Quakers' "open Insurrection against the sacred Order of the Ministry," which allowed anyone at all, "if they have but Confidence enough to pretend to an Inward Call of the Spirit, to invade these sacred Offices" and "to deliver what Doctrine they themselves please."[26] Another Virginian simply reminded his son not to be "like the Quaker, who presumes so much of light, that if himself now set, our world would be without a sun."[27] Despite their status as a tolerated minority, Quakers' seemingly arrogant disregard for community, tradition, and authority continued to represent the dangers of religious dissent and provided a useful negative referent for Anglican leaders who sought to emphasize the correctness and orderliness of their own faith.

The actual activities of Quakers in the early eighteenth century did not usually live up to this inflated rhetoric. In response to the persecution and hostility of the early Restoration period, Quakers in both England and America adopted a less confrontational, more inward religious style while at the same time developing legal strategies to fend off official interference and harassment.[28] In southeastern Virginia, as well as in North Carolina, Quakers remained a significant presence and caused little, if any, disruption. Local acceptance seems to have been the rule rather than the exception. Many Quakers became prominent citizens and merchants in the region, and the Virginia Yearly Meeting was usually held at Pagan Creek, in Isle of Wight County.

Southeastern Virginia Quakers also indirectly shaped the religious future of the region by nurturing a small Baptist community that would eventually be transformed in the fires of mid-eighteenth-century revivalism and become part of the wider evangelical movement (see chapter 2). In the first half of the eighteenth century, however, these southeastern Baptists were General Baptists, who had a strong historical and theological connection to the Quakers. Unlike Calvinist, or Particular, Baptists, General Baptists subscribed to the doctrine of general atonement, believing that Christ had died for all mankind's sins and that salvation through Christ was available to all who sought it rather than to just the elect, preordained few.[29] This view had influenced the emerging Quaker movement in the late 1640s, contributing to Quakers' tendencies toward universalism and perfectionism, and many early Quaker converts were drawn from the ranks of the General Baptists in England.[30] Fittingly, then, the first mention of Baptists in Virginia was in the journal of a Quaker, who reported that he had attended a 1699 meeting at the house of a Baptist preacher in Yorktown. By 1714 there were a sufficient number of Baptists living in southeastern Virginia to request ministerial assistance from England.[31] In response to their plea, a minister named Robert Norden arrived in Virginia later in the same year and established a church in Prince George County.[32] Norden's congregation met in a Quaker meetinghouse in the area for a year. In 1715 Norden was recognized as a dissenting minister under the Toleration Act, and the Prince George County Court licensed one congregant's home as an "ana-baptist public meeting house."[33]

Despite its powerful polemical utility, religious dissent was in practice a minor but real feature of Virginia's cultural landscape during the first half of the eighteenth century. It was also usually a geographically marginalized phenomenon, concentrated along the frontiers and in the backwaters of the Old Dominion, outside of the wealthier Tidewater counties. With its Quakers and Baptists, southeastern Virginia, along with northeastern North Carolina, formed a relative hotbed of religious dissent. In the Piedmont and the Shenandoah Valley, the substantial population of Scots-Irish settlers made Presbyterianism a majority faith. Various German groups of several different denominations and a small community of French Huguenots also settled in the Virginia backcountry. As long as they abided by the provisions of the Toleration Act, refrained from aggressive criticism of the establishment, and made no enemies among local elites, these groups remained uncontroversial. But when dissenters rejected the limitations imposed by the Toleration Act or directly challenged local officials and institutions, the situation could be very different.

Beginning in the 1740s, that is precisely what happened. The unexpected religious turmoil began modestly enough among a small group of worshippers in Hanover County, but it proved to be the beginning of a much wider transformation. The sudden appearance and rapid expansion of evangelical revivalism reinvigorated the tensions between establishment and dissent in the colony, giving those tensions new dimensions of meaning and significance. Ideas and practices associated with eighteenth-century Awakenings across the Anglo-American world interacted with Virginia's existing patterns of religious practice and its rapidly changing political, social, and economic environment at mid-century in unpredictable ways. The collision of these forces produced a distinctive dynamic of conflict focused on the mutually implicating political and racial dangers of dissent and religious liberty, which profoundly shaped the future of the colony's religious culture.

The Hanover County Awakening began among a small group of laymen who had become dissatisfied with the preaching at their parish church and begun meeting at the home of Samuel Morris, a local bricklayer, to read sermons and other devotional works that they found more inspiring.[34] The group read works by Martin Luther, John Bunyan, and the Anglican revivalist George Whitefield, who had preached in Williamsburg in 1739 and may have helped inspire their initial dissatisfaction. Morris reported that a book of Whitefield's sermons proved so affecting that "many were convinced of their undone Condition, and constrained to seek Deliverance with the greatest Solicitude. . . . The Concern of some was so passionate and violent that they could not avoid crying out, weeping bitterly, &c."[35] These were classic behaviors in the transatlantic wave of revivals that swept the English-speaking world in the middle of the eighteenth century, and they were commonly associated with Whitefield's preaching. Indeed, their very appearance in Hanover most likely reflected the dissenters' familiarity with this model of revival, whether gained through immersion in print culture, by word of mouth, or through contact with Scots-Irish Presbyterian communion-day practices.[36]

As this group grew, they attracted the attention of local authorities. The Hanover revivalists were called before the county court to explain their lack of attendance at the established church, and they claimed that they were dissenters and thus not subject to the penalties for nonattendance. The members of the court asked them their denomination, and in Morris's subsequent account, recorded by Samuel Davies, "as we knew but little of any Denomination of Dissenters, except *Quakers,* we were at a Loss what Name to assume. At length recollecting that *Luther* was a noted Reformer, and that his Doctrines were agreeable to our Sentiments, . . . we declared ourselves *Lutherans.*"[37] Perhaps embellished in Davies's retelling, this courthouse set piece purposely communicates the revivalists' emphasis on the new and, in Virginia, unprecedented nature of their own dissent and its contrast with the existing forms of dissent, as represented by the insular and theologically outré Quakers. At the same time, the story also connects their ideas to the founding moment of Protestantism in their invocation of Luther as a spiritual forerunner. Whether accurate in all its details or not, Morris's account captures the Hanover movement's self-construction as recapturing the vital and unmediated essence of true, Protestant Christianity, which it believed was missing from Virginia's larger religious tradition.

As the movement's connection to Whitefield and the print culture of revivalism suggests, however, the Hanover Awakening was not simply a spontaneous rediscovery of core Protestant principles; it was a local expression of a wider cultural phenomenon. These links to the larger world of mid-century revivalism became even more concrete as the Virginia dissenters encountered evangelical New Side Presbyterian ministers from the Middle Colonies. Led by William Tennent Sr. and his sons William Jr., Gilbert, Charles, and John, the New Side was the pro-revival faction in an acrimonious split among Presbyterians that began during the Awakenings of the 1730s and 1740s. Gilbert Tennent in particular became famous for his confrontational 1740 sermon *The Danger of an Unconverted Ministry,* which attacked members of the anti-revivalist Old Side for both their self-satisfaction and pride in their worldly education and achievement and their lack of a true, felt experience of God's saving grace, which left them merely outward professors with no real understanding of the vital heart of Christianity.[38] A series of ministers trained by the senior Tennent and his followers began visiting Hanover and surrounding counties in the 1740s. The first was William Robinson, who after a successful series of preaching engagements in 1743 persuaded the dissenters to adopt a Presbyterian denominational identity and put themselves under the care of the revivalist New Castle Presbytery in Delaware. Two of the Tennent brothers were among those who followed in Robinson's footsteps. This irregular ministerial assistance served as a supplement to Morris's and others' ongoing "Meetings for Reading and Prayer in sundry Places" to maintain the ongoing Awakening in the area.[39] Finally, in 1749 Samuel Davies, a gifted and politically astute protégé of Robinson's, settled permanently in Hanover to minister to the burgeoning evangelical Presbyterian community in Virginia.

Unlike geographically or ethnically bounded instances of religious dissent earlier in the eighteenth century, the revivalism in Hanover prompted a great deal of anxiety and hostility from Virginia authorities. In large part, this was owing to the revivalists' direct and personal confrontation with the established church and its local officials. The rector of the local Anglican parish, Patrick Henry (the uncle of the Revolutionary leader), complained that some of the dissenters, including Morris, held the view "that all true believers . . . have the spirit of discerning whereby they can distinguish a hypocrite or a formal professor, from a sincere Christian." Worse, "one Roger Shackleford . . . told those about him, that I had preach'd Damnable doctrine, and that he pitied me as being an unconverted graceless man."[40] Less personal but equally threatening was another dissenter's assertion to "one of his Neighbours that [the Anglican liturgy] contained abundance of lies."[41]

The New Side itinerants sometimes restrained the excesses of the Hanover movement. Morris, for instance, told Davies that William Robinson "successfully endeavoured to correct some of our *Antinomian* mistakes."[42] But as experienced controversialists the itinerants also engaged in aggressive criticism of what they saw as the complacency and corruption around them. John Roan, who visited Hanover in the winter of 1744–45, reportedly told his audiences "that all your ministers preach false doctrine, and that they, and all who follow them, are going to hell," and that "it is not the spirit of God" that motivated Anglican ministers, "but it is the spirit of the Devil, and no good can proceed out of their mouth."[43] While these reports may have been uncharitable glosses of standard revivalist tropes, even Morris admitted that Roan spoke "pretty freely about the Degeneracy of the Clergy in this Colony."[44] Such criticisms drew on Gilbert Tennent's heated rhetoric about "an unconverted ministry," but in Virginia they took on added meaning as an assault on the privileged status of the establishment, and Roan was indicted "for reflecting upon and vilifying the Established Religion."[45]

Roan's indictment was eventually dismissed, but Virginia authorities' response to the Hanover Awakening marked a new, aggressive phase in the colony's attitudes toward and strategies for dealing with religious dissent. Many of the arguments about the dangers posed by the New Lights, as revivalists and their supporters were called, recalled those made against Quakers. In his instructions to the grand jury hearing Roan's case, for instance, Governor William Gooch focused on the inauthentic and illegitimate nature of the religious authority claimed by revivalists, decrying the activities of "certain false teachers that are lately crept into this government; who, without order or license, . . . professing themselves ministers under the pretended influence of new light, . . . lead the innocent and ignorant people into all kinds of delusion." He also emphasized the divisive social effects of such delusion, claiming that as the revivalists "draw disciples after them, and we know not whereunto this separation may grow, but may easily foretel into what a distracted condition . . . this colony will be reduced."[46] False teachers, self-professed ministers, without order or license, pretending to divine inspiration in order to lead the ignorant into delusion and the colony to distraction—Gooch's language hammered home the themes of authority, legitimacy, authenticity, and community that had stood at the core of the debate since the seventeenth century. But the changing cultural and social environment of the mid-eighteenth century helped give these concerns new implications and expressions.

The expansionist bent of the evangelical movement and the geographic mobility of the itinerant ministers who promoted it became matters of great concern to the supporters of the Virginia establishment. This was no self-contained community of dissenters to be tolerated but an amorphous movement actively trying to draw men and women away from the established church, behavior that ran counter to most authorities' understanding of the intention of the Toleration Act. In 1747, responding to concerns expressed by members of the Council of State, Governor Gooch issued a proclamation that all magistrates should "discourage and prohibit as far as they legally can all Itinerant Preachers . . . from Teaching or Preaching."[47] But influential Virginians disagreed about exactly where that legal boundary lay. When Samuel Davies arrived that same year for his first tour in Virginia, he successfully gained license to preach at four different meetinghouses under the terms of the Toleration Act, with the support of Gooch and the seeming acquiescence of Commissary William Dawson, James Blair's successor.[48] Nonetheless, Davies's activities continued to cause concern and provoke complaints from the establishment's more anxious defenders. These defenders argued for a more restrictive conception of what the act permitted, insisting that dissenting ministers should be confined to a single location and congregation. Henry complained of Davies's well-publicized appointments to preach in additional locations, arguing that "the Govinor & Council never intended to encourage Itinerant Preachers" in licensing him.[49] When Davies returned in 1748 with his fellow minister John Rodgers, the General Court refused to give Rodgers a license and nearly revoked Davies's own license, despite the governor's support for the ministers.[50] Davies may have had Henry in mind when he credited the resistance to "the horrendous & shocking Reports spread Abroad concerning us by officious Malignants."[51]

By 1750 the dispute in Virginia had reached the Bishop of London. The bishop took Henry's position that "the Act of Toleration was intended to permit the Dissenters to worship in their own way, and to exempt them from penalties, but it never was intended to permit them to set up itinerant preachers, to gather congregations where there was none before."[52] Indeed, he implied that Davies's position reflected a more radical, extralegal philosophy: "If you judge the liberty granted not sufficient, and that you, and every body, have a natural right to propagate their opinions in religion in such a manner as they approve themselves, that is quite another point" from the purpose and limits of the Toleration Act. Surely, the bishop continued, Davies did not "suppose the Church of England to be . . . in the same state of corruption as the Romish church was at the time of the Reformation," but that was the only situation in which Davies's actions in "labouring to disturb the consciences of others, and the peace of the church" could be justified.[53] These arguments were designed to create an either-or choice between a narrow conception of the Toleration Act and a much more extreme position that, by rejecting the legitimacy of the Church of England, could expose Davies and his followers to serious legal repercussions.

In the face of such suspicious and hostile attitudes, Davies became a vocal advocate for an expanded vision of religious toleration in Virginia. Refusing the dichotomy offered by the Bishop of London, Davies pursued a more politic line of reasoning, insisting that his activities were the logical result of the requirements of the Toleration Act. In Davies's view, the act's goals of permitting dissenters to worship according to their conscience and exempting them from penalties required precisely the actions he had taken. Given the widely dispersed nature of the population and the presence of dissenters in many different counties, refusing to allow them a convenient meetinghouse was tantamount to denying them access to worship. "If this Liberty be denied them, are they not obliged, according to the *Act of Toleration* itself, to attend constantly on Worship in the established Church? And if so, where is their Toleration?"[54] Davies pointed out that Anglican ministers often served multiple churches or chapels of ease in their parishes, which sometimes spanned multiple counties, without "incur[ring] the odious epithet of an itinerant preacher, a pluralist, or nonresident."[55] His actions, he claimed, were simply the dissenting equivalent of the adaptations that the establishment had to make in Virginia. Serving multiple meetinghouses was not specifically prohibited by the Toleration Act and was, in fact, the only practical way to accomplish its intentions for the colony's scattered, clergy-poor population.

Davies also claimed that his movement did not seek to draw people away from the established church but rather sought to nourish those already disaffected as a result of ministers' neglect of "experimental religion."[56] He acknowledged the Church of England's legitimacy, praising its "excellent *Articles*" and denying that dissent arose from "any scruples about her ceremonial peculiarities," but he argued that the church's representatives in Virginia provided such "wretched Entertainment to hungry Souls" that the most devout churchgoers had turned away in search of more substantial spiritual sustenance.[57] Davies also downplayed the denominational elements of the conflict, arguing that he was not attempting to make *"Captures* from the Church of *England*, but . . . *sincere Proselytes to living Religion"* and that "it would inspire me with much greater Joy to see a *pious Church-man,* than a *graceless Presbyterian."*[58] In each case, he shifted the focus away from the Church of England in general to the actions and shortcomings of the Virginia establishment and its personnel.

To the supporters of the establishment who bore the brunt of Davies and his colleagues' heated criticisms these most likely seemed like meaningless distinctions, but for Davies they served to explain and justify his movement's place in Virginia's cultural, institutional, and legal order. Denying any desire to overthrow existing structures, he simply claimed to meet a growing desire for effective, spiritually compelling preaching and for an awakened, conversion-centered vision of Christian truth. Despite continued resistance from some quarters, he articulated a new vision of religious toleration in Virginia that moved beyond marginal, exceptional, or isolated cases to encompass an ongoing, expanding religious movement. By advancing such arguments, even though not always winning the debate, Davies, and the Hanover Awakening more generally, shaped the way in which both evangelicals and their opponents would understand the meaning and implications of religious dissent in the second half of the eighteenth century, setting the stage for Baptists' and others' more expansive arguments for religious liberty during and after the Revolution.

Another of Davies's innovations also had lasting implications. In 1751 Davies noted that "there is a great Number of Negroes in these Parts; and sometimes I see a 100 & more among my Hearers. I have baptized about 40 Adults of them within these three Years."[59] By 1755 Davies had baptized one hundred black men and women who had "given credible evidences, not only of their acquaintance with the important doctrines of the christian religion, but also of a deep sense of them upon their minds, attested to by a life of the strictest piety and holiness."[60] Such highly visible conversions marked the beginning of an extended process by which evangelical Protestantism became the primary religious idiom of African Americans in Virginia. Davies took his mission to black Virginians, nearly all of whom were slaves, very seriously. In order to give them greater access to God's word, Davies instructed them in reading and worked with the Society for Promoting Christian Knowledge to secure Bibles and books of Isaac Watts's hymns and psalms to distribute among them.[61] Other New Light leaders followed Davies's lead, as fellow Presbyterians John Todd, John Wright, and Robert Henry also made instruction of blacks a major element of their successful ministries across the Virginia Piedmont.[62] Black men and women in turn took seriously the message and the opportunities offered by Davies and his colleagues, even as they acted on their own understanding of the spiritual and social meanings of Christianity. The goals and aspirations of these men and women were not necessarily incompatible with those of New Light preachers, but they were not precisely the same either, and the tension and ambiguity produced by that divergence became a persistent element of religious interactions between blacks and whites.

The Anglican church had made very few inroads among Virginia's enslaved African and African American population in the first half of the eighteenth century. White resistance to the conversion of slaves dated back to the seventeenth century.[63] In the colony's early decades, statutes concerning slavery and servitude often differentiated in civilizational terms between European "Christians" and Indian or African "slaves." The disjuncture between religious identity on the one hand and social position on the other left the implications of slaves' conversion for their worldly status unclear. Some black men and women of this seventeenth-century "charter generation" successfully made the transition from "slave" to "Christian," gaining freedom and using their religious affiliation and the social ties they formed through participation in English institutions like the church to claim and protect their full membership in colonial society.[64] Others used their baptism and identity as Christians as supporting evidence in petitions and lawsuits to gain their freedom.

In the second half of the seventeenth century, however, a series of legal changes in Virginia worked to resolve the ambiguities of this situation by making birth and geographic origin rather than religious identity the primary categories of difference. In 1667 a new law specified that baptism did not affect the status of "slaves by birth," and other laws similarly sought to clarify and solidify the boundaries between slavery and freedom in these years.[65] Despite these changes, a lingering association between Christianity and liberty, or at least improved status, remained. Masters and clergy in Virginia frequently expressed suspicion about slaves' motives in seeking baptism, worrying that they did so to seek better treatment and that it would make them "proud and not so good servants."[66]

The changing character of Virginia's black population in the late seventeenth and early eighteenth centuries reshaped religious interactions between blacks and whites in the colony, changing the context and implications of the debate over black Christianization. Direct importation of African slaves dramatically increased the size of the black population in this period. The majority of these newcomers were captives from the interior of Africa who had little previous contact with Europeans and little interest in English religion. Moreover, the increasing size and ethnic and linguistic isolation of the slave population encouraged strategies of survival and resistance based on cultural independence rather than the selective assimilation practiced by earlier generations.[67] As in other parts of the Americas, if perhaps to a lesser degree, Africans in Virginia preserved, adapted, and combined their own regional or ethnic beliefs and practices to celebrate rites of passage such as marriage or death and to engage supernatural aid in rituals of healing and magic or conjure.[68] Many British officials and churchmen recognized that the persistence of such African practices provided alternate sources of meaning and authority for slaves, and they often proposed increased Anglican proselytization of the enslaved not simply as a religious duty but also as a form of social integration and control. Virginia masters remained reluctant, however, and ministers and their supporters frequently complained of white slave owners' "mistaken opinion that the Interest of the Master in his Negro or Servant, is taken away or Lessen'd by the Negro or Servant becoming a Christian."[69]

By the late 1720s, as the proportion of Virginia-born blacks began to increase, clergymen's arguments gained more traction. During this period Virginia elites began to refine and extend an ideology of "patri-archism" to explain and justify their position at the top of an emergent slave society, and slave baptism, particularly of infants born in the col-ony, fit with this vision and with the orderly, integrative principles of the established church.[70] African-born slaves may have seemed too for-eign to be incorporated into a cohesive, hierarchical society organized around masters' right to rule, but with the right instruction native-born slaves might be brought into the Christian community and turned into humble and dutiful servants. This shift in opinion was reflected in rising numbers of slave baptisms in the 1720s and 1730s, as masters sought to demonstrate their Christian benevolence and exercise their powers of patronage by sponsoring the baptism of their slaves.[71]

This interest in slave Christianization was quite limited, however. It tended to focus on children rather than adults and extended only as far as the process could be made to benefit masters. Thus, catechiza-tion was encouraged because it enjoined obedience and humility, but other forms of participation in the rites of the church that interfered with masters' authority or implied equality or authority on the part of blacks were not. Baptized slaves, for instance, did not get married in the church, and masters did not hesitate to separate slave couples when it served their interest. Despite the increasing number of slave baptisms, masters and church officials agreed that slaves were "not to be allowed to be Churched" in any more intensive sense.[72]

Regardless of what Virginia's masters wanted, however, black Virgin-ians attached their own meanings to Christianity and continued to draw on the long association between Christianity and liberty in the colony. A small minority of blacks did in fact adopt the Anglican faith, despite the hostility of most white planters. Some may have done so to create or solidify ties of sympathy and patronage with pious owners or ministers and to gain literacy and other insights into the culture of their masters. They may also have found genuine meaning and comfort in Anglican ideas of heaven and divine providence and exhortations to self-discipline and humility. But if they did, it is clear that they did not interpret these ideas and exhortations in the way their masters hoped.

In 1729 James Blair complained that despite the clear and carefu' struction of clergymen and masters, slaves who sought conversion mostly for their own reasons, including better treatment, and th persisted in the belief that "at some time or another Christianity them to their freedom."[73] In the summer of 1730 rebellious rumors circulated among Virginia's blacks that the king of England had ordered that all Christian slaves be freed but that the colony's leaders were concealing the order. Late in that year, slaves acting at least in part on the basis of this rumor organized an uprising in southeastern Virginia in which hundreds fled into the Great Dismal Swamp. Most of the rebels were eventually captured or killed, but for many members of Virginia's elite, slaves' evident willingness to interpret the meanings and implications of Christianity in direct opposition to the explicit instructions of ministers and masters highlighted the dangers of Christianizing their slaves and hardened their resistance to any large-scale attempts to do so.[74]

This standoff between masters and slaves over the terms on which Christianization of Afro-Virginians should proceed provided one important influence on the encounter between black Virginians and the emergent evangelical movement led by Samuel Davies in the 1740s and 1750s, but other factors shaped the encounter as well. Ongoing demographic and social trends continued to lower many of the linguistic and cultural obstacles to religious interactions between blacks and whites. The rate of natural increase of the colony's African and Afro-Virginian population increased significantly in the early eighteenth century, so that despite record numbers of African imports in the 1730s, the percentage of American-born blacks grew steadily from 56 percent in 1730 to 79 percent in 1750 and 91 percent in 1770.[75] At the same time, the total black population grew rapidly and spread into more recently settled areas outside the Tidewater. By 1755 blacks constituted about 37 percent of the combined population of Virginia and Maryland, more than 40 percent of Hanover County's population, and more than 50 percent in many neighboring counties.[76] The shift toward an overwhelmingly African American black population dispersed widely throughout a white population of roughly equal size entailed a type and degree of social and cultural interaction between blacks and whites that differed from anything in the colony's previous history.[77] These developments in turn set the stage for the reshaping of the dynamic of black Christianization in the colony as the expanding evangelical movement created a source of Christian authority and practice outside of the established church and brought new religious ideas, new social spaces, and new actors onto the scene.

Black men and women found attractions in evangelical varieties of Christianity as practiced by the Presbyterians, and later the Baptists and Methodists, that they had not found in Anglicanism. The oppositional rhetoric of these groups may have attracted those who were suspicious of Anglicanism's strong ties to the structures of power and hierarchy in Virginia society, and the creation of mixed-race congregations and informal prayer groups outside of the oversight of the established church reinforced this sense of opposition to Virginia's existing values and institutions for many participants, both black and white. Similarly, evangelicals' de-emphasis of doctrinal knowledge and theology and their increased use of oral, vernacular styles of communication made their variety of Protestantism accessible to nonliterate Virginians of both races and opened up new avenues of religious expression and authority to lay people.[78] From the perspective of black men and women who heard or heard about white evangelical leaders' criticisms of the establishment and their occasional rebukes to masters who mistreated or neglected the souls of their slaves, evangelical groups must have seemed to be offering a more sympathetic and engaged version of Christianity than the closely limited and tightly controlled Anglican attempts at instruction and conversion they had encountered. In all of these ways evangelical practice removed several important sources of black hostility toward Christianity.

At the same time, black Virginians most likely found the practices of evangelical Christianity more compatible with patterns of spirituality and engagement with the supernatural that had emerged from African roots in the colony's black communities. The central evangelical conception of conversion as a dramatic, often sudden or even instantaneous event differed dramatically from the lifelong process of gradual growth in faith envisioned by orthodox Anglicans and vaguely resembled many West and West Central African rites of initiation into adulthood, secret societies, or healing cults in which an initiate's social and spiritual identities were transformed. Baptism and the symbolic death and rebirth it enacted also had parallels or analogues in African ritual practice that could provide a point of entry into Christianity for blacks in Virginia.[79] Spontaneous prayer, singing, and, as time went on, the bodily exercises, trances, and visions that sometimes accompanied evangelical revivals all played a similar role in helping make Christianity accessible to the enslaved through at least superficial similarity to African and Afro-Virginian practices. As Sylvia Frey and Betty Wood argue, conversion still "involved a reorientation of beliefs and practices" for blacks in British America, but such rough parallels "provided continuity with the African past, making the transition to evangelical Christianity possible."[80]

Despite these changing demographic and religious contexts, the Christianization of Virginia's enslaved population proceeded slowly and unevenly. The motives of various participants and the meanings they attached to the process continued to differ, and although blacks and whites sought to create workable, shared understandings of this new version of Christian belief and practice in spite of these differences, these multiple goals and meanings often operated in tension with one another. Davies and other revivalists certainly wanted to save souls, but their mission to the slaves served other purposes as well. Most obviously, it was a significant part of their broader indictment of the establishment's complacency and carelessness about urgent religious and spiritual matters. In lamenting the ignorance and impoverishment of the enslaved in Virginia, Davies described them as "poor neglected negroes . . . whom their masters generally neglect, and whose souls none care for, as though immortality were not a privilege common to them with their masters."[81] When Davies enumerated the sins that had brought God's retribution to the colonies in the form of the French and Indian War, he included the fact that "Thousands of poor Slaves in a Christian Country, the Property of Christian Masters, as they will be called," remained "almost as ignorant of Christianity, as when they left the Wilds of *Africa*."[82] The revivalists' contrasting success among the slaves illustrated their own greater commitment to the cause of true Christianity, regardless of social station.

The evidence that *"Ethiopia has* also *stretched forth her Hands unto God"* also served to demonstrate the transcendent power of true Christianity for white evangelicals.[83] God's salvation did not respect worldly barriers of culture or status, and evidence of the progress of God's work among previously ignored and debased sections of the population highlighted that fact. Davies said that he had "never . . . been so struck with the appearance of an assembly" as when he saw "so many black countenances eagerly attentive to every word they hear, and frequently bathed in tears."[84] Because of their humble status and the cultural distance they had to travel to become Christians, sincere black converts, even more than whites, were "astonishing monuments to divine Grace."[85] A correspondent from Richmond County approvingly reported that despite the general religious apathy of Virginians, both black and white, "amongst Mr. Davies's people, religion seems to flourish; it is like the suburbs of Heaven. . . . It is very agreeable to see the gentlemen in those parts at their morning and evening prayers with their slaves, devoutly joining with them."[86] The image of masters and slaves praying together, united in their seriousness and humility before God, was a dramatic confirmation of evangelical principles, as was the transformation of Hanover County into the suburbs of heaven.

Davies owned slaves himself, and he did not intend for his work among the slaves to challenge the larger institution of slavery. "It is the object of my zeal," he wrote, "not to make them dissenters, but good Christians and good servants."[87] Like nearly all white Virginians, Davies saw slavery as a "domestic" relationship, and he thought that the proper regulation of that relationship was essential to society and government. Heads of household and their dependents had complementary duties, "and as it is the place of the latter to obey, so it belongs to the former both to rule and to provide."[88] Indeed, Davies argued that this form of orderly authority and subordination was essential to religion as well, because heads of household were obliged to provide not only for their dependents' "perishing bodies" but also for their "immortal spirits." In this role, heads of household could and should use their power to rule to make sure that subordinate members attended to their religious duties. Davies even went so far as to argue that "when it is unavoidable compulsive measures may be taken to oblige all our domestics to an attendance" upon family worship.[89] Far from seeking to overturn slavery or other relationships of household authority, Davies understood the highest goal of such authority, even in its coercive forms, to be the promotion of true Christianity.

Despite their own conviction that conversion made better servants rather than worse ones, Davies and his fellow revivalists seemed conscious of and even defensive about potential white criticism of their work among the slaves. Most white Virginians were dubious about slave conversion even under the auspices of the established church, and the idea of entrusting such a delicate task to unlicensed enthusiasts who could not themselves be trusted to respect duly constituted authority, much less inculcate that respect in slaves, seemed foolish to many observers. As "Peter Limits" worried in the pages of the *Virginia Gazette*, the dangers of slave Christianity and of religious dissent might compound and exaggerate each other, undermining the very foundations of social order. Davies verged on protesting too much when he chose to highlight the absence of resistance from slave owners in his letters. He thought that it was "very remarkable ... that notwithstanding the odium protestant dissenters lye under in this colony ... the Negroes in these parts are freely allowed to attend upon my ministry. . . . I cannot but wonder my attempts meet with so little opposition, and escape suspicion."[90] Another evangelical working among Virginia slaves noted that "some persons have objected against their learning, as if it made them worse, but that effect has not followed on any that have been with me, so far as I know; on the contrary, they come to serve from conscience, whereas before it was from dread."[91] In anticipating criticism for their activities' potential effects on slaves, even if only to reject it, such descriptions by evangelicals revealed an anxious awareness of the broader cultural connections between Christianity and freedom and dissent and disorder that underlay reactions like Philo-Bombastia's scathing satire.

The interests and motives of white revivalists and masters were not the only ones at work, however. Black men and women sought out and responded to evangelical preaching for their own reasons, and like Anglican officials, white evangelicals were not always certain that blacks received their message in the way it was intended. Even as he celebrated his successes in teaching slaves to read, Davies worried about their motivations: "Some of them, I doubt not, are excited to it by a sincere desire to know the will of God, and what they shall do to be saved: others, I am afraid, are actuated by the meaner principle of curiosity, ambition, and vanity."[92] Given the long and complex history of black Christianization in Virginia, the motives of slaves themselves did not necessarily divide so neatly into one category or the other. Some admitted to Davies that they sought baptism so "that they may be upon an *Equality* with their Masters." He claimed that "many such converse with me, whom I am obliged to exclude from that Ordinance." But others expressed a sincere and powerful desire for the kind of transformation that evangelical conversion promised, and this yearning affected Davies deeply. "Many of them only seem to have a desire to be, they know not what," he wrote, "they feel themselves uneasy in their *present* condition, and therefore desire a *change*."[93] Tellingly, though, Davies's evocative description did not distinguish between spiritual and worldly conceptions of slaves' "present condition" or make clear the precise nature of the change they sought. Slaves' search for transcendence and meaning could never be fully divorced from their worldly condition, but neither could it be reduced to that worldly condition, and their motives for exploring Christianity reflected both of these basic facts.[94] Davies in turn understood that many slaves sought what Frey and Wood describe as "a means of reversing, or at least attenuating, the terrible psychic damage done by enslavement," and he worked within what he considered proper limits to make evangelical Christianity answer that concern, both by instructing slaves in evangelical principles of faith and redemption through Christ and by adapting his own practices to make Christianity more accessible to the men and women he encountered.[95]

This complex mix of motives and understandings of Christianity's meaning on all sides meant that interactions between potential black converts and white evangelical leaders often took on the character of a negotiation. For their own reasons, both groups searched for common ground on which their interests in and hopes for evangelical faith and fellowship overlapped or could be made compatible. This process became most visible when black men and women sought baptism. Davies readily rejected candidates whose motives he considered improper—those seeking "equality," for instance—but for the "uneasy" others the situation was less clear. Davies found that many potential converts "have generally very high notions of the efficacy of baptism," believing that "they should become Christians instantaneously" as a result of the ceremony. "It is hard," he wrote, "to convince them of the necessity of proper preparatory qualifications for it." The attitude of prospective black converts may have reflected both the influence of African ritual practice and earlier Anglican conversion efforts that made baptism the primary marker of membership in the larger Christian community. For Davies, even more than for Anglicans, baptism by itself without the deeper marks of Christian faith was meaningless, and he struggled with how, and how strictly, to judge the sincerity and understanding of those who came to him for baptism. He worried about discouraging potential converts on the one hand and creating "only *nominal* Christians" on the other. His solution was to "make their temper and conduct, rather than their speculative notions, the standard of my judgment concerning them." Davies considered those who exhibited "the Feeling and Practice of a *Christian*" to be fit for church membership, "although they should be very ignorant of many of its important doctrines."[96]

This shift in emphasis away from doctrine and toward "feeling and practice" represented a compromise of sorts between black men and women's desire for "a change" through baptism and the minister's desire to assure sincerity and understanding. As Robert Calhoon notes, this "extraordinary" innovation "introduced into evangelical ministry an unpredictable new element" that further emphasized the experiential, or what Davies and his contemporaries appropriately called "experimental," dimensions of evangelical practice.[97] Davies highlighted examples of the success of this approach and claimed that "some of them seem to have made greater progress in experimental Religion than many sincere Christians of a fairer colour."[98] At the same time, however, a nagging element of uncertainty persisted in the relationship between white and black evangelicals. Even as he explained and justified his approach to conversion and praised the success and piety of black men and women, Davies admitted that "some of them, unpolished as they are, have had art enough to impose upon my charity."[99]

The rise of evangelical Protestantism and its role in the accelerating Christianization of Virginia's free black and enslaved populations added a new order of complexity to the intertwined issues of authenticity, legitimacy, authority, and community that pervaded the discourse of religion in the colony. In seeking out evangelical preaching, black men and women sought to join a Christian community based on authentic religious experience, and they perhaps hoped to gain a degree of authority through their mastery of a complex and compelling religious vocabulary. The conversion of black Virginians was, in turn, part of evangelicals' own claims to authenticity, as evidence of both the power and truth of God's word and their own commitment to a more pure, more faithful vision of that truth than that offered by the establishment. But as Davies's anxious description suggests, white evangelicals themselves wondered and worried about the authenticity of black men and women's professions of faith and the legitimacy of their interpretations of the meanings of Christianity. They certainly understood the potential for white backlash if their converts should prove "proud and not so good servants." Moreover, because the authority of evangelical ministers like Davies rested less on official license and more on their ability to inspire, recognize, and encourage the stirrings of divine grace, significant errors in judgment about black conversion could compromise that authority, opening them up to precisely the criticisms levied by defenders of the establishment: that they were unauthorized, self-professed preachers recklessly stirring social disruption through either deliberate design or deluded self-righteousness.

This was, in a sense, the same issue that revivalists confronted elsewhere in the Anglo-American world. Proponents of evangelical Awakenings sought to defend the authority of their own experience and religious judgment and the status of the revivals as authentic manifestations of God's grace, while their opponents emphasized what they saw as imposture, excess, and error.[100] In Virginia, however, these issues became linked to those of race and slavery in ways that proved difficult to control for those on any side of the debate. White and black evangelicals struggled to manage the multiple dimensions of these issues of authority, authenticity, legitimacy, and community as they engaged with one another and with the colony's larger cultural, social, and political environment. At the same time, critics like Philo-Bombastia manipulated these links to very different ends, complicating the efforts of evangelicals of both races to control the implications of their rhetoric and practice. The effect of evangelicalism on black Virginians was a vital part of white arguments both for and against the movement's legitimacy. The result was that the links between religious dissent, race, and slavery became even more firmly entrenched, even as disagreements about the meaning and significance of these links intensified.

The religious unrest that started with the Hanover County Awakening would continue throughout the eighteenth century. Revivalist Presbyterians remained a significant force in the colony, and Baptists and Methodists soon provided new elaborations of evangelical approaches to spiritual experience and communal organization that ultimately proved even more popular and disruptive to Virginia's established patterns of religious belief and practice. The patterns set during the Hanover Awakening and the period of elaboration and growth that followed shaped these later movements in important ways. By transforming the discussion of religious toleration from one focused on exempting ethnic enclaves and insular groups from penalties to a demand to accommodate an active and growing parallel religious movement, Davies and his colleagues created a new starting point for future arguments on the subject. Similarly, the links created between dissent and slavery in both public discussion and religious practice provided the basis for new rhetorical strategies, institutional practices, and social behaviors that continued to create new layers of meaning and new interpretations of evangelicalism's implications for Virginia's social and racial order.

LITTLE SOCIETIES

The Rise of the Baptists

IN 1778 THE Baptist ministers David Barrow and Edward Mintz were assaulted while preaching near Sleepy Hole, on the Nansemond River. Barrow and Mintz were members of a rapidly growing Baptist church in neighboring Isle of Wight County, which Barrow served as pastor, and they had recently constituted a branch of that church in Nansemond County.[1] As Barrow and Mintz began to lead the audience in a hymn, they were interrupted by a gang of men who climbed onto the stage erected for the preachers and "sung one of their obscene songs."[2] This group of "impious men" dragged the ministers from the stage down to the river. Mocking the Baptists' ritual of baptism by immersion, the men swore "as [the preachers] loved *dipping*, to give them enough of it." As the shocked audience looked on, the men repeatedly dunked Barrow and Mintz in the shallow, muddy water, holding them under for nearly a minute at a time. Each time they pulled Barrow's head above the water, they asked him if he believed. Barrow finally replied, "I *believe* you will *drown* me." The attackers relented and released Barrow and Mintz, who were soaked and humiliated but not seriously injured.[3]

The attack on Barrow and Mintz was just one of many legal and extra-legal measures taken against Baptists in late eighteenth-century Virginia. Preachers across the colony and new state were assaulted and insulted by angry crowds and individuals, and they were sometimes arrested, imprisoned, and fined as disturbers of the peace by local officials.[4] The Baptist preacher Samuel Harriss, for instance, was driven off by a Culpepper

County crowd wielding "whips, sticks, clubs, & c."[5] In a famous Caroline County incident, John Waller was viciously attacked and whipped by a mob that included the Anglican parson, the clerk of the parish, and the county sheriff.[6] On Virginia's Eastern Shore, Elijah Baker was seized by a mob and carried to a ship, where the captain was instructed to "make him work for his passage over the seas, and then leave him in some of the countries in Europe."[7] Ministers' audiences could also feel the sting of this harassment, as when a gang led by Robert Ashby repeatedly disrupted a church meeting by throwing a live snake and a hornets' nest into the congregation.[8]

These incidents and others like them indicate the deepening of the religious conflict that had begun with the Hanover County Awakening in the 1740s. The arrival and explosive increase in the number of evangelical Baptists in Virginia after 1760 brought new strains of eighteenth-century revivalism and new forms of religious community to the colony, reaching individuals and areas that had been unaffected by the Presbyterian Awakening. Even more than the Presbyterians, Baptists represented a challenge to the values and practice of the Virginia establishment. The ritual of believer's baptism by immersion served as a powerful marker of membership in a godly community symbolically set apart from the larger community. The movement's extensive efforts to enforce somber dress and sober behavior reinforced this sense of distinctiveness while rejecting precisely the social occasions and styles of display through which the gentry articulated their leadership within the larger community.[9] Moreover, Baptists rejected the need for a highly trained, educated ministry (which even New Side Presbyterians had maintained, despite their opponents' complaints to the contrary) and encouraged preaching and exhortation by all men who demonstrated inspiration and talent, including free blacks and slaves. The controversy surrounding the rise of the Baptists built on the dynamics of previous conflicts, including concerns about communal unity and traditional authority, as well as issues of racial order and slavery. But just as the Hanover Awakening had reshaped earlier discourses of establishment and dissent, the Baptist movement and the conflict it provoked changed the trajectory of Virginians' arguments about religion's place in their social order in significant ways.

Among other things, the dunking of Barrow and Mintz indicated growing familiarity as well as contempt. Over the course of the 1760s and 1770s both evangelicals and their opponents came to understand the contours of religious conflict in Virginia in similar ways, albeit from different sides of the issues. The violence against and intimidation of Baptists was not simply mindless or reflexive; it revealed a deep sense of the relationship between religion and social order and of the threat Baptists posed to that relationship. By silencing preachers, disrupting meetings, or lampooning rituals, anti-evangelicals took aim at what they perceived to be the most offensive elements of the growing evangelical movement: the proliferation of seemingly unregulated forms of speech, association, authority, and meaning outside of the traditional patterns of local communities and the established church. For Baptists themselves, however, it was precisely these new forms of authority and community that constituted the worldly expressions of true Christianity, and these new forms lay at the center of their efforts to live according to God's word. The interaction between Baptists and their critics served to highlight these categories and reinforce their significance.

The experience of conflict and persecution thus shaped the Baptist movement in important ways, with important long-term effects. Public criticism and persecution of preachers like Barrow and Mintz helped animate the anti-authoritarian dimensions of Baptists' Christian practice. The vehemence of local opposition often prompted Baptists to articulate more clearly their own criticisms of the establishment and its agents, to expand their institutional and associational structures, and to crystallize their more general sense of opposition and distinctiveness. The institutions, attitudes, and rhetoric produced by this confrontation in turn became parts of the larger evangelical tradition in Virginia, available for interpretation and application far beyond their original context. Baptists' aggressive rhetoric of liberty and liberation, for instance, gained a new level of resonance in a society based on racial slavery and, as Philo-Bombastia demonstrated with regard to the Presbyterians, could easily be conflated with Baptists' spiritually and institutionally inclusive attitudes toward black converts. For hostile observers, the perceived appeal of the Baptist movement to subordinate groups provided ammunition for accusations of racial and other household disorders. These accusations in turn prompted forceful defenses from Baptist spokesmen, who justified their movement's practices and attitudes in biblical terms that set forth a new standard of justice, authority, and morality and decried worldly prejudices against these godly standards.

But this powerful, confrontational rhetoric operated alongside Baptist efforts to shape orderly religious communities in ways that more often than not reinforced worldly hierarchies, and the creative tension between these impulses persisted throughout the Revolutionary era. Different groups and individuals within the Baptist movement understood the implications of these aspects of their faith differently. The intense, emotional sharing of religious fellowship across the lines of race, sex, and status dramatized the power of God's inspiration and mercy for Baptists of all sorts, but other meanings could coexist with that fundamental evangelical concept. Black converts brought with them the long-standing association of Christianity with liberty and improved status and thus could fix on elements of evolving Baptist practice that reinforced these ideas. Slaveholding Baptists, on the other hand, could believe, as Davies did, that shared fellowship between slaves and masters not only saved souls but also created better servants by sanctifying the duties that masters and slaves owed to each other. Efforts to apply the standards of Christian fellowship to other relationships of household and community contained similarly complex and often contradictory elements. Husbands and wives, children and parents, rich and poor, and neighbor and neighbor, as well as black and white and slave and free, sought to understand and apply the principles of evangelical faith in their lives and communities.

It is important to recognize that believers' understanding of that faith did not simply depend on or arise out of their social position. Despite the fears of Baptists' opponents, subordinates did not necessarily seek to use evangelical ideas to overturn their subordination; by the same token, superiors did not necessarily seek to reinforce their own authority in any straightforward manner. Nonetheless, it is equally important to recognize the ways in which worldly status and social relationships inevitably affected the meanings of faith. When Baptist ministers invoked Isaiah's call to "proclaim liberty to the captives," it mattered whether the listener was black or white, slave or free, not simply because some might take the promise of liberty literally, while others would not, but because these factors affected how believers imagined a world reshaped by God's power and mercy might look and what it might mean for them. Thus, Baptists and other evangelicals entered the contested religious terrain of the new United States with a number of powerful, unresolved tensions about the implications of evangelical ideas for the larger social order. And because of the multivalent, sometimes contradictory pulls of different evangelical principles, these tensions existed not just between the different groups that joined Baptist churches during this period but also within those groups.

At the core of this process, holding all of these conflicting impulses together, lay the shared complex of religious ideas, vocabularies, practices, and institutions that had emerged in the years after 1750 as the Baptist denomination established itself in the southern colonies. As the experiences of David Barrow and Edward Mintz suggest, by the 1770s the increasing visibility and distinctiveness of Baptist religious practice had moved the question of Baptists' relationship to Virginia's social order to the forefront of public and private debate. But Barrow and Mintz themselves, as well as the institutions and practices they represented, were both participants in and products of a long period of religious ferment and conflict that gave the Baptist movement its shape and character. This chapter traces this process as the Baptist movement grew and expanded from the 1750s into the early 1780s. It provides an account of the development and growth of the Baptist faith in southeastern Virginia and the doctrinal debates that produced the core beliefs and practices of the Baptist denomination in the new state. It then explores the meanings those beliefs and practices held in the context of eighteenth-century Virginia culture, the ways in which early converts experienced them, and the ways in which they shaped the relationships believers established between themselves. The patterns and tensions that emerged during this period provided the foundation for Baptists' post-Revolutionary battles over how to negotiate the religious, cultural, and political landscape of the early republic, and by the nineteenth century they had become deeply woven into the social and cultural fabric of Nat Turner's Virginia.

The Baptist movement that Barrow and Mintz represented grew out of a complex process of interaction between a variety of religious traditions in the second half of the eighteenth century. Like the Presbyterian Awakening centered in Hanover County, the Baptist movement in Virginia combined religious dissent native to the colony with revivalist missionization and organization from the northern colonies. The early history of the Baptist movement in southeastern Virginia provides valuable insight into these processes, as people, ideas, and organizations representing multiple Baptist traditions crossed and recrossed the border between Virginia and North Carolina in the decades before and during the American Revolution. Members of these groups sought not only to reshape their own religious life but also to establish links between themselves and like-minded dissenters in the region. In doing so, they argued and negotiated with one another about what constituted the essential aspects of evangelical faith and community and what was merely incidental. By the second half of the 1770s these negotiations had produced a rich and distinctive strain of Baptist doctrine and practice that elaborated a set of meanings of conversion, baptism, communion, and fellowship that provided the basis for Baptist solidarity and expansion in the Revolutionary era as well as for continued reinterpretation and reapplication in the early national period.

Three groups of Baptists shaped the emergence of the denomination in the southeast: General Baptists, Regular Baptists (also known as Particular Baptists), and Separate Baptists.[10] Each of these groups left its mark on the religious culture of eighteenth- and early nineteenth-century Virginia. As mentioned in chapter 1, General Baptists emerged in the early eighteenth century as a minor dissenting group in southeastern Virginia, nurtured by the region's Quakers, with whom they shared certain historical and theological affinities. By 1729 they had established churches in Prince George, Surry, and Isle of Wight counties in Virginia as well as in Chowan, Pasquotank, and Hertford counties in North Carolina.[11] The three Virginia churches had a total of about 90 members in 1730, but after that point the movement stagnated in Virginia.[12] In 1742 an epidemic and frustration at the continued hostility toward dissenters in Virginia prompted a number of members of the Isle of Wight church to move south to Halifax County, North Carolina, where they formed the Kehukee Baptist Church.[13] By 1750 North Carolina boasted thirteen churches with 676 members, while in Virginia the original Prince George County church had disappeared around 1745, and only the remnants of the Isle of Wight County church remained.[14]

Despite the decline of the General Baptists in Virginia, the growing group of churches in North Carolina attracted the attention of Regular Baptist missionaries affiliated with the Philadelphia Baptist Association, who began to spread the Calvinist doctrine of limited atonement and the conversion-centered practices of revivalist evangelicalism in the region in the mid-1750s. As with other instances of eighteenth-century revivalism, the most important element of this newly introduced vision of Baptist faith was the idea that a transformative experience of God's saving grace lay at the heart of Christian experience. Good intentions, doctrinal soundness, and upright behavior meant little without a true, inward, and deeply emotional experience of conversion. Preaching by "unconverted" ministers, no matter how well educated or well spoken, could not nourish hungry souls or produce more than the most transient positive effects. Like revivalists across the Anglo-American world, the Regular ministers sought to convince their North Carolina audience of their dangerous, unconverted state and their need for an outpouring of God's grace. John Gano, the first of the Regular missionaries, did exactly this when he visited northeastern North Carolina in 1754 and 1755. Gano succeeded in convincing many General Baptists of their "errors touching faith and conversion" and passed judgment on the conversions of those who "submitted to examination," including one minister of whom he proclaimed "this will not do: this man has yet the needful to seek."[15]

The Regulars' vision also entailed a shift in the meaning and function of baptism. The General Baptists practiced believer's baptism as an ordinance of the church, but in their evangelical focus on conversion, revivalists dramatically changed the standards of what counted as belief. Rather than "baptizing all who believed in the doctrine of baptism by *immersion,* and requested it of them," as the General Baptists did, the missionaries from the Philadelphia Association argued that an "experience of grace"—the inward change that made possible "belief" in a deeper and more fundamental sense—was the essential prerequisite to baptism and thus to church membership.[16] In 1755 and 1756 Peter Vanhorn and Benjamin Miller built on Gano's foundation of conversionist preaching by leading a wide-ranging "reformation" of the North Carolina churches, reconstituting them "upon the principles of the doctrine of *grace.*"[17] This meant requiring evidence of a true conversion experience for full membership, exercising disciplinary oversight over church members, and emphasizing the distinctive nature of the church community through practices such as covenants and constitution rituals.[18]

The Kehukee church founded by the Isle of Wight emigrants was the first to adopt this model. Six other North Carolina churches followed suit, but the transformation did not proceed smoothly.[19] The revivalists' confrontational style and efforts to distinguish the saved from the unsaved provoked anxiety and resistance in some quarters. When a group of General Baptist preachers hesitated to give him a hearing, Gano went to their meeting and "ascended into the pulpit, and read for his text the following words, *Jesus I know, and Paul I know but who are ye?*" making "some affraid of him, and others ashamed of their shiness."[20] Similarly, Vanhorn and Miller were quickly labeled "New Lights," and some "seemed to be afraid of them."[21] The tensions produced by their powerful yet exclusionary conception of true Christianity left many torn. The remaining members of the Isle of Wight church in Virginia wrote plaintively to the Philadelphia Association in late 1756: "We . . . confess ourselves to be under [a] cloud of darkness concerning the faith of Jesus Christ, not knowing whether we are on the right foundation . . . ; wherefore we desire alliance with you, and that you will be pleased to send us helps to settle the church and rectify what may be wrong."[22] Whatever help or advice they received seems not to have answered their concerns, however; by 1763 the Isle of Wight church had become inactive.[23]

The ongoing reformation of the northeastern North Carolina churches gained an additional layer of complexity from their interaction with a third Baptist group that settled in the region in the 1750s. A substantial group of Separate Baptists from New England had migrated south and settled in north-central North Carolina at about the same time that the Regular missionaries began visiting the General churches. The Separates gained their name from their origins among independent congregations that had withdrawn from other New England denominations in the revivals of the 1740s. Led by minister Shubal Stearns from Connecticut through northwestern Virginia, the Separates had finally settled at Sandy Creek in Guilford County, in central North Carolina, in November 1755, about one hundred miles to the west of the Kehukee group. The Separates pursued an active missionary program, and the movement spread rapidly, gaining new converts and planting numerous churches.[24] While theologically similar to the Regulars, the Separates brought from New England "a very warm and pathetic" style of preaching, "accompanied by strong gestures and a singular tone of voice," as well as "tears, trembling, screams, shouts, and acclamations" among the audience.[25] The Separates also brought a profound distrust of church hierarchy and a world-denying rejection of ungodly practices and people. These characteristics provoked confusion and hostility from unsympathetic observers and cautious admiration from sympathetic ones. John Gano commented "that although they were rather immethodical, they certainly had the root of the matter at heart."[26]

As Gano's comment suggests, some leaders saw substantial potential for uniting Separate and Regular churches into a single movement, but as the two groups grew and expanded from North Carolina into Virginia, both their substantial similarities and their lingering differences became clear. The Regular Ketocton Association, in northwestern Virginia, articulated its understanding of the groups' basic compatibility in 1769. "If we are all Christians, all Baptists—all *New Lights*—why are we divided?" the group asked, and quoted Psalm 133, "'Behold how good and how pleasant it is for brethren to dwell together in unity'; but how bad and how bitter it is for them to live asunder in discord."[27] Some Separates, however, "thought the *Regulars* were not sufficiently particular in small matters, such as dress," and objected to the Philadelphia Association's written confession of faith, to which the Regulars subscribed. Regulars in turn insisted that a confession of faith was necessary to maintain unity and clarity in doctrine.[28] The complex origins of the Regular group compounded the Separates' objections. In their view, the presence among the Regulars of former General Baptists who had been "baptized before they believed" constituted an insuperable barrier to communion. In both the Regular and Separate traditions, baptism was not valid or scriptural unless it occurred after a true conversion by an experience of God's grace. Otherwise, adult baptism was no better than infant baptism.[29] As a later commentator described it, "Men were to be baptized, not to make them in heart Christians, but because they were already such."[30] Thus, in the Separates' view, those former General Baptists who had been converted and joined the new Regular churches still had to undergo true baptism as believers. Moreover, the Separates thought that the Regulars were not strict enough in judging the conversions of those they did admit into the church.[31] In essence, these objections suggested that the reformation effected by Gano, Vanhorn, and Miller in the 1750s had not been sufficiently thorough.

Because of these issues, the groups remained independent of one another through the 1760s as each pursued its own program of expansion and institutional development. The Separates formed the Sandy Creek Association in 1760, and the Regulars formed their own Kehukee Association in 1765. The associational form distinguished both groups from the General Baptists, who, perhaps reflecting the Quakers' influence, "met at *yearly meetings*, where matters of consequence were determined."[32] Although Regulars and Separates maintained the principle of congregational independence, associations, which technically acted "only as . . . advisory council[s]," served vital organizational and spiritual functions.[33] They had important practical utility as mechanisms for exchanging information, advising on difficult issues, defining orthodoxy, and providing funds and ministers for "destitute" churches. But according to their supporters, associations also furthered more abstract religious ends by fostering unity, brotherly love, and communion—both as a general "sameness of love, mind, and rule" and as a literal sharing of the Lord's Supper—between churches.[34]

Participation in associational life also helped constitute a leadership class within the evolving Baptist movement. The ministers and prominent laymen who served as delegates to association meetings, despite their merely advisory status, began to craft a vision of proper Baptist order and develop a broadly denominational perspective on the issues that faced their movement. Associational life was the province of men, and nearly exclusively white men. Potential membership in this leadership class and access to the denominational perspective it provided were important elements that distinguished white male church membership from that of white women, black women, and, somewhat more equivocally, black men. Motivated white men could reasonably expect to have some influence on the official policies and institutions of their denomination, while white and black women and black men most often found their religious influence confined to families, households, quarters, or informal networks of association outside of formal denominational structures. These boundaries were not absolute, but they were real. Although the members of the emergent leadership class did not always agree—and major divisions would occur among them—the increasing importance of associational life tended to reinforce the collective power of white men within the churches. Thus, even as competing Regular and Separate traditions struggled to define the appropriate meaning of baptism and the boundaries of church community, they were developing similar institutional structures and systems of authority and leadership that shaped the dynamics of the movement's growth in important ways.

In the midst of this unsettled but fertile religious environment the Baptist movement returned to southeastern Virginia. Both Separates and Regulars sent itinerant preachers from North Carolina to Virginia, and

by the 1760s these efforts began to bear fruit. The Separates aggressively expanded into the Virginia Piedmont, while the Kehukee Regulars began a reconquest of the southeast.[35] After early Regular successes
in Prince George and Princess Anne counties, a 1770 revival in Sussex
County combined both Regular and Separate influences and reestab-
lished a strong and enduring Baptist presence in Sussex, Isle of Wight,
Southampton, and other neighboring counties. The converts made and
the churches founded during this revival provided the foundation for
Baptist growth in the region in the 1770s and 1780s and shaped a rap-
prochement between Regular and Separate traditions that helped define
the character of the Baptist movement well into the nineteenth century.

The Sussex revival exemplified crucial aspects of the mixture of traditions and backgrounds that informed the early Baptist movement in
the swampy, rural middle ground of southeastern Virginia. Although no
detailed accounts of the revival survive, the backgrounds of the men who
were most involved in sparking and maintaining it suggest the ways in
which it combined local and external influences, Regular and Separate
Baptist traditions, and small to middling farmers and locally prominent
converts. One of the most important ministers whose preaching helped
spur the revival was John Meglamre, the pastor of the Regular Kehukee
church in North Carolina. Meglamre (sometimes spelled McGlamre or
McGlamry) was a Maryland-born Presbyterian who had converted to the
Baptist faith after moving to North Carolina about 1760. In 1767 he was
ordained as a minister, and he became the pastor at Kehukee in 1768.[36]
Brothers Benjamin and James Bell were also major players in the Sussex
revival. Benjamin had become a Baptist after living somewhere south
of the Kehukee group, probably in South Carolina. His brother James
was a prominent citizen in Sussex County who at various times served
as militia captain, justice of the peace, sheriff, and General Assembly
representative. James's intelligence and talents "gained the general esteem of every respectable character in Sussex, and the adjacent counties." Under Benjamin's influence, James experienced the classic early
stages of evangelical conviction. He became deeply concerned about his
spiritual state and anxiously began to search for assurance of his salvation. He was converted and baptized by Meglamre during the revival and
soon became a popular and influential minister.[37] John Rivers, another
native of Sussex County, was also awakened during the 1770 revival. He
was baptized by the Separate minister Jeremiah Walker, who was active

in the counties to the west of Sussex, and became a member of Harper's Baptist Church in neighboring Dinwiddie County. Like James Bell, Rivers became a minister and active promoter of the ongoing Baptist resurgence in Sussex and surrounding counties.[38]

Two churches emerged out of the initial revival. Raccoon Swamp Baptist Church was constituted in June 1772 with eighty-seven members. Meglamre became the pastor, resigning from the Kehukee church to live among his new congregation in Sussex.[39] Sappony Baptist Church, also in Sussex County, was formed soon after Raccoon Swamp, in 1773. John Rivers served as the first pastor, and the church was "founded on what was then called the Separate order." After Rivers's death James Bell took over the pastorate of Sappony.[40] As the largest and most active church in the area, Raccoon Swamp formed several branches in Sussex and neighboring counties, many of which went on to become churches in their own right. The most important of these was a branch in Isle of Wight County on Mill Swamp, in the same neighborhood as the General Baptist congregation that had died out in 1763. Indeed, there is considerable evidence that the old General church provided at least some of the foundation for the Mill Swamp branch: as the denominational historian Garnett Ryland points out, "Five of the eight surnames of the signers of the [1756 Isle of Wight General Baptists'] letter to the Philadelphia Association appear among the earliest members of Mill Swamp."[41] In 1774 the Mill Swamp branch of Raccoon Swamp was constituted as a separate church, and David Barrow, then a newly ordained, twenty-one-year-old minister from Brunswick County, became the pastor. With the help of Meglamre and others, he organized branches of the Mill Swamp church at Black Creek in Southampton County and at South Quay, Western Branch, and Shoulder's Hill (near the site of Barrow and Mintz's dunking) in Nansemond County.[42] All of these branches had become separate churches by the middle of the 1780s. Several other branches of Raccoon Swamp formed during the 1770s would also become churches in their own right in the 1780s: Meherrin in Southampton County, Seacock and High Hills of Nottoway in Sussex County, and Otterdams in Surry County.[43] In less than a decade after the Sussex revival, then, the foundations of an enduring Baptist presence throughout southeastern Virginia had been firmly established (table 1).

The wave of conversions and expansion in the early 1770s built on both Separate and Regular foundations, as ministers and preachers

Table 1. RACCOON SWAMP AND MILL SWAMP BRANCH CONGREGATIONS, 1770–1780

Name of branch	County	Organized as branch[a]	Separate church
RACCOON SWAMP			
Mill Swamp	Isle of Wight	1772	1774
Meherrin	Southampton	1773	1788
Otterdams	Surry	1773	1787
Brunswick[b]	Brunswick	1773	
Seacock	Sussex	1779	1787
High Hills	Sussex	—	1787
MILL SWAMP			
South Quay	Nansemond[c]	1774	1785
Black Creek	Southampton	1774	1786
Western Branch	Nansemond	1777	1779
Shoulder's Hill	Nansemond	1779	1785

Sources: Raccoon Swamp [Antioch] Baptist Church, Minute Book, 1772–1837, LVA; Mill Swamp Baptist Church, Minute Book, 1777–1790, LVA; South Quay Baptist Church, Minute Book, 1775–1827, LVA; Black Creek Baptist Church, Minute Book, 1776–1804, LVA; Shoulder's Hill Baptist Church, Minute Book,1783–1923, VBHS; Semple, *Rise and Progress of the Baptists in Virginia;* Burkitt and Read, *Concise History of the Kehukee Baptist Association;* Gardner, *Baptists of Early America.*

[a] Estimated date.

[b] The Raccoon Swamp minutes mention a branch in Brunswick, but it is not clear that this body ever became a separate church. Raccoon Swamp [Antioch] Baptist Church, Minute Book, 1772–1837, 17 July 1773, LVA.

[c] South Quay was in Nansemond County until 1786, when an adjustment of county borders made it part of Southampton County.

from Separate churches to the west of Sussex worked alongside Regulars from the Kehukee Association to spread a Baptist vision of evangelical faith and community. This cooperation in a common enterprise intensified efforts to unite the two groups, particularly as influential Regulars came to sympathize with Separates' rigor in setting the boundaries of communion and fellowship. In 1772 delegates from each group visited the other's association in an attempt to negotiate a union, but the same difficulties remained. Individual churches gathered from the fruits of the mixed revival grappled with these issues as well. In 1773 the Raccoon Swamp church, whose pastor, John Meglamre, had been one of the Kehukee Association's delegates to the Separates, considered "whither it is legal to hold communion with a person Baptised before he Believ'd." After considering the query on Christmas Day 1773, the church conference, "except one voice," decided that they might hold such communion, upholding the compromise between the reformed present of the Kehukee churches and the group's more theologically diverse past.[44] But the matter was not settled. The Separates' objections to the Regulars' practices "operated strongly on the minds of many belonging to the Kehukee Association."[45]

In 1774 these concerns prompted a number of churches and ministers in the Kehukee Association to reconsider their position. Four churches, including Meglamre's congregation at Raccoon Swamp and David Barrow's new Mill Swamp church, decided that they could no longer hold communion with those who had been baptized before their true conversion and that they could not remain connected to churches that did. Several other churches later followed suit. It is not clear exactly how or why opinion at Raccoon Swamp changed so drastically between the December 1773 query and the 1774 decision.[46] One possibility was that Meglamre (the lone dissenting voice?) and perhaps others undertook to persuade the church to adopt the more strict position. Indeed, increased rigor and strictness in discipline and church practice were often part of religious revivals and intensified commitment within churches. Raccoon Swamp's reversal on the issue may have fit this pattern, serving as a type of revival or renewal of commitment within the church spurred by ministerial calls for increased rigor in enforcing the boundaries of communion.[47] Whatever the case, the decision of Raccoon Swamp and the other reformist churches provoked a bitter split in the Kehukee Association.[48] The traditionalists felt that questions about the meaning and appropriate application of believer's baptism had been resolved in the 1750s and that in bringing up the issue the reformers were being unnecessarily divisive. They argued that "more mischief might ensue by being too rigorous than by submitting to small inconveniences for the sake of peace."[49] But for the reformers and the Separates, this greater rigor at the expense of peace and complacency was precisely the point.

In 1777 Meglamre, Barrow, and the representatives of four other reformist Kehukee Association churches met with those of four Separate churches at James Bell's Sappony church in Sussex County. These representatives constituted their ten churches into a new Kehukee Association, uniting Regulars and Separates by combining aspects of both traditions. In a concession to the Regulars, they adopted a written confession of faith, but the contents of that confession reflected the Separates' vision of baptism and church community. It confirmed that "baptism and the Lord's Supper are Gospel ordinances, both belonging to the converted, or true believers," and, most importantly, "that [persons baptized in unbelief] ought to be baptized after they are savingly converted into the faith of Christ." Other articles emphasized the independence of individual churches on matters of discipline while at the same time maintaining the advisory utility of associations.[50] After establishing this confession as the basis of the new Kehukee Association, the representatives took up more specific issues on which their churches required advice: if an ordained Presbyterian minister converted and became a Baptist, was his ordination valid in the Baptist church? (no); what should a church do if a minister tried to persuade them that "difference in judgment about water baptism ought to be no bar to communion?" (deal with him "as an offender").[51]

With these principles established, the new Kehukee Association began a period of rapid development and expansion. Over the next decade, the association met frequently in both North Carolina and Virginia and received more than fifteen new churches into fellowship, including many that had initially refused to join the reformed group, as well as newly planted churches and established bodies seeking greater connection with their brethren.[52] By 1791 the association had grown so large that the churches in Virginia amicably split from the original group to form the Virginia Portsmouth Baptist Association, in which the veteran reformers and association builders Meglamre and Barrow played leading roles.[53] The reformed Kehukee Association also provided the template for a wider reconciliation of the Separate and Regular traditions in North Carolina and Virginia. In 1787 the two groups officially united on terms that reflected the issues and the settlement crafted by the Kehukee Association. The Separates agreed that the Regulars' confession of faith "holds forth the essential truths of the Gospel" and emphasized "that the doctrine of salvation by Christ and free, unmerited grace alone ought to be believed by every Christian and maintained by every minister of the Gospel." But Separates also maintained their scruples about written confessions by making it clear that "to prevent the confession of faith from usurping a tyrannical power over the conscience of any, we do not mean that every person is bound to the strict observance of everything therein contained."[54] In 1788 the Kehukee Association commemorated this move, recording their motion that "those *bars* which heretofore subsisted between the baptists amongst us . . . be taken down; . . . and that the names *Regular* and *Separate* be buried in oblivion, and that we should be henceforth known to the world by the name of the *United Baptist*."[55]

While celebrated as landmarks in denominational history, these later developments largely reflected transformations that had already occurred among southeastern Virginia's and northeastern North Carolina's Baptist communities from the 1750s to the 1780s. As General Baptists became Regular Baptists, and Regular Baptists united with Separate Baptists, leaders and churches negotiated and refined the essentials of Baptist faith, visiting and revisiting a series of central questions: What constituted true conversion? What was the appropriate relationship between conversion and baptism? What was and was not appropriate behavior for a Christian? How, and how strictly, should churches judge and enforce such behavior? How much disagreement and diversity on these issues could Christians tolerate while still remaining united with one another? These issues remained contested ones in Nat Turner's Virginia— in many ways living as an evangelical meant constantly confronting and evaluating these questions rather than definitively resolving them— but the concepts of conversion, baptism, communion, discipline, and fellowship that emerged from the region's complex doctrinal and institutional history formed the core of Baptists' conceptual and rhetorical vocabulary in the late eighteenth and early nineteenth centuries. Even though Baptists sometimes disagreed with each other about the application of these concepts, they generally agreed on their centrality and basic nature; to a large extent it was this agreement that made them Baptists.

To understand how this process worked and what its implications were for the social and cultural world of eighteenth-century Virginia, we need to explore as best we can how converts experienced church membership and the rituals and meanings of fellowship: what did it mean to become a Baptist? Ministerial writings and other personal accounts provide insight into the nature of conversion and of some of the most dramatic aspects of evangelical experience—revivals, preaching and prayer meetings, conviction of sin, and the new birth—all of which are vital to understanding the world of the Virginia Baptists. At the same time, these sources must be complemented with an understanding of the daily and weekly minutiae of belonging to a church community and living as a Baptist in late eighteenth-century Virginia. It is crucially important to understand the seemingly mundane and repetitive aspects of Baptist life, because the mechanisms, procedures, and ritualized language through which churches pursued their daily business constituted in themselves a discourse of religious and moral meanings. Church members of both races and both sexes drew on this discourse in their everyday interactions in church, learning the subtleties and the weight that different stock phrases could carry and learning how to interpret and apply those phrases to make meaningful statements themselves. The discourse of evangelicalism and the rituals of the church community created a standard of conduct, authority, and meaning that posited a source outside of worldly relationships; as they learned this language and the procedures of church government, converts could interpret and manipulate these concepts as ways of making claims to moral and spiritual authority, both within and outside of their churches.

Baptists in the southern colonies, like the Calvinist puritans of the seventeenth century and other eighteenth-century evangelical groups, placed direct experience of God and individual conversion at the center of their Christian vision. Baptist ministers described this experience in an evocative language of transformation: "We believe that none are saved by CHRIST but the regenerate, that is, such who are sometimes in this life born again, and made new creatures." The truly regenerate experienced "a real inward change of heart as well as of life and conversation" through the power of "an irresistible work of the holy spirit wrought in the soul."[56] Such a change could only come from faith in God, a faith that went beyond the outward forms of belief to something more fundamental and miraculous: "it is an act of the new creature, whereby he beholds the glory of the LORD and is changed into the same image."[57] For eighteenth- and nineteenth-century evangelicals, far more than for most seventeenth-century puritans, this direct experience of God's mercy and power took theological precedence over all other facets of Christianity.

Conversion, however, was a wrenching process, accomplished only by the grace of God. Baptist converts reported intense suffering under the conviction of their own sinfulness and the realization that their own corrupt nature prevented them from ever attaining or deserving salvation on their own merits. Because of Adam's original sin, all humans were "reduced to the vilest slavery; and are in perfect bondage to their spiritual enemies. Sin and Satan, and the world, and the flesh have an absolute dominion over them."[58] In such a state, there was nothing a man or woman could do to meet with God's approval; "all his performances, whether natural, or civil, or religious, are but just so many sins in the sight of GOD."[59] Some converts recounted their efforts to achieve salvation by observing the outward forms of religion. The minister James Ireland observed that "if heaven could have been obtained by the exercise of human endeavours and self-sufficiency I, perhaps, might have laid for such a claim." But he ultimately realized that his "groans and tears" meant nothing in themselves and "that the law [i.e., God's law] was spiritual and reached even to the discovery of my inbred polution."[60]

Upon reaching this nadir, prospective converts realized that they "stood in need of a better righteousness" than they could achieve through their own efforts, "a righteousness wrought out by the obedient life and rich atoning death of the Son of God."[61] The first glimmer of hope began with this realization, that despite their unworthiness, God had offered men and women the hope of salvation through the sacrifice of his son. But how could one be sure that one was among the elect? How could one know "that an application of the blood of Christ hath been made to his soul"?[62] After realizing the possibility of salvation, those in the throes of the conversion crisis anxiously sought evidence that they would be saved. Sometimes suddenly, sometimes gradually, assurance came. Indeed, relief from the anxiety itself was evidence that God had given the gift of faith, without which men and women would never truly be able to trust in God. As Ireland put it, God had entered his heart and "removed my burden of sin and guilt, giving me to possess that peace which was beyond understanding."[63] For the converted, anxiety and despair were replaced with "an unfeigned repentance, a supreme love to GOD, an honest zeal for his glory, deep humility, a lively hope, and a daily endeavour after sincere obedience to all the known requirements of the divine law."[64]

The idea of this personal, internal change lay at the heart of the Baptists' faith and provided much of the denomination's powerful attraction for those who joined. But despite the seeming individualism of its central theological tenet, the Baptist ethos was in practice social and communal rather than individualistic.[65] Even in the experience of conversion, Baptists understood that they were joining a collective body of the elect, becoming "Christians" in the fullest sense, fit for "that glory that is reserved for the followers of the Lamb" and part of both "the church *catholic* . . . all that have been, or ever will be saved" and "the church *militant* . . . the saints on earth."[66] On a less abstract level, of course, they also joined a "*particular* church . . . a little distinct and separate society, called out of the world, and professing faith in Christ Jesus."[67] Indeed, in many ways the Baptist movement was as much about creating these particular churches as it was about making converts. The languages of church community complemented and blended with those of conversion in shaping the movement. Fellowship, communion, and gospel order were concepts as essential to the development of the denomination as the burden of sin, the power of grace, and the new birth.

Most evangelicals created new forms of community and association, through prayer and reading groups, for instance, or through the Methodist class system, but Baptists gave this impulse its fullest and most elaborate expression. By making adult believer's baptism by immersion the gateway to church membership, they created a dramatic ritual process that simultaneously symbolized the concept of the new birth and that of a gathered church of saints. As the minister William Fristoe described it, "According to the scriptures, a death, burial, and resurrection is represented in a striking figure when a believer is immersed in baptism and raised up again; for thereby a death to sin and a resurrection to newness of life is represented."[68] Baptism was also usually a communal ritual. Prospective church members were "received by experience" after providing a detailed account of their conversion, from the crushing weight of their first conviction of sin to the joyous experience of God's saving grace. Once the experience was judged to be a true conversion, a time and place for the candidate's baptism would be appointed—most churches had a traditional spot at a nearby body of water. Sometimes the baptism occurred immediately, but more often it was set for the next Sunday morning, which was often the next day, since the church meetings at which experiences were received were frequently held on Saturday. At the appointed time, the minister, the candidate, and members of the congregation would assemble at the water, and the minister would speak a few words, lead a prayer, and then lead the candidate into the water, "where the whole body of the person is immersed in the name of the Father, and of the Son, and of the Holy Ghost."[69] The candidate emerged from the water symbolically reborn not only into a new life but also into a new community.

The Baptist church community was not literally separate from the rest of the world, of course. As Jewel Spangler points out, Baptist converts continued to participate actively in the political and economic life of their counties, and in many ways Baptist expansion built on "preexisting relationships of family, neighborhood, and friendship."[70] But the church was ritually set apart as a distinct cultural realm with rules for its members that differed from those of the outside world. Church members "joyn[ed] together in a gospel Church Relation and fellowship,"[71] and much of Baptists' energy and effort was spent in determining just how to make that abstract conception a social reality. Baptists knew that in theory God's truth was unitary and perfect and that unity and harmony among Christians was much to be desired, as when the Regulars appealed to the Separates on the grounds that true Christians, "all Baptists—all *New Lights*," should not live in discord. But in a fallen world even the saints had to struggle to see the truth, and disagreements and ambiguities abounded. While some sins were obvious and could result in a church member's suspension or expulsion, others were less clearly defined and their effects on fellowship harder to determine. Repentant sinners could be restored to the church, but how did the church judge repentance, and how much repentance was enough? The tensions between the abstract, unitary truth of God's law and the manifold, dizzying complexities of social reality gave rise to multiple interpretations of what it meant to follow God's law in the world. Church records reveal just how, through written covenants, queries in church, and disciplinary oversight of members' conduct, Baptists sought to define and to discern in practice the proper boundaries of fellowship between Christians and the proper conduct of Christians in the world.

Church covenants sought to capture the nature of Baptists' combined sense of sacred meaning and social interaction. Covenants were agreements signed by the founding members of a church and subscribed to by all new members that laid out the purpose of the church, the duties of the members to God and to one another, and sometimes a more detailed statement of faith and doctrine. The Baptist tradition of covenants went back to the British churches of the seventeenth century. In America, the Philadelphia Baptist Association popularized the form in 1742, when it published a version of the 1689 London Confession of Faith. The publication also included "A Short Treatise of Church Discipline," which included a discussion "Of the Manifold Duties of Christians, Especially to the Household of Faith." Because of this link to the Philadelphia Association, the use of covenants seems to have been most prevalent in the Regular Baptist tradition in Virginia, although many Separate-derived churches also used them.[72]

The earliest recorded covenant among the churches in Isle of Wight, Southampton, and Sussex counties is from David Barrow's church at Mill Swamp, in Isle of Wight County. Probably authored by Barrow himself, it was recorded at the church's constitution in July 1774. Later covenants at Mill Swamp's daughter churches, South Quay and Black Creek, were closely modeled on this one.[73] There is also some evidence of an earlier generation of covenants. Lemuel Burkitt and Jesse Read's 1803 history of the Kehukee Association provides an example of a covenant said to characterize those of the churches reconstituted "upon the principles of the doctrine of *grace*" by Gano, Vanhorn, and Miller in the 1750s.[74] The Raccoon Swamp "church constitution," which appears as a copy of a lost 1772 original in the minute book begun in 1837, is nearly identical to this Kehukee covenant.[75] This link is most likely attributable to John Meglamre, who was pastor of the Kehukee church in North Carolina in the late 1760s and then founder and first pastor of Raccoon Swamp in 1772. Although shorter and less literary, this early covenant has most of the same basic features as those from Mill Swamp, South Quay, and Black Creek, suggesting both the specific genealogical link between these churches and a more general conformity among them regarding the essentials of the "gospel Church Relation and fellowship."

Most of the covenants began with a statement that God had "called us out of our state of nature (in which state we were enemies to God by wicked works)" or "been pleased to call us out of darkness into his marvellous light."[76] Some covenants also contained a statement of the essentials of faith and a reference to the London Confession of Faith as adopted by the Philadelphia Association.[77] But the essential part of the covenant was that the church members agreed to "give ourselves to the Lord and to one another by the will of God."[78] This notion was at the heart of Baptists' conception of the church, fusing the individuality of evangelicals' emphasis on personal conversion and experience of God with collective organization, shared ritual practice, and a shared sense of meaning and purpose. Conversion and the experience of God's saving grace enabled church members to give themselves to one another through God's power, and this newly created community helped its members to live and worship together according to his laws.

The covenants also laid out more specific duties of church members to God and to one another. The members of Mill Swamp recorded that they

> do Solemly and Volintary and mutually Covenant with one another to meet to gather Every Lords Day as many as Can Conveniently to Celebrate the worship of God and to edify one another in his Servise

in the best manner we Can and doe promise to each other to keep
the [Lord's] day holy and to watch over Each of our family and Children under our Care that they doe the same and all times to behave
our Selves as becomes the gospel of our dear Redeamer Jesus Christ
. . . and jointly to maintain the worship of god and to Edify one another in Love and as god Shall Enable us by his grace to maintain
the doctrine of the blessed gospel and to Regulate by the word of
god and to watch over one another in the lord . . . and to admonish
and to Encourge and to Reprove if nead be according to Gospel Rule
in Love and to be admonished and Reproved by one another as the
word of god directs and as far as God Shall Enable us to perform all
mutual duties toword each other or to those that hearafter join with
us . . . and not to depart Irregularly from Each other without Regular dismission And that we Shall as god Shall give Means & ability
and Conveniancy & Opportunity to attend on the Means of Grace
Institutions & Ordinances of the Gospel hoping & Relying upon
Almighty God for grace Wisdom & Spiritual Guidance & ability to
Adorn this our Profession & to perform our duties & to bless us With
grace Suitable to our Privilages that he in his Mercy and Goodness
hath bestowed upon us in his house through Jesus Christ our Lord.[79]

The world invoked by church covenants was one in which the converted
joined together to maintain regular, orderly worship, keep the Sabbath,
perform and encourage family prayer, exercise disciplinary oversight
over members' behavior, perform the ritual of the Lord's Supper, and
regulate the boundaries of the church through admission, dismission,
suspension, and excommunication. It was this complex of duties, infused
with divine meaning and combined with the essential, evangelical fact of
conversion, that constituted the elusive but equally essential Baptist conception of fellowship. The phrase "Gospel Rule in Love" accurately reflected the charged combination of exaltation and submission that concept involved. Mutuality, discipline, divine inspiration and sanction, and
obedience to a higher law and set of moral and spiritual imperatives all
were part of this ideal, but none by itself encompassed it.

The exact manner in which these principles were to be pursued was less
clear, and much of the business in the early decades of Baptist activity in

southeastern Virginia was devoted to creating specific practices that enacted these ideals of fellowship. As the movement matured in southeastern Virginia, ministers and congregations faced constant queries about
the rituals, mechanisms, and policies of their churches. Much of this work
was essential but mundane, such as deciding the time and day of meetings, arranging for preaching and communion at far-flung branches of
large churches, and deciding the best method of collecting funds for the
support of the church.[80] Other issues required more consideration, however. What exactly were the proper boundaries of the church community?
To what extent did the rules of the covenanted church community differ
from those of the world, and in what ways? What did church membership
and true Christian fellowship mean for the relationships of household
and neighborhood that constituted rural society in eighteenth-century
Virginia?

One of the primary areas in which the churches actively confronted and
sought to answer these questions was the process of church discipline.[81]
Disciplinary concerns made up the majority of the business conducted
at church meetings, reflecting just how important discipline was in the
rhythms and rituals of Baptist church membership. Discipline reflected
one constellation of the church covenants' primary goals, "to Regulate by
the word of god and to watch over one another in the lord . . . and to admonish and to Encourge and to Reprove if nead be according to Gospel
Rule in Love and to be admonished and Reproved by one another as the
word of god directs." Church members sought to help one another live
according to God's laws, and they had a duty to prod their errant brethren firmly yet lovingly back onto the proper path. Doing so maintained
the purity of the church and reminded Christians of their duties to God.
At least in theory, the sins that ran rampant in the world—vanity, drunkenness, gambling, fornication, all kinds of disorder—were banned from
the church, where "Gospel Rule in Love" prevailed. Church members
were held to a different and higher standard—God's standard—and the
entire community of the church was dedicated to defining that standard
and seeing that its members upheld it as part of their duty to God.

In practice, discipline involved a set of more or less regular stages that
were meant to ensure justice and to reform members within the church
rather than drive them out.[82] When an accusation was presented against
a member, the church appointed a committee of members to investigate
the charge and, if necessary, cite the member to appear in church to an-

swer the accusation. If the charge was found to be groundless or the defendant confessed and expressed sincere repentance, the church usually stated its satisfaction and the member was retained in good standing. If the church determined that the defendant was guilty and he or she did not appear repentant, the defendant could be suspended from the rites of the church; if the offense was severe enough and the defendant's behavior seemed to warrant it, the congregation could pass a sentence of full excommunication, declaring the defendant "out of the watch and care" of the church. Even excommunication was not final, however; excommunicated members could still return to the church, acknowledge their faults, and be restored.

Through these processes, church discipline provided a regular forum in which church members confronted the world and one another and judged each according to the rules of gospel order. Historians have long noted that concerns about order were an important element of early evangelicalism in Virginia.[83] Evangelicalism's initial popularity in more recently settled and clerically underserved areas seems to reflect a desire for order, spiritual meaning, and community among early converts.[84] The language of church discipline highlights this concern. Many accusations involved unspecified offenses of "disorder" or "disorderly walking," suggesting that in many cases it was the violation of the rules of fellowship, rather than the specific nature of the violation, that concerned the churches.[85] The wide variety of cases in which an offense was specified reveal that this vision of gospel order entailed correct religious principles, moral behavior, and harmonious relations among Christians. Disputes between church members required investigation and mediation, and churches devoted a great deal of effort to reconciliation. The members of Black Creek spent more than a year, at least seven church meetings, and a specially appointed day of fasting and prayer in restoring fellowship between Henry Jones and Shadrach Lewis after a dispute over Jones's work on Lewis's house.[86]

Other forms of social or religious disorder were also monitored, and many of these also echoed both traditional standards of morality and traditional functions of church courts, such as sexual discipline. Thomas Oberry, for instance, was excommunicated from South Quay for fornication in 1783, while at Raccoon Swamp, William Roe was excommunicated for "whoredom."[87] Doctrinal and denominational matters also played a role in church discipline. The members of Raccoon Swamp wondered "what is to be done with a member, that holds, that God did not consider man a fallen creature, in making the covenant with his son."[88] And perhaps most unsavory of all these offenders, for her Baptist brethren at least, was Salley Harrison, who was "laid under censure for fellowshipping the Principles of the Methodist."[89]

Drunkenness was rampant among eighteenth-century Virginians, and church members appear to have been no exception. Drinking to excess was the single most common charge leveled against church members throughout the late eighteenth and early nineteenth centuries.[90] Sometimes drunkenness was a momentary lapse in discipline that was corrected by a communal reminder. In 1777 Joseph Lancaster's "excess of drinking" prompted Mill Swamp to appoint a committee of prominent members "to deal with him to try to Reclaim him," and he was soon restored to the church.[91] Many members, however, seem to have had recurrent problems with alcohol. At Black Creek, for example, Mary Johnson was dealt with for "Drinking to excess" in May 1776, and she was restored in September of that year. But she faced the same accusation again in November 1778 and was excommunicated from the church.[92] Drunkenness was also a frequent aggravating circumstance in or component of other offenses, as when James Gwin was expelled from Black Creek for excessive drinking and "other Crimes aledg'd against him" or when Sarah Savage was excommunicated from Mill Swamp "for Revelling and other disorders."[93]

The churches took aim at drunkenness not merely because it was so prevalent among Virginians of all stripes but also because it so easily led to other kinds of disorder. The tragic case of Matthew Womble served as a cautionary tale in this respect. Womble was an early member of Mill Swamp who was "chargd with drinking to an Excess and other Evle practices" in 1777.[94] He disappeared from Mill Swamp's records after that, most likely expelled from the church, but in 1784 he murdered his pregnant wife and four sons in a drunken rampage, and the Baptist minister John Leland composed a narrative poem about the incident that explained it in terms of evangelical concerns about drunkenness, household, family, and religion. The poem's simple rhyming couplets matched Leland's didactic purpose. Womble, Leland wrote, had once "walk'd in paths of righteousness" as a professed Christian, but "Westindia Rum and apple Brandy, / Shook his foundation, which was sandy." Womble got roaring drunk one night, and when his neighbor James Deford came to visit, "he got his axe and swore" that he would kill Deford where he stood. Deford escaped and ran to get aid, but before he could gather a sufficient force, Womble killed his wife and sons while his two daughters hid under the bed. Womble then fled into the swamp near his house, where he was captured after the party in pursuit heard him talking.[95]

Under arrest, his rage spent, Womble sadly explained that his actions had been the result of a religious delusion:

> I saw a man exceedingly bright,
> Like to an angel of the light;
> A splendid guard attend around,
>
> . . . .
> I thought it was the son of God.

This shining vision told him, "If you to heaven would e're attain, / Your wife and children must be slain." Womble claimed that, following this instruction, "I kill'd them all to get to heaven." After the murder, however, the bright man and his hosts "wanton'd in the human blood," and after conversing with the man in the swamp (which was how he was discovered) Womble realized "'twas Satan in disguise." Wracked with guilt, Womble "declared that he could hear the ghosts of his children, that seemed to be flying round him, crying daddy, mammy, & c." He was executed for his crimes, and Leland provided the moral:

> Let this a solemn warning be
> To those who use strong drink too free,
> And all apostates lend an ear,
> For their destruction draweth near.[96]

In the story as Leland framed it, drunkenness was not merely an inappropriately worldly behavior; it was a moral weakness that could provide a point of entry for the most shocking and fundamental perversions of religious and household order. By submitting themselves to the watch and care of the church, members of the Baptist community guarded one another from such weakness, but those who left the church had no such protection. Matthew Womble's fate was an extreme illustration of these dangers. While not all drunkards or apostates mistook the devil for Jesus or traded their role as protector and provider for that of murderer,

Leland's interpretation of the story implied that only luck and the grace of God prevented this. Moreover, by understanding the murders in terms of moral weakness and satanic manipulation, Leland and other evangelicals could make sense of a horrifying, disruptive, and seemingly senseless crime by making clear the principles of order that had been violated. Abandoning gospel order meant death and destruction in a spiritual sense, if not necessarily in the literal sense illustrated by the Womble murders. For believers, the fate was just as real and just as terrifying.

Even as Baptists worked to define and implement their own vision of gospel order, however, their opponents accused them of destroying the fundamental structures of household, family, race, and community that ordered Virginia society. Controversy and resistance dogged the Baptist movement from the beginning and gained strength as the movement expanded in the late 1760s and 1770s. As David Barrow, Edward Mintz, and many others found, this resistance could take the form of physical assaults, but it could also take the form of legal harassment, arrest, and imprisonment. While many Baptist ministers neglected or on principle refused to obtain a license to preach, local officials did not usually charge them with specifically religious offenses, preferring instead the more flexible charge of "disturbing the peace," which may also have more accurately reflected their sense of the Baptists' disruptiveness. In 1768, for instance, a Spotsylvania County prosecutor argued to local magistrates that a group of Baptist ministers were "great disturbers of the peace; they cannot meet a man upon the road, but they must ram a text of Scripture down his throat." A subsequent letter characterized those same ministers' offense as "running into private houses and making dissensions."[97] To those who opposed the Baptists, the order they envisioned and their means of pursuing it looked like the essence of disorder.

In 1772 the *Virginia Gazette* published "An Address to the Anabaptists imprisoned in Caroline County," most immediately aimed at preachers who had been jailed for disturbing the peace in that county but clearly intended as a broader condemnation of the movement itself. Its critiques echoed those expressed in the 1768 Spotsylvania controversy. The author of the address charged Baptists with using their emphasis on the weight of sin and the necessity of true conversion to "terrify and frighten many honest, and . . . pious Men, to forsake their Church and the cheerful innocent society of their Friends and Families, and turn sour, gloomy, severe, and censorious to all about them."[98] This somewhat petulant complaint may have been apt in its own way. Baptists themselves seemed to delight in telling similar stories of proud, careless men brought down by the sudden conviction of their own sinfulness. James Ireland presented his own conversion in these terms, as well as the stunned reaction of a worldly friend when he saw Ireland's "disconsolate looks, emaciated countenance, and solemn aspect."[99] The dramatic social encounters that for Baptists demonstrated the power of the extended conversion experience seemed profoundly dysfunctional to other Virginians.[100]

But the leveling of masculine pride was only the beginning of the disorders envisioned by the address's author. Baptists' irresponsible scare tactics were a means by which "Wives are drawn from their Husbands, Children from their Parents, and Slaves from the Obedience of their Masters. Thus the very Heartstrings of those little Societies which form the greater are torn in sunder, and all their Peace destroyed."[101] This critique got to the heart of the issue, for it linked Baptists' disregard for the establishment with the other fundamental structures of order in eighteenth-century Virginia. Baptists' threat to the "little societies" of orderly white households ultimately threatened "the greater" society of neighborhood, county, colony, church, and country.

A 1777 petition to the House of Delegates from Cumberland County recorded similar complaints and linked them to the long history of debates about dissent and disorder in Virginia. The petitioners complained that Baptists caused great mischief

by persuading the ignorant and unwary to embrace their erroneous tenets, which the petitioners conceive to be not only opposite to the doctrines of true christianity, but subversive of the morals of the people, and destructive of the peace of families, tending to alienate the affection of slaves from their masters, and injurious to the happiness of the public; that while such attempts are making, to pull down all the barriers which the wisdom of our ancestors have erected to secure the church from the inroads of the sectaries.[102]

Although they were aimed at the Baptists, these fears reached back to the history of dissent in colonial Virginia more broadly and echoed the concerns about error, authenticity, and order that pervaded the discourse of establishment and dissent. From the days of the Puritans and Quakers in the mid-seventeenth century to the Presbyterian Awakening led by Samuel Davies, the disorder of dissenters was seen as particularly dangerous to relationships of household and later racial subordination. By rejecting the rule of local Anglican elites and the accumulated wisdom of the establishment and by offering church membership and the intimate sharing of gospel fellowship to women, servants, free blacks, and slaves independently of fathers, husbands, and masters, Baptists activated this set of preconceptions and faced many of the same criticisms as their predecessors.

In responding to these critiques, Baptists themselves proved less than reassuring to their critics. Indeed, in the face of persecution and criticism, they developed an often confrontational language of liberty and righteousness that only heightened the seeming contrast between evangelical values and the old order. David Thomas, a Regular minister in Fauquier County, wrote his 1774 pamphlet, *The Virginian Baptist,* in part as a defense against accusations like those of the "Address to the Anabaptists." With that critique clearly in mind, Thomas sought to defend Baptists from charges of "making Divisions" between "slaves and their masters; children and their parents; yea, wives and their husbands" and breaking "the bonds of natural affection and bursted the strongest cords of relation asunder." Thomas responded that the peace that Baptists were so often accused of disturbing was "a false peace arising from ignorance and unbelief, and self love and carnal security." The gospel could break some out of this false peace, but others would only intensify their own attachment to the world as a result. "On this account, our SAVIOUR told his disciples that he 'came not to send peace on earth but rather division.'" If the relatives, masters, or neighbors of those awakened to God could not reconcile themselves to the truth, it was, sadly, only to be expected that they would vent "their malice against those who embrace the gospel."[103]

Though Thomas paused to reassure his readers that Baptists did in fact teach "that Subjects should bow to government; wives submit to their husbands; children obey their parents; and servants and slaves be in subjection to their masters," he added a qualification: "as far as their commands do consist with the word of GOD in all things." In this, Thomas captured the essence of the Baptists' complex attitudes toward the world, as well as the difficulty in reducing those attitudes to a single social or political point of view. Baptists held their members to a different standard. Members were to seek to understand and follow God's law in all things. God's law enjoined those in subordinate positions to submit to all legitimate authority; at the same time it gave them a standard for judging legitimacy that did not always accord with worldly standards. Thomas elaborated on the world-reshaping implications of this idea by drawing on biblical images that simultaneously resonated with the social world of eighteenth-century Virginia:

> Our religion in all its branches, tends only to love, and peace, and joy, and rest, and content, and felicity. And that it ever fails producing these and the like benign effects, is entirely owing to those that oppose its progress. . . . When the LORD JESUS displays the banners of his love, and his gospel trumpet sounds proclaiming liberty to the captives; Beelzebub will not fail making an horrible uproar, we may be sure of it. But is the captain of our salvation, or his honest soldiers to be blamed? . . . The strong holds must be demolished, the prison doors broken down, and the iron fetters dissolved. . . . The elect slaves must be redeemed, though others choose to hug their chains and even curse their best friends, who offer to set them free. . . . We raise no tumult; we cause no riot; we make no division, or disturbance at all.[104]

Rather than reaffirming Baptists' commitment to the existing social order or presenting disruptions of that order as exceptional cases, Thomas implied that disruptions came from those who would not acknowledge the righteousness of the Baptists' cause.[105] He insisted on the superiority of God's law to man's law and articulated a compelling vision of the former's triumph.

Thomas's use of the language of liberty and the extended metaphor of slavery could not have reassured his critics who worried about "making divisions." Thomas's vision powerfully linked liberation from sin with liberation from bondage. Although rooted in well-known biblical language, this was a potentially transformative vision in the context of a society based on racial slavery, and rather than eschewing it, Thomas embraced it. In many ways this rhetoric turned Philo-Bombastia's earlier criticism of Presbyterian calls for liberty on its head. While Philo-Bombastia had used the slippage in the language of liberty to discredit evangelical calls for toleration by linking them to threats to slavery, Thomas played on this same slippage, albeit somewhat less overtly, to dramatize the power of God's word. Similarly, language about how the truly converted soul "accepts of CHRIST . . . as a prince to rule over him" and "chearfully enlists under his banner; & heartily proclaims war with his enemies" had potentially dangerous political implications in a society in which the established church was headed by the king and dissent was associated with sedition. The turmoil caused by Virginians' evolving resistance to British imperial policies only deepened the dangerous implications of such language. Inevitably, these metaphors gained additional resonance from the ways in which the biblical languages of liberty and monarchy resonated with the institutions and hierarchies of eighteenth-century Virginia.

When Baptist ministers like Thomas talked about obeying God's law rather than man's or insisted that legitimate authority be consistent with the word of God, however, their most immediate meaning had to do with the establishment and Baptists' right to worship as they pleased. The spectacular acts of defiance his rhetoric seemed to invoke were mostly realized by those ministers and preachers who stood up to legal or extralegal persecution. The pages of the early denominational histories that form the basis for most subsequent interpretations are full of heroic accounts of ministers enduring abuse and imprisonment, the eventual triumph of their cause, and sometimes the tragic end of their persecutors. The dunking of Barrow and Mintz fit this pattern perfectly; one account even embellished the tale by claiming that "three or four" of their persecutors "died in a few weeks, in a distracted manner, and one wished himself in hell before he had joined the company."[106] Another early nineteenth-century chronicler used their story to illustrate a larger point about Baptists' success: "if persecutors did but know it, they take a wrong step to prevent the progress of religion by persecution: for persecution always whets the edge of *devotion*."[107] Persecutors' attempts to exercise illegitimate authority, contrary to the will of God, played right into Thomas's rhetoric.

But what did such heroic resistance and devotion really mean for the "little societies" of eighteenth-century Virginia? How literally could or did Baptist lay people, black or white, take the language of liberation

articulated by Thomas? Stories of subordinates defying worldly authority for the sake of religious truth made their way into Baptist lore, but
often as adjuncts to stories of ministers' own heroism. John Leland,
for instance, recorded the story of "a Mrs. Bailey," whose "husband had
told her, if she was ever baptized he would whip her within an inch of
her life, and kill the man that should baptize her." According to Leland,
she expressed her willingness to suffer for her faith—"if I am whipped,
my Saviour had long furrows ploughed upon his back"—and Leland
baptized her anyway. Leland "heard afterwards that he whipped her"
but boasted that "the head of John the Baptist is not taken off yet."[108]
The North Carolina minister John Tanner was not so lucky. He baptized
Mrs. Dawson against the wishes of her husband, "who was violently opposed to it, and . . . had threatened that, if any man baptized his wife,
he would shoot him." True to his word, the man ambushed Tanner at a
ferry landing and shot him in the thigh "with a large horseman's pistol."
Tanner survived, however, and "submitted to it patiently as *persecution
for Christ's sake*."[109] Such tales served to dramatize the struggle of common people for their newfound Baptist faith, but their rhetorical point
was less to celebrate the independent judgment of wives and more to
place the divinely ordained authority of ministers over that of ungodly
or tyrannical husbands.

In fact, alongside the heated rhetoric of public debate, most white
Baptist converts and the ministerial class that led them worked to craft
an evangelical community in ways that were more measured and accommodating of worldly relationships than either Thomas's defense or his
antagonists' criticisms suggested. The reshaped world most white Baptists envisioned resembled the one they lived in, except transformed by
the true faith, which would prosper and spread and bring harmony to
those relations that were now disrupted by "ignorance and unbelief." Indeed, despite the exaggerated fears of their opponents, promoting orderly, Christian households remained a central concern for white Baptists in Virginia, and church records reveal their attempts to work out
just how to do so. Through discipline and other practices, the churches
reached into even the most fundamental relationships of hierarchy and
subordination that constituted rural society, but the purpose of seeking to regulate church members in these relationships was neither to
reinforce the hierarchies of that society nor to replace them with more
egalitarian forms. Instead, it was to make sure that Baptists' conduct

in these worldly relations lived up to godly standards. Baptist leaders and the large majority of the laity intended no revolution in domestic arrangements, but they did seek to change the institutional and moral framework of those relations in ways that had complicated and sometimes contradictory implications.

Rejecting the Anglican establishment and infant baptism left Baptists in an awkward situation regarding the Church of England's quasi-governmental role in recording and legitimating both birth and marriage, and they struggled to craft and enforce alternatives that were consistent with gospel order. Baptist parents could no longer celebrate the birth of their children with christenings or have them recorded in parish registers. In fact, the churches disciplined members who attempted to do so. At Mill Swamp, for instance, Sister Hatfield was investigated "for being Forward in having her inphant Sprinkled," and similar investigations for "Sprinkling" occurred at other churches throughout the state.[110] Deprived of orderly access to this popular ritual, some of the churches sought other ways to include the children of members in the church communities. In 1778 David Barrow prompted the members of Mill Swamp and South Quay to order that the names and ages of members' children "be registered in the Ch[urch] B[oo]k," and in 1784 Shoulder's Hill Baptist Church, in Nansemond County, did the same.[111] Even after disestablishment, a query to the Kehukee Association at a 1789 meeting at Mill Swamp suggests that some Baptists may have sought to approximate Anglican practices of christening and godparenthood: "Is it the duty of a minister to take little children in his arms (at the request of their parents or others), and name them, and pray to the Lord to bless them?" The association rejected this idea, answering, "We think it duty for ministers to pray for infants as well as others, but not to take them in their arms or name them at that time."[112]

Baptists also sought to break the establishment's effective monopoly on marriage.[113] Civil marriage existed in Virginia, but high fees and the requirement to post bond placed it "out of reach for most Virginians." The only other legal way to get married was to post banns in the parish church, which required a fee to be paid to the parish minister or clerk, and only Anglican parsons were allowed to officiate at weddings.[114] These practices became a persistent, if not always prominent, item in Baptists' and other evangelicals' litany of complaints about the injustices inflicted by the establishment, and the demand that Baptist clergymen be permitted to conduct legal marriages often featured in their calls for religious liberty.[115] Within the church community, Baptists insisted on their own authority over marriage. In 1778 Raccoon Swamp declared that "a member, that utterly rejects the plan of Marriage, adopted by the Baptist Association, and Churches; and to enter into the Marriage state, by the Authority of a Priest; which we have no reason to believe was ever Called of God, to the Ministerial function" was to be declared "disorderly, and to be dealt with according to Gospel rule."[116] In removing marriage from the purview of the ungodly establishment, Baptists sought not to undermine it but to make it conform more precisely to God's plan.

In addition to their efforts to wrest institutional control of marriage away from the Church of England, Baptist churches worked to improve it by seeking to establish and police proper marital behavior. Harmony and proper Christian principles were at the center of this vision. At Mill Swamp, Thomas and Elizabeth Tynes were excommunicated "for living at variance betwixt themselves."[117] Shoulder's Hill excommunicated Priscilla Bruce for "disorderly conduct in marriage."[118] Albemarle Baptist Church, in the Piedmont, excommunicated Nathaniel Barlow after he remained "incorragable" in his "ill language, anger, and abuse of his wife."[119] But as always, the exact boundaries of the churches' authority and the appropriate implications of evangelical fellowship required careful attention and balance. In 1778 Raccoon Swamp advised Sister Tuder, who had left her spouse, "to abide with her husband, according to [1] Corinthians 7th and 13th": "And the woman which hath an husband that believeth not, and if he be pleased to dwell with her, let her not leave him."[120] Despite her husband's unbelief, the church thought that proper order required the household and her husband's authority to remain intact unless he actively opposed or rejected her. Similarly, when the minister Lemuel Burkitt asked the Kehukee Association whether "it is agreeable to God's word, for Christians to marry unconverted persons," the association stopped short of forbidding such marriages: "We do not know that God's word does actually prohibit such marriages, but we would advise the members of our churches to comply with Christian marriage as nearly as they can judge, for their own comfort and satisfaction."[121]

Rather than fundamentally remaking household relationships, then, white Baptists sought to ensure that existing forms of household authority were exercised in ways that were compatible with godly ends. According to this view, the power of heads of household, used properly, could have a profound effect in promoting the cause of true Christianity. Like Samuel Davies, Virginia Baptists placed a great deal of importance on the idea of family religion, and they expended considerable energy and verbiage promoting it. In 1777 Mill Swamp emphasized the centrality of household religion to the evangelical project. When asked "what shall be done with a member that is neglectful of performing the publick worship of god Night and Morning in his own family," the church declared that habitual neglect of family worship would subject members to discipline.[122] At Black Creek, Wist and Eliza Tynes were actually excommunicated for "neglecting Family Prayer & railing against the Brethren for dealing with them for the same."[123]

In many ways, this concern for familial order served to reinforce the power of heads of household. Although white Baptists did not go as far as Davies did in endorsing coercion, their vision was that godly authority embraced and even enhanced existing relationships of hierarchy and subordination. In 1783 the Kehukee Association was asked, "What shall the master of a family do with his slaves, who refuse to attend at the time of public prayers in the family?" The association responded that the slaves should be exhorted to attend, and given liberty to do so, but be left to decide for themselves.[124] In referring to "the master of a family," the Kehukee Association echoed and perhaps reinforced existing conceptions of slavery as a household relationship modeled on the family, conflating the two forms of subordination as a way of naturalizing and idealizing slavery.[125] In 1785 the members of South Quay used similar, albeit somewhat more inclusive language: "Is it a duty Assential to Church fellowship, for masters of Families, or Mistresses in husbands absence . . . to hold public prayer . . . ?"[126] Whether master or mistress, however, the head of a household had a duty to promote family religion both because of the authority he or she held and because the responsibilities of true Christianity actually increased that authority. The Kehukee Association elaborated on these themes in an 1800 circular letter to its churches, in which it considered "our duty to our *family* . . . not only as stewards, who have to give an account of our stewardship to God, but as it were, as *prophets, priests*, and *kings*." Like Christ, who was often described in these terms, heads of families had a threefold role to play. As prophets, they were to teach their dependents; as priests, to pray for their families; and as kings, to rule. "Every family," wrote the association, "should have one, and only one proper head, who should take the government thereof, and in all cases endeavor to rule with justice, having a particular regard for all about him, setting forth good examples, walking in the ways of godliness and true piety, praying with and for them oft."[127] In theory, at least, evangelical values would render the Christian household a powerful force for justice and piety.

Black converts' concerns and interests fit uneasily with white Baptists' focus on reforming and sanctifying household relationships. Although the most dramatic increases in black church membership did not occur until after the American Revolution, black men and women were a real, if not overwhelming, presence in the early years of the Baptist movement. Small groups of slaves were among the constituting members of a number of the Baptist churches formed in the late 1760s and early 1770s. In the Baptist communities of Isle of Wight, Sussex, and Southampton counties, black men and women represented about 10 percent of church members in the 1770s and an increasing percentage of new converts toward the end of that period (see chapter 4). Details about the identities and activities of these men and women are difficult to come by, but many, perhaps most, who became church members in these early years were the property of white Baptists, members of the very households their white brethren sought to remake according to Christian principles. Eleven of the thirteen surnames of enslaved members' owners that are legible on Raccoon Swamp's first membership list are shared with white church members.[128] At South Quay, sixteen of the first twenty-five black members were owned by white families that had members in the church, and several others were listed as belonging to families with connections to other Baptist churches in the area.[129]

The presence of enslaved black men and women as church members sometimes had awkward implications for white members' ideals of household order. White Baptists' concern over the proper forms of marriage, for instance, could only be partially applied to enslaved black Baptists, whose marriages were neither recognized by law nor sanctified by the established church. A 1778 query to the Kehukee Association sought to determine the proper Christian attitude toward these relationships, asking "Is the marriage of servants lawful before God, which is not complied with according to the laws of the land?" The association concluded that such marriages were lawful, but in subsequent years white Baptists shied away from the more difficult questions raised by this decision, such as whether masters could legitimately separate married slaves or whether slaves so separated could legally remarry.[130] Similarly, the children of black members were not included on any of the southeastern Virginia churches' lists of members' children. In the eyes of white Baptists, their black brethren were part of other people's households; they did not have households of their own. White Baptists' commitment to Christian fellowship and community did little to alter such basic conceptions of worldly relations in eighteenth-century Virginia, and those conceptions inevitably affected how Virginians of different races and sexes experienced church membership.

Thus, even as they adopted evangelical beliefs and joined in the rituals of Baptist community, black converts brought with them their own perspective and ideas, grounded in their own history and social position. Given the long-standing connections between Christianity and freedom in Virginia and their stubborn persistence among black communities in the colony, it is not surprising that some black converts may have anticipated rhetoric like Thomas's and put it to more literal use. In Sussex County, for instance, George Noble advertised for a runaway slave named "JUPITER, alias GIBB," identifying him by the "scars on his back from a severe whipping he lately had at Sussex court-house, having been tried there for stirring up the Negroes to an insurrection, being a great Newlight preacher."[131] Robert Munford, of nearby Mecklenburg County, advertised in 1766 for a runaway named Jack, who "it appears has been principally concerned in promoting the late disorderly meetings among the Negroes."[132] It is unclear exactly how these men gained their reputations or whether they were formally members of any church, but they seem to have taken hold of evangelical ideas and practices like mass revival meetings to craft and promote their own vision of the liberating potential of Christianity. Such activities may have helped spur complaints like the 1772 "Address to the Anabaptists" or the Cumberland County petition, but it seems unlikely that any white Baptists would have endorsed or knowingly encouraged such interpretations.

Within Baptist churches themselves, black converts' experiences and expressions of evangelical faith were shaped by the practices of fellowship, authorization, and discipline that had evolved since the 1750s and by the need to interact and communicate (in multiple senses) with their white brethren, who constituted a large majority of church members and denominational leadership. Even if they wished to, black men and women found little room to express more literal interpretations of the liberty proclaimed by Baptist ministers in this context. Some, however, mastered more orthodox modes of interpretation. In 1782 Richard Dozier, a white Baptist layman in Westmoreland County, recorded his positive impressions of the preaching of a slave named Lewis: "He spake by way of exh[ortatio]n to abt. 400. I think with the greatest sen[sibil]ity I ever expected to hear from an E[thiopia]n he pd out the state man was in by nature . . . & entreated them to rest not in an unconverted state but come & accept of X. by faith that they might be reconciled to God." In expounding on essential, orthodox evangelical themes such as the dangers of an unconverted state and the need for reconciliation with God, Lewis negotiated a world of shared meanings within the Baptist community, and his fluency in this language gave him authority and status within that racially mixed community despite his worldly station. Several years later Dozier again heard Lewis preach, and he noted that "his gift exceeded many white preachers."[133] The message Lewis preached was not necessarily incompatible with a vision of black liberation, and what Dozier heard and recorded might not have captured the full range of Lewis's meaning, but the ability of both men to focus on what evangelicals of both races understood to be universal spiritual truths helped maintain the links that held black and white Virginians together within the Baptist movement and minimized their differences.

Nonetheless, even when black preachers spoke on universal themes, their worldly status mattered. If men like Lewis provided models of spiritual power and authority for black converts to admire and emulate, they offered a slightly different message to white men and women. Soon after hearing Lewis for the second time, Dozier heard another black preacher named Jacob. Impressed with this "most wonderful preacher," he exclaimed, "Oh see God choosing the weak things of this world to confound the things that are mighty."[134] The humble social status of black preachers made for a powerful contrast with their exaltation and authority as preachers of God's word. This mattered to both blacks and whites in the audience, but because of their respective places in a society organized around the principle of racial slavery, it mattered in different ways. The psychological and spiritual impact of that contrast was real for all participants, but for those who were among "the weak things of this world" the leveling power of God's grace and inspiration implied a transcendence of worldly boundaries that could be interpreted as an improvement in status, while for those among the "mighty" this same transcendence meant abandoning worldly pretensions and attachments. In both cases, the central principles were man's reliance on God's mercy and the superiority of God's law to man's, but social context shaped the ways in which these principles were experienced and could be interpreted.

Preaching was not the only forum in which such complex interpretation occurred. Other practices of Baptist community also took on different meanings for different members of the church in ways that depended in part on their social status. In keeping with white Baptists' concern for gospel order within households, church discipline tended to reinforce rather than undermine hierarchical relations within the household. At South Quay, "Harrison's Pompey" (in the church records slaves were usually referred to in these possessive terms) was excommunicated "for continuing disobedience to his master," although he was later restored to membership.[135] But the role of the church was not simply to serve as an adjunct to masters' power; it was, as the Mill Swamp covenant put it, to "regulate by the word of god and to watch over one another in the lord." Pompey was disciplined not simply because he had disobeyed his master but because the church judged that in doing so he had broken with proper, gospel order. This may seem like a fine distinction, but it mattered to both the churches and their members, as another case suggests.

In June 1780 a slave named Nero stood before his fellow members of South Quay to face an accusation from his owner, John Lawrence, also a member of the congregation, "of disobedience & harsh language to him." Nero was censured by the congregation for his disobedience, but he responded by accusing his owner of "some misconduct" and succeeded in having Lawrence censured as well. Historians have cited this case as evidence of the evenhandedness and spiritual egalitarianism of evangelical communities, but the continuation of Nero and Lawrence's story complicates that conclusion, albeit without completely overturning it.[136] Although both men were restored to full fellowship in the following months, the conflict between them did not end.[137] In 1782 Lawrence again accused Nero of disobedience, and Nero was again censured by the church, but not expelled.[138] In 1786 Nero yet again faced "some accusations" from Lawrence. The congregation concluded that there was "no proof of his being guilty of a crime" and held Nero in fellowship. Two

months later the church reopened the case "on account of some dissatisfaction" expressed with the initial decision, most likely by Lawrence himself. "Brother Lawrence his [i.e., Nero's] accuser" was directed to "produce all the witnesses he has against [Nero]" for the next conference.
But when the church considered the matter, it again found "no proof"
against Nero and dismissed Lawrence's charges.[139]

Without in any way rejecting the idea that slavery was a legitimate
worldly relation, the members of South Quay, and particularly the white
men who governed the church, interposed themselves between master
and slave. By holding each accountable to the church's own rules of pro-
cedure and standards of conduct, South Quay as a church insisted on
its own independent judgment on the proper nature of the master-slave
relationship and its relationship to the duties of Christians to one another. Rather than accepting the master's view of the relationship, the
church investigated charges, weighed evidence and testimony from both
parties, and made its own collective judgment. At Black Creek and Mill
Swamp this process led to the disciplining of white members for "using
Barbarity" and "exercis[ing] uncommon cruelties" toward their slaves.[140]
At South Quay the church's insistence on its own judgment worked to
Nero's advantage in many cases, enabling him to withstand his owner's
accusations and even to have his owner censured. In 1791, however, the
South Quay church made clear its own vision of the moral boundaries of
the relationship between slave and master. At the church's April meeting Nero was "charged with refusing to obey his Master, and threatening
to leave him, and Deprive him of more of his Negroes; and other things
tedious to mention." The next day Nero was excommunicated, and the
church records reveal nothing more about what was clearly an ongoing
battle between slave and master.[141]

Such a confrontation hints at the ways in which evangelical conversion
and the institutions of Baptist life could carry very different meanings
for different members of the church. If slave owners could take comfort
in the fact that church discipline upheld the duties of slaves to masters,
slaves could take comfort in the fact that the church would hear their
testimony and could justify them against their masters' accusations, and
other church members could feel that the principles of gospel order had
been upheld. There was always plenty of evidence of the conjunction of
religious values with those of society at large: slaves were expelled for
disobedience to their masters, as Nero eventually was; wives were told
to obey their husbands, as Sister Tuder was; and church members were

urged not to reject civil authority, as Peter Butler of Black Creek was.[142] But it is unlikely that either enslaved or slaveholding Baptists viewed church membership or church discipline in such purely utilitarian, strategic terms. Both Lawrence and Nero remained in the church despite their recurring conflict and the frustration both must have felt at times. The story of Nero was primarily one of neither equality nor oppression, although it contained elements of both, but one of the ambivalent processes of Baptist community.

As Donald Mathews has recently argued, early southern evangelicals did not experience "equality" in church: "The experience, rather, was one of *fellowship,* which was itself revolutionary within a hierarchical society and one that could allow sharing across race, class, and gender lines."[143] The "revolutionary" nature of this experience must be understood in a qualified sense: evangelicalism did eventually utterly transform the religious landscape of the South and the nature of moral and civil discourse in the region, but its effects on fundamental social relations were far more indirect and attenuated. Nonetheless, unless we understand the subtle, internal dynamics of the churches and of the language of Baptist fellowship, we miss much of the import of what went on in the churches and how they provided a vital site of interaction and negotiation—power laden and unequal but no less important for that—between members of a changing southern society. Indeed, it was in part because the language of fellowship was shared, or at least by its nature presumed to be shared even when it was not, that evangelicalism became one of the dominant modes of expression and communication (again, in multiple senses) both among and between blacks and whites in the southern society that emerged in the decades after the Revolution.

Both the revolutionary experience of fellowship and the charged, confrontational language that Baptists invoked in their battles with a hostile, mocking world became part of the movement's character. The language of liberty and liberation, particularly when combined with the experience of entering and maintaining fellowship in church, provided Baptist converts with a new perspective on the world and worldly relations. This evangelical perspective did not inherently contradict worldly relationships, but it provided a kind of outsider's perspective on them, and the potential conflict that existed between the two could find expression as different individuals and social groups sought to shape their world according to these new values. Ministers and white men could draw on the powerful biblical imagery and the sense of righteousness their faith provided them to criticize aspects of their society, such as the oppressiveness of the establishment or the exaltation of wealth and gain over matters of the spirit. Such critiques often drew on potent metaphors and images that resonated with eighteenth-century Virginia society: monarchy and citizenship, duty and submission, family and patriarchy, household and community, bondage and freedom. This language helped spur the fears of the Baptists' opponents, but it also may have held special meanings, beyond those intended by the ministers and spokesmen who employed it, for other groups in the colony. Realizing those meanings in church was a more complicated affair, but church members were sometimes able to pursue those meanings, to a point, through the shared languages and institutions of evangelical spirituality and the Baptist church community. The conceptualization and practices of the church community allowed members such as Lewis or Nero to make assertions about meaning and value that claimed authority by being cast in terms of shared concepts of sin and salvation or gospel order and disorder, invoking the presumption that church members would or should subscribe to those meanings.

It is difficult, and perhaps even beside the point, to draw a conclusion about the "radical" or "conservative" or even "egalitarian" or "hierarchical" nature of the early Baptist movement. This is true both because the movement's proliferation of metaphors and meanings makes any single interpretation incomplete and because the terms themselves may misleadingly transpose spiritual beliefs and political or social ones. Even as Baptists sought to transform their world through faith, the material and social implications of that transformation were never clear. People of different races, sexes, and worldly status took hold of and reinterpreted evangelical concepts and institutions, but identifying these processes as central to evangelicalism's rise is not in itself an argument for the radicalism or egalitarianism of the Baptist movement; it is a way of exploring the nature and limitations of the negotiation process itself. At its heart, the Baptist movement was a powerful religious vision of personal transformation and collective unity. What it meant in social and political terms was in large part the product of the people who adopted it rather than of any inherent tendency or characteristic of the movement itself. To the extent that the Baptists' spiritual vision spawned officially sanctioned social or political manifestations, these appeared in ministerial criticisms of the establishment and in the church community itself, shaped in concert by ministers and lay people. It was from these ambiguous sources, along with their own sense of the injustices or apostasy of their society, that Baptists of different sexes and races shaped their own interpretations of their faith and its implications for their world.

In shaping these interpretations, they remained in constant dialogue both with one another and with the larger social, political, cultural, and military developments in Virginia. Nero's initial conflict with John Lawrence, for instance, took place during the closing stages of the American Revolution, a year after the port of South Quay narrowly escaped destruction by the British and a year before that destruction would become a reality. The military presence of the British affected race relations in southeastern Virginia in important ways, most notably by encouraging runaways, and perhaps this knowledge indirectly provided support for Nero's confident and confrontational stance. The subsequent charges and countercharges made by the two men through the rest of the 1780s coincided with other important developments. The Baptist denomination continued its rise to prominence and political and cultural power in the post-Revolutionary era, while at the same time a wide-ranging debate broke out among white evangelicals over the place of slavery within their churches. Both Baptists and Methodists took tentative steps to discourage slave ownership among their members and to promote the cause of manumission across Virginia. In doing so they provoked a backlash from white Virginians both within and outside of their movements that swamped this larger movement, if not individual anti-slavery commitments among some white evangelicals. At the same time, black men and women began to join evangelical churches in significant numbers and to shape their own local interpretations of scripture and Christian practice alongside their white brethren.[144] The experiences of Nero, Lawrence, and the other members of South Quay who watched and judged their conflicts were shaped by all of these forces as well as by the longer history of the Baptist denomination and evangelical dissent in the region. The Revolution and its aftermath thus only added to the complexities and multilayered significance of Baptist belief and practice in southeastern Virginia.

3

SACRED REGARD
TO THE RIGHTS
OF MANKIND

Confronting the Revolution

AFTER SURVIVING HIS 1778 dunking and more than twenty years of ministering to the Baptist churches of Southampton, Sussex, and Isle of Wight counties, in 1798 David Barrow left southeastern Virginia for good and moved with his family to Montgomery County, Kentucky. Barrow explained his decision in a circular letter modeled on the instructive missives circulated by Baptist associations to their member churches on matters of doctrine, practice, and faith. Addressing his "Very Dear Brethren, Friends and Fellow-Citizens," he sought to forestall any gossip or "ungenerous sayings, concerning the motives of my moving, the doctrines I have preached, and the principles I hold," by laying out in detail the motives and beliefs that had led him to emigrate.[1] One fact lay at the center of Barrow's reasoning and his intense concern to explain himself. In 1784 he had become convinced "of the iniquity, and . . . the inconsistency of hereditary slavery, with a republican form of government" and had manumitted his two slaves, Benjamin and Lucrecia Blackhead, at the Southampton County Court in March of that year.[2] In succeeding years Barrow found that "I cannot comfortably support my family, educate my children, and attend so much to public calls, as I have done, with my means, in this poor country, without falling into the line of speculation, or that of holding slaves, or sticking closely and personally to my farm." Barrow found speculation "incompatible with the work of the ministry," and "that of holding, tyrannizing over, and driving slaves, I view as contrary to the laws of God and nature." In short, Barrow found it impossible to attend simultaneously to his duties as the head of an orderly, Christian household and to his duties as a minister of God's word in the ways that he thought necessary. Hence, he hoped to sell his property in Southampton, pay off his debts, and move to a country "where the God of Nature has been the most liberal with his bounties."[3]

Barrow's decision echoed those of thousands of other Virginians in the post-Revolutionary era. Citizens of the Old Dominion moved west in astonishing numbers in the decades following the American Revolution, and Kentucky was perhaps the single most popular destination.[4] Ministers like Barrow enthusiastically joined this movement. David T. Bailey finds that nearly 57 percent of the clergy in the old southwest before the Great Revival were Virginians.[5] The magnitude of this clerical exodus prompted the Baptist historian Robert Semple to wonder in 1810, only slightly facetiously, "whether half the preachers who have been raised in Virginia have not emigrated to the western country," and particularly to "the vortex of Baptist preachers—Kentucky."[6]

Although Barrow's emigration reflected these larger trends, his motivation and ideology were far less typical. His particular vision of anti-slavery, republican, and evangelical values, although not unique, ran against the general trends within his home state and his denomination. Indeed, by 1800 a slow but inexorable reaction against such anti-slavery constructions of the Revolutionary legacy had begun. Influenced by Barrow and other anti-slavery ministers, Virginia Baptists' General Committee approved statements condemning slavery in 1785 and 1790, but in 1793 they retreated from this position in the face of both internal and external criticism, declaring that the issue of slavery was properly the responsibility of the state legislature, not the churches.[7] At the same time, the legislature proved itself equally uncomfortable with the moderate anti-slavery measures taken in the wake of the Revolution and began to restrict the ability of Quakers and other activists to promote manumission and to protect freed blacks from harassment and reenslavement.[8] Perhaps most ominously, by the mid-1780s white petitioners in a handful of counties, reacting against perceived threats to the peculiar institution, had already begun to articulate a defense of slavery in religious and republican terms.[9] For the men who signed these petitions it was the elimination of slavery rather than its perpetuation that presented a threat to their roles as fathers and masters of households. Barrow may have moved with the current of Virginians headed west, but on the issue of slavery he was standing against an almost tidal force of reaction and retrenchment.

Barrow's story, along with that of the black and white religious community he helped plant and nurture, reveals a great deal about the origins of Nat Turner's Virginia during the Revolutionary era. As we have seen, Barrow and the Baptist churches of southeastern Virginia stood at the forefront of evangelical doctrinal, institutional, and social development in these years. In many ways Barrow himself exemplified the aspirations of white evangelicals during this period. A virtuous, middling farmer and militia captain who overcame persecution to champion his faith and enthusiastically endorse the Revolution and republican ideals of liberty, Barrow personified white Baptists' desire to connect with and shape the central values of the emerging nation. Similarly, as a promoter of Baptist political activism, institution building, and respectability, he played a vital role in the denomination's continued rise and development in the new nation. Visions of orderly Christian households, energetic associational life, and strong ministerial leadership lay at the center of his program for the denomination, and all of these elements continued to be important to white Baptists in the post-Revolutionary era.

Perhaps the most central institutional issue for white Baptists was their ongoing struggle against the Virginia establishment. Barrow and other Baptist leaders seized hold of the language and ideology of imperial resistance and worked with remarkable success to make religious liberty a fundamental aspect of the independence movement in Virginia. This effort merged with the broader effort of religious leaders across the new nation to link the fate of Christianity to that of republican America as a strategy for gaining cultural influence and overcoming the marginalization of evangelicals in the pre-Revolutionary period.[10] Many of these efforts revolved around white masculinity and concepts of household authority. Christine Heyrman argues that white southern Baptist and Methodist preachers took up the mantle of republicanism and the martial legacy of the Revolution in order to assuage lingering fears about evangelicals' threat to social order, to appeal to male converts, and to achieve their own version of the aggressive, competitive mastery that characterized white masculinity in the South.[11]

But Barrow's anti-slavery commitment highlights the fact that the effects of republican and Revolutionary ideology and imagery were not always so easy to control. Baptist leaders' adoption of republicanism did serve many of the purposes Heyrman suggests, but the close association of evangelicalism and republicanism that offered white male evangelicals a path to authority in mainstream white culture also provided the foundation of a small but influential white Baptist anti-slavery movement in the early national period and led some white men to a more lasting commitment to emancipation—a tendency that considerably complicated the task of winning over the mainstream of white male Virginians. Barrow's career demonstrates that there was persistent disagreement about the meaning of the Revolution and the republican principles of the new nation even among the white men who were most devoted to Baptist institution building and political influence.

Nor did these debates exhaust the complexities of the Revolution's meaning for Baptist fellowship. The black men and women who joined the Baptist churches of southeastern Virginia in increasing numbers in the second half of the 1780s brought with them their own senses of the meaning and implications of both Christianity and the Revolution, which differed in important ways from those of their white brethren. The racial divisions caused by the Revolution loomed particularly large in southeastern Virginia. Virginia's royal governor, John Murray, fourth Earl of Dunmore, issued a proclamation of freedom for all rebel-owned slaves who took up arms for the British in November 1775, and throughout the war continuing confrontations between British troops, escaping slaves, loyalists, and colonial rebels profoundly disrupted the communities and social relations of the region. The black men and women who joined the churches in the aftermath of these disruptions sought not only soul salvation but also opportunities to create communities and provide ideological nourishment for their vision of freedom and justice, perhaps in part because both white Revolutionary commitment to natural rights and the solicitude of the British crown had proved to be unreliable supports in this regard.[12]

Even as white Baptist leaders in southeastern Virginia worked to meld evangelical and Revolutionary rhetoric to underscore the connections between civic and religious liberty, their churches were increasingly occupied by men and women for whom the Revolution itself carried very different, and in some cases directly opposed, meanings. Complicating matters further, after a handful of white anti-slavery Baptists like Barrow took full advantage of Virginia's 1782 liberalization of manumission and freed their slaves, some of these freed men and women joined the churches of their former masters, including Barrow's former bonds-

man Benjamin Blackhead in 1788. For these black Baptists the coincidence of Revolutionary and evangelical values had a very concrete result—freedom—which they continued to embody in the churches even
as white members retreated from such implications.

In this context the Revolution was simultaneously a challenge and
an opportunity for Baptists in Virginia, both black and white. The core
concepts of Baptist faith that had emerged over the previous three
decades—conversion, baptism, communion, discipline, and fellowship—
remained at the center of denominational identity, but their connection
to other emergent systems of meaning remained open to debate and interpretation. White Baptist leaders sought to lay claim to the legacy of
the Revolution; anti-slavery Baptists struggled to purge their churches
of the sin of slavery; enslaved African Americans sought to shape sus-
tainable communities of faith and to find support and recognition within
the white-controlled churches; free black men negotiated the discourses
of freedom and masculinity that structured ideas of church government
even as the privileges of whiteness grew in importance; and women of
both races learned and used Baptist languages of authority and righteousness to shape, as best they could, the conditions of their own subordination. Baptist leaders, then, could not simply adopt the language and image of the Revolution. They had to fight on at least two fronts—externally
to link their cause to national and state-level discourses of republicanism and internally to control the implications of those links within the
denomination—to claim, shape, and limit the meanings of Baptist republicanism.

The American Revolution in Virginia was shaped not only by imperial
politics and republican ideology but also by powerful social and racial
tensions within the colony, and the ways in which these tensions played
out over the course of the Revolutionary era had as much influence on
the social and cultural order of Nat Turner's Virginia as did more formal
political and ideological developments.[13] Like other mainland colonies,
Virginia experienced sporadic conflict and mounting hostility between
colonial leaders and the royal government in the decade after the Stamp
Act Crisis of 1765–66. These tensions were exacerbated in Virginia by
long-standing white concerns that social and political unrest in the colony could encourage slave rebellion.

By 1774 both white and black Virginians had come to suspect, and

blacks perhaps also to hope, that the British purposely intended to manipulate this threat to keep the colonists in check. Indeed, as the abortive uprising of 1731 demonstrated, an important radical strain of black
thought in colonial Virginia linked British authority to liberation, as an
almost millenarian force that could overturn the illegitimate authority of
Virginia's white leaders who perpetuated the system of slavery and offer
freedom and justice to the oppressed. This strain of thought may have
influenced black strategies on the eve of the Revolution, as slaves recognized the divisions within the white government and came to view British aid in their efforts for freedom as a realistic possibility. In fact, even
before the British took any concrete action, some slaves took the initia-
tive themselves. In mid-April 1775 slaves in several different communities, including Surry County, which bordered Isle of Wight, Southampton, and Sussex, plotted uprisings that may have been related to their
hope for British aid. It is unclear whether these plots were coordinated,
but white Virginians certainly worried that the coincidence of these local insurrections indicated a more general conspiracy and that British
actions encouraged such activity.[14]

Tensions began to boil over after April 21, when Governor Dunmore
sent British troops to remove gunpowder from the public magazine at
Williamsburg. While slightly less disastrous for royal authority than the
similar raid on Concord in Massachusetts two days earlier, this preemp-
tive move outraged many white Virginians, who viewed it as a prelude to
a concerted British attempt to crush American resistance and as a purposeful effort to leave white colonists unarmed and unprotected amidst
swirling rumors of slave uprisings. As angry and armed white colonists
gathered to demand the return of the powder, Dunmore chose to take a
hard line. A contemporary witness, Dr. William Pasteur, reported that
Dunmore warned that if the colonists attempted any violence against
British officials, he would "declare freedom to the slaves and reduce the
City of Williamsburg to ashes."[15] Such threats, although perhaps effective
in the short term, were largely counterproductive in the long term because they accelerated the alienation of white moderates and encouraged
the militarization of the resistance. The Sussex County patriot committee cited the removal of the gunpowder as the reason why it had formed
an independent militia company to put the county "into the best posture
of defence possible," and other counties did the same.[16]

As the standoff became more hostile, Dunmore abandoned the governor's palace in Williamsburg and set up headquarters on a ship at York-town, which only increased colonial fears of imminent attack. This un-stable situation lasted for months. Colonial leaders struggled to create a provisional government that bypassed the governor; Dunmore worked to rally loyalist support and to justify his conduct to his superiors; colonial volunteer militias patrolled to suppress loyalist activity and protect arms that might be needed in future conflicts; slaves who could sought to es-cape to the British, while others watched anxiously and sought to protect themselves, their families, and their communities in an unsettled situa-tion. After several small-scale skirmishes, including the burning of one of Dunmore's ships, which had been grounded in a hurricane, open hostili-ties began in October with a series of amphibious raids in the Norfolk and Portsmouth areas in which the British captured or destroyed caches of Virginian arms and gunpowder, as well as more than seventy cannon.[17]

Much of this early military action took place in southeastern Virginia, where it made a lasting impact on the black population. The British routed American defenders at Kemp's Bridge, south of Norfolk, in early November and occupied the city itself two weeks later. After the Kemp's Bridge victory, Dunmore finally issued a proclamation of rebellion that required all loyal British subjects to rally to the cause and declared free all servants or slaves "(appertaining to Rebels) . . . that are able and will-ing to bear Arms, they joining his Majesty's Troops."[18] Many slaves had already taken advantage of the disordered state of southeastern Virginia to escape to the British—the American commander at Kemp's Bridge suffered the embarrassment of being captured by a man who had been his slave—but Dunmore's proclamation firmly established and publi-cized this policy, intensifying anxiety among rebels across the South.[19]

While Dunmore's promise did not spur a full-scale, organized rebel-lion, hundreds of free and enslaved African American men joined the "Ethiopian Regiment," created by Dunmore, and many more attached themselves to the governor's forces in less formal ways. For Dunmore the measure was one of opportunity and expedience; he did not intend to free any slaves of loyalists, and certainly not his own slaves. Black Virgin-ians themselves, however, interpreted the meaning of the Revolution as a broader struggle against their own bondage, as members of the Ethio-pian Regiment demonstrated by wearing badges proclaiming "Liberty to Slaves." Moreover, although Dunmore almost certainly intended his offer to apply to men who could serve the British militarily, substantial

numbers of women and children, perhaps as many as half the total number of black escapees, took advantage of it.[20] Dunmore reported that
six to eight black Virginians joined his forces each day, and the total
was probably close to fifteen hundred, although as many as two-thirds of
these may have died from disease.[21]

In December, Dunmore decided that he could not hold Norfolk and
abandoned the city. The rebels similarly realized that Norfolk was essentially indefensible from naval attack and burned the city following British bombardment and a protracted skirmish on New Year's Day 1776.
This action was characteristic of the destructive yet indecisive nature
of the war in southeastern Virginia. During the next six years the region experienced an ongoing blockade of the Chesapeake, regular naval
harassment, occasional British occupation of useful ports, and periodic
offensives into the interior to destroy American supplies, particularly tobacco, which was traded for arms, salt, cloth, and other necessary materials. Significant British raids occurred in 1777 and 1779, and in the fall
of 1780 the British occupied the ports of Hampton, Suffolk, and Portsmouth. The last of these served as a base of operations for a series of
short, swift campaigns into the interior under Benedict Arnold until August 1781, when Lord Cornwallis and the main British force arrived from
the south and shifted the British headquarters to Yorktown.[22] Across
southeastern Virginia, black men, women, and children continued to
make use of these periodic opportunities to escape. More than half of
those who joined the British fled in family or extended kinship groups,
suggesting both the organized and premeditated nature of their flight
and the extent to which this exodus was driven by black desires for freedom rather than by British military expediency; the presence of women,
children, and grandparents among the refugees could only have added
to the logistical burdens the British faced.[23]

The specific experiences of the Revolution for residents of Isle of Wight,
Southampton, and Sussex counties are difficult to recover. For the most
part, these counties stood on the periphery of the major events. Except
for the stretch of Isle of Wight along the James River around the modest port of Smithfield, nearly all of the action took place just east of the
three counties. From this vantage point residents had a close, unsettling
view of the movements of the American Revolution in the South. Blacks
and whites in these counties anxiously observed the disruptions caused
by the war, and their own communities were often affected and some-

times even threatened. The small port and shipyard of South Quay, from which the Baptist church took its name, stood on the western bank of the Blackwater River in what was then Nansemond County (but became part of Southampton in 1786), and it briefly became an important center of American shipping and naval activity. Since the Blackwater flowed south into North Carolina's Albemarle Sound, ships and goods could circumvent the British blockade of the Chesapeake by sailing through the inlets of the Outer Banks to Edenton, North Carolina, and from there up the Chowan River to the Virginia line, where the Blackwater led north to South Quay. Goods could then be transported twenty miles overland to Suffolk, which gave water access to the James and the Chesapeake.[24]

This roundabout, makeshift route eventually brought the war even closer to home for Southamptonites. In the spring of 1779, when British troops occupied Portsmouth and Norfolk, they ventured up the Nansemond River and burned Suffolk and a number of rebels' houses in the area. Observers reported that the force then divided and headed for Smithfield in Isle of Wight County and South Quay. The South Quay shipyard was saved, but the entire region was deeply shaken by the raid.[25] Two years later South Quay was not so lucky, as the port was burned to the ground by forces under the command of Colonel Banastre Tarleton in the closing stages of the war.[26]

African Americans in Isle of Wight, Southampton, and Sussex had less opportunity to join the British than those living a day's ride to the east. Nonetheless, Dunmore's proclamation, combined with the intermittent threat and occasional reality of British incursions into the area throughout the war, powerfully demonstrated to them that the society they lived in could be overturned through military action and that freedom could be obtained through such resistance. Indeed, in 1783, when the British evacuated New York City, a handful of former Isle of Wight and Southampton slaves were among those departing for Nova Scotia to live as free men and women.[27] This experience gave the Revolution a lasting place in African American ideology and folklore in southeastern Virginia. In later years black Virginians not only appropriated the egalitarian language of American independence to challenge the legitimacy of their enslavement but also kept alive an association of British invasion with liberation, as when rumors circulated among slaves in the initial stages of the 1831 Nat Turner revolt "that the English were in the County killing white people."[28]

Baptist congregations in the counties were disrupted by the war. There are gaps in the records of Black Creek (February 1779–August 1783), Raccoon Swamp (1780–82), Mill Swamp (September 1779–June 1781), and the Kehukee Association (September 1778–May 1782), although, surprisingly, business seems to have continued as usual at South Quay.[29] (The other churches likely met when they could but did not keep records or did not transcribe them into their minute books.) There is thus little direct record of how Baptists in the region, black or white, responded to the military opportunities and challenges of the war. According to tradition, however, at least one local white Baptist played a particularly prominent role. The early nineteenth-century Baptist historian Robert Semple recorded that "in the time of the Revolutionary War Mr. Barrow was a warm Whig. He exhorted his countrymen to face the enemy and shake off the yoke of British bondage. . . . When dangers pressed, Mr. Barrow voluntarily shouldered his musket, joined the army and was found ready for the field of battle."[30]

Despite later Baptists' disavowal of his anti-slavery activism, Barrow represented an almost ideal vision of what mainstream white Baptists hoped the Revolution would achieve for them. The beginnings of his ministerial career coincided almost exactly with the outbreak of the Revolution in southeastern Virginia, and the trajectory of that career reflected the themes of piety, talent, leadership, and righteous political activism that shaped Baptist institutional development from the Revolution into the early republic. Born in Brunswick County in 1753, he was converted and baptized in 1770 by the minister Zachariah Thompson and joined the Fountain's Creek Baptist Church. At about the time of his eighteenth birthday Barrow "began to improve a gift" in preaching. A year later Barrow married Sarah Gilliam, of Sussex County, and joined Raccoon Swamp, where Sarah and her father, Hinchea Gilliam, were members. In 1774, amidst the upheaval of evangelical revival and the mounting imperial crisis, Barrow became the pastor of Mill Swamp and its branches in Southampton County.[31] Barrow quickly gained widespread respect for his preaching skill, piety, and character. As one biographer put it, "Jesus was with him and gave him many seals [i.e., converts]. His spotless character as a Christian greatly aided his pulpit labors. All who knew him at all knew he was a good man."[32] As we have seen, Barrow took a leading role in Virginia's growing Baptist movement and in the doctrinal and ecclesiastical reforms that clarified the relationship between conversion and baptism and shaped the union between Regular and Separate Baptists, first in the southeast and later across the state.

Barrow's role in the union between Regulars and Separates reflected his involvement in a larger set of issues that revolved around how Baptist ministers conceptualized their denomination and their own authority within that denomination. The union was really an agreement of fellowship and communication between various Baptist associations and churches, and in practice churches were represented in associations by ministers, preachers, and occasionally prominent laymen. Thus, despite very real disagreements that might occur and require mediation, associations ultimately represented a largely ministerial vision of the denomination. They reflected the ideals and goals of a white, male class within the church who had a particular interest in maintaining authority and influence in their own churches and across the denomination. From this ministerial point of view, the proper functioning and continued geographic extension of the associational form itself was just as important as the nature of the specific business that took place in associations.

Donald Mathews suggests the importance of such institution building to Baptists' visions for their denomination, observing that "through creating their own institutions and networks of communication, white Evangelicals finally achieved—in their own minds at least—the pinnacle of refinement and respectability."[33] In these years before Baptist mission societies and colleges, associations *were* the "institutions and networks of communication" that represented "the pinnacle of refinement and respectability" to white evangelicals. Barrow demonstrated his devotion to such institutions and networks throughout his career. He nearly always attended the annual meetings of his local association and frequently served as a messenger from one association to another, preached the introductory sermon, or served as moderator.[34] Later in his career, Barrow even revisited the institutional achievements of his earliest years. After he moved to Kentucky in 1798, he worked to unite Regular and Separate associations in that state, and in 1802 he reported success in uniting the two organizations.[35] In Kentucky, as in Virginia, Barrow was at the center of a ministerial effort to organize and extend the institutional reach of the Baptist Church.

Barrow embodied a rising concern for respectability among white

Baptists in other ways as well. In the 1780s he became a militia captain and served on the Southampton County Court, giving him a kind of social influence that very nearly epitomized the aspirations of the denomination in the new republic.[36] Unlike some prominent early Baptists, such as James Bell of Sussex County, Barrow was not a wealthy member of the gentry who happened to convert and use his influence to promote the cause. Instead, Barrow was a member of the broad middling swath of small-scale land and slave owners who rose to moderate prominence due to his talents, his service in the Revolution, and his involvement in post-Revolutionary political, intellectual, and religious debates.[37] This was exactly the image that Baptist leaders sought to project in the years immediately following the Revolution. In letters, in petitions, and in the denominational histories that appeared in the early nineteenth century, white Baptists depicted themselves primarily as virtuous non-elites whose political and religious interests were entirely compatible with those of the Revolution and who were dedicated to extending and preserving the Revolutionary legacy.

In this context, Baptists' humble origins became a badge of pride for subsequent chroniclers. The minister William Fristoe wrote in 1808 that most who joined the early Baptists in Virginia were "of the mediocrity or poorer sort among the people . . . and we have been encouraged to believe that it gave clearer proof of the genuine quality of religion among us." He went on to give biblical examples of Christ's teachings being accepted by the poor, while the rich and proud rejected him.[38] Barrow exemplified this white vision of Baptists' rise to cultural influence and respectability from within the Revolutionary tradition: his respectability was republican respectability. As his career intersected with the arc of the Revolution and its tumultuous aftereffects in Virginia, Barrow faced both the opportunities that a changing society presented and the limitations that the drive for republican respectability and the white, male, ministerial vision placed upon those opportunities.

As a denominational leader, Barrow also joined with other white ministers and laymen to shape Baptists' formal institutional response to the Revolution. The chaos of the opening stages of the conflict and concerns about loyalism, slave rebellion, and creating a legitimate government allowed white Baptists to claim an important place in any prospective coalition of interests and to shape the nature of that coalition and by extension the nature of post-Revolutionary society in Virginia. In 1775, for instance, the House of Delegates recorded a petition "from the Baptists of this colony" assuring them that Baptists shared in the common cause against Britain and that Baptists' religious beliefs in no way impeded them from serving as soldiers. After reassuring the House of their loyalty (or in this case their rebelliousness), they also requested that Baptist preachers be permitted to preach to the troops "without molestation or abuse."[39]

Baptists' public assertion of their willingness to participate in the war against Britain also provided an opportunity to pursue issues of religious freedom and to lay claim to a place in public religious culture. Members of the Occaquon Baptist Church, in Prince William County, sent a similar petition to the legislature in June 1776 that made the bargain even more explicit. The church members pointed out "that the strict[est] unanimity among oursel[ves] [is necessary?] in this most critical conjuncture of public affairs" and suggested that it was in everyone's best interest "that [every] remaining cause of animosity and division may if possible be removed." In order to prevent such animosity, the petitioners continued, perhaps Baptists could be allowed freedom of worship, be exempted from church taxes, and be allowed to conduct legal marriages and burials without recourse to the local Anglican parson. "These things grandted, we will gladly unite with our Brethren of other denominations and to the utmost of our ability promote the common cause of Freedom."[40] With almost embarrassing frankness, the Occaquon Baptists demonstrated the extent to which the connection between the cause of independence and the cause of religious freedom was consciously and purposefully pursued and shaped by evangelicals in the early days of the Revolution.[41]

Through such petitions, white Baptists sought to shape the Revolution to serve their own ends and to give their denomination a central place in the newly independent state. The Revolution occurred amidst an ongoing, multifaceted contest over establishment, dissent, and toleration in Virginia, but the relationship between independence from Britain and religious freedom was not a straightforward or obvious one. Most Revolutionary leaders favored at least some form of toleration that would allow non-Anglicans to worship without legal molestation and to assign their taxes to the support of a licensed minister of their own denomination. Some leaders, like Thomas Jefferson and James Madison, came to favor a more extensive vision of religious freedom that would abolish the establishment and end all state support of religion. But the practical implications and implementation of these views on the establishment, public support of religion, and the place of evangelicalism in Virginia's cultural life played out over decades and were very much up in the air in the early days of the Revolution.[42] Indeed, Jefferson's bill establishing religious freedom, drafted in 1777, was not passed by the legislature until 1786, and even then issues about what to do with the property of the formerly established church lingered into the nineteenth century. From the very beginning, however, Baptists shaped their discussion of and participation in the Revolution according to their own strong advocacy of religious freedom.

In addition to straightforward petitioning, white Baptists sought more subtly to combine the terms of their struggle with those of the independence movement, thus integrating the idea of religious liberty with other Revolutionary conceptions of independence, liberty, and justice. A poem by the Baptist minister David Thomas published in an October 1776 issue of the *Virginia Gazette*, signed only "COUNTRY POET," demonstrates some of the rhetorical strategies that accomplished this convergence:

> FREEDOM we crave with ev'ry breath;
> An equal freedom, or a death.
> The heav'nly blessing, freely give,
> Or make an act we shall not live!
> Tax all things, water, air, and light,
> If need there is; yea tax the night!
> But let our brave heroic minds
> Move freely, like celestial winds.
> Make vice and folly feel your rod,
> But leave our consciences to God.
> To mortal power she never bows,
> For Heav'n alone claims all her vows.[43]

Thomas addressed the issue of religious freedom, but he drew on the language and conceptual framework of the Revolution. Thomas's "equal freedom, or a death" echoed Patrick Henry's influential and religiously resonant 1775 exhortation, "give me liberty or give me death." Henry had been brought up in Hanover County, in the heart of the Presbyterian Awakening of the 1750s, where his uncle and namesake was Samuel Davies's Anglican nemesis. Henry himself was less influenced by his uncle than by Davies's stirring, popular rhetoric, and in the "Liberty or Death" speech he deployed a similar popular style and freely studded his oratory with biblical references. Although Henry was not an evangelical himself, his successful use of evangelical styles of communication highlights the ways in which common themes linked the evangelical and Revolutionary movements despite their different social composition. As Rhys Isaac suggests, both "seem to have met a general need for relief from collective anxiety and perceived disorder," and "both called for positive individual acts of affirmation as the basis for a new moral order."[44] In reappropriating Henry's rhetoric for evangelical purposes, Thomas took advantage of the connections that had been forged between the two movements for Revolutionary leaders' purposes to further Baptists' campaign for religious liberty. Thomas's poem also sought to recast Revolutionary ideas on the issues of taxation that ran through both the imperial crisis and the religious controversies of the era by suggesting that the injustices of British taxation paled in comparison with the injustice of taxing freedom of conscience in the form of state support for a religious establishment.

Of course, evangelicals were after more than just religious freedom. One of the ironies of the religious history of the late eighteenth and early nineteenth centuries was that as evangelicals agitated for religious freedom, and Baptists in particular for a rigorous and thorough separation of church and state, they were at the same time actively working to move closer to the center of public culture in the new nation. They believed that the separation of church and state would increase the public profile and influence of Christianity rather than decrease it.

Much of this rhetorical and cultural work also played on the trope of the Revolution. In an untitled poem composed "shortly after the Declaration of Independence," James Ireland, a Baptist minister in central Virginia, captured many of the dimensions of this strand of evangelical argument.[45] In the poem, Ireland connected American success in the Revolution with God's providence and presented the spread of religion across the nation as the natural fulfillment of the Revolution, as the proper way to express gratitude for God's favor. At the outset, Ireland reminded "America" that God, "thro' scenes of war and blood, / Display'd to thee salvation," by responding to American prayers and permitting victory over the British, "That thou should be / A nation free / From their unjust oppression." In the second stanza, Ireland purposely conflated American freedom from Britain with freedom from the bondage of sin. He called on "sons of liberty" to "own thy Independence" by accepting God:

> Replete with peace, valiant we stand
> Freedom the basis of our land,
> Blest with the beams of gospel light,
> Our souls emerge from sable night;
> Jehovah's heralds loud proclaim,
> Eternal life in Jesus name,
> > Points out his blood,
> > The way to God,
> For our complete salvation.

Echoing his earlier reminder of God's salvation of the American cause, Ireland thus called for a more "complete salvation" by embracing evangelical Christianity. The poem's third stanza outlined the risks of not accepting God's dominion over the new nation. Like many republican writers, Ireland believed that the main danger to the new nation was pride, and he described how the sin of pride insidiously undermined the foundations of liberty, bringing oppression and despotism. Only proper obedience to God could bring the humility and virtue necessary to sustain a free, republican society.

Finally, again capturing an important dimension of the fusion of Christian and republican rhetorics forged during the Revolutionary era, Ireland concluded with a millennial vision of a triumphant American empire, ruled by God:

> Thy guardian care we now implore,
> Be thou our King for ever
> > May gospel rays,
> > Divinely blaze,
> With an immortal lustre,
> > And teach us how,
> > Our hearts to bow,
> To the Redeemer's sceptre.

> O may the silver trump of peace,
> Within our Empire never cease,
> Until the ransom'd purchas'd race,
> Are called in by sov'reign grace,
> Then may the conflagration come,
> And sinners rise to hear their doom;
> > Thy chosen ones
> > In endless songs
> Will shout forth hallelujah's.

In this vision, the triumph of America would truly initiate the millennium, the thousand-year rule of Christ culminating in the final judgment, separating the chosen from the sinners for eternal reward or eternal punishment.

Ireland's metaphor of the "ransom'd purchas'd race"—by which he simultaneously invoked Christ's atonement for human sins, which "purchas'd" the salvation of the elect; a sense of Americans as a chosen people leaving behind the dual bondage of tyranny and sin; and millennial prophecy about the conversion of the Jews and the restoration of Israel—suggests other dimensions of Virginia Baptists' broad appropriation of republicanism and the image of the Revolution. The vagueness of the language that linked republican and evangelical concepts and its sometimes disquieting resonance with the social institutions of eighteenth-century Virginia helped give this language its power but also meant that it was susceptible to interpretation and reappropriation by a variety of groups with a variety of goals. Perhaps the most challenging of these interpretations appeared in the relatively short-lived anti-slavery movement among white evangelicals in Virginia. Understanding the white evangelical anti-slavery movement as an alternate interpretation of the evolving links between Christianity and republicanism provides insight into its cultural power while at the same time acknowledging its more limited, albeit real, political and social influence.

Among Virginia Baptists, some of the most prominent white anti-slavery spokesmen were also leading activists for religious liberty and architects of the Christian version of republicanism that emerged during and after the Revolution. John Leland, a New Englander who lived and preached in Virginia for more than a decade during and after the Revolution, later gained fame for presenting President Thomas Jefferson with a "monster cheese" made by Baptists in western Massachusetts as a token of their esteem for Jefferson and his views on religious freedom.[46] During his time in Virginia, Leland, a prolific writer, actively campaigned for disestablishment and asserted the Baptists' radical position on church-state relations: "The liberty I contend for, is more than toleration. The very idea of toleration, is despicable; it supposes that some have a pre-eminence above the rest, to grant indulgence; whereas, all should be equally free, Jews, Turks, Pagans and Christians."[47] Leland was also very conscious of the way that religious liberty had accompanied the increasing popularity of evangelicalism, and he exulted in this dual political and religious victory over the establishment. "The subject of religious liberty," he claimed, ". . . has so far prevailed, that in Virginia, a politician can no more be popular, without the possession of it, than a preacher who denies the doctrine of the *new birth*."[48] But like James Ireland and other spokesmen for the evangelical vision of American destiny, he insisted that both true republicanism and true devotion to the new birth required more than just lip service; it must be sincerely lived out. For Leland this meant that those politicians who supported religious liberty should grant it to their wives, children, and slaves by allowing them to worship as they pleased.[49]

As that argument implies, Leland combined his strong Baptist and republican principles with anti-slavery activism. One of the greatest injustices of slavery, in his view, was the denial of slaves' rights to freedom of conscience. Thus he combined fundamental Baptist political and religious principles into a critique of Virginia's peculiar institution.[50] In 1790, spurred by a handful of influential activists within the ministerial ranks, the Virginia Baptist General Committee even adopted a resolution written by Leland "that slavery is a violent deprivation of the rights of nature and inconsistent with a republican government, and therefore [we] recommend it to our brethren to make use of every legal measure to extirpate this horrid evil from the land."[51] On his departure from Virginia, Leland expanded on this statement, asking his perhaps skeptical audience "whether Heaven has nothing in store for poor negroes than these galling chains."[52] The intertwined republican and evangelical principles that Baptists used to shape their place in newly independent Virginia led Leland to argue for a further fundamental reshaping of post-Revolutionary society.

Like Leland, David Barrow was a crucial figure in the Revolutionary Baptist movement, and he came to question slavery for very similar reasons. Along with Leland, Barrow was also an activist in the Baptists' battles over religious liberty in the post-Revolutionary period. At a Kehukee Association meeting in May 1785 Barrow raised the issue of a bill in the legislature that would impose a general assessment to support religion in the new state. Leland, also in attendance, read a petition from Charles City County against the assessment, and the association agreed to circulate a similar one.[53] A month later such a petition was read and approved at Mill Swamp, and a committee was appointed to circulate it generally to residents of Isle of Wight County.[54] Similar approval was recorded at Black Creek.[55] A decade later, Barrow corresponded with the New England Baptist leader and religious-liberty activist Isaac Backus about Virginia Baptists' campaign for the sale of former Anglican glebe lands to support public education and poor relief.[56] According to nineteenth-century denominational historians, Barrow "most eloquently vindicated the right of all men to worship God according to their wishes, and urged his brethren to maintain a united and immovable stand against those enactments which took away this right."[57]

Perhaps even more than Leland, Barrow used his influence and his association with Revolutionary ideas to oppose slavery. When Barrow freed Benjamin and Lucrecia Blackhead in 1784, he recorded a deed of manumission with the Southampton County Court:

> Whereas an act of General Assembly Intitled an act Concerning the manumission of Slaves, gives free liberty to all persons holding slaves under Certain Restrictions to manumit or set them free. Therefore be it known to all whom it may Concern that I David Barrow . . . being duly Sensible and fully pursuaded that freedom is the Natural and Unalienable right of all Mankind; and also haveing a Single eye to that Golden Rule prescribed in Sacred Writ Vizt "do to all Men as ye would they should Do to you" Do hereby Agreeable to the above recited Act Manumit or set free . . . a Negro Man Named

Ben Blackhead, of about twenty three years of age, and a Negro
Woman named Lucrecia Blackhead of about Eighteen and I do
freely and Voluntarily from a Sacred regard that I have to the rights
of Mankind Acknowledge & declare them the Above named Negroes
to be free Citizens of the State.[58]

With this economical combination of words and action, Barrow made
his vision of what republican and Christian values meant for slavery concrete. Barrow's language drew on a familiar formula—the overwhelming majority of Southampton and Isle of Wight county manumissions
included a statement similar to Barrow's that combined a natural-rights
argument against slavery derived from the rhetoric of the Revolution
with a religious statement, usually based in the Golden Rule.[59] These
statements reflect the influence of local Quakers. Quaker anti-slavery
had been cast in terms of the Golden Rule as early as 1688, and throughout the period of legal private manumission from 1782 to 1806, when the
legislature effectively quashed further manumissions by requiring freed
men and women to leave the state, a substantial minority of manumitters
in Southampton and Isle of Wight were Quakers.[60] Barrow's exact language was his own, however, departing significantly from the identical,
formulaic language of most other manumitters. Barrow's reference to
the General Assembly act and his "free liberty" to manumit was distinctive. He also embellished the standard formula a bit by adding *unalien-
able* to the natural-rights language—certainly an intentional echo of the
Declaration of Independence—and by referring directly to the Golden
Rule rather than simply stating it. Most significantly, Barrow's declaration of his "Sacred regard" for the "rights of Mankind" and his assertion
that the Blackheads were "free Citizens of the State" were unique to his
formulation. Despite the Quaker influence, then, his use of the language
of republicanism and Christianity had its own particular valence.

Quakers' pacifism and close ties with their British brethren often
prompted suspicions of loyalism during the Revolution, and they held
an ambivalent relationship to the new political order and ideologies that
emerged in its aftermath. White Baptists' active evangelical activities,
their eager participation in the Revolution, and their insistent efforts to
influence the nature of the Revolutionary settlement through the campaign for religious liberty distinguished them from the pacifist and qui-

etist Quakers. As we have seen, white Baptist anti-slavery was enmeshed in the larger denominational project of adopting and adapting the image of the Revolution as a part of a strategy of gaining greater acceptance and cultural influence in the emerging republican world. These differences found subtle expression in the anti-slavery ideas of each denomination. The Golden Rule lay at the heart of Quakers' anti-slavery thought, even as they incorporated Enlightenment and Revolutionary ideas into their arguments. For white Baptists such as Barrow, republican arguments played a much more prominent role. When Quaker anti-slavery activists employed republican arguments, they spoke to some extent as outsiders critiquing the shortcomings of the Revolutionary tradition. When Barrow did so, he self-consciously spoke as a participant in that tradition, calling for its extension to what he saw as its natural outcome. But white Baptist anti-slavery was also ultimately compromised and limited by its participation in this tradition, at least as it evolved in the South. Quakers eventually succeeded in persuading their members to abandon slavery; the 1782–1806 era of manumission represented the culmination of that process. White Baptist anti-slavery advocates like Barrow and Leland could not persuade their white co-religionists or their fellow white Virginians that slavery was incompatible with either Christianity or republicanism. Instead, the majority of white Baptists eventually chose a different configuration of republican and Christian values that facilitated accommodation to slavery and slaveholding and eased the way to cultural influence in the antebellum South.

In 1784, however, this outcome was not so clear. For Baptists in Virginia the era of manumission represented the beginning of their denominational struggles over slavery, not the end, and Barrow's manumission of Benjamin and Lucrecia Blackhead initiated a period of sometimes open debate on the issue of slavery in his churches. Barrow's manumission did not immediately inspire a wave of emulators, but in September 1785 John Johnson, a member of Black Creek, emancipated a woman in her mid-twenties named Milly. It seems likely that Milly was Milly Blackhead, Benjamin Blackhead's wife, who became a member of Black Creek in August 1788, soon after Benjamin.[61] Johnson's language in his deed of manumission was identical to Barrow's highly distinctive formulation, strongly suggesting Barrow's direct influence on Johnson's decision.[62] Although no other identifiable white Baptists in Isle of Wight or

Southampton counties manumitted their slaves in the several years following Barrow's act, other events clearly indicate that the issue of slavery had become a matter of serious attention.

In February 1786 the members of Black Creek considered a query whether it was "a Ritious thing for a Christain to hold or Cause any of the Humane Race to be held in Slavery." After debating the matter for several sessions, the church decided that it was "unrighteous." The following year, the congregation considered a more complicated query whether "a person who hires Slaves can be Consider'd as one who hold or Causes any part of mankind to be held in slavery." The church debated this query for several sessions, including a session specially appointed for urgent business, at which the query was withdrawn without an answer.[63] In confronting the difficult and significant issue of hiring slaves, the members of Black Creek demonstrated not only their serious engagement with the complexities of living in a slave society but also their ultimate inability to agree on an anti-slavery policy that was equal to those complexities. As Sarah Hughes has demonstrated, hiring slaves was not "an incidental or peripheral aspect of the slave labor market" but in fact a central aspect of the institution. Particularly in areas like the counties of southeastern Virginia, which were not devoted to staple-crop agriculture but exhibited "a diversified rural economy with low profit margins," hiring slaves provided crucial flexibility in the use of labor and helped tie non-slaveholding (but not necessarily non-slave-using) whites to an economic and social system of racialized slavery.[64]

Many Black Creek members may have participated in this practice, for in 1787 only about half of the white male members owned any slaves, and those who did averaged two to three slaves, both figures slightly below county averages.[65] It is significant, then, that Black Creek's efforts foundered on the issue of hiring slaves. White church members were willing to condemn the peculiar institution in principle, but they were less willing to threaten their own strategies of economic survival. Indeed, Barrow's emigration to Kentucky demonstrates the difficult economic decisions facing even the most committed anti-slavery Baptists. Like many white Virginians, Barrow sought greater economic opportunity to the west. Others did not have the resources or the desire to relocate to accommodate their scruples and remained in Virginia, moving uneasily toward a de facto accommodation with slavery.

The controversy over slavery at Black Creek disappeared from the church minutes for several years after the 1787 query on hiring slaves, but it did not go away. In the years immediately following the 1787 query several more members of Black Creek manumitted their slaves. On February 14, 1788, Henry Jones recorded a deed that manumitted two young men, significantly named Jimes [James?] Fredom and George Liberty. The same day, Giles Johnson manumitted James Blackshins and Dick Blackshins. Both Jones and Johnson used the exact same language that Barrow and John Johnson had used.[66] (Another manumitter during this period, Benjamin Beal Jr., who freed a man named Mingo in February 1789, was also probably a Baptist.)[67] George Liberty and Dick (or Richard) Blackshins both eventually became members of Black Creek in the early years of the nineteenth century.[68] Giles Johnson was a long-time deacon at Black Creek, and the church had licensed him to preach just months before he manumitted his slaves. Henry Jones was also a licensed preacher in 1788, and in 1802 he was ordained as a minister. And John Johnson, who had manumitted Milly Blackhead in 1785, was chosen as a deacon in May 1788.[69] In the late 1780s, then, an influential group of members at Black Creek evinced a commitment to manumission and a hostility to slavery that appear to have been deeply influenced by Barrow's thinking on the matter.

On the statewide level, Baptist anti-slavery efforts also reached their peak during this period. In 1785 the Virginia Baptist General Committee approved a resolution condemning slavery as "contrary to the word of God." In 1790 the committee further pursued this issue, appointing a committee of several prominent ministers, including Barrow, to draft a resolution on slavery. Unable to agree on the wording, the committee adopted the resolution written by Leland "that slavery is a violent deprivation of the rights of nature and inconsistent with a republican government, and therefore [we] recommend it to our brethren to make use of every legal measure to extirpate this horrid evil from the land."[70] This statement, particularly the reference to "every legal measure," was clearly an endorsement of manumission for church members as well as an encouragement of political actions such as petitions and lobbying, which were pursued by Quakers and some Methodists.

But as in Black Creek's debates, it was unclear exactly how this recommendation would affect the policies of churches or the boundaries of fellowship between church members. The General Committee's resolution had no binding authority over any churches, church members, or slaves, and the reactions from the local Baptist associations that bothered to respond ranged from wary to hostile. The Roanoke Association, for instance, warned against emancipating slaves "promiscuously" and suggested that slavery should be left to individual consciences. The Strawberry Association suggested that the General Committee should not "interfere" with slavery. Faced with these reactions, the General Committee decided in 1793 that decisions on the issue of slavery were most properly the responsibility of the legislature.[71] Thus, any anti-slavery action was left in the hands of those members who felt moved to take it, as was the burden of persuading their fellow Baptists to emulate them.

The tensions this denominational ambivalence provoked emerged in the Black Creek church. A group of members including Barrow's wife, Sarah, John Johnson, Benjamin Beal, Elizabeth Beal, and Noel Vick did not take communion with the church in the early spring of 1791. When the church examined them to find out why at a June 24 meeting, these members stated their renewed dissatisfaction "with a Part of the Church for holding Slaves and hiring them which caused a Debate which took up the greater Part of the Day." The church could not reach a resolution that day, and the matter was debated extensively over several meetings. Eventually all five dissenters returned to the church, but a definitive statement was never made; the church considered slaveholding unrighteous, but it did not go so far as to sanction breaking fellowship because of it. John Johnson retained his influence in the church and was ordained as a deacon (in which capacity he already served) in August 1793, but Noel Vick continued to be troubled by slaveholding within the church. In November 1793 he was brought before the church again for "absenting himself from the Lords Table on account of Slaves being held by some of the Brethren." At the next meeting Vick agreed "to content himself as much as possible," but he continued to come into conflict with the church. Finally, in 1802 the church excommunicated Vick for his "ungodly life and conversation . . . and his long absence from attending our appointed meetings."[72]

In both its participants and its underlying ideology, Baptist manumission in Southampton and Isle of Wight counties was intimately tied to the more general white Baptist anti-slavery movement. The Mill Swamp church never faced the type of division that Black Creek did, but several members, including the future minister John Gwaltney, manumitted their slaves in the 1790s.[73] Although manumission could express a purely personal aversion to slavery or simply operate as a gift to a particular slave or slaves, this was not the case for the handful of Baptists who freed their slaves during Virginia's era of legal manumission. David Barrow, John Johnson, and others intended to lead by example, to encourage their co-religionists to follow suit and realize the incompatibility of slavery with the intertwined political and religious creeds to which they subscribed. For these men, manumission presented the opportunity for white Baptists voluntarily to free themselves from the sin of slavery and take a leadership role in the ending of slavery in the new nation as a whole, fulfilling the Christian and republican promise of the Revolution and furthering white Baptists' rise to influence and power in the new order. Manumission was a concrete and public point at which these men's belief in the association of Christianity, republicanism, and freedom was realized.

Beyond the evidence of his views expressed in his deed of manumission, Barrow left a handful of more expansive documents that provide a deeper glimpse into his thinking and the nature of his anti-slavery beliefs, including the 1798 *Circular Letter,* a manuscript journal of a trip to Kentucky in 1795, and a lengthy anti-slavery pamphlet published in Kentucky in 1808.[74] Although all of these documents came after the crest of the manumission movement, there is no indication that Barrow's views changed significantly over this period, and the documents serve as a reasonable guide to his anti-slavery thought from the mid-1780s on. In these writings Barrow condemned slavery as both *"inconsistent* with . . . the *principles* of the *American Revolution"* and "a *spawn* of the *devil, begotten* of *he himself,* by an *unnatural commerce* on *fallen human nature."*[75] Barrow braided the strands of evangelical belief and republican principles into a powerful argument that slavery was contrary to God's will, dangerous to the health of the new nation, and threatening to the purity of the church. And echoing the broader Baptist concern over the fate of new nation, Barrow also implied that those three dangers were intimately related.[76]

As James David Essig suggests, Barrow linked the concepts of political tyranny and the tyranny of sin through the idea that both deviated from divinely ordained fundamental principles. Slaveholders, in Barrow's view, were despots just as kings were, because they exercised illegitimate, arbitrary, and absolute authority over their fellow men.[77] This issue of despotism and the sins that slavery promoted in both slave and master echoed James Ireland's fears that pride and an unwillingness to submit to God would undermine the republican experiment and cause rapid backsliding into tyranny and oppression, and Barrow linked such fears explicitly to slavery. He claimed that "there are few *evils* or *sins*, now existing, in church, state or families,—but what rise out of, or are connected with *slavery*." In addition to the peculiar institution's degrading effects on slaves, it caused a litany of sins in the masters, including imperiousness, covetousness, idleness, effeminacy, pride, hard-heartedness, cruelty, "superfluity of naughtiness," intemperance, fornication, adultery, prevention of lawful marriage, and disobedience to parents. Not only did these sins threaten the virtue of the republic but they could raise a bar to church membership, making slavery a threat to the prosperity of the church.[78]

On a 1795 trip through the northern Virginia town of Winchester, Barrow found a corresponding model of what a society without slavery might look like. Barrow recorded in his journal that Winchester was inhabited

> by the most independent farmers I ever saw. . . . The inhabitants are mostly immigrants fr: the Northward. they have few slaves, and are consequently industrious. The women think it no shame to attend to their household and kitchen affairs, w. their own hands, & the men steadily at their business. This part of Va: promises [for?] greatness and independency. . . . The manners and morals of the people are agreeable in general. I also find several religious denominations livg: peacably in those regions; as Baptists, Pbyns:; Lutherians, Quakers, & c.[79]

In Barrow's view, familial and social order and the fulfillment of proper gender roles were threatened by slavery, and they prospered in its absence. As Barrow's list of sins suggests, gender and familial order were fundamental to his understanding of the problems of slavery and of the nature of a republican society. His description of Winchester suggests how. "Greatness and independency" for a society depended upon industrious application to the gender-specific tasks of an agrarian household; slavery diverted men and women from these tasks by encouraging laziness, covetousness, disobedience, and sexual misbehavior. In a prosperous farming community like Winchester, which was not dependent on slaves, family and gender roles not only led naturally to proper republican independence but also led to the prosperity and harmony of several flavors of Protestant Christianity—"Baptists, Pbyns:; Lutherians, Quakers, &c." Thus, in addition to the powerful impulses of religious liberty and republican political philosophy, Barrow's anti-slavery vision drew on a particular understanding of the importance of gender, family, and household to the health of both religion and nation. This distinctive vision of household and gender eventually ran headlong into a different conception that underlay the powerful resistance of many Virginians to Barrow's message.

Despite the rhetorical force of the anti-slavery arguments of men like David Barrow and John Leland, it is important to remember how unpersuasive they proved to the majority of the Baptist rank and file. Leland's 1790 General Committee resolution was a fairly shallow high-water mark of the statewide anti-slavery movement among white Virginia Baptists. Leaders like Leland and Barrow never succeeded in persuading more than a handful of lay members to take any concrete action, and that handful could provoke bitter divisions within the churches. Even at Black Creek, probably the most strongly anti-slavery Baptist church in eastern Virginia, those Baptists who sought to cleanse the church of the sin of slavery could not persuade their fellow church members to do so and ultimately had to compromise or face expulsion. This did not entirely preclude action based on personal anti-slavery commitments, but whenever anti-slavery activists sought to pursue their beliefs in a broader forum, they provoked reaction from the mainstream of the church.

In 1825, for instance, slavery resurfaced as a divisive issue at Black Creek. At a meeting in December of that year the church's minister, Jonathan Lankford, abruptly "declared to this conference that he cannot in Justice to his conscience administer the Ordinances of the Gospel to this Church any longer owing to his oppesition [*sic*] on the subject of Negro Slavery, a part of the church being Slave holders." After debating the matter for more than a year, lamenting the divisive effects of Lankford's statement, and dismissing Lankford's motives as petty self-aggrandizement, the church expelled him.[80] Although few, if any, of the members of Black Creek in 1825 had been around for the church's earlier controversies over slavery, their decision clearly reflected the implied outcome of those decisions. The church committee's report on the Lankford case asserted that slavery was a matter best left to individual consciences and that anti-slavery action within the church threatened fellowship between church members who held slaves and those who did not. In this configuration, anti-slavery agitation was a form of willful divisiveness and unchristian confrontational behavior that was unacceptable among fellow church members.[81]

The outcome of this case, like the Roanoke and Strawberry associations' reactions to the 1790 General Committee resolution, reflected a very different interpretation of the staples of Baptist republican ideology than the one put forward by Barrow and Leland. In all of these cases, the reaction against anti-slavery agitation implied that religious freedom and freedom of conscience—the very ideas that had been central to Baptists' interpretation of the Revolution and to the ideology of anti-slavery activists—should prevent religious agitation on issues of slavery. Such decisions should be individual, and religious organizations, along with their ministers, should steer clear of issues deemed political. It was this interpretation of freedom of conscience and the separation of church and state, not that of Leland and Barrow, that gained sway in Virginia at the beginning of the nineteenth century, and it was this interpretation that persisted.

Among non-evangelicals, popular reaction against Virginia's 1782 legalization of private manumission and a 1785 Methodist petition in favor of general emancipation suggest several other dimensions of republicanism, Christianity, and gender that would eventually come to predominate in Virginia. In 1784 and 1785 a series of petitions mostly from Southside counties just to the west of Isle of Wight, Southampton, and Sussex reached the state legislature. The hundreds of men who signed these petitions argued that they had, in confronting British usurpations, "seald with our Blood, a Title to the full, free, and absolute Enjoyment of every species of our Property, whensoever, or howsoever legally acquired." How unfair, even tyrannical, then, were attempts to deprive them of "the most valuable and indispensible Article of our Property, our Slaves." Such a plan was not only inconsistent with the rights of free citizens, it was worthy of "a *Bute*, or a *North*, whose Finger is sufficiently visible in it."[82]

In this view, emancipation and manumission were part of a last-ditch conspiracy by the British designed to bring misery to Americans and again deprive them of their rights. (This view was slightly more plausible than it may seem because of the powerful negative impression that Quaker and Methodist loyalism and/or neutrality left on many Americans, a problem that did not afflict the Baptists, who eagerly hitched their own fortunes to the American cause.) The petitioners also argued that slavery was biblically justified and "That it was ordained by the Great and wise Disposer of all Things, That some Nations should serve others."[83] Finally, most of the petitions included complaints about the disorders caused by the blacks who had already been freed, including the "Insolences, and Violences so freequently of late committed to and on our respectable Maids and Matrons, which are a Disgrace to Government."[84] Together, these arguments and objections added up to a dramatically different interpretation of the intertwined meanings of the Revolution, Christianity, and gender than the one Barrow had put forward. Natural rights became white male property rights; the Golden Rule became divinely ordained servitude; industrious farm women became potential rape victims. While the interpretations were different, the common perception that the legacy of the Revolution, the dictates of Christian scripture, and the health and safety of the white household were the most important categories defined the ground on which most of the ideological battles among white Americans in the early national and antebellum periods would be fought.

To the extent that they articulated a positive defense of slavery, the Southside petitioners were ahead of the curve. Many, perhaps most, Virginians continued to harbor doubts well into the nineteenth century about the desirability of slavery in their republican society even as they rejected all significant anti-slavery activity as disruptive and unworkable. The churches of southeastern Virginia held on to anti-slavery beliefs longer than most, apparently in large part because of Barrow's influence. In 1796 the Virginia Portsmouth Baptist Association, moderated by Barrow, considered *"the present wretched and distressing times"* experienced by the churches and decided that one reason was that *"covetousness,* leads Christians, with the people of this country in general, to hold and retain, in *abject slavery,* a set of our poor fellow creatures, *contrary to the laws of God and nature."*[85] This vision was entirely consistent with Barrow's view that slavery caused sins that undermined the health of the church. (In addition, the typography was consistent with his fondness for italics, suggesting that he may have actually authored the minute.)

Moreover, other reasons given for the decline—that a similar covetousness led ministers "to neglect their sacred work; turn into their farms, merchandize; leading some to embrace civil offices; and thus 'entangling themselves with the affairs of this life, they displease him who hath chosen them to be soldiers'"—reflect both the details of Barrow's biography and his own expressed concerns about his inability to fulfill his dual roles as minister and father without embracing slavery.[86] The Portsmouth Association's deliberations and conclusions unquestionably reflect Barrow's influence and preoccupations: in January 1797 Barrow reiterated the concerns expressed by the association, complaining to Isaac Backus that "from twenty five years Experience" he "never knew altogether so dull a Time" and admitting that "it has of late, often led me to enquire into the Cause."[87] He left for Kentucky the following year.

Ultimately, Barrow found Kentucky little more hospitable than Virginia; many of the same trends he had faced in his home state persisted in his adopted home. In October 1806 he was expelled from the North District Association of Baptists, in Montgomery County. He had been charged in 1805 by a neighboring association of "Meddling with emancipation," and his refusal to refrain from "preaching the Doctrine of emancipation to the hurt and injury of the feelings of the Brotherhood" over the past year had caused them "to expel him from his seat in the Association." In the course of the debate over Barrow's actions, his ministerial brethren were forced to clarify their attitudes toward slavery and toward anti-slavery activism in the church. They articulated an argument that the Bible "enforc[ed] different duties on various characters in their different stations in the present world" and exhorted church members to perform "those relative duties enjoined on us in the word of God to perform in our several stations [in] which God in his wise providence has been pleased to place us." But that argument was almost overshadowed in the association by arguments that focused on the effects of anti-slavery activism on fellowship within the church. Barrow was expelled, not so much because of theological or doctrinal error, but because his actions had caused "hurt and injury" to his brethren and were "pernicious to peace and good order."[88]

The irony was that in both Virginia and Kentucky Barrow himself had been an architect of the peace and good order that united Baptist churches. His uniting of Regulars and Separates in both states and his regularly attending, preaching at, and moderating associational meetings had been fundamental to the institutional expansion of the denomination.[89] In Barrow's view, his anti-slavery activity was cut from the same cloth, establishing proper Godly and republican order in denominational institutions, in families, and in society more broadly. In 1774 Barrow had determined that baptism before conversion was inconsistent with fundamental Christian principles and had worked to reform his church and his association. For him, the issue of slavery was analogous: it was contrary to the basic principles of Christian religion, and therefore churches that sanctioned slavery needed to be reformed. In his parting letter Barrow recorded his prayers for the church, including the wishes "that she may *keep the ordinances, as they were delivered to her at the first*," "that she may maintain a regular and gospel discipline," and that "all false doctrines and heretical principles, may clearly be discovered, and sink into darkness, where they belong." Barrow implied that the toleration of slavery was among these false doctrines when he pointedly asked masters of slaves "whether in this particular, they are *doing, as they would others should do to them!*"[90]

Even after his expulsion from the North District Association, Barrow pursued this reform through the same Baptist institutions that he had helped develop. In 1807 he helped form the anti-slavery Baptized Licking-Locust Association, Friends of Humanity, which continued to follow the forms of Baptist institutional practice, bringing ministers and preachers together, creating links between churches, giving advice on doctrinal and disciplinary matters, and establishing terms of fellowship.[91] As a later denominational historian put it, "He soon brought order out of confusion. The churches and fragments of churches that held to the emancipation scheme were organized, and a respectable Association was formed."[92] "Peace and good order," as well as associationalism, remained fundamental to Barrow's vision of the Baptist mission.

David Barrow died in Kentucky on November 14, 1819. According to tradition, his last words were from the Twenty-third Psalm.[93] Perhaps they were the familiar and conventional first verse of the Psalm, "The Lord is my shepherd; I shall not want," or perhaps the equally familiar and apt fourth verse, "Yea, though I walk through the valley of the shadow of death, I will fear no evil. . . ." But Barrow's experiences of activism, frustration, and even persecution may have led his mind to other passages and phrases, perhaps "he leadeth me in the paths of righteousness for his name's sake" or "Thou preparest a table before me in the presence of mine enemies: thou anointest my head with oil; my cup run-neth over." However he chose to conclude, his career expressed aspects of the Baptist experience of the Revolutionary era that, although gradu-ally marginalized and suppressed, help illustrate the negotiations that shaped Baptist republicanism and illuminate the mainstream of Baptist thought by demonstrating some of the alternatives.

Even as Barrow and other white anti-slavery activists despaired of achieving their vision of a truly Christian and republican society in Vir-ginia, other men and women took hold of evangelical and republican values that emerged in the wake of the Revolution and interpreted and used them in their own ways. Black Virginians' experiences of the Revo-lution differed profoundly from those of their white neighbors, but they too understood the era as a struggle for liberty and self-determination. Some six thousand or more ran away to the British, but most black men and women in Virginia had to seek these goals through other, less direct means.[94] Many chose to make evangelical Christianity part of this effort, not necessarily to achieve freedom from bondage, although some did at-tempt just that, but to find meaning, respect, authority, and community through the beliefs, rituals, and institutions of this emerging religious movement.

The cultural, social, and political environment of the 1780s and 1790s may have reduced the perceived distance between the material and the more symbolic or psychic potentials of evangelicalism for black converts. Both the Methodist and Baptist anti-slavery movements peaked in the second half of the 1780s—Methodists in Sussex County freed more than one hundred slaves at one session of the county court in 1787–88—and across Virginia white legislators and Revolutionary leaders sought to de-termine what place, if any, slavery had in a republican society.[95] Private manumission was just one aspect of this larger quest, compromised and self-interested though it may have been, on the part of white Virginians to come to terms with the contradictions in their society. As Ira Berlin puts it, "If their handwringing often served as a cover for inaction, it nev-ertheless helped to put the door ajar," and black men and women sought to open or squeeze through this door in whatever way they could.[96]

These efforts were facilitated by a changing economy in which wheat and livestock increasingly replaced tobacco as the mainstay of many

Virginia farmers, by increasing industrial production in some regions, and by the growth of towns and cities like Richmond, Petersburg, Portsmouth, and Norfolk, which serviced this new, more diverse economy. All of these developments increased the demand for a skilled and mobile workforce, giving slaves, especially men, greater flexibility in their work and greater leverage to negotiate the conditions of their service.[97] Combined with the military challenges and ideological developments of the Revolutionary era, these economic changes reshaped both the strategies and the tactics that enslaved men and women used to shape their own lives and, sometimes, to gain their freedom. Indeed, through manumission, self-purchase, freedom suits, military service, escape, and countless other strategies, the free black population of Virginia grew dramatically in the post-Revolutionary era, from about two thousand in 1782 to twelve thousand in 1790 and thirty thousand in 1810.[98]

It was in this context that black men and women began to join evangelical churches in significant numbers. Black Christians remained a minority in Virginia's African American population well into the nineteenth century, but the 1780s and 1790s were an important turning point in the Christianization of the black population. Perhaps inspired by the resonance between evangelicalism's promise of personal and communal transformation and the larger social transformations of the Revolution and its immediate aftermath, African and African American men and women who joined the Baptist and Methodist movements during these years provided a critical mass of black converts who took hold of evangelical religion, made it their own, and helped spread it to the black (and to an extent also the white) population of the new state.[99] We saw in chapter 2 how black preachers like Lewis, whose talents Richard Dozier thought "exceeded many white preachers," spoke to mixed audiences and illustrated, in ways that may have differed for blacks and whites in the audience, the power of God's word to level worldly distinctions. In Gloucester County a black minister named William Lemon even served as pastor of a biracial church for a time.[100] On a somewhat less exalted level, the entry of black men and women into mixed congregations had similar meanings that could be interpreted in different ways by different participants. Indeed, the post-Revolutionary growth of the Baptist churches in Isle of Wight, Southampton, and Sussex counties was due in large part to increasing black membership, and while it is impossible to know for certain whether, or to what extent, the attraction had anything to do with Barrow's or other

white Baptists' anti-slavery sentiments, Barrow's ideas would have resonated with the deep-seated themes of liberation in black interpretations
of Christianity.[101]

Black men and women also began to develop their own distinctive
interpretations of evangelicalism's message outside the bounds of white
oversight, sometimes in ways very directly related to the political and
social turmoil of the post-Revolutionary era. In more densely settled,
urbanizing areas like Richmond, Petersburg, Williamsburg, Norfolk,
Portsmouth, and their hinterlands, where free blacks and urban slaves
led lives somewhat more flexible than those of rural slaves, independent
black churches developed. Many of these churches split off from white
bodies because of frustration with restrictions placed on black preaching
and officeholding, and their relationship to the white-controlled denominational structures was a subject of careful negotiation on both sides.[102]

Black Baptists in Williamsburg, for instance, supported the independent preaching of Moses, "who was often taken up and whipped for
holding meetings," despite the hostility of white denominational authorities. A free black preacher named Gowan Pamphlet then moved into
the neighborhood "and began to baptize as well as preach." In defiance
of an associational ban on black preaching, "the blacks were rebellious,
and continued to hold meetings," and as a result Pamphlet and many
others were excluded from the white church. Pamphlet continued to
preach and to baptize those he converted. About 1781, appropriating
the forms of Baptist ecclesiastical practice, Pamphlet "formed a kind of
church of some who had been baptized, who, sitting with him, received
such as offered themselves. Gowan baptized them, and was, moreover,
appointed their pastor. Some knowing how to write, a church book was
kept." In 1791 the same association that had previously excluded the
members of Pamphlet's Williamsburg church received them into fellowship and reported the church's membership as five hundred.[103] It is unclear how, when, or by whom Pamphlet himself was converted and baptized, but from the fragments of his history that survive it is clear that
he drew on the forms of authority, communication, and association created by white Baptists in their struggle for recognition and community
in Virginia, adopted them for his own ends, and ultimately persuaded
white authorities to recognize both him and the institutions he created.
Whatever his differences with white Baptists, Pamphlet demonstrated
his religious authority in terms that they could understand as legitimate.

Preaching, baptism, overcoming persecution, organizing churches, and keeping records were as important to Pamphlet's story as they were to David Barrow's or Edward Mintz's.

Perhaps less spectacularly or successfully than Pamphlet's career, that of Jacob Bishop, a free black minister from Northampton County, illustrates the tensions between black desires for independence and self-government and white concerns over racial and doctrinal order. Moved by the power of Bishop's preaching and his potential as a servant of God, white Baptists in Northampton helped Bishop purchase his and his wife's freedom. In 1795 he moved to Norfolk, where "his preaching was much admired by saints and sinners for some time wherever he went." The Portsmouth and Norfolk church, a 1789 offshoot of the church Barrow and Mintz had planted at Shoulder's Hill in 1779, was embroiled in a controversy over its substantial black membership's desire to have a vote in church conferences. White advisers from other churches suggested that black members be considered a "wing" of the larger body, apparently so that they might have a degree of self-government but not full voting authority within the biracial church itself, which, given their numbers, would compromise white control of the church. Bishop was appointed "to take the oversight of them."[104] For reasons that remain unclear—vaguely described by white ministers in 1803 as black members' concern "that matters might turn up disagreeably to them and dishonoring to God"—the black branch of the church later agreed to "be subordinate to the white brethren, if they would let them continue as they were," and a series of white pastors, including Jacob Grigg, who would later join Barrow among the "Friends of Humanity" in Kentucky, and then Davis Biggs, were appointed to oversee the black branch of the church.[105] The 1798 minutes of the Portsmouth Association, however, record that Grigg and Bishop together represented the Portsmouth church that year, and Bishop is listed alongside Grigg in the capital letters the minutes used to denote pastors and ordained ministers.[106]

It is impossible to know precisely what black ministers like Pamphlet or Bishop preached or how it differed from what white Baptists heard from the pulpit, but their experiences and actions, as well as those of the congregations they formed and served, highlight the degree to which independent religious judgment and access to religious authority mattered to black men and women. This is easier to discern in the semiurban, independent black churches that formed during the 1780s and 1790s, but as we shall see in chapter 4, it was no less important to black Baptists in rural, biracial churches, even though the process of interaction and negotiation with their white brethren differed in many ways. James Sidbury has recently argued that historians of black Christianity should pay more attention to "the local interpretive vitality that formed the base for the broad 'slave church' that modern scholarship has uncovered."[107] While the details and content of local interpretive processes often elude us in all but the most exceptional moments, the outlines of such processes are apparent in the controversies that emerged as Pamphlet's and Bishop's "textual communities" intersected and overlapped with those of white Baptists. Their relative institutional successes demonstrate that white and black Baptists did, in fact, have a great deal in common, even as the tensions that remained demonstrated the very real and persistent differences between black and white interpretations of Baptist principles.

At least some black Baptists saw the political turmoil of the 1780s and 1790s as providing an opportunity to extend the liberating potential of the Revolutionary era in more literal ways. There is circumstantial evidence that Gowan Pamphlet was involved in the shadowy "Secret Keeper" conspiracy in 1793, an apparently widespread black plot to take "the hole country" that drew its inspiration from the Haitian Revolution.[108] If real, this scheme proved ephemeral. No major uprising or arrests of conspirators occurred despite the fears of white Virginians. In 1800, however, Gabriel's Rebellion, the far more concrete conspiracy led by Gabriel, an enslaved Henrico County blacksmith who belonged to Thomas Prosser, provided both black and white Virginians with evidence of just how radical the intersection of evangelical and republican values could be in certain hands.

Gabriel and his co-conspirators developed a detailed plot to take and hold the city of Richmond and force whites to abolish slavery. On a prearranged night one group of rebels would set fire to the city's warehouse district, and while Richmond's able-bodied white men rushed to fight the fire, two other groups would capture the city armory and take the governor, James Monroe, hostage. Hoping that some portion of a politically, socially, and religiously divided white population might support them, or at least sympathize with their desire for liberty, they would then negotiate for freedom and abolition. On the appointed day, however, heavy rains flooded the bridge the rebels intended to take into the city, preventing the execution of their plan. Meanwhile, informers had alerted white authorities, who, once convinced of the plot's reality and seriousness, mobilized the militia and questioned suspects until the details of the plot emerged.[109]

Gabriel's Rebellion reflected slaves' keen, if incomplete, awareness of the political context of the times. As they saw many northern states begin the process of abolition and saw rising white anti-slavery sentiment within Virginia itself, slaves very clearly understood and appropriated the rhetoric of liberty and liberation in the post-Revolutionary era. One conspirator claimed that Gabriel planned to carry a flag with the slogan "death or Liberty" on the night of the revolt.[110] Moreover, the example of the Haitian Revolution and the presence of both white and black refugees from Saint Domingue in Virginia in the 1790s suggested to the rebels the ways in which slaves might take advantage of a divided white master class to achieve their own freedom, and the bitterly intense battles between Federalists and Republicans in the late 1790s leading up to the election of 1800 suggested that such a moment had come.[111] The rebels reportedly planned to spare "French men," who, at least in their revolutionary incarnation, slaves believed supported black freedom, as well as Quakers and Methodists, who were also "friendly to liberty."[112]

In organizing for the rebellion, Gabriel and his followers took advantage of both the institutions and the languages of evangelical Christianity. Many of the rebels attended the Baptist Hungry Meeting House, and they recruited participants at religious meetings across the Richmond area.[113] Gabriel's brother Martin had gained a reputation as someone who knew the Bible well, and when challenged by another conspirator, he invoked a scriptural defense of the rebellion. At a planning meeting for the uprising, Ben Woolfolk challenged Gabriel's leadership and argued that the plan should be postponed. He pointed out that when Moses led the Israelites out of bondage, "God had blessed them with an Angel to go with him, But . . . I could see nothing of that kind in these days." Woolfolk seems to have meant that despite his name, Gabriel was no angel who could lead black people out of bondage. Martin replied by playing on several verses from Leviticus (26:6–8) to counter Woolfolk's point: "I read in my Bible where God says, if we will worship him, we should have peace in all our Lands, five of you shall conquer an hundred and a hundred, a thousand of our enemies." After the leaders of the conspiracy consulted for a time, they seem to have agreed with Martin, who then chose the day the revolt should take place.[114] This discussion, and the apparent seriousness with which the leaders took the competing biblical references, suggests that Christianity had deeply pervaded at least some influential black leaders' thinking by 1800. It also clearly shows the ways in which black Christians interpreted biblical language to apply directly to their own social position. The debate between Martin and Woolfolk provides a narrow window into the often irrecoverable substantive process of interpretation that must have occurred in quarters, workshops, fields, and churchyards across Virginia as more and more black men and women found meaning in evangelical Christianity.[115]

Gabriel's Rebellion and a subsequent set of insurrectionary scares along the Virginia–North Carolina border in 1802 prompted aggressive white reprisals and helped catalyze the already increasing conservatism of white Virginians on the issue of slavery. In 1806, for instance, the Virginia legislature undercut the effect of the 1782 legalization of private manumission by requiring all newly freed people to leave the state within a year. Other laws passed in the early nineteenth century attempted to address the conditions whites thought had led to the uprisings: black education, freedom of movement, and unsupervised assembly and whites' laxity in supervising their slaves and policing the black population in general. Many of these laws proved difficult to enforce and inconsistent in practice, but their very existence reflected the shifting mood of the white population.[116] In Petersburg, the nominally biracial Davenport's Baptist Church collapsed about 1802, apparently because the few white members could no longer abide being part of an almost entirely black church. White members attached themselves to rural biracial churches, while black members reconstituted themselves into an independent body. About the same time, in the wake of the Portsmouth church's decision to reinstitute white oversight of the black members, Jacob Bishop left Norfolk for Baltimore, and he eventually moved on to New York, where he became pastor of the black Abyssinian Baptist Church.[117] Black and white Baptists in Isle of Wight, Southampton, and Sussex counties continued to interpret the meaning of their faith in ways that were shaped by individual preferences, local conditions, and interactions with one another as much as by larger forces, but with Barrow's migration to Kentucky and the reaction to Gabriel's Rebellion and the 1802 conspiracies, the waters of the Baptist mainstream had narrowed considerably. Neither Barrow's nor Gabriel's vision of the liberating potential of evangelical and republican beliefs proved equal to the task of transforming Virginia into a free society.

In 1808, at the end of his history of the Ketocton Association, in north-western Virginia, the Baptist minister William Fristoe turned to his final section, "Reasons why the Baptists, generally, espouse Republicanism." "It is well understood by our neighbors," Fristoe wrote, "that the baptists with us are generally republicans," and he went on to explain why. He cited the oppressions of the British government and the Anglican establishment and recounted traditional republican arguments against monarchy, including the inevitable, greedy expansiveness of tyranny and the virtue and wisdom of an informed population. But Fristoe was most interested in establishing a strong and necessary connection between political republicanism and Baptist forms of church government. Mo-narchical systems invariably went hand in hand with ecclesiastical des-potism, Fristoe claimed, but in the new republic "our religious educa-tion agrees with and perfectly corresponds with a government by the people." Not only was Baptist church government the most purely scrip-tural method of organizing Christian communities, but its rules and government—the right of church members to choose officers and con-duct discipline, the independence of congregations, the lack of priestly hierarchy—accorded most directly with the values of a free society.[118] Fris-toe played on and extended the fusion of republicanism and evangelical-ism forged during the Revolutionary era, but the presumption of unity that informed his approach—the seamless harmony of Baptist faith and republican government and the easy translation of Revolutionary agita-tors for religious liberty into a peaceful, contented citizenry—masked the controversies and conflicts within Baptist republicanism. In reality, Baptists espoused republicanism for many different, sometimes conflict-ing reasons.

Robert Semple, who completed the first official history of Baptists in Virginia in 1810 (a task he inherited from John Leland), faced exactly this challenge of incorporating the linkage of republicanism and evan-gelicalism in his vision of the denomination's place in society, while limit-ing and rejecting any alternate interpretations of that linkage that would jeopardize Baptists' growing mainstream legitimacy. Semple's *History of the Rise and Progress of the Baptists in Virginia* remains the standard source on the early Baptist movement, and while he was not overtly hostile to the anti-slavery past, he clearly wished to emphasize its marginality within a larger celebratory narrative of Baptists' "rise and progress." Semple took extensive notice of the Baptists' Revolutionary political activities, both as supporters of the patriot cause and as shapers of religious freedom in Virginia. When discussing David Barrow's contributions, however, Semple walked a fine line. He celebrated Barrow's "spotless character," his talents and achievements as a preacher, and his service in the Revolution, but when discussing Barrow's anti-slavery views, he gave the story the tone of a cautionary tale. Semple wrote that Barrow "carried his opinions of liberty so far as to think it criminal to hold negroes in slavery. . . . Although this measure proved his disinterested zeal to do right, it is questionable whether it was not in the end productive of more evil than good. While it embarrassed his affairs at home by lessening his resources for the maintenance of a large family, it rendered him suspicious among his acquaintances, and probably in both ways limited his usefulness."[119] Semple presented Barrow's anti-slavery activities and beliefs not as censurable in themselves, but as detracting from his more important duties as a father and a Baptist minister, thus implying that such activity was not really appropriate. Semple's vision of the denomination's past and future was one of religious purity, republican virtue, and institutional development, which left little room for activities that distracted from those goals.

For these reasons and more, Semple also treated the subject of black religious authority delicately. He briefly described the careers of men like Gowan Pamphlet, William Lemon, and Jacob Bishop, but he did so in ways that emphasized God's power in elevating such humble men and minimized the independence and controversy that were often evident in these men's careers. He recounted Pamphlet's independent activities but emphasized that before accepting his church into fellowship, the Dover Association had made sure "to appoint persons to visit them and set things in order."[120] Semple's acute racial consciousness shone through when he described Lemon's pastorate as something "it would hardly have been supposed would have been done by Virginians" and claimed that "though not white in his natural complexion," Lemon "had been washed in the laver of regeneration; he had been purified and made white in a better sense."[121] Semple expressed similar surprise at what he took to be Bishop's pastorate: "This, as might be supposed, could not answer in Virginia." Instead, under Davis Biggs's leadership, "the church has moved on in a much more tranquil manner."[122] As with Barrow, Semple did not openly disapprove of these men, and he praised their piety and talent. But he framed each man's story to justify, however reluctantly, white Baptists' acceptance of the racial hierarchies of Virginia society.

But even as men like Fristoe and Semple sought to channel the rising Baptist emphasis on respectability toward the mainstream of white Virginia's public culture, developments within the churches ensured that this desire could never be entirely unproblematic. As the pace of black conversion increased in subsequent years, the fundamental composition of the Baptist laity in Nat Turner's Virginia began to change. Black and white men and women confronted one another in church in increasing numbers, and as they did so they sought to sort out the implications of evangelical values for the community they increasingly shared, albeit in complex and sometimes partial ways. In this context, the defeat of the Baptist anti-slavery movement represented the closing off of one potential interpretation of the intersection between evangelical fellowship, gospel order, and republican values, but many other tensions and ambiguities remained. Chapter 4 takes an extended look at the evolving practices and discourses of church membership and evangelical authority in Nat Turner's Virginia as men and women of both races worked to understand and shape their communities' shifting patterns of inclusion and hierarchy according to their own conceptions of gospel order.

SOMEWHAT LIBERATED

Baptist Community and Authority in
Nat Turner's Virginia

ON OCTOBER 4, 1788, at a church conference at South Quay, David Barrow motioned for the church "to fall on some method to somewhat liberate Bro'th Tom (Porter's)."[1] After considering Barrow's motion, the church decided to postpone the decision on Tom's "liberation" for further consideration. Tom was one of the earliest African American members of South Quay; he had converted and undergone baptism sometime before 1777, when the congregation was still a branch of Mill Swamp. He may have been the property of a fellow member of South Quay, Abraham Porter.[2] When the church considered "liberating" Tom, however, it was not attempting to fix on a means of obtaining his emancipation or otherwise lessening his condition of worldly servitude. Despite Barrow's 1784 manumission of Benjamin and Lucrecia Blackhead, his ongoing anti-slavery activism, and the contentious debates taking place at South Quay's sister church, Black Creek, the liberation he sought for Tom was of a different sort. Barrow was asking that Tom receive license to preach in public from the church. In November the church again considered Barrow's "motion . . . respecting the liberation of Broth. Tom . . . & though[t] [it] expedient to let it lie over for better information of our Judgts respectg his Gifts." Whatever information the church received was not recorded, but the motion was never revived, and Tom never received what the church often termed "liberty to preach."[3]

The case of Porter's Tom illustrates the powerful but subtle ways in which race and gender shaped Baptist institutional and spiritual practice in the decades after the Revolution. Beginning in the 1780s, the Baptist churches of Isle of Wight, Southampton, and Sussex counties grew from small alternative communities into powerful religious institutions in which a diverse variety of Virginians interacted and pursued their visions of evangelical faith. As the churches expanded and diversified, most notably as African American membership increased, members struggled to reconcile Baptist spiritual and ecclesiastical practice with both the conflicted influence of Revolutionary ideals and the constraints of an evolving society based on racial privilege and chattel slavery. The deeply ingrained privileges of whiteness and masculinity and the enduring restrictions of blackness and femininity in eighteenth-century Virginia influenced Baptist practice from the outset of the movement. In the changing context of the post-Revolutionary era, however, many white church members, particularly white men, felt increasing pressure to work out these influences in a more concrete and formal way, while black members and white women, who felt the brunt of these changes, sought to resist or to mitigate any loss of status as best they could with the repertoire of Baptist discourse and practice available to them.

This process took place within an institutional and ideological framework that shaped its limits and possibilities. On the one hand, white men already controlled the churches themselves as institutions. Unlike in the pre-Revolutionary New England Baptist churches described by Susan Juster, there is no evidence that white women ever had a formal vote in the Baptist churches of southeastern Virginia.[4] Although the Philadelphia minister Morgan Edwards recorded the existence of the office of "deaconess" in some Virginia Separate Baptist churches when he traveled through the colony in 1772, the Regular churches of Isle of Wight, Southampton, and Sussex counties do not appear to have had such an office. (Edwards did not visit any of the southeastern Virginia churches; his path took him further west, through the Southside.)[5] From the beginning of the Revolutionary era, the government of the churches, like that of the nation, rested in the hands of white men and reflected, both intentionally and unintentionally, their preoccupations and prejudices. On the other hand, the men who controlled the formal channels of power in the churches attempted to govern them according to the ideals of Christian fellowship, religious liberty, and individuals' equal access to conversion and an ongoing relationship with God that shaped Baptist community. In the process of attempting to interpret and apply these principles in practice, the churches presented members of all sorts with a language of divine justice, human morality, Godly community, and ultimate meaning that had a basis separate from worldly standards. The significance of this process lay not so much in the fact that the decisions and practices of the churches diverged dramatically from worldly ones — in certain select ways they did, but in most ways they did not — but rather in the very existence of an alternate set of values to which men and women of different worldly status could appeal. From these materials, Baptist men and women of all races who felt inspired to do so could construct a critique of the inequalities, injustices, and apostasy of their society in terms that demanded a hearing from their brethren.[6]

The abortive liberation of Porter's Tom is particularly revealing in this context. Tom was a member of the inclusive religious community at South Quay, a "brother" in a church of siblings. Like other members, he had experienced God's saving grace and joined the church by relating his experience and undergoing the ritual of baptism. When he appeared before the church in 1802 and "gave satisfaction" for an accusation of excessive drinking, Tom participated in the cycle of discipline, confession, and repentance that was essential to creating and maintaining the community of believers that constituted a Baptist church.[7] But he was also marked by his race and his gender: on the South Quay membership list, Tom appears in a section for "male blacks," and in the minutes his name always bears the possessive modifier "Porter's," marking his enslavement. Thus, the inclusive ideal of Baptist fellowship and participation in the churches' rituals of godly community did not preclude distinctions of race and gender that shaped the character of black men's membership, a fact borne out not only by their categorization on membership lists and in minutes but also in concrete ways, such as the exclusion of enslaved men from the largely white and male government of the church.

The operation of race and gender in the churches did not always or automatically mean exclusion, however. Despite his status as a black man and a slave, Tom's gender provided him potential access to a formal channel of power in the church as a licensed preacher. The rituals and rules of the Baptist Church involved processes of authorization and discipline of certain kinds of speech, ranging from conversion relations, disciplinary testimony, and preaching on the one hand to gossip, swearing, and lying on the other, and these processes were intimately linked to gender. Short of ordination as a minister or deacon, formal license to preach represented one of the most significant forms of spiritual and social authorization in the churches. It was open only to men, but theoretically it was open to all men to whom God had granted the inspiration and ability.[8] Black men from "Jupiter alias Gibb" to Lewis to Gowan Pamphlet and Joseph Bishop took advantage of this inspiration in a variety of ways, both with and without the approval of white churches. In some cases, such as Pamphlet's, their fluency in Baptist discourses and practices persuaded white officials to confirm and legitimize black preachers' self- and community-appointed religious authority within the larger structures of the denomination. Tom's manhood made him, at least potentially, a fit voice for God's word in the eyes of other church members and a possible recipient of the masculine "liberty" to preach.

As Barrow's awkward phrase "somewhat liberate" suggests, however, white church members were not entirely comfortable with the implications of such "liberty" for African or African American men in their communities and thus felt it necessary to qualify and constrain its meaning. Over the course of the late eighteenth and early nineteenth centuries white Baptists in Isle of Wight, Southampton, and Sussex counties granted license to preach to black men only reluctantly and attempted to exercise close oversight over those to whom license was granted. Most recorded cases resembled Tom's, ending in a refusal to license the candidate. But even white members' attempts to control and delimit the meanings of church practice could not prevent black men and women from drawing their own meanings from the churches' shared rituals of spirituality and authority. Indeed, evidence of unauthorized black preaching in the church records suggests not only white efforts to control but also independent black judgments about who deserved "liberty to preach." Perhaps not as impressive as the independence demonstrated by black churches in urban areas, this was nonetheless highly significant for black men and women in the rural backwater of Nat Turner's Virginia.

Race and gender thus shaped members' experience of Baptist institutions and Baptist spirituality in subtle and sometimes contradictory ways as the churches expanded in the years after the Revolution. Tom's case, and the issues of race, masculinity, and preaching it traces, is just one example of this process, but it provides a useful template for understanding the fundamental ambivalence and interpretability of Baptist practice in this period. Barrow's phrase "somewhat liberate" captured the instability in a key term of Baptist discourse that allowed multiple meanings to coexist in the church and permitted members to build their own interpretations of the intertwined social and spiritual implications of their faith. White Baptist ideas of "liberty" ranged from long-standing Christian and evangelical theological principles to the powerful religio-social critique of Virginia society put forth by early crusaders such as David Thomas to the anti-slavery arguments of Barrow, John Leland, and others. Black Baptist ideas included those ideas but also drew on the long-standing association of conversion with freedom and status among black Virginians, their own distinctive experience of the Revolutionary struggle for "liberty," and even the radical ideas of men like Gabriel and, perhaps, Pamphlet. These sometimes conflicting meanings overlapped and intersected in so many ways that it was difficult to disentangle them. Operating in these multivalent terms, the liberation that Baptist churches offered their members was always, inevitably, partial and incomplete. Such dynamic tensions in Baptist language and practice provided the foundation for the contentious but very real Christian fellowship forged among the diverse group of men and women who joined the churches of southeastern Virginia in the post-Revolutionary era.

After the conclusion of the Revolution, the Baptist churches of Isle of Wight, Southampton, and Sussex counties began a period of expansion and institutional elaboration that continued, fitfully, well into the nineteenth century. Of the thirteen Baptist churches that existed in these counties from 1770 to 1840, five were officially constituted during the 1780s. Most were long-standing branches of the existing churches. South Quay and Black Creek, which had been branches of Mill Swamp, became independent bodies in 1785 and 1786, respectively. Seacock and High Hills grew out of Raccoon Swamp in 1787, and Meherrin became a separate church in 1788 (table 2). In becoming separate churches these branches gained an independent institutional existence that facilitated the continued growth of the congregations and better enabled them to adapt to local conditions and develop their own homegrown leadership. This impulse found a broader regional expression in 1791, when the churches of southeastern Virginia amicably split off from the Kehukee Association and formed the Virginia Portsmouth Baptist Association.[9]

Table 3 shows two significant periods of growth for the churches of Isle of Wight, Southampton, and Sussex, in the 1780s and the first decade of the nineteenth century, interrupted by a period of stagnation and de-

Table 2. BAPTIST CHURCHES IN ISLE OF WIGHT, SOUTHAMPTON, AND SUSSEX COUNTIES, 1770–1840

Church	County	Begun[a]	Separate church	Records for period
Raccoon Swamp	Sussex	1770	1772	1772–1892
Sappony	Sussex	1770	1773	
Mill Swamp	Isle of Wight	1772	1774	1777–1840
Black Creek	Southampton	1774	1786	1774–1862
South Quay	Southampton	1775	1785	1775–1899
Seacock (Elam)	Sussex	ca. 1779	1787	1819–1889
High Hills	Sussex	—	1787	1787–1845
Meherrin (Sturgeon's)	Southampton	1773[b]	1788	
Tucker's Swamp	Southampton	1804	1806	1818–1857
Beaver Dam	Isle of Wight		1828	1828–1894
Smithfield	Isle of Wight		1830	1830–1894
Millfield	Southampton		1836	
Newville	Sussex		1836	

Sources: Raccoon Swamp [Antioch] Baptist Church, Minute Book, 1772–1837, LVA; Mill Swamp Baptist Church, Minute Book, 1777–1790, LVA; Black Creek Baptist Church, Minute Book, 1776–1804, LVA; Black Creek Baptist Church, Minute Book, 1804–1818, VBHS; South Quay Baptist Church, Minute Book, 1775–1827, LVA; Shoulder's Hill Baptist Church, Minute Book,1783–1923, VBHS High Hills [of Nottoway] Baptist Church, Minute Book, 1787–1845, LVA; Beaver Dam Baptist Church, Minute Book, 1828–1894, LVA; Smithfield Baptist Church, Minute Book, 1830–1894, VBHS; Gardner, *Baptists of Early America;* Burkitt and Read, *Concise History of the Kehukee Baptist Association;* Semple, *Rise and Progress of the Baptists in Virginia;* Jones, *History of the Virginia Portsmouth Baptist Association;* Lumpkin, *History of the Portsmouth Baptist Association.*

[a] The year is an estimate of when there was first an active Baptist congregation or significant revival in the neighborhood, based on minutes and published histories.

[b] Several sources date this congregation only to the mid-1780s, but a 1773 minute from the Raccoon Swamp Minute Book states that "a Certain number of members living in Southampton, on Meherrin" petitioned for permission to hold communion quarterly in their neighborhood. Raccoon Swamp [Antioch] Baptist Church, Minute Book, 1772–1837, 8 May 1773, LVA.

cline in the 1790s. In the second half of the 1780s nearly all of the newly founded churches grew rapidly from their initial membership, more than making up for the decline in size of the established parent churches, Raccoon Swamp and Mill Swamp, owing to the loss of the branches.[10] Although the churches were inconsistent in recording individual baptisms, both their running minutes and their membership lists suggest the dynamism of the late 1780s. The South Quay church minutes, for instance, regularly note men and women "rec'd by experience" or "rec'd and baptized" in the years after the church's constitution in 1785.[11] The Black Creek church's membership list became a running list in this period, noting four new members in June 1788, including David Barrow's former slave Benjamin Blackhead. The wave of new receptions continued for the rest of that year, peaking in August with seventeen names added to the list during that month, including Blackhead's wife, Milly, who had been freed by the church member John Johnson in 1785.[12]

About 1790 this rapid growth tailed off. Although most churches

Table 3. Baptist church membership in Isle of Wight, Southampton, and Sussex counties, 1772–1810

				MEMBERSHIP			
Church	County	Consti- tuted	At consti- tution	1777	1791	1800	1810
Raccoon Swamp	Sussex	1772	87	209	140	117	188
Sappony	Sussex	1773	6	200	34[a]	26	59
Mill Swamp	Isle of Wight	1774	11	142	112	110	197
South Quay	Southampton	1785	24		79	60	103
Black Creek	Southampton	1786	70		100	90	92
Seacock (Elam)	Sussex	1787	18		32	14	51
High Hills	Sussex	1787	—		31	23	31
Meherrin	Southampton	1788	—		85	85	139
Tucker's Swamp	Southampton	1807	15			27	
Total				551	613	525	887
Total without Sappony				351	579	499	828

Sources: Figures for membership at constitution are from Semple, *Rise and Progress of the Baptists in Virginia*, 442–43. Figures for 1777 are from Burkitt and Read, *Concise History of the Kehukee Baptist Association*, 50. Figures for 1791, 1800, and 1810 are from the minutes of the Virginia Portsmouth Baptist Association for those years, VBHS.

[a] The dramatic decline in membership at Sappony is probably the result of the early death of minister James Bell in September of 1778, which left the church with no regular preacher for many years.

continued to receive a few new members each year over the next decade, new receptions did not keep pace with dismissions, excommunications, and deaths. It was during this period of stagnation that the Portsmouth Association lamented the covetousness that its members believed undermined the cause of Christ and David Barrow decided to emigrate to Kentucky. James David Essig argues that white Baptists' very success in shaping and joining the post-Revolutionary mainstream undermined their sense of distinctiveness and mission, prompting a period of stagnation and fears of excessive worldliness that contributed to their short-lived but important attempts to confront the issue of slavery and slaveholding in the churches from 1785 to 1797.[13] There is much to recommend this view; as we have seen, white Baptists' concerns about slavery were clearly related to their uneasiness about worldliness, and political success certainly changed the dynamic of their relationship to the world and to civil authority. But in Isle of Wight, Southampton, and Sussex counties, at least, the timing of the most widespread Baptist antislavery activities coincided far more with the period of expansion in the late 1780s than with the stagnation of the 1790s. Indeed, a closer look at the growing membership in these counties suggests important modifications to this interpretation of the Baptist movement in early national Virginia.

The 1780s saw not only the general growth of the Baptist churches of southeastern Virginia but also the beginning of an influx of African Americans into the churches. Table 4, drawn from church minutes and membership lists, shows that blacks made up about 11 percent of the total membership at the combined congregations of Mill Swamp, Black Creek, and South Quay from 1774 to about 1777 (the latter two were still part of Mill Swamp) and about 10 percent at Raccoon Swamp from 1772 to 1783. Among the men and women who joined Mill Swamp and its branches from 1777 to 1788, however, blacks constituted 37 percent of the total. This trend continued into the early 1790s, as African Americans ranged from 23 percent of new members at Black Creek to 49 percent at Mill Swamp after 1788. At Raccoon Swamp a similar trend must have occurred, because a membership list created in 1789 indicated that blacks made up 39 percent of the total membership of the church, in part because of the loss of white members, presumably to the newly constituted churches of Seacock and High Hills in 1787 and Meherrin in 1788 (no membership records from those churches survive for this period), but also because of a significant increase in the actual number of black members.[14] The 1780s, then, were more than simply years of growth or an extension of pre-Revolutionary revivalism among Virginia Baptists: they represented a turning point in the racial composition of Baptist communities in Isle of Wight, Southampton, and Sussex counties that would have lasting effects on the nature of the Baptist faith and its implications for church members.

Within the churches, the impact of increasing black membership was reflected in the efforts of white members to determine just how to incorporate free and enslaved African American men and women into the body of the church. As Jewel Spangler points out, white Baptists seem never to have considered admitting slaves as members on identical terms with free white members.[15] We should not be surprised at such inequality in a society in which slavery and racial privilege had been firmly established for a century. The crucial task is to examine the specific dynamic of inclusion and exclusion, in both material and discursive terms, and its significance for the people involved. The incorporation of a growing African American membership into the Baptist churches of southeastern Virginia did not take place in isolation. The consideration of the place of blacks in church intersected with other issues of gender and religious

Table 4. Baptist church membership in Isle of Wight, Southampton, and Sussex
counties, by race, 1772–ca. 1795

Church	Dates	Members counted	White N	White %	Black N	Black %
Mill Swamp, Black Creek, South Quay*a*	1774–ca. 1777	All	152	89	19	11
	ca. 1777–1788	New	70	63	41	37
Mill Swamp, Black Creek, South Quay total	1774–1788		222	79	60	21
Mill Swamp	1788–ca. 1790	New	24	51	23	49
Black Creek	1788–1794	New	62	77	19	23
South Quay	1788–ca. 1795	New	19	59	13	41
Raccoon Swamp*b*	1772–1783	All	170	90	19	10
	1789	All	86	61	56	39

Sources: Mill Swamp Baptist Church, Minute Book, 1777–1790, LVA; Black Creek Baptist Church,
Minute Book, 1776–1804, LVA; South Quay Baptist Church, Minute Book, 1775–1827, LVA; Raccoon
Swamp [Antioch] Baptist Church, Minute Book, 1772–1837, LVA.

Note: Where data internal to membership lists or from church minutes permit, I have calculated the
number and racial profile of new members for a given period rather than the total church membership
for the whole period of the list. This provides a more nuanced picture of the changing shape of Baptist
membership than a single list covering a longer period.

a Because South Quay and Black Creek were branches of Mill Swamp until 1785 and 1786, respectively, their early membership lists overlap significantly. I have calculated all three churches' membership together by cross-checking lists and eliminating duplications. Beginning in 1788 the data permit
separate counts for each church.

b The 1772–1783 Raccoon Swamp list is badly torn. I could identify the race of 189 members, but
roughly 48 names are either missing or illegible due to tears and holes in the manuscript. Thus, these
totals should be considered very rough approximations. When this estimation of the number of missing names is included, the membership percentages are 71.73 percent white, 8.01 percent black, and
20.25 percent unknown.

authority that infused the churches during this period, and the potential
meanings and possibilities of Baptist faith for church members reflected
the tensions between and interaction among these different factors.

Throughout the period of this study, the majority of white male
members in nearly all of the churches were slaveholders, and within the
churches, at least, white men collectively always had the final say about
issues of policy, doctrine, and membership.[16] The white men who controlled the churches generally seem to have believed that African Americans represented a separate class of members in significant ways, in
part because of their worldly status—most were slaves, which made
certain practical differences—but also because of the ideologies of racial difference that had become essential to the operation of southern
society.[17] As we shall see, this thinking sometimes left free blacks in an
awkward position. But even slaveholding white members did not form
a monolithic group, and the presence of slaveholders in the churches
did not automatically lead to an unproblematic embrace of slavery and

racial distinction. Unlike David Barrow, John Leland, or, conversely, the Southside proslavery petitioners discussed in chapter 3, most white Baptists had little desire to confront the morality of slaveholding directly. Rather, they sought more indirect ways to make the practice of slavery and sincerely held Baptist principles of fellowship, morality, and discipline compatible with one another. In this context, the ways in which racial difference and slavery should affect the operation of the church, its rituals, and its rules of order were not clear. When queries from members or advice from denominational institutions pressured the churches to establish definitive policies, the results were often equivocal. Moreover, actual practice in the churches reflected a diversity that left a great deal of room for interpretation and negotiation in specific instances.

Even before the upsurge in black membership, white and black Baptists struggled to work out how worldly distinctions should translate into the basics of church membership. In 1777, for instance, Mill Swamp considered the query, "What shall a Church do with her Minister if he will not Baptise a servant until his or her master or Mistress be willing."[18] This query and the manner in which it was posed reveal tensions between white Baptists on the issues of race and slavery in the church. The query suggests that the worldly status of African Americans was an issue for at least some powerful church members: a minister had refused or threatened to refuse to baptize a slave without a master's permission. At the same time, however, the query focused on the minister's reluctance rather than on the issues of masters' permission and slave membership, implying that the minister's position was a departure from standard practice and that some members of the church objected to his stance. Although no response to the query was recorded, none of the churches in Isle of Wight, Southampton, or Sussex regularly required masters' permission until the 1830s. Baptism by immersion was the most distinctive ritual of the Baptist denomination, and by preserving at least theoretically unfettered access to that ritual for slaves the churches made an important statement about the spiritual equality of their members.

In other aspects of church life, similar questions arose about black members' access to the rituals that lay at the heart of the religious world of the Baptists, and these questions became more urgent as black members came to constitute a larger portion of church membership. In 1778 the South Quay church posed the query, "Is it duty for our black Brethren to attend Conferences, when convenient." The church "answered yes they ought to attend for instruction" but did not suggest that black members would have any positive role in the government of the church. In 1785 South Quay again raised the issue of black attendance, with similar implications, unanimously agreeing "that our black brethren attend our Conferences when they can obtain leave from their owners."[19] In referring to "their owners," the white brethren at South Quay equated black membership with slave membership—not inaccurately in this particular case, because there were no free black members of South Quay in 1785—and strengthened the implied equation between blackness and unfreedom more generally. The church was in one sense being realistic—because of slaves' obligations to their masters it was difficult for them to attend daytime meetings on Saturdays, when church conferences were usually held—but in both of these cases it was also constructing and maintaining a vision of black members as occupying a separate category of membership with a marginal, passive role in church government.

South Quay's 1785 decision on slave attendance immediately followed an almost identical motion on women's attendance: "A move made that the female members attend our appointed conferences, agreed to by all."[20] Together, the two motions established an analogy between women's and African Americans' status in the church that emphasized the passive nature of their participation in church government. At a meeting of the Kehukee Association in October of that same year, for instance, delegates from across southeastern Virginia and northeastern North Carolina addressed a query about women's authority in church that clarified the nature of their role in church business. Asked whether a woman had "any right to speak in the church in matters of discipline, unless called upon," the Association answered, "We think they have no right unless called upon, or where it respects their own communion."[21] Although the white men who governed the church wanted women and blacks to attend church conferences at which business and discipline were conducted, they were to have a largely passive role, speaking only when called upon.

Even this rather strict view of the exclusively white and male right to church government allowed a significant loophole: "where it respects their own communion." Baptist discourse and practice gave individuals a degree of spiritual authority based on their conversion and their own relationship to God. In turn, the church-centered ideals of fellowship and communion gave that authority a social, interactive dimension. Speaking concerning one's own communion could provide a limited but real avenue for discussing specific grievances or even the state of the church more generally. Absenting oneself from communion, for instance, could be a pointed expression of nonfellowship with a member or members of a church. In 1791 the investigation of a number of members at Black Creek who had "absented themselves from the Lord's Table last Communion" revealed that some members, both men and women, had a "Difficulty . . . with a Part of the Church for holding Slaves and hiring them." More prosaically, in 1825 Black Creek excommunicated Catharine Jones, who had continually absented herself from communion because of her inability to "reconcile herself to the desition [decision] of the Church in holding Sister Elizabeth Jones in fellowship, whom she cou'd not fellowship."[22] The ultimate legitimacy of such claims was determined by the reaction of the rest of the church, usually embodied in the white male members, who controlled the official voice of the church, so it depended both on the member's own persuasive use of Baptist religious and institutional language and concepts and on the general weight of opinion among the enfranchised members. South Quay's and the Kehukee Association's construction of black and female membership excluded these members from official power in the church, constituting that power as white and male. But their construction also provided a means by which marginalized members could use their spiritual authority to make claims on the main body of the church and from which they could draw their own interpretations of the meaning of Baptist faith.

Indeed, High Hills Baptist Church institutionalized this process when it treated the role of women in its rules of decorum. After carefully laying out how many male members constituted a quorum for which kinds of business, the rules took up the role of women: "Females shall have a voice in the Church in Certain cases, such as chooseing officers, Delegates, in giving information, receiving to fellowship, or rejecting any who are unworthy, but shall not have the government in their power."[23] Women's status as church members gave them a voice but not "government." Most other churches did not make formal rules equivalent to those of either the Kehukee Association or High Hills on these issues, but as the Black Creek cases suggest, in practice there must have been a great deal of room to maneuver between these two poles.

South Quay was also unusual in establishing such definitive rules on race so early on. As with gender, in other arenas and in other churches more equivocal practices predominated. Eighteenth-century church membership lists, for instance, suggest that the formula that became common in the nineteenth century—separate sections for white male, white female, black male, and black female members—evolved only gradually. Raccoon Swamp's first list, covering the period 1772–83, appears to have been a running list and does not segregate members at all by race or by gender. At Mill Swamp, the membership list begun in 1774 categorizes members by gender but not by race, and Black Creek followed a similar practice in its first list. Among these first-generation lists only South Quay's, which covers members from 1775 to 1827 but was created in 1786, is fully segregated by both race and gender. A 1789 list for Raccoon Swamp divides white and black members and has separate sections for white men and white women, while it lists blacks by their owners' names. By the second decade of the nineteenth century a combination of racial and gender categories had become standard at most churches, although some divided black members into free and slave sections. This systematic categorization of members had not existed from the outset, however; in the earlier years gender appears to have been the characteristic that seemed most immediately relevant to the white male members who created such lists.

In the more formal rules of the churches, the privileges of masculinity sometimes intersected uneasily with the disabilities of race in ways that contradicted the easy conflation of blacks and white women into a general category of passive membership at South Quay. From the founding of the Isle of Wight, Southampton, and Sussex churches, maleness seems to have been the key to formal power in church. Such a role was, in fact, a duty of male church members. In 1777, for instance, Mill Swamp emphasized that "a mail member that dos not attend publick Conference" would be liable to discipline unless the rest of the Conference judged his excuse satisfactory.[24] While all churches appear to have excluded male slaves from official power in church government, most church constitutions, including that of South Quay, gave the vote to "members," "male members," or "free male members," constructions that theoretically left participation in church government open to free black men.[25] The Portsmouth Association confronted this issue directly in 1794. "Is it agreeable to the word of God, and that decency which ought to be observed in the church of Christ," the delegates wondered, "to send a free black man [as] a delegate to the Association?" The very existence of this query, especially the concern for "decency" it expresses, suggests that the idea of a black delegate was unsettling in certain ways to the other representatives to the association. But ultimately the group determined that "we can see nothing in the word of God, nor any thing contrary to the rules of decency, to prohibit a church from sending as a delegate, any male member they shall choose."[26]

During the same period, several free black men at Black Creek, including Benjamin Blackhead, enjoyed the full privileges of membership. Although the records do not show actual votes, so there is no direct evidence that these men had the franchise (to be fair, for the same reason there is no direct evidence that anyone had the franchise), Blackhead and Samuel Blackman were counted with the white male members when the church took attendance or noted absentees, and Blackhead even contributed to the church fund for the upkeep of the meeting house.[27] And when Black Creek created a new membership list in 1804, Blackhead, Blackman, and several other free black men who joined the church in the early nineteenth century were listed along with the white men in a section for the free male members of the church; free black women, however, were listed with the slaves. For the Portsmouth Association and the Black Creek congregation, freedom and masculinity were the keys to an official voice in church government, which ran counter to the conflation of "black" with "slave" and the casual association of slaves with women that underlay white male church government at South Quay.

As the eighteenth century drew to a close, the members of Mill Swamp sought to chart a course through these various constructions of race, gender, and the nature of church membership. In September 1799, in the context of a revival in which twelve blacks, including several free men and women, were received into fellowship, the church sought to answer the query whether "the free Male Members (of the Black)" had "an equal right to sit with us in Conference, or not."[28] In contrast to South Quay's 1778 and 1785 queries on black attendance, this query was not about religious duty or opportunity to attend conferences "for instruction"; it was more political in nature, dealing with free black members' right to participate in the government of the church. The governing white members' reaction to the query revealed both the complex intertwining of ideas of freedom and race in the church and the church's equivocation on the issue. At the March 14 meeting the following year, Mill Swamp again considered the query, "being again propose[d] to this [Conference], as tho it had not been rec'd in consequence of the Querist being desired to withdraw it, which Query was rejected by a large Majority."[29] The exact meaning of the church's action in this case is not entirely clear, and the convoluted language of the minute is in some ways as revealing as the resolution of the question. Although the minute could signify the church's decision that free black men did not have the right to sit in conference, it appears that by "rejected" the minute means, not that the query was answered in the negative, but that instead of considering the query and formulating an answer, the church asked the querist to withdraw and re-submit the query, at which point the church refused to consider it. Thus, it seems that the church refused to set a firm policy or make a definitive ruling on the question. Even if such a ruling was intended, the church's language in recording it indicates a level of discomfort about making a straightforward statement of racial exclusion.

At the same March 14 meeting, however, the church pursued the same end by different means. Mill Swamp's new "Rules of Decorum," drawn up at the meeting, specified that "the Names of the free born Male Members shall be called over by the Clerk" to determine whether a quorum was present, thus implying that voting membership would similarly be restricted to "free born" men.[30] This roundabout definition most likely had the effect of disenfranchising free blacks at Mill Swamp, since most free blacks in the neighborhood had been manumitted by Quaker or Baptist masters in the 1780s.

This strangely indirect debate highlights several important aspects of the churches' collective attitudes toward ideas of race and the place of African Americans in the church community. Mill Swamp's inability to formulate a clear answer to the initial query suggests that the church's white members were seriously divided on the issue of free blacks' participation in church government. Although there seems to have been a clear sense that black members, including free blacks, constituted a separate or potentially separate class within the church, the white members of Mill Swamp could not agree on a way to set church policy in those terms. Instead, they chose to define authority within the church in terms of freedom, masculinity, and birth, but unlike Black Creek or the Portsmouth Association, they did so in a way that most likely served to exclude black men. Even among the churches that excluded free black men from church government, the rules of order remained vague; no church explicitly limited participation in church government to white men until 1813, and most did not do so until the 1830s.

During the 1780s and 1790s, then, the white male Baptists who controlled the government of the churches in Isle of Wight, Southampton, and Sussex counties struggled to cope with the implications of the changing racial profile of church membership. While evangelical and Baptist concepts gave all believers spiritual authority and brought them into Christian fellowship, formal institutional authority in the churches rested on masculinity and freedom. As black membership increased and Virginia's free black population grew in the closing decades of the eighteenth century, it was unclear how these principles of authority would or should affect African American church members. It is clear that much of the time white Baptists thought of blacks as a separate class of members. It is equally clear that they resisted making direct public pronouncements on these issues of race in church. Both the queries themselves and the churches' equivocal answers suggest the churches' uneasiness about either including African Americans as members on the same terms as whites or explicitly excluding African Americans from certain privileges or duties of membership. The query on baptism shows that most white members who set church policy wanted to create an inclusive community based on rituals that emphasized the individual experience of salvation and were not restricted by worldly status. But white members also indirectly made clear that the privileges of voting and control over church government were the provenance of free men, which most of the time meant white men. A great deal of ground lay between these two poles, however, and it was on this broad middle ground that most of Baptist church life took place.

If white Baptists' seeming openness to black religious authority and their potential support for black liberty attracted this first wave of black men and women to the churches, the structures of authority and governance they found in the churches tended to reflect rather than to challenge worldly hierarchies. White men such as David Barrow, John Johnson, and John Gwaltney reconsidered the implications of republican and evangelical values for slavery in the 1780s and 1790s and concluded that slavery was incompatible with those values, but others sought to carefully delimit the implications of evangelical spiritual fellowship to preclude such erosion of worldly distinctions. Black men and women in the churches could seize on the more radical strains of Baptist theology and practice if they wished, but their ability to pursue and elaborate those meanings in church was limited by the weight of opinion among white members.

Both the contest over the place of black men in the churches and the conflict over slavery more generally addressed questions about the meaning of white manhood in addition to those about the meaning of blackness and bondage. As Barrow's view of virtuous white farm families in Winchester suggests, anti-slavery Baptists were concerned about the effects of the peculiar institution not only on slaves but also on masters and their families. Likewise, the construction of formal authority within the churches depended not only on the disabilities of female and black members but also on the privileges of white men. That is why free black men in particular posed such a quandary for the white-controlled churches. Did white men's authority in church stem from their freedom or from their whiteness? What weight did freedom carry without whiteness?

The strange debate at Mill Swamp highlights these issues. The practical effect on free black men was the same whether the exclusion was explicitly based on race or on free birth, but the ideological effect on the construction of white male identity in the church was quite different. White men at Mill Swamp chose to identify their status as men who were born free—perhaps a particularly white construction of the republican values that became so important to Baptist leaders' efforts to claim an influential place in the cultural order of the new nation—as the basis of their right to rule in church. At Black Creek, however, freedom and masculinity, rather than birth, remained the decisive factors, as Benjamin Blackhead and Samuel Blackman demonstrated. Increasing black membership, as well as increasing black freedom, raised powerful questions about freedom, masculinity, and the rights of church government in the closing decades of the eighteenth century, but the Baptist churches of southeastern Virginia provided only equivocal answers.

In 1800 the circular letter of the Portsmouth Association proclaimed that "some of our churches have experienced a little reviving in their bondage, which encourages a hope that the Lord hath not utterly forsaken us, but that he will yet shew compassion according to the days wherein he hath afflicted us." Even more exciting, "we have also been favoured with reviving news from a number of churches around us in Virginia, where King Jesus is reigning and triumphing gloriously . . . by the wonderful displays of his love."[31] The next decade proved this optimism entirely warranted. After the lull of the 1790s, the first decade of the nineteenth century marked a significant Baptist revival in Isle of Wight, Southampton, and Sussex counties. Table 3 indicates this growth, and the minutes and membership lists of the churches illuminate its character. In the years 1802–7, for instance, South Quay's minute book recorded about thirteen new white members and seventy-three new black members. Black Creek's membership list suggests that thirty-six whites and twenty-nine blacks joined the church from about 1803 to 1810, and in 1806 a branch of Black Creek split off to become Tucker's Swamp Baptist Church. (Unfortunately, no records survive for Tucker's Swamp from before 1818.) And according to church minutes, Mill Swamp added approximately seventy-eight white members and thirty-one black members in the period 1798–1807, while Raccoon Swamp added fifty-four whites and sixty-five blacks.

Because the churches were inconsistent about recording new baptisms, these figures probably understate the number of men and women who joined the churches in this era. But the general impression they convey is certainly accurate: the churches grew rapidly in the decade after 1800, and much of that growth came from the continued influx of African Americans and, upon closer inspection, of women. Table 5 illustrates the effect of this period of growth on the overall racial profile of Baptist membership. By the second decade of the nineteenth century, blacks made up more than 30 percent of all Baptists at Mill Swamp and Black Creek, probably more than 50 percent at South Quay, and nearly 70 percent at Raccoon Swamp. Table 6 demonstrates that the churches also became more female during this time period. From church minutes, it appears that women tended to form a majority among both black and white members. This pattern continued throughout the first four decades of the nineteenth century. By the 1830s, white men constituted 20–25 percent of all members at most of the southeastern Virginia churches and only about 10 percent at Mill Swamp and Raccoon Swamp, after making up 30–40 percent from the 1770s to the 1790s (see table 7).

Clearly, white women, black women, and black men found something compelling in Baptist churches despite the realities of white male control

Table 5. BAPTIST CHURCH MEMBERSHIP IN ISLE OF WIGHT, SOUTHAMPTON, AND SUSSEX
COUNTIES, BY RACE, 1802–1820

Church	Dates	Members counted	White N	%	Black N	%
South Quay	1775–1820[a]	All	141	51	137	49
	1802–1820	New	63	40	96	60
Black Creek	1805–1810	All	103	66	52	34
	1810–1818	New	21	54	18	46
Black Creek total	1805–1818		124	64	70	36
Mill Swamp	1812–1820	All	186	69	82	31
Raccoon Swamp	1813	All	60	32	127	68

Sources: South Quay Baptist Church, Minute Book, 1775–1827, LVA; Black Creek Baptist Church, Minute Book, 1804–1818, VBHS; Mill Swamp Baptist Church, Minute Book, 1812–1840, LVA; Raccoon Swamp [Antioch] Baptist Church, Minute Book, 1772–1837, LVA.

Note: Where data internal to membership lists or from church minutes permit, I have calculated the number and racial profile of new members for a given period rather than the total church membership for the whole period of the list. This provides a more nuanced picture of the changing shape of Baptist membership than a single list covering a period of twenty or more years.

[a] The South Quay membership list covers the years 1775–1827. It is possible to determine new members added during a particular period, but because there is no consistent record of deaths, excommunications, or departures, figures for total membership can only be calculated for the whole list up to a chosen end date.

over church government. As historians have revised their assessment of the early Baptist movement's radicalism with regard to race, class, and gender, they have also undermined long-standing assumptions about the source of the movement's attraction for marginalized members of Virginia society.[32] If Baptists did not offer an unusual degree of equality in church, what was it that brought so many white women, slaves, and free blacks into the denomination? In her study of Baptists in Kentucky, Ellen Eslinger provides part of the answer. Exploring African American church membership, she argues that opportunities for separate worship and independent black community life rather than egalitarian treatment within the churches spurred African Americans' interest in Baptist church membership.[33] This was almost certainly part of the appeal of Baptist churches for blacks in Isle of Wight, Southampton, and Sussex counties after 1800, and the church community may have held a similar appeal for white women. But this useful correction to earlier, simplistic ideas about the relationship between treatment in church and the appeal of the Baptists to subordinate groups has the potential to dismiss too easily the religious and ideological dimensions of evangelicalism's appeal. Indeed, part of the attraction of separate worship and independent community life was the opportunity to explore and express dimensions of Baptist faith that might not receive a hearing in church. Acknowledging the limitations of white Baptists' egalitarianism leaves open equally important questions about the content of blacks' and white women's experience in the churches—about how Baptist religious concepts and rituals shaped that experience, how men and women in the church interpreted those concepts and participated in those rituals, and how their participation in turn shaped the Baptist community more broadly.

The evolution of the Baptist churches of southeastern Virginia in the early decades of the nineteenth century was not marked by dramatic political and symbolic issues like the containment of the anti-slavery movement of the 1780s and 1790s, but the influx of blacks and white women into fellowship after 1800 makes this era equally important for our understanding of evangelicalism in Virginia. As historians move away from a straightforward interpretation of southern evangelicalism that emphasizes radicalism in the eighteenth century and capitulation to southern norms in the nineteenth, we need to turn our attention more fully to the ongoing process of interpretation and interaction that constituted Christian fellowship in the churches. The rituals and language of the church could mean different things for the different church members. Not unexpectedly, the general drift of Baptist practice over the course of the early nineteenth century was toward the more definitive enshrinement of worldly standards of race and gender in the church. But these standards never converged exactly, and the enduring ideals of evangelical community provided members of all sorts with material to make claims on the church community and, in some cases, to act out their vision of their faith.

The ritual process of discipline through which Baptist and other evangelical churches defined Godly behavior and maintained the boundaries of their communities is perhaps the most obvious and visible example. Discipline focused on different offenses for members of different races and sexes, expressing church members' recognition of worldly differences, but the churches also placed great emphasis on maintaining the consistency and fairness of the process itself, at least according to their own criteria. Moreover, discipline constantly implicitly referred to Baptist religious values that were not always reducible to worldly categories, most notably notions of God's law, divine order, and fellowship among Christians.[34] In the process of discipline, then, Baptists of different worldly standings found an expression of community in which

Table 6. Baptist church membership in Isle of Wight, Southampton, and Sussex counties, by race and sex, 1772–1840

Dates	Members counted (source)[a]	White men N	White men %	White women N	White women %	Black men N	Black men %	Black women N	Black women %
Racoon Swamp									
1772–1783	All (list)	58	40.6	85	59.4	10	76.9	3	23.1
1789	All (list)	25	29.1	61	70.9	29	51.8	27	48.2
1813	All (list)	14	23.3	46	76.7	50	41.7	70	58.3
1815–1824	New (minutes)	4	44.4	5	55.6	17	37.0	29	63.0
1837	All white (list)	24	29.3	58	70.7				
1828–1840	New (minutes)	11	19.6	45	80.4	28	39.4	43	60.6
Mill Swamp									
1774–1790	All (list)	103	48.1	111	51.9	27	46.6	31	53.4
1812–1820	All (list)	43	23.1	143	76.9	30	36.6	52	63.4
1835	All white (list; minutes)[b]	34	19.1	144	80.9				
South Quay									
1775–1796	All (list)	35	44.9	43	55.1	27	65.9	14	34.1
1802–1820	New (minutes)	27	42.9	36	57.1	46	47.9	50	52.1
1824–1829	New (minutes)	39	40.6	57	59.4	15	53.6	13	46.4
1827–1840	All (list)	70	38.9	110	61.1	42	44.7	52	55.3
Black Creek									
1775–1795	All (list)	60	47.2	67	52.8	12	57.1	9	42.9
1805–1818	All (list)	56	45.2	68	54.8	35	50.0	35	50.0
1818–1827	All (list)	60	36.8	103	63.2	27	44.3	34	55.7
1829–1840	All white (list)	65	30.7	147	69.3				
High Hills									
1807–1820	All (list)	8	30.8	18	69.2	2	40.0	3	60.0
1820–1827	New (list)	17	35.4	31	64.6	8	61.5	5	38.5
1832–1840	New (minutes)	24	48.0	26	52.0	27	50.9	26	49.1
Tucker's Swamp									
1818–1830	All (list)	19	40.4	28	59.6	44	48.4	47	51.6
1830–40	All (list)	61	33.7	120	66.3	30	40.0	45	60.0
Beaver Dam									
1828–1840	All (list)	93	46.5	107	53.5	15	35.7	27	64.3
Smithfield									
1830–1840	All (minutes)	7	50.0	7	50.0	7	36.8	12	63.2
Seacock (Elam)									
1838	All (list)	12	22.6	41	77.4	5	38.5	8	61.5

Sources: Raccoon Swamp [Antioch] Baptist Church, Minute Book, 1772–1837, LVA; Raccoon Swamp [Antioch] Baptist Church, Minute Book, 1837–1892, LVA; Mill Swamp Baptist Church, Minute Book, 1777–1790, LVA; Mill Swamp Baptist Church, Minute Book, 1791–1811, LVA; Mill Swamp Baptist Church, Minute Book, 1812–1840, LVA; South Quay Baptist Church, Minute Book, 1775–1827, LVA; South Quay Baptist Church, Minute Book, 1827–1899, LVA; Black Creek Baptist Church, Minute Book, 1776–1804, LVA; Black Creek Baptist Church, Minute Book, 1804–1818, VBHS; Black Creek Baptist Church, Minute Book, 1818–1862, VBHS; High Hills [of Nottoway] Baptist Church, Minute Book, 1787–1845, LVA; Tucker's Swamp Baptist Church, Minute Book, 1818–1830, VBHS; Tucker's Swamp Baptist Church, Minute Book, 1818–1857, VBHS; Beaver Dam Baptist Church, Minute Book, 1828–1894, LVA; Smithfield Baptist Church, Minute Book, 1830–1894, VBHS; Seacock [Elam] Baptist Church, Minute Book, 1819–1839, VBHS; "Minutes of the Virginia Portsmouth Association, Held at Otter Dams Church, Surry County, Virginia, May the 26th, 27th, and 28th, 1832," 11, VBHS.

[a] Calculations are based on available data, which vary significantly over time and from church to church. When membership lists with discoverable dates are available, I have used those. When no membership list is available, I have calculated the numbers of new members during a particular

period from church minutes or, in some cases, from internal evidence within a list covering a much longer period.

  b An 1835 list in the Mill Swamp minute book gives the names of 34 white male members but provides no data about other groups. In 1832, however, the Portsmouth Association reported that Mill Swamp had 178 white members and 120 black members. The gender breakdown among whites given here is based on subtracting the 1835 figure of 34 white men from the church records from the 1832 figure for total white membership from the Portsmouth Association minutes. No comparable data on the gender breakdown among black members are available. See Mill Swamp Baptist Church, Minute Book, 1812–1840, "Free white male members belonging to the Church at Mill Swamp, [Sept.] 1835," LVA; "Minutes of the Virginia Portsmouth Association, Held at Otter Dams Church, Surry County, Virginia, May the 26th, 27th, and 28th, 1832," 11, VBHS.

worldly hierarchies were neither overtly rejected nor explicitly endorsed, but refracted through the principles of evangelical faith.

As the Kehukee Association's 1785 decision on women's speech in matters of discipline suggests, the institutional practice of discipline reflected the churches' more general mixture of white male institutional control and shared spiritual authority. The white male cast of church government in general meant that discipline too was run by and voted on by white men. In cases where disciplinary records include the name of the accuser along with the accusation, the accusers were overwhelmingly white men: of 158 such cases, 136 accusations came from white men, and only twice did anyone other than another white male accuse a white male of any offense (see table 8). This predominance was in part due to the fact that accusations were often declared publicly by the deacons even if the charges did not originate with them; regardless of the origin of an accusation, an official charge was nearly always filtered through white male authority. Similarly, the committees appointed to investigate charges were usually composed of white men, although the churches occasionally appointed black men or white women to investigate offenses alleged against black or female members. At Black Creek, for instance, Benjamin Blackhead was appointed several times to cite black members to attend disciplinary proceedings.[35] Overwhelmingly, though, the institutional power in the ritualized process of discipline belonged to white men.

In an equally powerful but perhaps more subtle way, distinctions of gender and race also found expression in the types of discipline faced by white and black men and women over the entire period. Certain offenses recurred relatively frequently in most groups: drunkenness, nonattendance, disputes with other church members, and generalized "disorder" (see table 9). But even among these offenses, drunkenness occupied a far more prominent place in the discipline of white men than in that

Table 7. White men as a percentage of total Baptist church membership in Isle of Wight, Southampton, and Sussex counties, 1772–1840

Church	Dates	Members counted (source)[a]	White men N	White men % of total
Raccoon Swamp	1772–1783	All (list)	58	30.7
	1789	All (list)	25	17.6
	1813	All (list)	14	7.5
	1828–1840	New (minutes)	11	7.9
Mill Swamp	1774–1790	All (list)	103	37.9
	1812–1820	All (list)	43	16.0
	1835	All (list; minutes)[b]	34	11.4
South Quay	1775–1796	All (list)	35	29.4
	1802–1820	New (minutes)	27	17.0
	1824–1829	New (minutes)	39	31.5
	1827–1840	All (list)	70	25.5
Black Creek	1775–1795	All (list)	60	40.5
	1805–1818	All (list)	56	28.9
	1818–1827	All (list)	60	26.8
High Hills	1807–1820	All (list)	8	25.8
	1820–1827	New (list)	17	27.9
	1832–1840	New (minutes)	24	23.3
Tucker's Swamp	1818–1830	All (list)	19	13.8
	1830–1840	All (list)	61	23.8
Beaver Dam	1828–1840	All (list)	93	38.4
Smithfield	1830–1840	All (minutes)	7	21.2
Seacock (Elam)	1838	All (list)	12	18.2

Sources: See table 6.

[a] Calculations are based on available data, which varies significantly over time and from church to church. When membership lists with discoverable dates are available, I have used those. When no membership list is available, I have calculated the numbers of new members during a particular period from church minutes or, in some cases, from internal evidence within a list covering a much longer period.

[b] An 1835 list in the Mill Swamp minute book gives the names of 34 white male members but provides no data about other groups. In 1832, however, the Portsmouth Association reported that Mill Swamp had 178 white members and 120 black members. The proportion of white males given here is based on the 1835 figure of 34 white men from the church records and the 1832 figures for total white and black membership from the Portsmouth Association minutes. See Mill Swamp Baptist Church, Minute Book, 1812–1840, "Free white male members belonging to the Church at Mill Swamp, [Sept.] 1835," LVA; "Minutes of the Virginia Portsmouth Association, Held at Otter Dams Church, Surry County, Virginia, May the 26th, 27th, and 28th, 1832," 11, VBHS.

of other groups; 30 percent of all disciplinary investigations of white men from 1772 to 1840 resulted from accusations of drunkenness. Disputes with other members made up 11 percent of all charges against white men but only 1–3 percent of charges against other members. Conversely, nonattendance accounted for 17 percent of the discipline faced by white women but only 10 percent of that faced by white men and far less for black men and women. These differences may suggest different behaviors among church members and certainly suggest different social situations that could have influenced perceptions, if not actual behavior.

Table 8. ACCUSERS AND ACCUSED IN CHURCH DISCIPLINE, BY RACE AND SEX, 1772–1840

		ACCUSED				
Accusers	Accusations	White men	White women	Black men	Black women	Other[a]
White men	136	75	25	24	8	4
White women	11	1	6	0	0	4
Black men	8	1	0	4	3	0
Black women	3	0	0	2	1	0
Total	158	77	31	30	12	8

Sources: Raccoon Swamp [Antioch] Baptist Church, Minute Book, 1772–1837, LVA; Raccoon Swamp [Antioch] Baptist Church, Minute Book, 1837–1892, LVA; Mill Swamp Baptist Church, Minute Book, 1777–1790, LVA; Mill Swamp Baptist Church, Minute Book, 1791–1811, LVA; Mill Swamp Baptist Church, Minute Book, 1812–1840, LVA; South Quay Baptist Church, Minute Book, 1775–1827, LVA; South Quay Baptist Church, Minute Book, 1827–1899, LVA; Black Creek Baptist Church, Minute Book, 1776–1804, LVA; Black Creek Baptist Church, Minute Book, 1804–1818, VBHS; Black Creek Baptist Church, Minute Book, 1818–1862, VBHS; High Hills [of Nottoway] Baptist Church, Minute Book, 1787–1845, LVA; Tucker's Swamp Baptist Church, Minute Book, 1818–1830, VBHS; Tucker's Swamp Baptist Church, Minute Book, 1818–1857, VBHS; Beaver Dam Baptist Church, Minute Book, 1828–1894, LVA; Smithfield Baptist Church, Minute Book, 1830–1894, VBHS; Seacock [Elam] Baptist Church, Minute Book, 1819–1839, VBHS; Seacock [Elam] Baptist Church, Minute Book, 1832–1889, VBHS.

[a] Couples of either race or individuals of unknown race or sex.

Male drunkenness was probably more likely to be publicly visible than female drunkenness, for instance; women may have had more difficulty attending church conferences because of their household duties or the risks of traveling while pregnant or with small children; and black attendance may have been viewed more flexibly because of legal restrictions on slaves' movement.

Not only did common charges have different weights but black and white men and women faced different accusations among the less frequent offenses as well. Most noticeably, fornication and bastardy featured far more prominently for white women than for white men, while a collection of offenses that white men faced, including fighting and economic conflicts, did not appear at all for white women. African American men and women faced accusations of theft far more frequently than whites, and black men were especially vulnerable to this charge. Slavery-related offenses like disobedience and running away also featured prominently in the discipline of black Baptists, although these were not inevitably decided in favor of the master, as suggested by the conflict between John Lawrence and Nero discussed in chapter 2. Sexual and marital offenses like adultery, fornication, and marital irregularities also accounted for a far greater proportion of black discipline than of white discipline.

Together, these disparities added up to significantly different disciplinary profiles for men and women in the churches of Isle of Wight,

Table 9. OFFENSES IN CHURCH DISCIPLINE, BY RACE AND SEX, 1772–1840

Offense	White women N	White women %	White men N	White men %	Black women N	Black women %	Black men N	Black men %
Adultery	3	1	0		14	10	12	4
Assault	0		0		0		1	0
Bastardy	11	4	1	0	2	1	1	0
Criticizing church	1	0	3	1	0		2	1
Dishonesty	0		0		0		1	0
Disobeying church	11	4	20	4	0		1	0
Disorder	38	13	28	6	20	14	32	11
Disputes	12	4	55	11	4	3	3	1
Doctrinal issues	8	3	7	1	2	1	0	0
Drunkenness	26	9	142	30	9	7	37	13
Economic issues	0		10	2	0		1	0
Familial disorder	2	1	3	1	0		0	
Fighting	0		11	2	1	1	6	2
Fornication	19	7	10	2	14	10	6	2
Idleness	2	1	1	0	0		0	
Immorality	3	1	4	1	2	1	1	0
Improper disposition	7	2	10	2	4	3	4	1
Lying	5	2	8	2	4	3	4	1
Marital disorder	5	2	2	0	6	4	8	3
Membership issues	8	3	17	4	2	1	4	1
Miscegenation	0		0		1	1	1	0
Murder	0		0		0		1	0
Nonattendance	50	17	47	10	2	1	12	4
Preaching	0		0		0		2	1
Roguishness	0		0		0		1	0
Sexual disorder	0		2	0	0		3	1
Shooting at someone	0		1	0	0		0	
Slander	0		1	0	0		0	
Slavery-related issues	0		6	1	4	3	12	4
Swearing	1	0	5	1	0		1	0
Tattling	2	1	0		2	1	0	
Theft	2	1	4	1	13	9	48	17
Uncleanliness	0		1	0	1	1	1	0
Whoredom	0		1	0	0		0	
Wife abuse	0		3	1	0		2	1
Worldliness	8	3	13	3	0		4	1
Unknown	63	22	64	13	31	22	67	24
Total	287		480		138		280	

Sources: See table 8.

Note: Percentages do not always add up to 100 due to rounding.

Southampton, and Sussex counties. Social offenses like drunkenness, disputes, worldliness, and fighting—especially drunkenness—dominated the charges against white males, constituting 56.3 percent of all cases (see table 10). White women's charges were divided more evenly among social, religious, and sexual charges. Religious offenses, including nonattendance, accounted for 27.2 percent of the discipline of white women,

Table 10. Categories of Offenses in Church Discipline, by Race and Sex, 1772–1840

Category	White women N	White women %	White men N	White men %	Black women N	Black women %	Black men N	Black men %
Social	67	23.3	270	56.3	41	29.7	125	44.6
Religious	78	27.2	94	19.6	6	4.4	21	7.5
Sexual	38	13.2	20	4.2	38	27.5	34	12.1
General/unknown	104	36.2	96	20.0	53	38.4	100	35.7
Total	287	100.0	480	100.1	138	100.0	280	99.9

Sources: See table 8.

Note: Percentages do not add up to 100 due to rounding.

while social charges accounted for 23.3 percent and sexual charges for 13.2 percent. In the aggregate, then, Baptist churches in southeastern Virginia tended to discipline white men for public, masculine behaviors that conflicted with evangelical ideals of piety, humility, and temperance. The collective meaning of discipline for white women was more complex. The slight plurality of religious offenses in their overall disciplinary profile suggests that women's membership was taken seriously by the churches and that their religious views and behaviors mattered to the men who controlled the disciplinary process. But the disproportionate representation of sexual offenses among white women compared with white men suggests the degree to which traditional ideals of femininity, including a powerful sexual double standard, continued to inform Baptist ideas of evangelical womanhood. Bastardy accusations among whites, for instance, were overwhelmingly directed at women—eleven times as often as against men. In this very broad view, Baptist church discipline seems to have been more transformative for white masculinity than for white femininity.

Like white women, black men and women found that in general the charges they faced reinforced their worldly status. Theft, drunkenness, and slavery-related charges largely account for the predominance of social offenses for black men, making up 78 percent of all such offenses. Charges against black women were divided more evenly between social and sexual charges. Their social offenses resembled black men's, although offenses suggesting general unruliness—lying, disputes, and improper disposition—figured more prominently. This disciplinary profile reveals the types of disorder to which Baptists thought black men and women particularly prone, and these ideas conformed with standard white visions of blacks.

Black women faced sexual discipline more often than any other group, and black men faced it significantly more often than white men. These charges differed somewhat in composition and meaning from those against whites. Black men and women were accused of adultery far more often than white men or women, which may not have reflected white preconceptions of black lasciviousness so much as it reflected the obstacles facing black marriage in this era. White Baptists' oversight over slave marriages, which were not legally recognized, can be read as an effort to enforce conformity to unrealistic, Eurocentric standards, but a more sympathetic and realistic reading suggests that white Baptists were genuinely (if somewhat naively, given their general complicity in the system of slavery) concerned about these relationships and discerning the proper Christian attitude toward them.

In 1778 the Kehukee Association had taken up the query "Is the marriage of servants lawful before God, which is not complied with according to the laws of the land?" and answered that such marriages were lawful.[36] But churches had difficulty confronting the implications of this decision. The second annual meeting of the Portsmouth Association, in 1792, attempted to confront such questions directly: "Is it lawful, and agreeable to the word of God, for a black man-servant, (or slave) who has been married to a wife, who is removed from him a great distance, without his, or her consent, to marry another woman during her life or not?" After debating this question and reaching no answer, the association referred it to the following year's meeting.[37] At the 1793 meeting the association again debated the question and eventually agreed to appoint a committee, including David Barrow, to rewrite the query in such a way that it could be answered. Barrow's query reversed the implication of the question, asking, "What ought Churches to do with Members in their Communion, who shall either directly, or indirectly separate married Slaves, who are come together according to their custom as Man and Wife?" This query also "was thought by a Majority to be so difficult, that no answer could be given it."[38] At the next meeting, a delegate pointed out that the revised query should have been expunged from the records but had not been (perhaps because Barrow had been in charge of collecting and publishing the records), suggesting just how divisive such questions were for the churches.[39]

The cases of adultery that actually came before the churches suggest that black members themselves may have used the disciplinary process to attempt to protect their marriages. Most of the charges include a phrase such as "taking another man's wife" or "taking another woman's husband."[40] These accusations may have made their way to the church through the aggrieved partners or through their friends. Other marital situations were more complicated. When Mill Swamp investigated "Mrs. Clark's Beck" for "leaving her husband," they eventually reported that "her conduct [was] thought to be justifiable" and retained her in church. However, when she soon took "a husband while [her] former husband yet lives," she was excommunicated.[41] White Baptists seem to have considered black marriages binding and worth protecting. This could cut both ways for black members. Those who wanted assistance in maintaining a stable relationship could find it in the disciplinary process, along with toleration for separations caused by sale or removal. But those who sought to change or dissolve relationships for other reasons found themselves held to the idealized standards of the white community.

In the practice of discipline itself, the general patterns faded into the details of particular cases and particular situations that carried meanings even more complex and ambivalent for the men and women who shaped them. The overall tendencies in discipline were just that: tendencies rather than absolute rules. And individual cases could easily diverge from the general pattern. Even when cases fit these patterns, the details and complexities of the ways in which the church pursued them suggest the power of discipline as a religious ritual. And tracing the extended disciplinary career of particular individuals suggests the tensions between this power and the racial and gendered expectations of Virginia society more broadly.

Ethelred Gardner was one of the most wealthy and influential members of the South Quay church. In 1810 he owned thirteen slaves, making him one of the largest slaveholders in the church.[42] The Gardner family name recurred frequently in the church minute book, and Ethelred was a constant presence in the church from the first decade of the nineteenth century. In 1813 he was ordained as a deacon.[43] Family, office, and wealth made Gardner a very important man within the local Baptist community. Despite his standing, in 1811 Gardner went before the church to face accusations that ultimately led to an emotional break with the church. In recording the accusations, the clerk of the church captured the essence of what would become a recurring difficulty between Gardner and his brethren. The church complained "that [Gardner's] general conduct and conversation in public companies is too light and airy, and calculated at sometimes to exite mirth and laughter amongst the ignorant and wicked part of mankind, and at other times to exite anger and strife, and thereby bringing upon himself disputes, quarrels, and (sometimes) fights, to the great dishonor of our Holy religion." There were two events behind these accusations. In May, Gardner had attended court day and amused a crowd "by playing very uncommon and ludicrous pranks with a stud horse." He had compounded this violation of Baptist standards of behavior by assaulting a man "at the letting of the poor at Hardy Cobbs store" in August.[44]

Gardner had engaged in exactly the type of aggressive, worldly behavior against which Baptists defined themselves at the very public events the Baptist community sought to replace.[45] When his case came before the church, Gardner acknowledged the charges, but he "attempted to justify them—whereupon he was expelled by the unanimous voice of the church."[46] Rather than participating in the ritual of humble submission and sincere repentance by which discipline restored fellowship between Christians, Gardner faced excommunication for his continued adherence to the assertive values of wealthy male Virginians in the early nineteenth century.[47] This punishment must have had its effect, because less than a year later Gardner adapted his demeanor and voice to the standards of evangelical community. He "came forward, confessed his faults for which he was expell'd," and was restored to fellowship.[48]

Unfortunately, Gardner continued to have serious difficulty controlling his behavior on public occasions. In March 1814 he was in "an affray at Solomon Dardins sale," but he managed to reconcile with the church. Gardner drank too much and got in a fight at an estate sale in 1815; after expressing "deep repentance ... he was forgiven, on his promising to refrain in future." In December of the same year, however, he "was charged with drinking to excess and other disorderly conduct on last Southampton court day." These repeated offenses made the church wary of Gardner's performances of repentance. In April 1816 Gardner appeared before the church and "professed to have repented, and said that he had again resolv'd to try to get the powers of regulating himself in the use of Brandy—which he found to be a great evil." Rather than restoring him, however, the church "agreed to wait with him longer in a state of Suspence, to see if he should succeed in his resolution and agreed to unite in prayer to God to assist him." In August, after again voicing his acknowledgment and repentance, Gardner returned to the church.[49]

Gardner's extended disciplinary career suggests the powerful attraction of the Baptist community for even elite men in early national Virginia. One of the most remarkable aspects of these cases is that Gardner kept coming back to the church despite his evident attraction to the sometimes lewd, aggressive, and brandy-sodden world of court days and estate sales in Southampton. Baptists required white men to forgo this version of masculinity and substitute one based on piety, sincerity, and restraint. The ritual of discipline encapsulated this contrast, both by rejecting worldly behaviors and by requiring a sincere expression of repentance and humility before one could rejoin the community. In all of these ways, Gardner's offenses—fighting, drunkenness, disputes, and excessive worldliness—and his struggles to regain his standing in church represent the main themes in the discipline of white men in the Baptist churches of Isle of Wight, Southampton, and Sussex counties.

Of course, not all cases fit the general patterns as well as Ethelred Gardner's. Despite the overall disproportion in sexual offenses, for instance, white men, even powerful white men, could be disciplined for sexual and marital misbehavior. John Holms, a traveling preacher licensed by Mill Swamp, was excommunicated for attempting to seduce local women by promising to marry them even though he already had a wife and for "acting uncomely towards two Married Sisters in our church, or in other Terms discovering . . . unchaste intentions to them."[50] Several men were also disciplined for abusing their wives. In 1787 Mill Swamp recorded that David Jones "acknowledges that he has bin provokt to beat his Wife," which was "gotten over by confession."[51] The church was less lenient when confession was not forthcoming. Another member of Mill Swamp, Brother Goodrich, was excommunicated for "Drunkenness, Profanity, and abusive conduct towards his wife and treating the church with contempt" in 1808.[52]

In some cases the disciplinary process could authorize women's voices, even against those of their husbands. At South Quay, when James Saunders was excommunicated for "abusing his wife," Ann, she was "cited to attend . . . to give the church what information she can respecting the . . . charge."[53] South Quay's intervention into the relationship between husband and wife, to the extent of calling on Ann Saunders to testify against her husband, suggests the churches' sincere desire both to regulate misbehavior and to treat husband and wife as separate individuals and independent members of the church. In the right circumstances, church discipline provided a forum for women's voices to be heard and justified. Such cases illustrate one of the ways in which women's status as church members allowed them to speak in the disciplinary process both on their own account and in support of the churches' efforts to reform white masculinity. Evangelical men remained patriarchs, but their churches expected them to be responsible ones, subject to the rules of gospel order, and women's testimony and participation helped encourage white Baptist men to fulfill their duties as heads of Christian households.

But this authorization of women's voices remained limited to particular situations in the disciplinary process, and unauthorized speech or assertion could result in discipline. The extended disciplinary career of Rhoda McClenny demonstrates the ways in which women's authority as church members intersected with issues of Christian fellowship and the gendered enforcement of evangelical femininity. McClenny was a white woman who joined South Quay by relating her experience of conversion and undergoing baptism in 1805.[54] In March 1810 she was "charged with some improper conduct, which probably amounts to theft." The church assigned a committee to investigate, and in June, "upon hearing the circumstance of the case it was agreed that she be restor'd to full fellowship." But one powerful member of South Quay did not agree with this decision. Brother Cutchings Council, a founding member of the church and a deacon, refused to sit with the church in fellowship unless the case was reheard. A motion was made to do so, but it was defeated, "whereupon Bror Council rose from his seat, withdrew himself and, amidst the most earnest and warm remonstrances and solicitations of the church, refused to be considered as one of us." The church then charged Council with disorder and called on him to justify his conduct.[55]

In September, Council seemed to relent. He acknowledged "his error as to the manner of his withdrawing from us, and was restored to his priviledges." But once accepted into fellowship, he immediately charged McClenny with lying. McClenny was present and debated with him on the matter, but the church concluded that "it would not be decided, so as to give satisfaction to the Church and Bror Council." The matter was postponed, and helps were called in from other churches. Three months later the matter was again taken up by the church, "and upon a full examination, she [Sister McClenny] was restored to her priviledges." Council again withdrew from the church, but he did not succeed in forcing the case to be reheard, and in February 1812 he acknowledged "his error, and professes sorrow for the same," and was restored.[56]

Unfortunately, the South Quay minutes do not record the exact nature of the conflict between these two members, but the overall dynamic is telling. In these cases the church upheld both McClenny's membership and her right to speak in church "where it respects her own communion." She successfully confronted and debated a powerful white male officeholder who had attempted to bring the weight of his own vision of fellowship and communion to bear on her. By refusing to sit in fellowship with the church if it fellowshipped McClenny, Council hoped to force the church to choose between his membership and hers. But after examining the circumstances, the other white men who controlled the disciplinary process decided that McClenny's actions were more compatible with the values of the Baptist community, despite Council's own weight within that community. In such circumstances the church provided white women with a voice, and the resources to give that voice force, that they seldom found elsewhere in antebellum Virginia. For white women, as for the rest of the church, of course, this process was not about power or gender, at least not directly; it was about the values of the church and the nature of fellowship. But these religious meanings drew at least some of their effect from worldly distinctions of power and gender. Seeing the powerful humbled and the humble justified dramatized the ways in which God's law superseded man's law and confirmed the Baptist churches' efforts to live by that higher law.

Thus, the authority white women found in the disciplinary process was real, but it was limited by the values of the church community, as Rhoda McClenny found when she faced the other side of South Quay's attitudes toward female speech. In June 1819 Jordan Edwards accused McClenny "of being in the habit of talebearing or tatling, contrary to Gospel order." A committee investigated and found that McClenny had "used very unbecoming language or filthy conversation, in the presence of Bror Edwards, his family and others." The church expelled McClenny in December.[57] In this case, McClenny's speech, outside of authorized channels and expressing quintessentially female forms of disorder— "tale-bearing and tatling"—conflicted with evangelical conceptions of femininity. Of course, church discipline relied on information church

members provided about one another, but the church distinguished between legitimate charges or testimony and "filthy conversation" by gaug-
ing the context and spirit of such speech and its consistency with Baptist
values. This process could offer women a voice in church equal to that
of any other member, but it could also enforce traditional restrictions on
and expectations of women's behavior.

A final example of the complex ways in which church discipline operated in individual lives is the career of Benjamin Blackhead at Black
Creek. In June 1788, four years after being manumitted by David Barrow, Blackhead joined Barrow's church at Black Creek. He almost immediately had his first encounter with church discipline, which illustrated
one of the church's major concerns about black members. In August the
church suggested that Blackhead, "having taken a woman for his wife
in the time of his bondage and they both now being free," should now
"for his safty and c[omfort?] . . . Comply with the form of matrimony."[58]
Blackhead and his wife, Milly, apparently did so, because there is no record of further action on the case.

Much of Blackhead's early experience with church discipline involved disputes with other church members. In 1799 he faced a "matter
of difficulty" with another free black member, Samuel Blackman, that
continued for several months until it was "happily settled." In 1800 another "matter of difficulty" arose with another free black church member,
Dick Blackshins, but it was "settled between themselves." In 1801 Henry
Jones, a minister, accused Blackhead "of being unjust in his dealings."
At the next meeting, "the Brethren agreed to look over it." A similar dispute arose with Wilie Griffin in 1803, and Blackhead was again retained
in fellowship (Griffin apparently died).[59] Although there is little information about any of these cases, it is tempting to read the mediation of
disputes as a positive function of church discipline for Blackhead, particularly since all of these cases were successfully resolved. A free black
man in a slave society must have welcomed a friendly arena in which to
present the conflicts and disagreements that arose from doing business.
None of the disputes seems to have been bitter, and Blackhead's actions
suggest that he felt a strong desire to remain in the church despite the
difficulties doing so began to cause him.

In 1805 Blackhead was accused of drunkenness and "after lengthy
debate" was declared out of fellowship. Although there is no record of
his restoration, he must have returned to the church and made amends,

because his name appears in the records for 1807, when he was accused of lying and stealing. The church formed a committee to "call together for Infirmation any person or persons that know anything concerning Ben's character relative to the charge." The committee must not have liked what it found, for Blackhead was declared out of fellowship at the next meeting.[60]

Blackhead returned to the church in 1811. At the December meeting, the clerk recorded that he was once again "received in fellowship and is immediately under the watch and care of the church." His return to the church suggests that Blackhead, like Ethelred Gardner, truly valued what he had found in the Baptist community despite the surveillance of his conduct that church membership entailed. But Blackhead did not manage to retain his membership for long: six months after his restoration, he was accused of "receiving stolen property of a slave which was found in his house," and he was excommunicated.[61]

The details of Blackhead's experiences are inaccessible, but there are several suggestive aspects of his disciplinary career. Blackhead was a free black man; he occupied one of the most problematic categories in southern society. Baptist ideals of spiritual egalitarianism and the extent to which those ideals were practiced within the community at Black Creek must have helped ease some of the tensions associated with the complexities of his status. Blackhead also obviously engaged in trade of some sort. His early disciplinary cases involved disputes, some of which were related to business, and he was successful enough to make a contribution to the church fund that was equal to those of other respectable church members.[62] The church's role as a mediator and its evenhanded treatment may have influenced Blackhead's desire to remain in the church, evinced by his two restorations. Moreover, Blackhead's freedom had real meaning in the Black Creek church. He was a voting member of the church conference, along with the white male members and other free black men like Samuel Blackman and Richard Blackshins, and he sometimes served as an agent of the church in disciplinary investigations of other black members. Church membership and the church community provided Blackhead with a degree of institutional support and authority, along with the spiritual authority that accompanied his conversion and entry into fellowship with other Christians.

But if the attraction of Baptist life for Blackhead was related to his problematic status in southern society, so too were the events that led to his expulsion from that life. One can only imagine the events and re-lationships that led Blackhead to conceal stolen property in his house, but the circumstances do not have to have been exceptional. Blackhead had been a slave himself, so he must have had relationships and friend-ships within the slave community. Whether he was hiding stolen goods for a slave or had bought them from the slave, the events are entirely plausible. It is even possible that the "lying and stealing" that led to Blackhead's 1807 excommunication may have been a similar incident. In any case, theft was an offense that was often connected with the cir-cumstances of slavery, and it was certainly connected with blackness; blacks as a group faced 90 percent of all accusations of theft, and black men alone faced 71 percent. Blackhead was excommunicated twice for crimes associated with blackness and slavery, and the second time the connection was quite direct.

Along with communion and baptism, church discipline was one of the main rituals that expressed the values of Baptist institutional and spiri-tual life. Discipline operated in at least three dimensions simultaneously: it instantiated the ideals of "a Gospel Church relation and Fellowship";[63] it gendered and racialized spiritual and social experience within the churches; and it helped shape evangelicalism's public face in Virginia society. In the first of these dimensions it validated the spiritual author-ity and the power of Christian fellowship among members. In the second dimension it brought worldly distinctions into tension with evangelical spiritual values. This often worked to reinforce social differences be-tween members, but it could also dramatize the power of Baptist fellow-ship, as in the humble submission demanded of Ethelred Gardner or the justification of Rhoda McClenny against Cutchings Council. The final dimension was intimately related to the changing character of Baptist membership in the early nineteenth century.

Many aspects of the overall character of discipline for the different groups in the churches were products of the period after 1810. Indeed, it seems that the increasing presence of women and blacks in church and the declining proportion of white men among church members in-tensified the distinctively racialized and gendered patterns of discipline. This phenomenon was most marked for white men and women. The en-forcement of traditional restrictions on women became an increasingly important component of the discipline of white women over the course of the early national and antebellum eras. The disproportionate representation of sexual offenses in the discipline of white women compared with white men was largely a phenomenon of the period after 1810. In each decade from 1770 to 1810, sexual cases constituted 3-6 percent of all disciplinary cases for white women (see table 11), percentages comparable to those for white men during these years. In the decades after 1810, however, sexual offenses came to account for 18-24 percent of disciplinary cases for white women, compared with 2-8 percent for white men. This shift coincided with a moderate but definite increase in the percentage of cases of drunkenness among white male offenses. Up to 1810, accusations of drunkenness made up 24 percent of all charges against white men; after 1810 that proportion increased to 31 percent.[64]

These changes reflected larger changes in the structure of the church communities during the same period. White male Baptists seem to have countered their declining numerical presence with more strictly exercised control over church government and with an increasing emphasis on distinctive practices of masculinity as the public face of evangelicalism in the antebellum period. Church discipline reflected this preoccupation in several ways. For white men, discipline increasingly emphasized temperance and proper public comportment; for white women, it increasingly focused on sexual continence. By enforcing proper conformity to patriarchal norms among white women, white male Baptists could enact a distinctive evangelical identity in antebellum Virginia without compromising their masculinity or mastery in more fundamental terms.[65]

It is important to understand that this change in patterns of discipline was gradual and often subtle. Members of both sexes continued to face discipline for a variety of offenses; even as overall emphases shifted, white men could be (and were) disciplined for sexual offenses, and white women, like other members, regularly faced discipline for drunkenness. Moreover, despite white male control over the institution of church discipline, the process never became a straightforward application of social control. Churches sought to apply consistent standards, investigate charges, and consider evidence carefully, and by the standards of the time they were relatively successful in doing so. Donald Mathews may have exaggerated slightly when he noted "the dignity, fairness, and probity of these investigations," but not by much.[66] The main point of the process of discipline for the majority of the men and women who

	1772–1780		1781–1790		1791–1800	
	N	%	N	%	N	%
WHITE WOMEN						
Social	7	35.0	8	21.6	6	17.6
Sexual	1	5.0	1	2.7	2	5.9
Religious	1	5.0	13	35.1	10	29.4
General	11	55.0	15	40.5	16	47.1
Total	*20*	*100.0*	*37*	*99.9*	*34*	*100.0*
WHITE MEN						
Social	16	50.0	31	49.2	28	57.1
Sexual	2	6.3	3	4.8	2	4.1
Religious	0	0.0	9	14.3	8	16.3
General	14	43.8	20	31.8	11	22.5
Total	*32*	*100.1*	*63*	*100.1*	*49*	*100.0*
BLACK WOMEN						
Social	0	0.0	5	38.5	4	23.5
Sexual	0	0.0	1	7.7	6	35.3
Religious	0	0.0	1	7.7	1	5.9
General	6	100.0	6	46.2	6	35.3
Total	*6*	*100.0*	*13*	*100.1*	*17*	*100.0*
BLACK MEN						
Social	2	22.2	10	37.0	16	34.8
Sexual	0	0.0	4	14.8	6	13.0
Religious	0	0.0	1	3.7	1	2.2
General	7	77.8	12	44.4	23	50.0
Total	*9*	*100.0*	*27*	*99.9*	*46*	*100.0*

Sources: See table 8.

Note: Percentages do not always add up to 100 due to rounding.

participated in the process was to dramatize the ongoing act of belonging to a church of the converted and to give meaning to the fellowship that church members shared.[67] Even as the nature of their participation reflected the gender politics of evangelicalism in southern society and thus shaped their experience of discipline in different ways, white men and women continued voluntarily to submit themselves to the judgment of the churches of southeastern Virginia and to find meaning in the fellowship they found there.

The discipline of black men and women does not seem to have been marked by clear patterns of change over time in the way that white discipline was. Investigations of adultery and theft increased over time in absolute terms, but that was to be expected given the increasing number of African Americans in the churches. Indeed, discipline of black members appears to have declined in proportional terms as their membership in-

1801–1810		1811–1820		1821–1830		1831–1840	
N	%	N	%	N	%	N	%
13	38.2	13	35.1	5	14.7	15	16.5
2	5.9	9	24.3	7	20.6	16	17.6
6	17.7	7	18.9	7	20.6	34	37.4
13	38.2	8	21.6	15	44.1	26	28.6
34	100.0	37	99.9	34	100.0	91	100.1
42	64.6	23	65.7	37	58.7	93	53.8
2	3.1	2	5.7	5	7.9	4	2.3
10	15.4	8	22.9	14	22.2	45	26.0
11	16.9	2	5.7	7	11.1	31	17.9
65	100.0	35	100.0	63	99.9	173	100.0
7	33.3	5	25.0	7	18.9	13	54.2
4	19.1	7	35.0	14	37.8	6	25.0
0	0.0	1	5.0	3	8.1	0	0.0
10	47.6	7	35.0	13	35.2	5	20.8
21	100.0	20	100.0	37	100.0	24	100.0
24	52.2	15	41.7	23	37.7	35	63.6
4	8.7	10	27.8	7	11.5	3	5.5
0	0.0	3	8.3	9	14.8	6	10.9
18	39.1	8	22.2	22	36.1	11	20.0
46	100.0	36	100.0	61	100.1	55	100.0

creased. This was part and parcel of the increasing focus on distinctive white evangelical masculinity; discipline focused on white men even as the churches became more black and more female. But despite this decreasing attention in disciplinary cases, the character of African American experiences of Baptist fellowship appears to have been changing over the course of the early nineteenth century. There is evidence that as black membership increased, black men and women created their own interpretations of the meanings of evangelical fellowship and that these meanings built on the tensions and ambivalences of Baptist concepts and rituals as they evolved in Nat Turner's Virginia.

The issues of preaching, liberty, and liberation raised by the case of Porter's Tom in 1788 provide a useful case study of these tensions and reveal something of the process of interpretation that was so central to forging fellowship across the lines of race in the churches. Tom's case was not unique; several other black men applied for license to preach in the period 1780–1830. Taken together, these cases demonstrate that black members and the largely white "body of the church" often disagreed about who deserved "liberty to preach." They also cast the tensions inherent in the language of liberty into sharp relief, as the multiple meanings of liberty became more apparent when applied to an enslaved church member. In order to understand how these tensions operated in cases of black members seeking license to preach, it is useful first to examine how Baptists used the term *liberty* and the variety of interpretations to which that term was susceptible.

In Christian tradition, *liberty* resonated with a host of implications. In the Old Testament tradition it recalled the Israelites' liberation from bondage in Egypt and Isaiah's divine commission "to proclaim liberty to the captives" (Isa. 61:1), which had served David Thomas as such a powerful metaphor for Baptists' campaign against what they saw as the religious complacency and oppressive actions of the pre-Revolutionary establishment. In the New Testament, the idea of liberty was linked to liberation from sin and the possibility of salvation: "where the Spirit of the Lord is, there is liberty" (2 Cor. 3:17).[68] In the Reformed Protestant traditions that informed American evangelicalism this notion of liberty gained strength from the intertwined principles of God's absolute sovereignty and man's absolute depravity: true liberty from sin and from suffering could only come from and through God.[69]

Virginia Baptists drew directly on these various uses. The Portsmouth Association's 1801 circular letter on Baptists' distinctive Calvinist belief in salvation by grace alone, for instance, concluded by urging members to "stand fast in that liberty wherein Christ Jesus hath made you free, and be not entangled again with the yoke of bondage."[70] These theological traditions also carried with them a host of more radical associations, including an antinomian rejection of secular law and authority.[71] Indeed, the *Oxford English Dictionary* recognizes this tension inherent in religious ideas of liberty, defining the term as "freedom from the bondage of sin, or of the law."[72] The linkage in religious use between spiritual liberty and political or social liberty had a long history, and evidence of these linkages ran through the early Baptist movement in Virginia.[73]

As previous chapters have shown, Baptists in colonial and Revolutionary Virginia drew on the biblical language of liberty both as an argument for religious freedom and as a critique of a society that they saw as being in bondage to sin. Some Baptists, like David Barrow, wove these associations into a critique of slavery in Revolutionary and early national Virginia. Opposition to Baptists and other evangelicals often seized on this issue, along with the disorders Baptists were purported to cause in families and households, in order to emphasize the fundamental threat to social order that evangelicals represented. Of course, the truth of the matter was far more complex and compromised than either anti-slavery activists hoped or anti-evangelicals feared. White Baptist proclamations of "liberty to the captives" held primarily spiritual and symbolic meanings, and their translation into more transformative social messages was always partial and incomplete. At the same time, the powerful metaphorical meanings of Baptist uses of *liberty* remained accessible for those who sought them. African American church members understood both the social and the spiritual meanings contained within the religious language of liberty and white church members' tentative anti-slavery activities. Indeed, some church members embodied the intersection of these different meanings. Among the early nineteenth-century members of Black Creek were the free black couple George and Cherry Liberty. George Liberty had been freed in 1788 (along with Jimes Fredom) by Henry Jones, a member of Black Creek, and joined the church himself about 1805.[74] In George Liberty's person and in his entry into Baptist fellowship, liberty from the bondage of slavery and liberty from the bondage of sin coexisted and overlapped to the point of being indistinguishable.

When Baptists used the term *liberty* in their records, however, they were usually referring to other matters. They most often used it to denote license or permission obtained from the church or from God. Often this was structured as a relief from normal restraints, as a particular privilege or freedom to act granted in particular circumstances, synonymous with *leave* or *permission*. In church rules, for instance, members were not allowed to speak more than three times to one subject without obtaining "liberty" from the church. Members were denied the "liberty of laughing, or whispering, in time of Publick speaking."[75] In some uses, then, *liberty* spoke as much of restraint as of freedom, and sometimes it spoke directly to the restraints and hierarchies of southern society. The 1800 rules of Mill Swamp, for instance, stated that "no Woman shall

speak in conference, but when called upon . . . except she should be bur-
thend in which case she shall have liberty to tell her grievance." When
slaves were cited to come to disciplinary meetings, churches asked "the
Liberty of their Master for them to attend our Next Conference." The
Kehukee Association, to which the churches in southeastern Virginia belonged until 1791, advised its churches, "We think it is the duty of every
master of a family to give his slaves liberty to attend the worship of God
in his family."[76]

Liberty obtained from God was more transformative. When preachers felt particularly inspired or saw that their words had particularly
good effect, they felt that they had preached with "liberty." John Williams
recounted that after itinerant John Waller was assaulted and whipped
while preaching in 1771, he "Went Back Singing praise to God, Mounted
the Stage & preached with a Great Deal of Liberty." When asked about
the beating, Waller "answer'd that the Lord stood by him . . . & pour'd
his Love into his Soul without measure, & the Brethren & Sisters Round
him Singing praises . . . so that he Could Scarcely feel the stripes . . . Re-
joicing . . . that he was Worthy to Suffer for his Dear Lord & Master."
Waller experienced liberty as God's love filling his soul, freeing him from
and through suffering and turning him into a vessel for God's message.[77]
Williams himself often described his own preaching in similar terms.
When he became ill on a preaching tour, he was tempted to "quit & never
proceed another step in a Christian life." After a disappointing session of
preaching "with but little liberty," he returned to the pulpit and began to
preach again. "I had not spoke very long before my soul got intirely released . . . & went forward with as great liberty as ever I had. The Christians seem'd to git much matter, the unconverted visible impress'd, &
one particular old soldier for the Devil . . . scream'd out & fell down, after
some time to rise upon her knees . . . hollowing out & sometimes crying
to God for pardon."[78]

Liberty from God could also apply to a religious community as a
whole. In 1818 the Black Creek church recorded in its covenant that "we
will as God shall give us means, ability, Conveniency, & opportunity, attend on the means of Grace, Institutions, & ordinances of the Gospel,"
but later replaced *ability* with *liberty*.[79] Running through these uses is
the idea that liberty from God, like grace, was what enabled fallen humans to behave in godly ways. By granting liberty, God released men
and women from the normal restraints of sinful, worldly life and gave

them the ability to preach God's word effectively, to hear and receive that word in meaningful ways, and to live and worship together as a church according to his laws.

When members obtained "liberty" to preach, they drew on all of these meanings. In church covenants members agreed not "to break the order of the Gospel Church by taking upon ourselves any Office or Dignity in the same, of the Ministry or others, till thereunto called by the Voice of the Church."[80] Only the church could grant liberty to preach, and it only did so after a trial period in which the church could judge the candidate's abilities and adherence to doctrine, as the case of Porter's Tom illustrates. But Baptists also unfailingly referred to the ability to preach as a "gift" that, like grace or mercy, came from God. So while on one level preaching was a liberty or license granted by the church, it maintained strong overtones of liberty granted by God. Moreover, "liberty to preach" involved freedom of movement and freedom of expression that implicitly combined permission granted by the church with inspiration directly from God, as when James Delk received license from Mill Swamp "to exercise his ministerial gift publickly wherever the Lord may cast his lit [light]."[81]

Given the long history and distinctive valence of black interpretations of Christianity dating back to the colonial period, African American church members certainly understood the multiple meanings of liberty that permeated southeastern Virginia's Baptist movement as well as the ways in which preaching intersected with those meanings. The only members of the churches of Isle of Wight, Southampton, and Sussex counties ever charged with preaching without license from the church were slaves. White members sometimes were denied permission to preach after a trial period or had their licenses revoked when charged with another offense, but only slaves faced direct charges of "exercising publick functions contrary to the rules of this Church," as Tom of Battle was at South Quay in 1810.[82] The church's objection to Tom may have been in part because of his excessive drinking, for which he was excommunicated in 1811, but Tom's offense also involved many aspects of the churches' uses of *liberty*. In finding a time, place, and audience for his preaching, he must have exercised the freedom of speech and movement that were associated with the "liberty to preach," all without "liberty" granted from the church.

Tom's assertiveness in claiming the right to preach may have spurred

South Quay's white members to consider the matter of black preaching more broadly. In December 1812 a church conference considered "the propriety of permit'g our black brethren to preach." They referred the query to the Portsmouth Association, and the next year the church directly took up the matter of licensing black preachers. In December 1813 the church decided to allow Tom, who had been restored to membership soon after his excommunication and who "profess[ed] to be call'd of God to preach," to "exercise his gift" in the church at the February meeting. In February the church also considered the candidacies of "Abra'm (of Manny) and Aaron (of Blackledge)." The church was not convinced, however: "The question about our black brethren candidates for liberty to preach was taken up and considered, whereupon it was agree'd to that Bro. Darden, on behalf of this Church, strictly forbid Bro'r Tom (of Battle) to exercise at all in a public way, and that he admonish the other Brethren, not to attempt to preach untill thereunto call'd by the Church, and that he exhort them to try to [do] good by doing Justly, loving Mercy, and walking humbly with God."[83] The church was uncomfortable with the ways in which these members exercised their "liberty" and felt that they could best express their religious calling in ways more in tune with their worldly station. For Tom, Abram, and Aaron this message must have seemed distressingly familiar to the stereotypical refrain of the white Christian message to slaves—submission, humbleness, obedience—and a far cry from whatever spiritual or temporal liberty preaching had represented.[84]

As far as the churches were concerned, preaching, particularly among black members, was a privilege granted only to those of unquestioned religious and moral character. While it is unclear whether it was moral or doctrinal failings that undermined Tom's, Abram's, and Aaron's attempts to gain license from South Quay, "Capt. Drew's Harry," a member of Black Creek, found his authorized preaching career cut short for very specific reasons. In March 1812 Harry was charged with "going to bed with another woman besides his wife—which woman goes by the name of Charolt Diggs." A committee of prominent white members was appointed to investigate the charge and to "silence him [Harry] from preaching." Although in September the committee reported that "their appears to be no Positive evidence in the case," and the church "agree[d] to hold him in fellowship And that he shall enjoy all the Privildges of the Church," they also decided that Harry should be "Restrained from Preaching untill They think Propper to give him Liberty again."[85] Similarly, in 1810 the Portsmouth Association warned churches "that Arthur Byrd (a man of color) who has been excluded from the Baptist society, is imposing on the churches as a Baptist preacher" and cautioned them "against any further imposition by the said Byrd."[86] The church maintained particularly careful watch over those whom it permitted to preach in order to ensure that church-sanctioned "liberty" was not tainted by association with liberties of any other sort.

Nonetheless, white Baptists' suspicion of black men's religious authority in the early nineteenth century was not an impenetrable barrier to official legitimacy. Indeed, despite hardening white attitudes during this time period, such legitimacy could even extend to baptizing converts and creating enduring communities of believers. In 1821 the Mill Swamp church accepted as members "sundry negroes . . . who were Baptized by a Man of Colour from Williamsburg by the name of Going, pastor of the African Church near that place."[87] "Going" was almost certainly Gowan Pamphlet, who had died sometime before 1810.[88] In receiving these men and women into fellowship as an existing body rather than receiving them by experience, the white members of Mill Swamp implicitly recognized not only Pamphlet's authority to conduct legal baptisms but also the fact that these unaffiliated black Baptists had been leading orderly, Christian lives for years after their pastor's death. Mill Swamp's willingness to accept these men and women as members suggests their ability to maintain a recognizably Baptist theology and practice that was acceptable to the white governors of the church, and the persistence of this group highlights the vibrancy and distinctiveness of black Baptist life outside of the white-controlled churches. At the same time, their desire for a connection with Mill Swamp may have reflected a sense of vulnerability and a need for the institutional legitimacy that a white-controlled church could provide as the social and political environment became more hostile in the early decades of the nineteenth century.

Two later cases of attempts to preach by black members at South Quay provide useful contrasting examples of the line between legitimate and illegitimate attempts to claim religious authority in the eyes of the white church. They also demonstrate how the liberty to preach was almost inevitably tinged with other meanings of liberty. On November 30, 1822, the church considered the cases of two aspiring black preachers. The church heard evidence "that Bro'r York (of Saunders) has been in the habit of exercising as a preacher, without the permission and contrary to the rules of this Church." York was cited to appear at the next church conference, in March 1823, at which the church agreed "that he be admonished not to exercise in publick, until the Church shall have an opportunity of being better informed of his call, his talents, and his moral character, and shall thereupon grant him permission." That same day in November 1822, however, the church agreed "that Bro'r Davy (of Norfleet) be Licensed to preach as he may be call'd upon, and his master may permit him."[89] These two cases differed in several ways at the out-set. York had already claimed liberty to preach without the church's per-mission, perhaps drawing more strongly on liberty from God or claiming his own de facto liberty to act as he pleased, rather than relying on liberty granted by the church. This must have raised the church's suspicion both of potential heterodoxy in his reluctance to follow prescribed forms and of potential rebelliousness as a slave's taking liberty for himself. They did not reject York's becoming a preacher out of hand, but insisted that the church, rather than York himself or informal gatherings of listen-ers, should be the judge of his call, talent, and character. Davy, however, received license in an orderly way from the church, and the church tell-ingly modified the idea of a preacher's freedom of movement and call from God by invoking his master's permission as part of his call.

The conclusion of each man's story (as far as the church records are concerned) extends this initial divergence in important ways. The church investigated York's moral character in 1823 and 1824, and while he was retained as a member of the church, he was not licensed to preach. In 1828 York was again "charged with having gone forward to preach, Con-trary to a former order or rule of this Church." The church also found "that he at one time attempted to exercise the gift of the ministry while so much intoxicated, that the audience were greatly disgusted with his Conduct and Conversation." York admitted that he had violated church rules, and the church expressly forbade him from preaching any more. While he accepted the judgment in church, it must not have sat well, for in 1829 York was charged with "having reproach'd the Church, and slandered its members," and was expelled.[90] Davy, on the other hand, found that the liberty granted by the church and by his master extended beyond preaching: "At a special conference, call'd and held the 24th of July 1824; Bro'r David of Norfleet . . . who has lately been emancipated by his master (Jno. Norfleet of Nansemond co.) being about to remove to Philadelphia, petitioned for a letter of dismission, which was granted him."[91] The change from "Davy" to "David" may have indicated his changed status in the eyes of the church clerk who recorded the minute. By accepting the formal, restrained liberty granted by the church and by his master, David had attained a more complete liberation than nearly any of his fellow church members.

The church most likely knew Jonathan Norfleet's predispositions, so perhaps it knew that restricting David's call as "his master may permit him" was no restriction at all. Indeed, perhaps that helped make it easier for David to obtain license to preach in the first place. York's attempts to create his own liberty to preach and to act may have stemmed from a realization that such liberty would never actually be granted to him. Eventually, by speaking against the church, he at least implicitly (and perhaps explicitly) condemned the system of restraint and order that gave *liberty* an important part of its meaning for the church. In both York's and David's cases, though, we see the white members who directed church government attempting to define the boundaries and implications of "liberty to preach."

Despite the cases' differing outcomes, both point to the process of negotiation and interpretation at work in the churches. York, like Tom of Battle, acted on his own as a preacher without waiting for "liberty" from the church. York's and Tom's ability to find an audience for their preaching, most likely among their fellow slaves, is an important indicator that the black members of the church were exercising their own judgment about who should receive "liberty to preach." Even after being explicitly forbidden to preach, York found an audience. Even if the audience disapproved of his preaching, as the church minutes suggest, York himself and to some extent his audience were willing to test or even ignore the church's institutional authority to control their own religious experience. We have less information about David's case, largely because it provoked less controversy, but it must have served as an important example to the enslaved members of the church. For David, the multiple meanings of liberty aligned to produce both spiritual and material freedom, a fact that could not have been lost on his fellow church members. David's example must have reinvigorated many of the implications of the language of liberty in the church.

Even as African American church members sought and found their own meanings in the shared language and rituals of the churches, the churches themselves were reconfiguring their relationship to their black members in ways that gave such alternate meanings less support from the white body of the church. As black membership increased in the early nineteenth century, some churches began to balk at the idea of leaving church government open to black men, regardless of their status. South Quay, for instance, changed its rules to reflect changing white concerns. The church's 1791 rules of order had not specified any racial categories for participation in or attendance at church conferences, but in 1813 a motion was approved specifying that the clerk should "call the names of the White male members . . . at the opening of each conference."[92] Even though South Quay had no free black male members, the church went even farther than Mill Swamp had in its 1800 decision to limit government to "free born" male members, overtly embracing a racial definition of authority within the church. The new rule made little practical difference at South Quay, but the ideological shift toward race was important.

Similar changes gradually took hold in the region's other churches as well.[93] Even Black Creek, where Samuel Blackman and George Liberty appear to have kept their voting rights into the 1820s, was affected by this trend. When the church began a new membership list in 1818, the names of the free black men were initially listed together with those of the white men. This was consistent with the previous list, begun in 1805, which had included all free male members together. But on the new list, the clerk went back and crossed out Blackman's and Liberty's names and placed them alongside the male slaves on a list of "black male members." Interestingly, no such confusion occurred regarding the free black women, who had long been listed alongside their enslaved sisters.[94] Because maleness was the essential prerequisite to governing authority in the church, black women's status as free or slave had held far less significance to white record keepers than black men's. As race came to replace freedom as the primary division between men in church, however, such distinctions came to matter far less for white attitudes toward black men as well.

This shift in the place of free black men within the church was only one of many gradual modifications in the racial practices of southeastern Virginia Baptist churches in the early nineteenth century. White church leaders instituted a number of other top-down changes in church organization that further asserted and increased white control. These changes did not prevent blacks in southeastern Virginia from joining evangelical churches, but they served to mark black Baptists as a separate and subordinate group and to place white members in a position of oversight over blacks. In 1813, for instance, the voting members of Black Creek called on "all the White & Black Brethren" to attend a specially appointed conference "in order to give the Black Brethren some instruction."[95] South Quay appointed a similar meeting in the same year, agreeing to "hold an extra conference on the third Sunday in Aug't for the purpose of settling any matter of difficulty with the black members."[96] By the 1820s the practice of separate meetings for the discipline of black members had become common in churches across southeastern Virginia, and concern for policing the black membership was a recurring theme of church business.[97] In 1826 Raccoon Swamp emphasized the importance of white oversight of the growing black community attached to the church by appointing four white men "to preserve good order at this place and to disperse the Blacks as soon as worship may be concluded."[98]

The increasing separation and marginalization of black congregants had contradictory effects, reflecting the largely unintended consequences of the interaction between the different priorities of white and black church members. White Baptists wished both to segregate black members and to control their collective religious activities, as Black Creek's intention to "give the Black Brethren some instruction" and Raccoon Swamp's appointment of whites to police the black membership suggest. But in practice this segregation encouraged and perhaps increased the independence of black Baptists and allowed them a freedom of action and interpretation that might not have been possible if they had been more fully integrated into the white-controlled churches. The churches increasingly treated black members as a collective group, an adjunct to the main, white congregation, and engaged with them less frequently as individual believers. This practice gave black men and women greater leeway to work out their own ways of being Baptist in their own communities rather than relying primarily on their experiences in church. Indeed, both the evidence of unlicensed black preaching and the numerical realities of growing black membership in the churches of Isle of Wight, Southampton, and Sussex counties hint at the development of black community and religious life affiliated with, but to a certain extent independent of, Baptist churches that Eslinger identifies as crucial in attracting African Americans to the denomination.[99]

The white-controlled churches seemed to recognize the tensions inherent in their changing approach to their black membership, and the sought ways to reconcile the marginalization of black members with what they saw as proper oversight and subordination. Sometimes the churches delegated authority to conduct certain aspects of church business within the black congregation to trusted black members in good standing. When it arranged the separate meeting in 1813, South Quay appointed "Brethren Ben of Copeland and Harry of Battle . . . to watch over our Black Brethren and Sisters, and to assist them in settling any matter of difficulty or (if need be) to bring their cases before the conference."[100] But this delegation of authority did not connote white acceptance of black autonomy, as the prosecution of unlicensed black preachers demonstrates. It became clear, sometimes quite rapidly, that the separation of white and black members could both facilitate white oversight of black members' church activities and move those activities to the margins of the larger church. By 1817 South Quay's meetings "for the benifit of Black members" were run entirely by white members, as were nearly all disciplinary investigations. Later that year, South Quay decided that black members would be required to attend the separate meetings arranged for them or face disciplinary action.[101] South Quay formalized this arrangement earlier than many other churches, but by 1825 Black Creek and Tucker's Swamp were both following similar procedures. The equivocally inclusive model of evangelical community that white Baptists articulated in the late eighteenth century began to give way to an equivocally exclusive one. Through this gradual shift in the institutions of church life—the conferences and disciplinary process that helped give Baptist community and faith their meaning—white church members tacitly stated the separateness and inferiority of African American church members far more firmly than they had in the eighteenth century.

A wrenching controversy at Black Creek in 1825 revealed another dimension of this gradual process. At the church's December conference in that year the minister, Jonathan Lankford, "openly declared to this conference that he cannot in Justice to his conscience administer the Ordinances of the Gospel to this Church any longer owing to his oppesition on the subject of Negro Slavery, a part of the church being Slave holders." Other white members of the church expressed their surprise at Lankford's declaration, noting "that he has so long, and so very lately administered both Baptism and the Lords Supper to the Church," including the slaveholders.[102] In September 1826 a majority of the church's members voted to expel Lankford "untill he has fellowship with the Church."[103] As in earlier conflicts over slavery, the opposing sides framed the issues within the church in the particularly Baptist and evangelical terms of fellowship, baptism, and communion—the sinews of Christian community. Lankford expressed his opposition to slavery by withholding "the Ordinances" because he could not fellowship slaveholders or those who held fellowship with them. Likewise, his opponents expressed their surprise and suspicion of his motives by pointing out that until his declaration he had actively engaged in the rituals of fellowship with all members of the church.

As they debated "the Novel and difficult case of Brother Jonathan Lankford" over the course of a year and a half, church members elaborated on these themes. Eventually the key group of men most concerned in governing the church articulated a ringing condemnation of Lankford, and by implication all attempts at anti-slavery activism in the church, by strategically redeploying the key concepts of Baptist community. In September 1827 a committee of prominent lay members of Black Creek presented a final "report and resolution" of Lankford's case that detailed and justified the church's actions. They reiterated their earlier arguments about the abruptness of Lankford's actions and explained that "the Church contained slave holders when he became a member thereof, has continued to do so ever since, and notwithstanding there has been a small majority of non slave holders the Church has moved on harmoniously, each member regulating this subject to his own conscience . . . without interfering with that of his brothers, untill the present case." In emphasizing the harmony between slaveholders and non-slaveholders in the church, the committee was both repudiating Black Creek's contentious eighteenth-century anti-slavery debates and working toward a conception of Christian community that elevated unity between (white) Christians over other dimensions of faith—righteousness, moral purity, spiritual equality—that also informed Baptist doctrine and practice. In the committee's view it was dissension and divisiveness that lay at the heart of Lankford's plan: "Jonathan Lankford has . . . yielded too much to the delusion of Satan, and thereby lost sight of the duties of the Gospel," and "his sole object from the first to the last, has been, to split the Church asunder, in order to Promote, in some way or other, his own self-ish views and Purposes." The committee then spelled out exactly what those purposes were. Although Lankford had ministered to the church for many years, he had never officially been called to be the church's pastor. According to the committee, Lankford, with "the knowledge that a Majority of the Church were non slave holders, and wou'd therefore Probably sustain him," had attempted to split the church and then, with the majority on his side, would have "expelled every slave holder, considered him self the leader, and therefore entitled to ev'ry Promotion, which the Church cou'd confer," including the pastorate.[104]

Throughout their report, the language the committee used to describe Lankford and his actions expressed their fears of division within the church over the issue of slavery and asserted an interpretation of concepts of "the duties of the Gospel," Christian order, and church practice that would preclude such division. Lankford's "improper motives" were evinced by "the obstinacy of his conduct" while the church considered his case: "He wou'd neither fellowship the Church, nor leave the Church when requested to withdraw from it." In the view of the committee, he purposely undermined the ritual process of discipline, which was designed to preserve order and harmony through either reconciling church members to one another through acquittal or repentance or purifying the membership by expelling those who could not be fellowshipped.[105] His "unbrotherly (and we think) unchristian" actions, his "self interested" motives, and his appeal to "Party spirit" would reduce the church "to a state of the utmost disorder, discord, and confusion." And if that was so, the committee asked, "were not his motives impure? And has he not for such an impudent and immoral course, lately forfitted the confidence of the Church?"[106] This rhetorical turn implicitly emphasized the converse of Lankford's behavior—order, harmony, assurance, purity, modesty, morality—as ideals of Christian community and linked them to quiescence on the issue of slavery. The church minutes that recorded the committee's report reinforced this point and, perhaps seeking to plaster over the division in the church that Lankford had caused, noted that the committee's report "was read and *unanimously* received."[107]

While Lankford's own views are more difficult to analyze, mediated as they are by church minutes recorded by his opponents, it is clear that he too drew on both the literal and the ritual vocabularies of evangelical faith, albeit in very different ways than his opponents. Lankford's initial challenge to the church rested upon his refusal to administer communion—the central ritual of fellowship—to a church that contained slaveholders. Lankford's most powerful source of religious authority and his best means of spreading his message was his status as a preacher and minister. Preaching was a particularly charged form of speech, and being licensed as a preacher required not only particular talent but also inspiration from God and license from a church. As the churches' experience with black preachers indicated, this inspiration could be difficult for institutions to control. Lankford was also an ordained minister and therefore had certain authority in the Baptist world. He could administer the rituals of baptism and communion, and although he was not the pastor of Black Creek, ministers like Lankford oversaw churches and congregations, giving advice and to some extent directing the churches' spiritual life. The committee recognized these potential sources of authority and influence for Lankford and sought to undermine them by criticizing Lankford's behavior and by constructing their alternative vision of Baptist community, based more strongly in the values of the white laity. The committee concluded their report on exactly this note. Lankford, they claimed, "was at Perfect liberty to enjoy his own opinion; but they cou'd not suffer him to controul them, upon an important question, over which they considered he had no cognizance, further than as regarded his own conscience."[108] The committee thus asserted yet another meaning of liberty, restricting it to individual conscience and thereby preserving church members' freedom to endorse slavery.

White church members' attitudes toward slavery and the ways in which they treated their black brethren operated in parallel. Both reflected attempts by a majority of white Baptists to shape the language and rituals of their church in ways that firmly inscribed worldly hierarchies into religious practice. Black Creek's decision in the Lankford case reaffirmed the broad precedent that such hierarchies were not to be questioned in church. The church's most influential white members insisted that the morality of slavery was not a religious question, and by casting anti-slavery agitation as "unbrotherly and ... unchristian," they laid an implicit foundation for more positively proslavery sentiments based in Baptist doctrine and church practice. At the same time, the churches' general trend toward separating white and black members made a more direct statement about the place of certain worldly hierarchies in Baptist religious practice. Separate meetings and an increasingly explicit emphasis on white oversight of black members' participation in the churches carried a clear message of white superiority and black sub-ordination, even as they emphasized white church members' duties to foster the faith and enforce the orderliness of their black brothers and sisters. In combination, white church members' rejection of anti-slavery activism and their embrace of increasingly segregated church practices reflect the ongoing reinterpretation of Baptist language and practice in the biracial churches of southeastern Virginia. Drawing on particular elements of evangelical and Baptist discourse, white Baptists gradually constructed a religious vision that simultaneously reflected their belief in the spiritual equality of all souls, their ideal of harmonious relations between Christians, and their investment in their own racial privilege.

The construction of this interpretation did not go uncontested, however. Although church records provide frustratingly limited access to the content of black Baptists' religious vision, the records do contain evidence that African American church members expressed dissatisfaction with the churches' decisions and policies. This evidence demonstrates that black church members could and did use the language and practices of the Baptist Church to challenge decisions made by white members, or at the very least to register their disagreement with those decisions. And while there are only hints of what positive religious visions lay behind particular incidents, the records convey an overall sense of divergence and conflict between black and white interpretations of the implications of Baptist fellowship.

In most cases such conflicts come to light only briefly. At South Quay, for instance, "Ben of Britt," who had been appointed by the church "to exercise an oversight with the Black members in his neighborhood" in 1814, found himself accused of "improper conduct towards the Church" in 1821. Ben was restored to the church in 1822, but he was expelled again in 1826 for neglecting his duties of oversight, at least in the eyes of white members. Despite these ongoing tensions, he returned to fellowship in 1827. In 1830 another black member, "Abel of Harrison," was charged with disorderly conduct. Abel had previously served the church in 1825 by citing Ben to appear for discipline.[109] But now he stood before the church "for having spoken disrespectfully of the Church or some of its members because Will of Harrison Daughtry was not admitted to the Ordinance of Baptism." Will had initially been "received by experience" into the church in 1829, but the white church members in charge of such decisions had judged "the said Will's Conduct to be unchristianlike and therefore our Pastor refused to Baptize him." Abel was absent in October, perhaps registering his continued unhappiness with the church's decision and with the fact that he faced discipline because of it, but he appeared at the church's November conference and "expressed sorrow for his imprudence and asked the forgiveness of the Church," which was granted.[110]

The authority these men received from the white-controlled church did not prevent them from coming into conflict with and even publicly criticizing that church. Abel's disagreement with South Quay's decision went to the heart of Baptist practice and fellowship, touching on the issues of spiritual experience, baptism, and Christian conduct. The language in which Abel's offense was described—"having spoken disrespectfully of the Church or some of its members"—echoed York of Saunders's "having reproach'd the Church, and slandered its members" after being forbidden to preach the previous year. Both men felt that the church had improperly restricted access to its rituals and sources of spiritual authority. For Ben and Abel, as for York, at least temporarily, running afoul of the rules of the church did not necessarily mean abandoning evangelicalism as a larger religious orientation. Ben's and Abel's decisions to return to the church represented an ongoing negotiation between their own view of their faith and that of the institutional church. Both ultimately reconciled themselves to the church's requirements, as York ultimately could not, but the experiences of all three men hint at the complexities of individual decisions in a context in which the white-controlled church was just one aspect of a larger evangelical community.

A case at Black Creek is both more suggestive of general dissatisfaction and more tantalizingly incomplete. In December 1822 the church conference investigated a complaint "that there is great negligence and apparent falling off amongst the black members of this Church in the discharge of their duties as Church Members, and especially as respects their absenting themselves from communion." While the church minutes cast this question as a matter of inattention to religious duties, there may have been something more at stake. The black members of Black Creek seem to have been drawing on the power of withholding fellowship in order to express dissatisfaction with the church, although the substance of the disagreement is unclear. In March 1823, at a conference specially appointed for investigating "the state and standing" of the noncommunicant black members, the church conference "requested that if there were any complaints among them [the black members] touching communion that they would make them known. Whereupon several of them rose and stated their greviances." The conference decided that none of the grievances were serious enough to be a bar to communion and dismissed the charges, the black members "being exhorted generally to be more vigilant in the discharge of all their Christian duties."[111] Despite the conference's conclusion that their concerns were insignificant, the black members' expression of dissatisfaction through basic Baptist ritual practice demanded attention from the church and left its trace, however faint, in the minutes.

The substance of disagreements between white and black members usually remains hidden in the church records, but one case at South Quay reveals the extent to which worldly relationships gave rise to fundamental moral conflicts between white and black church members. In January 1830 William M. Jones, South Quay's clerk, presented a charge against "Dick of Elias Daughtry a member of this Church for having violently and without the fear of God before his eyes assaulted him with an axe in his hand." Jones, who owned Dick's wife, had been searching Dick's wife's house for stolen property. He found Dick at the house with stolen "bacon, pork, brandy and Cider in Dicks possession." Jones confronted Dick, who was drunk at the time according to Jones's report, and Dick responded with "very insulting language—such as 'had you given out to your folks as you ought to have done' this would not have been." When Jones ordered him to leave, Dick responded, "I come here before you did and I shall not go away." According to Jones, Dick then attacked him with the axe (but apparently did not harm him). Jones "asked him what he meant by such menaces, [and] he [Dick] looked him wishful in the face and gave him no answer." Jones "then ordered Dick to give him the axe [and] he answered 'I shall not' with much more insulting language." The church conference unanimously found Dick "guilty of theft, or accessory thereto, and of Drunkenness" and expelled him from the church.[112]

Dick's case is remarkable in many ways, not least because the minutes purport to record his actual words, a rarity in Baptist church records. Moreover, most disagreements between white and black church members did not result in either actual or threatened violence. But the case does reveal a moral contest between two members of the same church whose worldly status differed dramatically and suggests how that contest intersected with the values of the Baptist church community as constructed by its white members. It is clear from what Jones chose to record of their meeting that Dick's rejection of Jones's authority was as much at the heart of the matter as Dick's assault with the axe. Each of the quotes attributed to Dick reflects his refusal to be directed by Jones or to recognize Jones's right to direct him. Dick justified his actions by referring to Jones's deficiency as a master—"had you given out to your folks as you ought to have done"—and by suggesting that Jones had no right to control his movement or his presence in his wife's house—"I come here before you did and I shall not go away." Such resistance to authority challenged not only the master-slave relationship but also the Baptist church community. This community was based on members' agreement to submit to the authority of the church, particularly in church discipline. Rejecting that authority in any way was grounds for expulsion, whatever the specific offense involved. Dick, unlike Ben, Abel, or the Black Creek members who expressed dissent but ultimately reconciled themselves to the decisions of their churches, expressed no concern for Jones's authority either as a white man and master or as a fellow church member and officer of the church. Thus, in Jones's view, Dick's resistance to authority was a religious offense as well. Not only had Dick committed theft and assault but his obstinacy when confronted showed that he had done so "without the fear of God before his eyes."

Although we can only speculate about Dick's own view of the situation, his actions can be understood to a certain extent in terms of the principles, discourses, and practices that shaped the Baptist community. In defending his right to be in his wife's house, he was asserting his own authority as a husband, something for which evangelical discipline would have held him accountable had he abandoned it. Indeed, Baptist churches' rhetorical support for black marriages, equivocal as it sometimes was in practice, was likely an appealing aspect of the faith for many black men and women. Just as important, Dick was challenging Jones's evangelical self-conception as a good master, arguing that Jones's deficiencies as a master, not his slaves' moral failings, were at the root of the disorder. The principles of gospel order required a great deal from masters as well as from slaves, and if Dick knew he was in the wrong, he asserted that Jones was too.

Thus, the obvious anger, violence, and atypicality of Dick's case should not blind us to the larger context in which it occurred and the ways in which it reflected issues that pervaded the churches and sometimes made biracial fellowship deeply problematic from both black and white perspectives. While most other African American church members neither committed assault nor utterly rejected the authority of the church, the issues that provoked Dick's case and the moral universe behind it were central aspects of the churches' relationship to their black members. Theft and drunkenness, the two main offenses for which Dick was expelled, were the first and second most common offenses specified against black men in the churches between 1772 and 1840. Indeed, theft was an almost entirely African American category of crime in the churches. And offenses relating to slavery, clearly an important issue in Dick's case, were also among the offenses for which black men were most commonly disciplined.

More broadly, black members' willingness to use the rituals and practice of the church to challenge and question the authority of decisions made by white church members may have drawn on the same moral background as Dick's more radical, personal rejection. Black church members must have noticed white members' failures to live up to their own standards of mastery and in fact must have understood those standards and what constituted living up to them quite differently than did their white brethren. Moreover, their sense of community and of their right to their own spiritual and social experiences despite white efforts at control probably drew on a sense of authority and justice similar to Dick's. Indeed, in attacking Jones's provision for his slaves and in defending his own right to be in his wife's house Dick expressed a kind of frustrated masculinity analogous to the masculine authority of the unlicensed slave preachers. Masculine roles, as preachers or as providers, might underlie both subtle and overt forms of resistance in the slave society of Nat Turner's Virginia. Turner's own actions suggest that Tom of Battle or York of Saunders might not have been as distant from Dick as white church members wished to believe.

Between 1780 and 1830 the Baptist churches of Isle of Wight, Southampton, and Sussex counties became large, complex institutions with an enduring place in the society and culture of antebellum Virginia. White men gradually asserted their control over church government even as the body of the church became increasingly black and female, and the fellowship the churches offered women and African Americans became more definitively marked by their worldly station. As this transformation occurred, the white men who governed the churches sought to make a reformed, evangelical white masculinity, pious, restrained, and temperate, the public face of the denomination in the state. In this idealized view, temperate, pious, white Baptist men would rule confidently and lovingly over dutiful, modest wives, children, and servants. The changes in church discipline and in the institutional structure of black membership over the course of the first decades of the nineteenth century played into this program in many ways. But the meanings of Baptist community could not be so easily controlled by a single group within the church. The records of the churches not only reveal the general drift of official church policy but also hint at the ways in which men and women of both races sought to shape their denomination to different, sometimes conflicting ends. Evangelical principles offered, at the very least, a standard of justice and divine meaning to which members could appeal and through which their voices carried authority in their communities. The growth of increasingly independent African American congregations attached to the churches provided the most remarkable manifestations of this process, although they were not the only ones. In the records of authorized and unauthorized preaching and of church discipline more broadly, black men and women left powerful evidence of their own vision of the liberty that an evangelical and republican faith could and should offer its adherents. Much of the time, these meanings coexisted in uneasy, submerged tension with those of the white mainstream of the churches. But they carried with them the potential for a more fundamental divergence between white and black religious worlds, as the ensuing years would demonstrate.

REBELLIOUS AND UNGOVERNABLE

Nat Turner and the Religious World of Antebellum Virginia

ON THE FIRST DAY of November 1831 Nat Turner sat in his cell in the Southampton County jail and explained to Thomas R. Gray the "history of the motives which induced me to undertake the late insurrection, as you call it." Instead of a detailed indictment of slavery or a narrative of personal or collective injustice, Turner provided his religious biography as his sole explanation for his actions. Turner recounted a childhood in which his uncanny intelligence and supernatural knowledge of hidden things had indicated to his parents that he "was intended for some great purpose." Born in 1800, Turner spent his youth in the biracial, rural world of lower Southampton County at exactly the time that African Americans began joining the evangelical movement in large numbers and the relationship between white-controlled institutions and black congregants was becoming most contentious. Turner's vision of the meanings of Christianity seems to have incorporated influences from both black and white sources, including "my grandmother, who was very religious, and to whom I was much attached," as well as his then master, Benjamin Turner, "who belonged to the [Methodist] church, and other religious persons who visited the house, and whom I often saw at prayers." Like his parents, these observers noted Turner's intelligence and "singularity of . . . manners" and commented that he "would never be of service to any one as a slave." Through such interactions, Turner's sense of Christianity merged with his more general sense that he was destined for something more than a life of worldly servitude. In pursuit of this destiny, Turner cultivated his spiritual authority within the local black community, which already deferred to his intelligence and inspiration, by "wrap[ping] myself in mystery" and "by the austerity of my life and manners, which became the subject of remark by white and black."[1]

Turner's sense of special purpose was reinforced by his reading of scripture and by his own experience of direct revelation. He recounted to Gray how "as I was praying one day at my plough, the spirit spoke to me, saying 'Seek ye the kingdom of Heaven and all things shall be added unto you.'" Questioned by Gray, Turner claimed that by *spirit* he meant "the Spirit that spoke to the prophets in former days." This experience was repeated several years later. Turner began to communicate the revelations of the spirit to other slaves and determined to fulfill "the great promise that had been made to me."[2] As Mechal Sobel points out, Turner's emphasis on continued communication with the "spirit" fit not only with Christian conceptions of God, particularly as the Holy Ghost, but also with African conceptions of supernatural power and methods of human interactions with that power, despite Turner's own expressions of "contempt" for "conjuring and such like tricks."[3] This ambiguity highlights the ways in which Turner's religious outlook was not simply a product of evangelical churches themselves but rather one of the fertile religious culture that emerged as evangelical language, concepts, and practices became widespread among southeastern Virginia's black population.

Beginning in 1825, Turner's visions became increasingly urgent and violent: "I saw white spirits and black spirits engaged in battle, and the sun was darkened—the thunder rolled in the Heavens, and blood flowed in streams—and I heard a voice saying, 'Such is your luck, such you are called to see, and let it come rough or smooth, you must surely bare it.'" In response to this vision and other revelations, Turner "sought more than ever to obtain true holiness before the great day of judgment should appear, and then I began to receive the true knowledge of faith." He "discovered drops of blood on the corn as though it was dew from heaven," and he "found on the leaves in the woods hieroglyphic characters, and numbers with the forms of men in different attitudes, portrayed in blood, and representing the figures I had seen before in the heavens." Turner came to understand this as a sign of impending judgment, "that the Saviour was about to lay down the yoke he had borne for the sins of men, and the great day of judgment was at hand." Turner communicated these visions to both whites and blacks in his neighborhood, and one white man, Etheldred T. Brantley, was deeply affected. "He ceased from his wickedness, and was attacked immediately with a cutaneous erruption, and blood ozed from the pores of his skin," an affliction of which he was healed by a regimen of fasting and prayer. The spirit then informed Turner that "as the Saviour had been baptised so should we be also—and when the white people would not let us be baptised by the church, we went down to the water together, in the sight of many who reviled us, and were baptised by the Spirit."[4]

In 1828 the spirit appeared to Turner again "and said the Serpent was loosened, and Christ had laid down the yoke he had borne for the sins of men, and that I should take it on and fight against the Serpent, for the time was fast approaching when the first should be last and the last should be first." Gray interjected himself into Turner's narrative here, asking the defeated and imprisoned prophet, "Do you not find yourself mistaken now?" But Turner did not retreat from the messianic implications of the vision, asking in response, "Was not Christ crucified?" The spirit instructed Turner to wait for a sign that he should "commence the great work" and then to "arise and prepare myself, and slay my enemies with their own weapons." The February 1831 solar eclipse served as the sign, and Turner began to gather a handful of trusted lieutenants to help organize the uprising. After much planning and several delays, another strange atmospheric phenomenon finally spurred the rebels to action.[5]

Early in the morning of Monday, August 22, a few miles west of the settlement of Cross Keys, Turner and seven others entered the house of Turner's master, Joseph Travis, and killed the entire family. The group moved on to other farms, systematically killing the white people they encountered and gathering supporters, arms, and supplies as they went. By noon from fifty to sixty people had joined the revolt, and approximately fifty-five whites had been killed. In the same period, however, word of the uprising had spread throughout the county, and the white population had mobilized to subdue it. The rebels attempted to cross the Nottoway River and enter the county seat of Jerusalem, but they found the roads and bridges into town heavily defended. After this setback, facing increasingly well-organized resistance, the rebels turned back, and the revolt began to lose momentum, morale, and organization. Several skirmishes on the morning of the twenty-third ended the revolt, and most of its leaders were captured or killed. Turner himself escaped and went into hiding near the Travis farm, where the revolt had begun. He was captured at the end of October and hanged on November 11.[6]

Turner's religious biography and his apocalyptic vision were unique and intensely personal, but they were also clearly products of the larger cultural and social processes unleashed by the changing religious landscape of post-Revolutionary Virginia. In this sense, despite Turner's individual distinctiveness, which both he and Gray emphasized for different purposes, his motivations and his actions had wide-ranging ramifications for the nation, for the state of Virginia, and for the communities in which the rebellion occurred. For Baptists in Southampton, Sussex, and Isle of Wight counties, the uprising and its aftermath represented a turning point in the evolving relationship between black and white religious communities and in the relationship between evangelical values and those of mainstream white culture in Virginia. In responding to the revolt itself, white Baptists joined with other white Virginians in a massive effort at ideological containment of the uprising and worked within their churches to restrict the religious activities of their African American brethren. But the contradictions and inconsistencies in the larger white reaction weighed particularly heavily on white evangelicals, who felt pressed to defend their churches and denominations from association with the rebels.

Given the extent and force of the white reaction, black men's and women's first priority in the wake of the rebellion was to develop strategies that would protect them, their loved ones, and their communities from harm. They also had to determine what to expect from their white brethren and to restructure their religious communities accordingly. In the process of negotiating the complex ideological terrain created by Virginians' reactions to the revolt, white and black Baptists redefined their faith and their practice in ways that helped make evangelicalism a fundamental part of both white proslavery southern culture and the "invisible" black church of the antebellum South.

Beyond Turner's specific prophetic motivations, the rebels' violent campaign represented a powerful ideological assault on the ideals of white Virginians. The revolt not only revealed hidden dimensions of African American thought and culture but also brought to the surface the barely suppressed nightmares of white southerners by giving the lie to the evolving myth of paternalism that blended religion, republicanism, and gender into a seamless justification of southern society.[7] Turner and his fellow rebels turned these justifications on their head, drawing on evangelical Christianity and the heritage of the American Revolution to expose the illegitimacy of white southern mastery and the inability of white masters to protect their families and dependents.[8] White Virginians unintentionally revealed the depth of this challenge as they struggled to reassert military and ideological control in ways that contained the revolt's implications and denied its legitimacy. Concern over the uprising's larger significance reached the highest levels of Virginia political life. In the winter following the revolt the state legislature anxiously examined the place of slavery in Virginia society and even considered the possibility of gradually abolishing slavery in the state. The rulers of Virginia ultimately rejected that course and indefinitely deferred any action on the various conservative schemes of gradual emancipation and colonization that had been proposed, opting instead for a renewed commitment to policing the slave and free black population. Meanwhile, Virginia conservatives articulated an increasingly influential defense of slavery as a positive good in both Christian and republican terms.[9]

The Southampton revolt shook Baptists and other evangelicals in southeastern Virginia with particular force. Most immediately, the uprising disrupted and traumatized the communities, black and white, in which Baptists lived. It also exposed fundamental tensions in the religious and ecclesiastical culture of the region. Both Nat Turner's messianic leadership and the patterns of recruiting and organization that seem to have accompanied it revealed that the shared religious world of southeastern Virginia was not shared in the way envisioned by most white evangelicals. Rather than finding in evangelical doctrine a message of pious submission and spiritual fellowship with their white masters, many blacks in southeastern Virginia seemed to have found messages of power and divine retribution. Rather than finding in evangelical churches a loving community of humble fellow Christians, they seemed to have found networks of rebellious communication and organization. Despite decades spent persuading themselves and the white public that true Christian religion contributed to peace and harmony between slave and master and loving mastery and orderly obedience within households, white evangelicals found themselves faced with powerful evidence to the contrary that exceeded the direst warnings of either contemporary northern abolitionists or an earlier generation of southern anti-slavery activists like David Barrow.[10]

As we have seen, white Baptists experienced sharing religious fellowship with slaves and free blacks as an important but ambiguous aspect of their faith. Fellowship across lines of class and race dramatized the power of God's message by temporarily suspending worldly distinctions and substituting a leveling spiritual order. To some extent, however, the effect of this dramatization depended on the actual existence of such worldly distinctions, and this fact imbued the whole process with powerful countervailing impulses. For decades, Baptist interracial fellowship had been built on delicately balancing these tendencies and maintaining at least the illusion that black and white Baptists understood their shared spiritual communion in the same way. The Turner revolt, however, caused many whites to question whether such fellowship was truly possible and to reassess the relationship between whites and blacks in church. In doing so, they so alienated many of their black brethren that the bonds of fellowship strained to, and sometimes beyond, the breaking point.

The broader white reaction to the Turner rebellion also created particular problems for evangelicals in southeastern Virginia. The themes of delusion, imposture, authority, and legitimacy that had once pervaded Virginians' discussions of religious dissent and social order reappeared in public debate with a vengeance, albeit in a context very different from their colonial origins. The sincerity of African American religious beliefs became an object of intense scrutiny, as did the wisdom of white religious practices that encouraged black spiritual autonomy. One of the ways in which white commentators sought to contain the unsettling implications of the uprising was to focus on Turner himself as the leader of the rebellion and on his religious vision—his "gloomy fanaticism"—to the exclusion of all other aspects of the revolt. Gray, Turner's jailhouse amanuensis, exemplified this approach. In his framing of Turner's *Confessions,* Gray followed Turner's lead in focusing on the rebel leader's religious biography and downplayed the possibility that revolt had been more widespread or had its roots in any other source. Seymour L. Gross and Eileen Bender have argued that Gray intended this narrative to be psychologically reassuring to white readers, for whom this vision of Turner's religious madness seemed safely distant, as opposed to any explanation that implicated the system of slavery or white supremacy in general.[11]

Gray's narrative and others like it may have served this purpose for some white Virginians, but for Baptists and Methodists—the vast majority of white churchgoers in Virginia by 1830—who sat in church every week with African American slaves and who disciplined them for unauthorized preaching or for conflicts with their masters, this narrative increased rather than decreased their anxiety and sense of implication in the revolt. For these evangelicals, the focus on Turner's religious motivations as a source for the revolt was profoundly unsettling, as was the more general white concern about black religion and preaching as actual or potential mechanisms of revolutionary organization. Thus, even as white Baptists in Southampton, Sussex, and Isle of Wight counties confronted the same ideological challenges facing other white Virginians, they also took on an additional burden of defending and ultimately transforming their denomination and its place in southern society. Black Baptists in turn increasingly drew on many of the same elements that had made the rebellion possible—independent worship and segregation within the churches, unauthorized and covert preaching—as they found white-controlled churches deeply inhospitable to any but the most conventional and submissive religious expression.

In the days immediately following the revolt, word of the "insurrection," as it was immediately termed by white observers, prompted both massive military mobilization and wide-ranging public speculation about its motivation, extent, and meaning. Troops from surrounding areas poured into Southampton to assist in suppressing the rebellion. Governor John Floyd dispatched six militia companies to Southampton, along with arms and ammunition for the Sussex and Southampton regiments. Meanwhile, the mayor and council of Norfolk mobilized the militia there and requested further help from nearby federal naval and army bases.[12] A turn-of-the-century historian of the revolt estimated that by August 25 "there were three thousand troops on the way to Southampton and more preparing to set out."[13] Across southeastern Virginia and northeastern North Carolina more informal reprisals resulted in uncounted deaths. John Hampden Pleasants, editor of the *Richmond Constitutional Whig* and a member of the Richmond militia group dispatched to Southampton, noted that "summary justice in the form of decapitation has been executed on one or more prisoners." "Some of these scenes," he reported, "are hardly inferior in barbarity to the atrocities of the insurgents."[14] Another witness grimly recorded on August 27 that *"many negroes are killed every day:* the exact number will never be ascertained."[15]

In this atmosphere of panic and violence reliable information was hard to come by despite the flood of newspaper articles and oral rumor that followed the revolt. One newspaper advised its readers "to take *every report* with many grains of allowance—he will scarcely be safe if he believes a fiftieth part of what he hears."[16] Nonetheless, early newspaper accounts uneasily combined sensationalistic, exaggerated news of the revolt with confident reassurances that there was no serious danger. Reports placed the number of rebels at up to four hundred or suggested that they were runaway slaves who had burst out of the Great Dismal Swamp, "incited by a spirit of plunder and rapine."[17] Whites anxiously wondered whether the revolt was part of a larger conspiracy, and in the following weeks reports and rumors of uprisings or unruly behavior among blacks sprung up across Virginia and North Carolina, often resulting in brutal reprisals. In the weeks after the revolt white commentators overlaid this background of white panic and violence with a facade of calm reassurance, and these twin impulses created uneasy tensions in the white response considered as a whole.

The military mobilization of southern Virginia's white population was more than matched by a kind of ideological or discursive mobilization that sought to understand and contain the implications of the revolt and to restore ideological and psychological order for white Virginians. In the months that followed the revolt several themes emerged in the white public reaction that illustrate exactly the kinds of anxieties and tensions the revolt produced and revealed in the state, in the South, and in the nation itself. One of the ways this tension surfaced in the early press coverage was in depictions of the gendered and familial dimensions of the rebels' violence. White observers emphasized the violence of the revolt, as well as what they viewed as its illegitimacy and cowardice, by highlighting the fact that most of the white victims of the uprising were women and children. But such representations sometimes worked to conflicting ends. While they were intended to inspire chivalrous sympathy among observers and emphasize the viciousness of the revolt, they also served to highlight just how effective the rebels' assault on Southampton's mythic paternalism had been. As white ideologies of family and gender were deployed to condemn the rebellion and rally support, they simultaneously revealed the deep vulnerability of southern society and the racial and gendered fictions on which it was based. Moreover, the deployment of these ideological constructions of the revolt, its effects, and its meaning affected different groups in different ways, revealing conflicts and tensions within Virginia and southern society that those ideologies were meant to conceal. The very language and concepts intended to discredit the revolt as vicious, mindless violence of the worst sort thus unintentionally demonstrated the rebellion's effectiveness and ideological power.

The earliest reports of the Southampton revolt described the carnage in terms that revealed this process. Newspapers almost inevitably calculated white deaths in terms of families, reporting "that several families had been murdered" or "that several white families had been destroyed" or even, with some exaggeration, that "from twenty five to thirty families are said to have fallen victims to [the rebels'] ferocity."[18] As more detailed information became available, these reports gained a powerful, graphic intensity. John Hampden Pleasants observed "whole families, father, mother, daughters, sons, sucking babes, and school children, butchered, thrown into heaps, and left to be devoured by hogs and dogs, or to putrify on the spot."[19] In addition to the violence itself, correspondents often depicted the broader effects of the uprising and subsequent panic in terms of the disruption of families and the dislocation of women and children. A letter from Jerusalem, the county seat, published in the *Richmond Enquirer* reported that "every house, room and corner in this place is full of women and children, driven from home, who had to take [to] the woods, until they could get to this place. We are worn out with fatigue."[20]

In the minds of white observers, then, the horror of the revolt was wrapped up in its assault on and disruption of white families. The family was the crucial ideological unit of southern society. The ideology of family, which combined ideas about gender roles and relations with the economic and political unit of the white male–headed household, was the foundation for the public status of white men in the southern community. Family also served as a template for conceptions of mastery and submission more broadly, representing and naturalizing the paternalist quid pro quo of white male protection and provision in return for submission and obedience.[21] Nat Turner's revolt struck directly at this institution not only by revealing black men's unwillingness to play by the rules of the paternalist bargain but also by exposing the impotence of white men's promise of protection to other dependents. Moreover, the shocking violence of the revolt and the rebels' willingness to kill white women and children also demonstrated the distance between familial relationships of subordination and racial ones, undermining the familial metaphor that served to naturalize slavery as a benevolent, reciprocal, paternalist system, a domestic relationship like any other. Thus, the revolt suggested that the ideology of mastery was illusory in almost every sense and raised, as one member of the Virginia House of Delegates put it, "the suspicion that a Nat Turner might be in every family."[22]

The image of exhausted white women and children fleeing for their lives through the woods to Jerusalem dramatized these fears and elicited responses of sympathy and outrage from whites across the nation. But in order to contain the unsettling implications of such images, white Virginians simultaneously engaged in a rhetorical assault on the rebels themselves that echoed the violent retributive justice that occurred across the region. Although they lacked the theatrical eloquence of the severed head displayed at at least one rural Southampton crossroad, these printed attacks similarly denied the humanity and masculinity of the black men who had struck for their freedom and reasserted the power and status of white men.

Over and over again the rebels were referred to as "wretches," a word whose connotations of debasement and contempt in a culture devoted to masculine honor and mastery marginalized and delegitimated the rebels.[23] White writers often combined this characterization with assurances that the danger was past or that the revolt was doomed to failure: "Serious danger, of course, there is none. The deluded wretches have rushed on to assured destruction"; "The wretches who have conceived this thing are mad. . . . The ruin must return on their own heads—they must fall certain sacrifice to their own folly and infatuation"; "the further progress of these wretches has been arrested"; "several of the deluded wretches have been killed, and some taken prisoners."[24] Some reports echoed this general approach while at the same time emphasizing the effect on women and children. The *Richmond Enquirer* observed, "What strikes us as the most remarkable thing in this matter is the horrible ferocity of these monsters. They remind one of a parcel of blood-thirsty wolves rushing down from the Alps; or rather like a former incursion of the Indians upon the white settlements. Nothings is spared; neither age nor sex is respected—the helplessness of women and children pleads in vain for mercy." Nonetheless, the paper continued, "the danger is thought to be over."[25]

The white shapers of public opinion thus employed a series of images and associations that collectively served to mark the rebels as inhuman or as a particularly degraded species of humanity. (The trope of delusion evident in several of these images was also important to the white reaction to the Turner revolt and is discussed in more detail below.) As "wretches" the rebels again became slaves. As "monsters" or "wolves" they became inhuman, deformed, or animalistic. And perhaps most interestingly, as "Indians," whose apparent distinguishing characteristic was indiscriminate violence toward white women and children, the rebels became uncivilized, outside of the boundaries of society. These images expressed a negative image of "bad" slaves as threatening outsiders, in contrast to whites' idealized (and illusory) view of slaves as contented, subordinate members of white households. Moreover, by linking this constellation of images to the fate of white women and children during the revolt, the public reports emphasized the ideological contrast between white masculinity and paternalism and the aberrant, defective masculinity of the rebels.[26]

For some white commentators, these qualities marked the revolt as destructive, criminal, and mindless rather than revolutionary or transformative. The *Richmond Compiler* reported of the rebels:

> What an abandoned set of banditti these cut-throats are! Their steps are everywhere marked with the blood of women and children: An astonishing fatality seems to have attended these helpless classes. Neither infancy nor the female sex is spared in their blood-thirsty wrath! What they expected to gain; whether the brigands sought blood or plunder, how much they stole, etc., etc., seems less known, of course, than how many they murdered. . . . It is astonishing that such a parcel of wretches should have dared the murderous deeds which they have committed.[27]

Such representations denied or concealed the potential ideological impact of the revolt by linking the rebels' family-centered violence to their supposed wretchedness and by using terms like *banditti, cut-throats,* or *brigands* to impute baser motives of blood lust or theft. And as noted above, published reports reinforced this strategy of containment and sought rhetorically to restore order by combining these representations with reassurances that the rebellion was doomed to defeat, that the danger was past, and that the offenders had been captured or killed.

Even as they sought to dehumanize and delegitimate the rebels, white Virginians also sought to rehabilitate white masculinity and the promise of protection that the revolt had undermined. One of the main ways in which this proceeded in the press was in descriptions of the military operations in the aftermath of the revolt. Early news of the revolt was accompanied by reports of militia movements from nearly all of the nearby counties and cities.[28] More important than the reports of the movements themselves was their reassuring tone of confidence, competence, and self-congratulation. The *Petersburg Intelligencer* wrote, "Our friends at a distance may rest assured that we are prepared to meet any emergency. The Governor and Council have taken prompt and efficient measures to put a speedy end to the disturbance."[29] John Hampden Pleasants, himself a member of the Richmond militia, reported from Southampton that "the highest approbation is expressed of the admirable conduct and spirit of the militia, who has every where turned out with the utmost . . . , and given the most unquestioned evidence of their ability, instantly and effectually to put down every such attempt [at rebellion]."[30] The mobilization of volunteer companies and federal troops was less important militarily, since the revolt had already been turned back by local forces by the time other troops arrived, than it was psychologically and ideologically. It reassured white Virginians that the government possessed sufficient force to quell such uprisings, and it provided an ideal display of martial masculinity—of white men in their roles as agents of legitimate, disciplined violence in the face of the illegitimate, indiscriminate violence of the black men who conducted the revolt, as the protectors rather than the murderers of white women and children.

Significantly, this image of disciplined violence also countered the reality of vicious, undisciplined violence that emerged in widespread white vigilantism in the aftermath of the revolt. Peter H. Wood describes the vigilante reprisals as "a counter-terror intended to offset the panic aroused by the brutal rebellion and to shift the fear of awesome vengeance back onto the black population."[31] The imposition of military order and the curtailment of the worst excesses of white vigilantism lent legitimacy to the overall structure of white rule, at least to white minds, while still allowing the lingering message of vigilante reprisals to have its effect. Press coverage complemented this process not only by openly decrying vigilantism but also by portraying the military response in glowing terms. This praise of disciplined, martial white masculinity was a necessary counterpoint to the rhetorical assault on the rebels' masculinity in the overall attempt to rehabilitate and relegitimate white rule, just as military order was a necessary complement to vigilantism.

Some accounts addressed these issues directly, reporting instances of the gallantry, condescension, and reciprocity that were essential to the image of proper southern masculinity and mastery. A Norfolk paper recorded that "the officers of the expedition speak in the strongest terms of gratitude of the kindness and attention received from many persons on their line of march. . . . Of the generous hospitality of the beautiful little town of Smithfield they will ever cherish a lively remembrance, they cannot speak of it in measured terms."[32] An early September letter to the *Constitutional Whig* from the Southampton County seat of Jerusalem reported that "families are returning home, and opening their doors to the weary soldier as he passes, with the grateful acknowledgement for the promptness [with] which the same came to our relief." (The author completed this reassuring picture with his concluding sentence, *"We commence hanging tomorrow."*)[33] John Hampden Pleasants elaborately thanked nearly everyone involved (although he publicly excoriated a taverner who he felt had overcharged the militia men in an effort to profit from the suffering of his neighbors):

> To Gov. Floyd, South East Virginia owes a large debt of gratitude, for the prompt and silent energy with which he threw arms and men into all the supposed affected districts; and to Brig. Gen. Eppes, we tender the respects of those lately under his command, for the vigilance and fortitude with which he surmounted difficulties, arising not from the strength of the enemy, but the novelty of the situation, and the alarm and agitation of the inhabitants. To the Ladies of Southampton we want words to express the warmth of gratitude

inspirited in the breasts of the Richmond Troop, by their unremit-
ting kindness and attention.—All that the troop regrets is, that some
occasion had not offered, in which they could have manifested, by
deeds, their zeal for the public safety, and their devotion to their hospitable and amiable countrymen of Southampton.[34]

Pleasants spoke approvingly of behavior on the part of superiors that
matched masculine ideals of command and mastery, and he expressed
an elaborate condescension toward inferiors, particularly "the Ladies,"
thus enacting his part in the reciprocal relationships of paternalism.

Such a call begged for a response, and within a few weeks a notice appeared in the *Constitutional Whig:*

The Ladies of Southampton, having in a great measure recovered
from the shock, caused by the unexampled butcheries lately per-
petrated in their county, seize the earliest opportunity of returning
their thanks to the different volunteer companies throughout our
State, and sister State North Carolina, who gallantly came forward
to defend them. . . . They will ever cherish the most lively gratitude
for their services.[35]

It is perhaps significant that this notice did not appear until more than
a month after the revolt, and several weeks after Pleasants's statements.
"The Ladies of Southampton" may have delayed performing their public
role until the panic spawned by the revolt had subsided and they were
finally able to return to their homes, thereby ensuring that the other side
of the bargain had been restored. Nonetheless, in making such gracious
acknowledgment they enacted a ritual of willing, grateful submission to
white male protection and authority that was vital to the reconstruction
of white manhood in the aftermath of the revolt. Such moments helped
to restore a sense of white masculinity and of the coherence of the ideal
of mastery that the rebels' concerted assault had threatened. Indeed,
there is some indication that white men had an interest in portraying
the panic itself as more of a female affair, which would serve multiple
purposes: it would reinforce their own role as protector, deny or down-
play their own fears, and dismiss the panic of the revolt as overstated,
as something that women feared but that men felt they could handle.
The *Lynchburg Virginian,* for example, published a letter from South-

ampton to gentleman in Richmond dated September 4 stating, "We expected you would be a little ineasy about us, from the many rumors that were abroad in the land. It came upon us as unexpectedly as anything possibly could, and produced a pretty general panic, especially among the females."[36]

While the relationship between white men and white women was crucial to the ideological underpinnings of mastery, it was also only one of the intertwined relationships challenged by the Turner revolt, and not necessarily the most significant. For the reconstitution of white male mastery to be complete, the analogy between the different relationships of familial and racial subordination had to be restored. Just as white women appeared in the press acknowledging their gratitude for the protection of the region's white men, stories of the loyalty of African American slaves appeared that served to highlight the aberrance of the rebels' behavior and to reconfirm in white minds blacks' willing participation in the paternalist bargain of slavery.

The most prominent of these stories was the defense of Simon Blunt's house on the morning of August 23, in the waning stages of the rebellion. According to newspaper reports, Blunt, "who was very unwell with gout" and unable to flee his home when reports of danger arrived, armed himself, his son, his overseer, several white neighbors, and his slaves and repelled an attack by the remnants of Turner's force. In the narrative of the revolt that developed, this vigorous defense, conducted by loyal slaves against bloodthirsty but cowardly rebels, marked the final battle of the rebellion, with several of Turner's remaining band killed or captured.[37] This incident not only illustrated to white commentators the courage of Blunt and his family—one newspaper recommended Blunt's son, "a lad about 15, distinguished for his gallantry and modesty," to "Gen. Jackson, for a warrant in the Navy or at West Point"[38]—but also provided the opportunity to reflect on the meaning of slaves' loyalty. According to white observers, Blunt's slaves, "who nobly and gallantly stood by him," exemplified the larger allegiance of the vast majority of enslaved African Americans. Many slaves, "whom gratitude had bound to their masters," assisted in quelling the rebellion. Throughout the county, "a fine spirit had been shown in many of the plantations of confidence on the part of the masters, and gratitude on that of the slaves."[39]

It is especially telling that this white version of the story differs significantly from Turner's own account in the *Confessions*. Turner placed far less weight on the incident at Blunt's and did not mention slaves defending the house. Turner stated that his men fired on the Blunt house to see if anyone was there—expecting it to be deserted—and that when their fire was returned, they retreated. He mentioned that he left several men behind and that he did not see those men again.[40] Despite claims for its significance, the narrative built up around the confrontation at Blunt's in the white press had less to do with its military importance than with its potential as an ideological set piece. The story of the defense of Simon Blunt's house emphasized the reciprocal relationship between the bravery and confidence of masters and the gratitude and loyalty of slaves and, in the figure of Blunt's son, infused this relationship with the overtones of the white household and family (and of course also hierarchy—no one suggested recommending any of the Blunt family slaves to West Point).

Despite such attempts to limit the revolt's implications and present a picture of powerful, functional white paternalism in the wake of the revolt, serious tensions remained. Not only did lingering doubts about the security of the white family and the sufficiency of white male protection find expression in a variety of social, cultural, and political arenas, including the debates of the Virginia House of Delegates the following winter, but aspects of the martial reconstruction of white male authority were unstable even on their own terms. One Southamptonite, for instance, testily remarked that "there is one idea gone abroad, in relation to the occurrences here, which I think deserves correction." Public reports of the revolt could "produce the impression that the people of this county, unaided, would not have been able to put down the insurrection." This correspondent insisted that while he was grateful to the citizens of other counties for their prompt aid and concern, "it is due to truth as well as the just confidence which the people of every county ought to feel in themselves, to state that the insurrection was effectually and completely suppressed by the citizens of this county."[41] Some aspects of the military mobilization, self-congratulation, and ritualized courtesies that helped reaffirm white Virginians' faith in the paternalist bargain thus threatened to undermine the authority of local masters.

Such issues of territorial precedence and military credit played out on a larger stage as well. Virginia Governor John Floyd, for instance, reacted with displeasure when he was informed that the mayor of Norfolk had called on the assistance of federal forces stationed there. "I felt reluctant to ask of the United States that which we could so easily do ourselves," Floyd explained. Using unnecessary force would actually increase the public's and the slaves' perceptions of the state's vulnerability, he argued. If federal troops were needed to quell this uprising, "it is not difficult to perceive the train of thought which would be indulged, should the United States at any future day have use for their forces in the prosecution of a foreign war."[42] Assessing the seriousness of the threat and assigning credit for its suppression were delicate ideological acts that simultaneously had to balance the claims of regional and local forces without discrediting either one—allowing everyone to have "the just confidence which the people of every county ought to feel in themselves."

Similar issues bedeviled attempts to formulate a program of policing the slave population in order to prevent future uprisings. One commentator, possibly Thomas R. Gray, argued uneasily that mercy, scrupulous justice, and discretion in the use of force, rather than massive force or violent retribution, were the best means for restoring order and expressing white male authority. "It becomes us as men to return to our duty," he wrote. "Without manifesting a fear of the blacks, by keeping a stationed armed force in any section of our country, let us adopt a more efficient plan, by keeping up for some time, a regular patrol, always under the command of some discreet person, who will not by indiscriminate punishment, goad these miserable wretches into a state of desperation."[43] This statement reveals the fears that lay behind such arguments: fear of the black population and a paradoxical fear that showing fear would increase the danger. Mirroring the larger dynamic of white reaction, this author sought to contain the resulting anxieties within a conception of dutiful, confident, competent white masculinity and degraded, desperate black manhood.

The gendered and familial nature of the rebellion's violence constituted, intentionally or not, a wide-ranging attack on the ideal of white mastery and provoked an equally wide-ranging reaction by whites intent on shoring up that ideal. Other overt or subliminal ideological challenges met with similarly complex responses of containment and denial from white authorities. The rebellion's relationship to the ideas and values of the American Revolution became a crucial point of contention in the fall and winter of 1831–32. A great deal of this discussion came from white commentators, who sought either to criticize or to defend the revolt and, more importantly, the South's racial and political outlook and the system of slavery itself. Northern abolitionists took the occasion of the uprising to reflect on the injustice and danger inherent in slave society and highlighted its inconsistency with the democratic and egalitarian values associated with the Revolution. Southern spokesmen took issue with these attacks and developed a defense of southern institutions that criticized abolitionist interpretations of Revolutionary principles as "inapplicable and mischievous," asserting instead southerners' rights of property and self-determination.[44]

In an address to the Virginia legislature, Governor Floyd suggested that the uprising had in fact been sparked by "unrestrained fanatics in some of the neighboring States" who circulated "inflammatory papers and pamphlets . . . amongst our slaves."[45] William Lloyd Garrison's *Liberator* and David Walker's *Appeal to the Colored Citizens of the World* were, respectively, the most prominent paper and pamphlet that Floyd had in mind, and in taking aim at them he sought to defuse and delegitimate the connections their writers drew between Revolutionary ideals of natural rights, including the right to rebellion, and slavery.[46] Thus, Turner's uprising provided the occasion for an open ideological clash between emergent abolitionist and proslavery interpretations of the legacy and significance of the Revolution.

But there is also evidence that the rebels themselves, and other slaves who knew about the revolt but did not participate in it, made associations between Turner's uprising and the Revolutionary era that differed strongly from those of their white neighbors. And these associations seem to have been rooted at least as much in the particular experience of southeastern Virginia during the Revolution as in later, nineteenth-century abolitionist texts, suggesting that an ongoing, independent African American memory and interpretation of the Revolution played a significant role in the rebellion. Turner himself claimed that he had originally planned the uprising for the Fourth of July 1831 but that illness and indecision had delayed its execution.[47] It seems likely that the initial choice of July 4 was intentional, although its meaning is not altogether straightforward. Did Turner intend it as an appropriation of American independence by enslaved African Americans—seizing hold of the Revolutionary promise of freedom? Or did he choose the date as a direct assault on the values of the slaveholding society he sought to overthrow, an effort to efface the white celebration of freedom altogether? Perhaps it was both.[48] In any case, the rebellion did not begin until August, and the July 4 reference appears as a brief mention in the *Confessions*, which suggests that Turner wanted readers to make a connection despite the uprising's actual date.

There are also hints that another, perhaps more significant, subversive interpretation of the Revolutionary legacy circulated among Southampton slaves before and during the revolt. Several accounts, including the testimony of one black witness at the trial of one of the rebels, imply a parallel between the rebellion and the British occupation of southeastern Virginia during the Revolution. An article in the *Norfolk Herald* written after Nat Turner's capture reported that Turner had claimed that his prophetic visions had led him "to believe that he could succeed in conquoring *the county of Southampton* (what miserable ignorance!) as the white people did in the revolution."[49] Similarly, an account in the *Liberator* from a northern observer in Norfolk and Richmond during the rebellion and its aftermath observed that "it appears that the negro children had been taught to repeat that the British, or some other foe, were coming to Virginia to massacre all the white people: for some time before the insurrection, they had often been overheard repeating such a story to each other. Many blacks not particularly concerned in the rebellion, and living quite remote from the scene, have been apprehended for uttering similar predictions."[50]

The significance of these rumors, and their meaning for at least some of the rebels, was suggested at the trial of Hardy, a slave implicated in the uprising. At the trial a slave named Harry testified that he "heard at Mr. Jones' that the English were in the County killing white people, that he told [this] to [the] prisoner [Hardy] & Berry Newsom—prisoner made light of it and said it was nothing and ought to have been done long ago—that the negroes had been punished long enough."[51] These few hints suggest that the Revolution represented something very different for many blacks in southeastern Virginia than it did for either their white neighbors or northern abolitionists, not virtuous republican government, self-determination, or even Jefferson's equivocal declaration of equality but something far less abstract that drew on the actual experience of the Revolution in the region: war against white slave owners.

Thus, while the Revolution had come to symbolize self-determination and virtuous, independent white male government for the white population of Virginia, the Southampton rebels' use of the Revolution served as a reminder of the racial divisiveness and destruction that the war had visited on the region. That this memory of the Revolution could resurface among African Americans two generations after the conflict itself suggests just how deeply the conflict affected the black community and how deeply their understanding of the Revolution diverged from that of their white neighbors. Even as white Virginians fought off the challenge of northern abolitionist interpretations of the Revolution in the context of the Turner rebellion, they had to suppress a more fundamental challenge much closer to home.

The main way in which white Virginians sought to defuse the multiple challenges of the Turner rebellion was to focus on the figure of Nat Turner as a religious fanatic. For the most part, focusing on Turner himself and his religious motivations helped assure white southerners that the rebellion had not been widespread and that its ideological significance did not extend beyond Turner's supposed delusions and his ability to gain influence over his followers. This became the primary narrative of the revolt, shaped by newspaper reports and especially by Gray's publication of *The Confessions of Nat Turner*, which detailed Turner's religious visions and his belief that he had been chosen to lead a war of retribution against the whites. But this narrative did not succeed entirely in quieting white anxieties. It did not completely suppress other interpretations of the revolt, as many interested observers, including Governor Floyd, continued to suspect that the initial conspiracy had extended far beyond Turner and his six associates; in fact religion and the influence of black preachers was one of the main grounds on which these suspicions of a more extensive conspiracy rested. Moreover, for Baptists and other evangelicals, both the focus on Nat Turner and the larger concern about black religion proved troubling. As white accounts of the revolt came to emphasize issues of religion and fanaticism and articulated defensive interpretations of the gendered and Revolutionary dimensions of the revolt, Baptists had to deal not only with the difficult implications of the rebellion itself but also with the tenor of the larger white reaction.

Early hints of Turner's role emerged in the days following the rebellion but were not published or widely known until the end of the week. On August 27 the *Richmond Compiler* published an August 24 letter to Governor Floyd from Brigadier General Richard Eppes, of Sussex County, naming "General Nat Turner (a preacher and a slave)" as one of the leaders of the revolt; and on August 29 a Norfolk paper published an August 25 letter "from a gentleman attached to the Richmond Cavalry" reporting that "one of the ring leaders who is mortally wounded and will probably die tonight . . . says the insurrection was urged and headed by a black preacher, who is not yet taken."[52] "Who is this Nat Turner?" asked the *Compiler,* reflecting both the public's curiosity about the origins of the revolt and the gradual personalization of the white interpretation of those origins, "Where is he from?"[53] As Turner's role became widely publicized, attention increasingly concentrated on his background and personality, particularly his status as a preacher and "fanatic." The *Richmond Enquirer* wrote that Turner "had been taught to read and write, and permitted to go about preaching in the country. . . . He was artful, impudent and vindicative without any cause or provocation, that could be assigned." Instead, his motivations were wrapped in his (deluded or feigned) religious beliefs. "Nat . . . pretends to be a Baptist preacher—a great enthusiast" and "declares to his comrades that he is comissioned by Jesus Christ, and proceeds under his inspired direction," claiming "that the late singular appearance of the sun was the sign for him."[54]

Other observers concurred in this judgment of Turner's central role and his motivation. John Hampden Pleasants recorded his impression "that [the rebels] acted under the influence of their leader, Nat, a preacher and a prophet among them; that even he had no ulterior purpose, but was stimulated exclusively by fanatical revenge, and perhaps misled by some hallucination of his imagined spirit of prophecy."[55] By construing Turner's motivations in this way, newspaper accounts continued their earlier pattern of depicting the revolt as the result of what they saw as madness or infatuation, thus attempting to contain its implications within a relatively narrow sphere, limited at its most extreme to the delusions of one particular individual.

Following immediately on the heels of Turner's capture and execution in the early weeks of November, Gray's publication of the *Confessions* largely worked toward similar ends. Gray's pamphlet, like the newspaper accounts, attempted to establish Turner's fanaticism and to attribute the revolt to that fanaticism. As noted earlier, Seymour L. Gross and Eileen Bender argue that Gray's emphasis on Turner's religious visions represented an attempt on Gray's part to construct a narrative that was psychologically reassuring to white readers. By understanding Turner's motivation as religious madness, they argue, white readers did not have to implicate themselves or the system of slavery in the horrors of the rebellion.[56] Although this was almost certainly Gray's intent, we should not so readily dismiss the religious aspects of the *Confessions* or take for granted the success of his (and other whites') efforts to contain the implications of the revolt.

The literary scholar Eric J. Sundquist argues persuasively that Turner exercised a complex but significant degree of control over the *Confessions* despite Gray's attempts to shape the reader's reactions and interpretation. In Sundquist's view, the trope of fanaticism served, not to obscure Turner's original motivations entirely, but rather to "mediate intentions or emotions that hid in plain sight, as it were, and were constituted less by concealment than by the master's misunderstanding." Thus, Turner "submitted to Gray's objectification while at the same time donning it as a mask, achieving by contrast his own dynamic and articulate subjectivity."[57] In short, Turner represented his visions and motivations more or less accurately, knowing that Gray and his white audience would misinterpret them as deluded fanaticism. The account of Turner's religious beliefs and motivation in the *Confessions* should be seen as largely Turner's own creation, operating in the text much as it did in "historical reality," combining African and American/Christian "spirituality and ideology" to assert an underlying demand for and justification of freedom.[58]

Several scenes in the *Confessions* illustrate this process. When Gray pressed Turner on his denial of any connection to a plot in North Carolina that followed the Southampton uprising, Turner responded, "Can you not think the same ideas, and strange appearances about this time in the heaven's might prompt others, as well as myself, to this undertaking."[59] On one level, Turner's reply fit with Gray's vision of him as a fanatic and as the sole cause of the revolt. Turner denied any connection with other real or rumored unrest and referred to the supernatural signs that had spurred him to action, the mark of his delusion. But Turner's response also undermined Gray's efforts to isolate and confine the meaning of the rebellion; it asserted that both the power of religious inspiration and the desire for freedom were universal and that Turner was not, in fact, an isolated fanatic but rather one of many who would bear similar witness against slavery. Indeed, Turner's success in recruiting dozens of supporters in his home counties and, if white fears are to be counted (and in this case they should be, since it is white confidence and sense of implication that are at issue), hundreds more across the state suggests just how ineffective white efforts to contain the revolt within Turner's own religious vision were. That vision clearly resonated with his fellow bondsmen regardless of what men like Gray thought of it, and other whites confronted this issue directly.

Just as Turner succeeded in communicating his own ideas via Gray's text, alternative interpretations of the revolt worked their way into the broader discourse of the rebellion's origins in Turner's fanaticism. Evidence surrounding the revolt suggested that religion and religious networks beyond Turner's own beliefs had played an important role in organizing the uprising. Although the official verdict on the revolt echoed Gray's conclusion that the uprising had been limited to a small area and had its origins in Turner's personal religious delusions, both the evidence itself and the range of white responses to the revolt made this conclusion less than persuasive even at the time. The initial suspicions of many observers about the causes of the revolt indicate the degree to which African American religion was suspect in many whites' eyes. One report, which proved inaccurate in nearly every dimension, claimed, "I have been diligent in my inquiries to obtain information that can be relied on. The result is, about 250 negroes from a Camp Meeting about the Dismal Swamp, set out on a marauding excursion, and have, for the sake of plunder, murdered about 60 persons."[60] John Hampden Pleasants similarly reported that "the prevalent belief is, that on Sunday week last, at Barnes' Church in the neighborhood of the Cross Keys, the negroes who were observed to be disorderly, took offence at something; (it is not known what) that the plan of insurrection was then and there conceived."[61] This account had a bit more substance to it, since Benjamin and Samuel Turner, Nat's former masters, had been devout Methodists and Nat most likely had attended Barnes' Methodist Church on occasion.[62] But both suggestions highlight the fact that whites suspected black religious activity of rebellious tendencies.

These suspicions had the weight of experience behind them—both Gabriel's Rebellion around Richmond and the Denmark Vesey plot in South Carolina had drawn on religious networks and religious ideology to recruit and organize participants.[63] This was exactly what Governor Floyd suspected to be the case in Southampton. Floyd claimed that black preachers in Virginia, inspired by northern abolitionist propaganda, had organized and conducted the revolt. "I am fully convinced," he wrote, "that every black preacher in the whole country east of the Blue Ridge was in [on] the secret" and that "head men in the Church" had inspired their congregations to join the rebellion.[64]

Newspaper reports reflected a similar concern on the part of other white Virginians and suggested that black religion, both independent and attached to white-controlled churches, contributed to the Turner rebellion. Whether or not all of these reports were entirely accurate, their plausibility to whites suggested that Nat Turner's personal religious vision had a context and a system of institutional support that the most extreme "fanaticism" interpretation of Gray and others discounted. In the first week of September, for instance, the *Richmond Enquirer* reported that "not the slightest circumstance has transpired, unless it be the arrest in New Kent of a slave from Prince George, who said that he had been carrying dispatches (verbal message) *through* a black preacher in P. George to the opposite side of the river—which dispatches were said to come from another black preacher below."[65] Several weeks later, covering the trials of alleged rebels in surrounding counties, the paper mentioned that one slave in Nansemond had been sentenced to death: "It was said that *he* was present of the blacks; at which a black preacher (from the Isle of Wight or Surrey) had asked such as were willing to join, to hold up their hands—this fellow was identified as one of those who held up their hands." The same report recorded the fate of the preacher in Prince George, who was also sentenced to death.[66]

If these accounts were not disturbing enough for Baptists in Isle of Wight, Southampton, and Sussex, the testimony of one witness placed responsibility for the rebellion at their very doorsteps. A young woman named Beck, who was owned by Solomon Parker, testified "that she has heard the subject discoursed about among her master's slaves, and some of the neighboring ones, for the last eighteen months: and that at a meeting held at Racoon meeting-house, in May and August last, some eight or ten expressed their determination to unite in the scheme." The woman's testimony was not supported by anyone else, and after her first round of testimony the slaves she named were acquitted, given the rules of evidence used in the trials. The white correspondent who reported on the trials interpreted this to mean "that we have, as yet, had no sufficient reason to believe that there was a 'concert or general plan' among the Blacks. I have no doubt, however, that the subject has been pretty generally discussed among them, and the minds of many prepared to cooperate in the design."[67] This suspicion gained more credibility several days later, when the same correspondent sent word that "there had been three convictions since the date of my letter, upon the evidence of the girl of Solomon Parker, who had been previously repudiated by the Court. If her tale was true, the plot was more extensive than we had previously believed."[68] The prospect that slaves at Raccoon Swamp had been actively discussing the rebellion and may have "determin[ed] to unite in the scheme" shook the white members of the church and its sister churches throughout southeastern Virginia. Only one black church member, a free member of Raccoon Swamp named Will Archer, was excommunicated for participation in the revolt, but the implication that knowledge of the revolt, as well as the dissatisfaction that contributed to it and the actual recruitment of participants, existed within Baptist congregations fundamentally challenged both white Baptists' vision of fellowship with blacks and their vision of the place of their religion in southern society.[69]

Part of the problem was that these issues were never fully resolved. Many whites who initially believed Beck's testimony later repudiated it, claiming that their own prejudices and fears had caused them to be uncritical.[70] Ultimately the hints at a wider religious network remained inconclusive and problematic, and they were never developed into a compelling or reliable picture of a larger conspiracy. As a result, white Virginians themselves remained divided and inconsistent on the question of the rebellion's larger implications and underlying causes, and this left Baptists and other evangelicals of both races vulnerable to suspicion but unable to respond in a definitive manner. Whether such connections existed at all, and what their nature was if they did, remained the subject of speculation, driven more by commentators' own preconceptions and agendas than by actual evidence. Opened-ended religious debate flourished in this context.

White Baptists in the region faced considerable criticism from other white commentators on the revolt. Despite their long history of fostering Christian ideas of household order, family religion, and due submis-

sion to authority, the idea that evangelical Christianity fostered rebelliousness in slaves, promoting inappropriate ideas of equality and justice, re-
gained currency in the months after the uprising. Many of these criticisms
had enough basis in the denomination's history in southeastern Virginia
to sting all the more. S. B. Emmons, who reported on the rebellion itself
and on the local reaction for William Lloyd Garrison's *Liberator,* claimed
that "at Richmond, the whites were heard cursing the Quakers or Baptists, whom they declared would ruin the State."[71] More directly, the influential September 26 account of the revolt in the *Constitutional Whig,*
which some historians attribute to Thomas R. Gray, criticized white evangelicals both for allowing blacks to preach without sufficient supervision
and for their own "misguided" message to blacks. The author argued that,
unlike the free black population of Saint Domingue, Virginia's black population was too ignorant and uneducated to present any real danger of
concerted collective rebellion. The only danger of such organization came
from religion:

> But if any desire there was to increase this spirit [of rebellion]
> among our slaves, I would advise our citizens, to permit coloured
> preachers to go on, as they have for several years past haranging vast
> crowds, when and where they pleased, the character of their sermons
> known only to their congregations—Nor do I think some of our
> white brethren, exempt from censure, when they fill their discourses
> with a ranting cant about equality.—If our insurrection was known,
> beyond the neighborhood of its commencement—its cause must be
> attributed to the misguided zeal of good men, preaching up equal-
> ity; and to ignorant blacks, who again retail the same doctrine, with
> such comments as their heated imaginations may supply, to their
> respective circles of acquaintance.—For my own part, I think when a
> minister goes into a pulpit, flies into a passion, beats his fist, and in
> fine plays the bloackhead, that he gives a warrant to any negro who
> hears him, to do whatever he pleases provided his imagination, can
> make God sanction it. . . .
>
> But I would caution all missionaries, who are bettering the condi-
> tion of the world, and all philanthropists, who have our interest so
> much at stake, not to plague themselves about our slaves but leave
> them exclusively to our own management.
>
> Our insurrection[,] general, or not, was the work of fanaticism.[72]

Even though this author rejected the possibility of a general insurrection—"they are ignorant who believe in the possibility of such a thing"— a tension existed between his dismissal of the revolt as fanaticism and his concern that religion could serve as both an ideology and an institutional framework of rebellion.[73] This same tension ran through the overall white response. Distinguishing fanaticism from religion more generally was a difficult task, made more difficult by the different interests at play in the aftermath of the revolt. As the reactions of the *Constitutional Whig* correspondent and Governor Floyd suggest, fanaticism and delusion were not the end of the story even for those who wished they were.

White Baptists and other religious spokesmen thus faced manifold challenges when they entered the discussion of the Southampton revolt. Not only did they have to face the evidence that their black brethren might have participated in, known about, or sympathized with the revolt but they also had to confront the public suggestions of their unwitting complicity in the rebellion. These religious spokesmen also participated in the discourse of fanaticism and delusion, but they sought to be more rigorous in distinguishing between these aberrant forms and proper religious activity. Indeed, this distinction was crucial in creating and maintaining distance between the religious background of the revolt and the religious world of white evangelicals that had gradually gained legitimacy over the past decades. Commentators like Pleasants, Gray, and Floyd allowed some degree of ambiguity in considering the extent to which Turner's fanaticism intersected with the more general religious world of southeastern Virginia, but those who felt more implicated by such associations could not afford to do so.

At the core of this challenge was the undeniable fact that Turner, his style of leadership, and his language of righteousness and divine justice really did emerge to a significant degree out of the evangelical culture that had evolved in southeastern Virginia over the course of the revolutionary and early national eras. His interpretation of evangelical discourses was undeniably personal and unique in its violent, messianic nature, but important aspects of it also had real parallels and precedents in the movement's history. From the aggressive language of liberty invoked by David Thomas against a hostile religious establishment to David Barrow's and John Lankford's anti-slavery interpretations of Baptist values, evangelical ideals had persistently provided the basis for profound critiques of worldly hierarchies and injustices. Even though white church members repudiated certain applications of these ideas or qualified them to the point of irrelevance, the development of increasingly independent black evangelical communities in the nineteenth century provided fertile ground for alternative interpretations. None of this is to deny the unique and exceptional quality of Turner's vision or even the possibility that he was truly insane, but it clearly suggests that white evangelicals had good reason to feel implicated in the revolt.

Turner's religious biography placed him in a class of frustrated black spiritual virtuosi like the unauthorized preachers Tom and York. He had become fluent in evangelical ideas and vocabularies in biracial churches and religious households, and he cultivated his own leadership and his own interpretations of those ideas and vocabularies along the margins of the black communities attached to evangelical churches. But like Tom and York, Turner found his claims of divine inspiration and religious authority checked by skeptical white authority figures. His own account of converting Etheldred T. Brantley and then being "baptised by the Spirit" with him while the white church that had rejected and "reviled" them looked on suggests pride in his spiritual authority's overcoming racial boundaries and institutional limitations, an evangelical trope that reached back at least as far as Samuel Davies. Similarly, his separation from other slaves and his purposeful abstemiousness suggest that he may have been crafting his own version of evangelical masculine leadership to underscore his spiritual power. Like white evangelical preachers of an earlier generation, Turner attempted to transmute his many experiences of rejection into heroic masculine leadership. In constructing his own leadership as divinely inspired while denying the authority of white-controlled churches, Turner upset the delicate balance white evangelicals sought to maintain between unfettered access to spiritual authority and the communal regulation of that authority. Further, in ignoring the formalities of church governance, he was also rejecting the paternal oversight of white male evangelical leaders. The possibility that Turner's co-conspirators Hark Travis, Will Francis, and Henry Porter were also preachers suggests that this pattern may not have been unique among the rebels.[74]

In response, white evangelicals sought to discredit Turner and ciate white religion from the revolt by deploying many of the sa of authenticity and legitimacy that had originally been used dissenters in Virginia. One such commentator defensively a almost circular fashion, that religion could not have contributed to the revolt, because true religion would not produce such effects:

> It has been said by some (in consequence, I presume, of the leader of this murderous banditti calling himself a Prophet, and pretending to receive immediate revelations from Heaven,) that it proceeded from what is called religious fanaticism. But let such persons be assured, that it was in consequence of the absence of all religious feeling, and the leader of this banditti and his associates being given up to the natural lusts and passions of their depraved and wicked hearts, that produced the dreadful atrocities of which they were guilty. True religion has its seat in the heart, and has the effect of subduing all these horrid, natural passions and inclinations, and producing in the place of them, love to God and love to man, a sincere, heart-felt desire to do all the good we can to our fellow-creatures. Where these fruits are not produced, there is no religion.[75]

This commentator, who styled himself "Old Virginia," took the religion out of "religious fanaticism." Instead of true religion, which white evangelicals insisted could only produce harmony and peace in households, families, and communities, Old Virginia laid the blame for the revolt on the promotion of emancipation by northern abolitionists and the Colonization Society. No mention was made of evangelicalism's own complex history in this regard.

Another commentator took up a more specific issue in the coverage of the uprising. A letter from a Southampton resident "to a gentleman in Richmond" excerpted in the *Lynchburg Virginian* complained that "this fellow [Turner] is very improperly represented to be a Baptist preacher. I wish you to see the Editors of your paper on the subject, and say to them that that account, from the best information I can obtain, is an entire mistake."[76] This correspondent reflected Baptists' more general concern to determine, as best they could, that none of the rebels was a member of their denomination. In its circular letter on the revolt, for instance, the Portsmouth Association declared that "we believe none of them were Baptists," despite the imprisonment of William Archer and the suggestion that blacks at Raccoon Swamp discussed the revolt.[77]

Baptists accomplished this distancing move in part by focusing on the formal requirements and rituals of membership and licensing. The

Southampton writer pointed out that Turner "never was a member of the Baptist, or any other Church; he assumed the character of his own accord, and has been for several years one of those fanatical scoundrels, that pretended to be divinely inspired; of bad character, and never countenanced except by a few of his deluded black associates."[78] By emphasizing the institutional measures of Baptist faith and adherence, such commentary also emphasized a particular white, largely male view of what it meant to be a Baptist. As in the expulsion of Jonathan Lankford at Black Creek and the regulation of black preaching at South Quay, white church members used their control of church government to mark certain interpretations of the evangelical message and certain religious activities as illegitimate, as being outside of the circle of sanctioned Baptist activities. This dynamic of Baptist life made it possible for spokesmen to assert more or less truthfully that none of the rebels were Baptists, at least in the sense that they considered most important. This claim could then function more generally to distance white Baptists and their faith from the revolt in the face of evidence of significant associations between Turner's uprising and less official forms of evangelical and Baptist belief and community.

White Baptists similarly used their control over their denomination's institutional life in dealing with the implications of the revolt for the internal dynamic of their churches and communities. In addition to their potential threat to the public image of the denomination, Turner's status as a religious visionary and preacher and the implication of religious networks in the revolt deeply challenged evangelicals' ideal of harmonious Christian fellowship between blacks and whites in a society dedicated to racial slavery. Among Baptists in southeastern Virginia this challenge prompted white church members to take steps to resolve existing tensions in church practice and exercise an even greater degree of control over black members' participation in and experience of the church community in the decade following Turner's rebellion. Working through the key institutions and rituals of Baptist life, most notably baptism, communion, and discipline, white church members distanced themselves not only from the Turner rebellion but also from their black brethren. While the tensions between black and white religion, and more generally between an evolving authorized orthodoxy and all other interpretations, in the Baptist churches of southeastern Virginia were not new, the aftermath of the Turner uprising increased the separation between black and white religious worlds in the region and reaffirmed white male control of the churches.

The immediate reaction of the churches varied, but Black Creek's reaction reflected the way in which the event went to the heart of the rituals of biracial fellowship. In the immediate aftermath of the August 22 revolt, the church in September "agreed that the sacrement be Postponed in consequence of the unpleasant feeling the white Brethren have towards the black Brethren."[79] Similar suspensions of communion occurred at Mill Swamp and Raccoon Swamp.[80] When communion resumed at Mill Swamp almost a year later, the church instituted a change in its administration: "Resolved that the coloured members of this Church at all future times of communion seat themselves in that part of the house that they now occupy, and that the present Deacons carry the bread and wine and deliver it to one of the Black members who shall distribute to the balance."[81] Even this did not satisfy all of the church's white members; at the same meeting Matthew Cofer requested "liberty to withdraw from the Church," and nine other members followed suit. At the next meeting it became clear that these men had left the church because they "do not fellowship the Colured members of this Church." It took more than a year for the church to reconcile the dispute.[82] In the immediate aftermath of the rebellion the coherence of the church community and the rituals that embodied and sustained it dissolved in the face of such pervasive "unpleasant feeling."

In their reports to the Portsmouth Association in 1832 churches across the region noted again and again the "painful dissatisfaction" the white members felt toward their black brethren. Clearly, white members felt that the insurrection had revealed a potentially explosive divergence between their interpretation of the evangelical message and that of their black co-religionists despite the public efforts to distance the denomination from the revolt. In its annual letter to member churches the association reflected these complaints and took a grim view of the future of the biracial religious community that had existed in the churches:

> The high character of godliness claimed by many of the insurgents, and the extensive religious influence they actually possessed, (though we believe none of them were Baptists,) have destroyed,

with many of our Brethren, all confidence in the professions of that class of persons. . . . Some Churches have complained to the Association, that since the insurrection, the great body of their coloured members have constantly exhibited a most rebellious and ungovernable disposition, and which, wherever it has existed, has resulted in the worst consequences. Whether in those Churches a union can ever be restored between our white and coloured members, or whether they must be separated entirely, and continue to exercise toward each other no feelings of fraternity or communion, are questions which can be decided only by the great Head of the Church.[83]

Like the churches' suspensions of communion, the Portsmouth Association's letter indicated that the Turner rebellion had broken the bonds of fellowship linking black and white Baptists in the region. White church members were no longer confident that the shared language of the church—the rituals of baptism, communion, and discipline and the spiritually and socially charged concepts of fellowship, gospel order, and liberty—carried the same meanings for African Americans that it did for them. The interpretability of Baptist language and practice that had been the basis of biracial fellowship had reached the breaking point. The association's dismay at the Southampton rebels' "high character of godliness" and "extensive religious influence" caused it to question the very possibility of fellowship across racial lines.

But the Portsmouth Association and its member churches across southeastern Virginia still sought to reconstruct that community through the deployment and restructuring of Baptist rituals in ways that would solidify white control over the churches and inscribe racial hierarchies more firmly in religious practice. In doing so, the churches built on the trends toward segregation and white oversight that had been developing piecemeal in the early nineteenth century. In the aftermath of the Turner rebellion, however, these trends gained momentum and an overt sense of purpose. The Portsmouth Association recommended that each of its churches appoint a meeting at which all of its black members would "undergo examination and receive instruction in relation to Church Government and their duty to their owners, and in case they refuse the instruction and government of the Church, the Association advises that they shall be expelled."[84] Even before the association gave this general advice, most of the churches had summarily suspended all of their black members for the purpose of investigating their attitudes toward, and conduct during, the rebellion. At Tucker's Swamp, for instance, the church launched a full-scale inquiry "into the state and standing of our Coloured Members . . . and also Request their owners (if expedient) to Give the Church information should they know them Gilty of any immoral Conduct."[85] Over the next year or so black members were readmitted to the churches, but the membership rolls had been purged of any members whose behavior was in any way suspect. Church discipline strictly exercised by white members was thus a crucial step in restoring fellowship between black and white Baptists, and it did so on much narrower terms than before the rebellion. While there was never room for outright rejection of church government, the ability to challenge and question the decisions of the church, as the black members of Black Creek had in 1822 or as Abel of Harrison had at South Quay in 1830, was severely restricted after 1831.

The Portsmouth Association also recommended that its churches definitively close off other potential avenues by which African American Baptists could assert their own interpretations of fellowship and liberty. Nat Turner's reputed status as a preacher, one who claimed to have baptized himself and a white man, had intensified white Virginians' suspicion of black preachers. Echoing the actions taken by the state legislature, the association advised its churches "to refuse license to coloured persons to preach, and to interdict their holding meetings."[86] While regulating black preaching had clearly been a concern for white church members in the years before the revolt, the institution of a blanket prohibition changed the terms of the relationship between the white-controlled church and its black members. In the past, African American men theoretically had had the same access to religious authority and the same status as fit mouthpieces for God's word as white men, and their preaching had been judged, again theoretically, based on its effectiveness and orderliness. By making race a defining factor in determining who had liberty to preach, the churches drew a stronger distinction between white and black members and their access to God's word than had existed before the revolt.

At the same time, white church members continued their pre-rebellion trends toward separate meetings and white oversight of black members' participation in the church, and they increasingly sought to direct the interpretation of the religious messages that black members heard toward obedience and submission. In 1832 Raccoon Swamp appointed several white members to serve "for a Patrool, to preserve Or[der among] the B[lack members] at our Aug't Meeting." South Quay appointed "the 3rd Lords day in April [1833] . . . for the purpose of Lecturing and admonishing the Colour'd members." This process of "lecturing and admonishing" became a regular feature of church meetings for black Baptists in the decades after 1831. At a separate conference for black members at Black Creek in 1841, for instance, the white moderator "[gave] them a charge respecting their duty to their God, to the church and to their owners."[87]

The reconfiguration of church practices affected even the most basic rituals of community and fellowship. A baptism at the recently formed church in the town of Smithfield illustrates how that ritual was changed to reflect slaves' subordinate social status as much as their spiritual equality. After "Sam (a man of Colour)" and "Sarah of Soloman Pastures" recounted their experience of grace, the church gathered by the waterside, and Sam and Sarah, "each prepared for the ordinance and presenting to the Minister letters from their several earthly Masters, giving consent, they were duly Baptised."[88] An 1841 scene at South Quay presents the effects of this change in practice even more dramatically: "Aesop a servant of the Hon. Richd. H. Bakers presented a note from his master granting his consent and recommending him to this church. Whereupon he related an experience of Grace and was received for baptism and on the next sabbath morning was baptised and received in full fellowship by the Church."[89] Although the church considered Aesop "in full fellowship," it was his owner's permission and recommendation that took priority, over even the experience of grace. These changes were neither unprecedented nor ubiquitous in Baptist churches in the decade after the rebellion, but their increasing prominence reflected a new, more thoroughgoing emphasis on the subordinate status of black members and on the authority and discretion of their masters in shaping their participation in Baptist communities.

Thus, the long-term effect of the Turner rebellion on Baptist communities was to make more explicit and concrete racial practices that had been implicit or evolving in the period before the uprising. In the decade or so after the revolt, the churches separated black members from white more rigorously than before and became far more straightforward about white male control of church government. While most churches probably practiced segregated seating at least as early as the second decade of the nineteenth century, in the later 1830s, as churches raised money to build new buildings or refurbish old ones, several also made explicit provision for the separate seating of black members. High Hills Baptist Church, for instance, "agreed that the railing which now stands in the house be moved across the end of the house Cutting off 8 feet to the South end for the Negroes to occupy."[90]

The churches also codified the specifically white and male rights of church membership. In response to a proposal from the Portsmouth Association, the Elam Baptist Church (formerly known as Seacock), "resolved that it is the unanimous opinion & wish of this Church that the constitution of the Portsmouth Association be so altered that where ever the words male members are inserted the word white should precede, so that it should read white male members." Several other churches recorded similar approbation.[91] This attitude affected the language of the churches as well. In 1844 Tucker's Swamp for the first time recorded that it had called the names of the "free white male members" rather than just the "free male members," which had been the standard phrase for years. The church cleared up what must have seemed to be a redundancy in the new language in 1853, when the moderator simply called the names of the "white male members."[92]

Clearly, Nat Turner's "religious madness" did not seem as safely distant or as incomprehensible to antebellum white Virginians as it might to twentieth- and twenty-first-century scholars. As we have seen, whites and blacks in southeastern Virginia shared, albeit uneasily, an evangelical community based on common but ultimately interpretable discourses and rituals of conversion, baptism, discipline, and fellowship. Whites fluent in these languages could empathize with Turner's religious vision, with his use of scripture and revelation to understand the world and his place in it, even as it horrified them. The centrality of religion to the revolt, compounded by specific references to Methodist and Baptist churches and practices in the evidence surrounding it, implicated the churches even as they sought to constrict the ways in which the evangelical message could be interpreted. The revolt, and its religious dimensions in particular, challenged the biracial evangelical community and the presumption of mutual intelligibility on which it was based. White evangelicals in the region thus felt both implicated in and challenged by the revolt. White Baptists clearly took pains to distance themselves from the rebellion and from their black co-religionists.

In part because the exact parameters of black participation in the rebellion remain unclear, the black reaction is more difficult to judge. In later decades "Ole Nat" entered local folklore as a kind of trickster figure, exemplifying the fact that, as one former slave put it, "de niggers could always out-smart de white folks."[93] But the real, historical Turner was a more problematic figure for blacks in southeastern Virginia, whose decisions in the days and months surrounding the rebellion could be matters of life and death. Although there is little record of most of the individual decisions made or the reasons behind them, the history of the contentious development of linked black and white evangelical communities provides enough context to engage in a degree of informed speculation on these issues.

Even as Turner and his followers drew on the racial and gendered tensions within southeastern Virginia's increasingly biracial evangelical world to shape their revolt, the vast majority of black evangelicals remained on the sidelines, and the degree to which they sympathized or identified with Turner remains difficult to determine. The white churches' reports that their black members had become "exceedingly refractory and ungovernable" suggest the ways in which the religious community that had been forged in the early decades of the nineteenth century had been shaken by the uprising, but they should not necessarily be taken as evidence of rebellious tendencies along the violent lines pursued by Turner.[94] This "ungovernable" behavior of black members may have been solely a matter of white perception. But it may also have reflected very real black resentment of the white backlash that threatened the modicum of independence and respect black evangelicals had carved out over the preceding decades. Black members had expressed disagreement with the white-controlled churches before, sometimes in aggressive, confrontational terms, but in the context of the rebellion such conflict may have seemed deeply threatening to white members in a way that it previously had not. Moreover, whites may have been more likely to treat individual cases of confrontational disagreement as symptomatic of a collective rebellious tendency. At the same time, such conflicts with white members must have increased as black members reacted to the curtailment of their access to religious authority and self-determination in the form of license to preach and independent meetings. Thus, by changing the perceived implications of long-term tensions within southeastern Virginia's evangelical communities, the Turner rebellion provoked a religious crisis for both blacks and whites.

In this context, Turner's heroic, prophetic model of evangelical masculine leadership most likely lost whatever appeal it had for blacks in southeastern Virginia. The failure of the revolt, the crushing white backlash, and the potential destruction of black religious communities dramatically illustrated the risks involved in open rebellion. In a 1937 interview, the former slave Allen Crawford claimed that his grandmother had confronted Nat Turner soon after he was captured: "Grandma ran out and struck Nat in the mouth, knocking the blood out and asked him 'Why did you take my son away?' In reply Nat said 'Your son was as willing to go as I was.' It was my Uncle Henry dat they was talking about." Passed down through several generations, this story, strictly true or not, can be seen as one family's encapsulation of the revolt's complex meaning, simultaneously giving voice to the grandmother's pain and frustration and to Turner's defiant pride in Henry's willingness to risk all to resist slavery. It also suggests that gender remained a dividing line in black attitudes toward the uprising and toward Turner himself. Women like Crawford's grandmother may have found Turner's vision less compelling than did men. Turner's leadership was based on largely masculine forms of authority, and his appeal to his followers seems to have built on grievances that were felt particularly strongly by black men. It is thus not surprising that his forces were entirely male and that there is almost no record of female participation in the uprising.[95]

Even for black men, decades of experience in sharing religious institutions and fellowship with whites provided other models of evangelical masculinity and other strategies for dealing with white power. Some may have followed the path of Dick and York, rejecting the controls imposed by the white-controlled churches and surrendering their own links to the officially sanctioned religious community those churches provided. Dick and York were not prophets of revolution as Turner was, but they both asserted their own construction of their rights as men, Dick as a husband and York as a preacher, against the church's construction of those rights. If they retained allegiance to evangelical ideas of salvation and fellowship, they did so outside of institutional channels, without either the limitation or the protection of an alliance with whites. For others, though, the model of Ben and Abel may have provided the most relevant guide to coping with a difficult situation. Despite conflict with the white-controlled church, both of these men ultimately accommodated themselves to its disciplinary and doctrinal requirements. It is difficult to determine whether this move reflected a genuine belief in the church as the sole source of legitimate religious authority or whether it was a more strategic decision designed to preserve personal status and communal integrity as best as possible under the circumstances. For most, perhaps, there was some combination of the two. Perhaps many black evangelicals reinterpreted the stoic, day-to-day righteousness enjoined upon them by their white brethren, not as a reflection of their appropriate station and abilities, but as a meaningful expression of the reality of the world in which they lived and its contrast with the more profound reality of divine truth. Perhaps they heeded white exhortations "to try to [do] good by doing Justly, loving Mercy, and walking humbly with God," not because they did not hope for freedom, but because they understood the results of doing otherwise.[96] Endurance of persecution, after all, was another key component of evangelical manhood.

The interrelated issues of race, republicanism, gender, and household that lay near the heart of Turner's uprising were precisely the issues that had come to pervade the Baptist churches of Isle of Wight, Southampton, and Sussex counties over the course of the previous half-century. The revolt itself exacerbated and shaped these tensions. White Baptists faced the same pressures as other white Virginians to confront the gendered nature of the revolt and its manipulation of the Revolutionary legacy. In these arenas, their response mirrored the larger white response, bringing white Baptists into closer communication with the southern mainstream.

Indeed, aspects of this response actually facilitated a convergence of evangelical and "southern" values. Baptists' conceptions of family and family religion could provide both reassurance to individuals in the wake of tragedy and an ideological rallying point for white Virginians seeking to condemn the revolt and valorize their own way of life. Likewise, the Baptists' long-term efforts to link their cause with the legacy of the

Revolution helped connect the issues of gender, family, and religion with those of nationalism and, in this context, its peculiar incarnation as southern sectionalism. In the 1830s, emerging southern sectional arguments about the distinctiveness and superiority of the southern way of life drew on a potent combination of familial, religious, republican, and racial ideologies that presented that way of life as a more pious, more virtuous, and more pure incarnation of American and Revolutionary principles than degraded, hypocritical northern ways, shot through with universalism and abolitionism. Baptists and other white evangelicals provided a powerful way of linking these themes through their infusion of familial relations with religious and emotional meaning, their linkage of "true" religion with "true" Americanness, and their emphasis on harmonious relations between slave and master, relations that were also infused with religious and familial meanings.[97] The aftermath of the Turner revolt, charged with these very issues of race, family, gender, republicanism, and religion, provided a fertile ideological environment for the melding of certain evangelical ideas into an emerging southern mainstream.

Accomplishing this convergence meant drawing sharp distinctions between proper and improper expressions of evangelical faith, as the purposeful deployment of labels like "fanaticism" and "delusion" in the rebellion's aftermath illustrates. By manipulating the discourses of authenticity, legitimacy, authority, and community that were central but contested elements throughout the religious evolution of Nat Turner's Virginia, white Baptists worked to restore the equilibrium not only of their churches but also of the white household itself. Promoting the centrality of religious discourses and institutions in this process also meant asserting unequivocal white control over the churches and the subordination of black members to the oversight of the white congregation. As white Baptists sought the same kind of reconstruction of their society and their ideological world that other whites sought in the wake of the Turner uprising, they also faced the added dimension of reconstructing their religious community in ways that reassured both themselves and their white neighbors that their faith had nothing to do with the rebellion. This meant addressing the place of their denomination in white society and the place of African Americans within their denomination; accomplishing the first goal entailed, at least to some extent, accomplishing the second. Thus, as we have seen, white-controlled Baptist churches thoroughly marginalized their black members in the decades after 1830, restricting black members' privileges and their involvement with white church life.

White and black Baptists still shared a religious world in southeastern Virginia. African Americans continued to join the churches and to participate in the newly constrained rituals of baptism, communion, and discipline. But the boundaries of that world and the ways in which it was shared had changed drastically since the 1770s. The religious world of Baptist churches revolved around distinctive rituals—relation of conversion, baptism, communion, discipline, preaching—that dramatized the spiritual processes of repentance and salvation, the presence and inspiration of God in one's life, and the process of joining and maintaining a community of the godly that held itself separate from the world. In the eighteenth and early nineteenth centuries these rituals and their openness to African Americans had provided materials for a particular interpretation of the evangelical message that emphasized the linkage of spiritual and social autonomy and authority. Although most white church members would not have subscribed to this interpretation as it applied to African Americans, and although they indeed viewed their black brethren as a distinct and different group from themselves in many ways, church language and practice were diverse and inconsistent enough to allow and even encourage such an interpretation. Indeed, Baptist fellowship was in large part built on this interpretability. It allowed blacks and whites to share a religious language and sense of community without either overtly challenging or unquestioningly endorsing existing social relations.

This changed in the wake of the Turner revolt. White reaction and efforts at ideological containment of the uprising (and the increasingly self-consciously "southern" ideological counteroffensive) catalyzed the emerging alliance between white evangelical religion and white southern culture, and it simultaneously increased the distance between black and white religion in the region's Baptist churches. Both of these trends were evident in the churches even before the Turner revolt, but in its aftermath they became more self-conscious, explicit, and unequivocal. The period of the Turner revolt, then, marked a watershed in the racial and cultural dynamics of evangelicalism even though the issues involved were by no means novel. It contributed to powerful, lasting patterns in southern religious life. White evangelical religion became an increasingly significant part of a developing sense of white southernness in the antebellum era, an identification that persists even today. Perhaps even more importantly, the actions of white evangelicals in the aftermath of the Turner revolt played a powerful contributing role in shaping the persistent division between white and black religion in southeastern Virginia and across the South.

EPILOGUE

IN HIS STUDY OF Southampton County through the long Civil War era Daniel W. Crofts provides a powerful illustration of the ways in which the Old Dominion remained Nat Turner's Virginia. In August 1867 the Cool Spring Baptist Church in Southampton County was accepted into the Colored Shiloh Regular Baptist Association. Eighteen sixty-seven was an auspicious year for the association and for black Virginians more generally. The preceding March, the Reconstruction Act of 1867 had confirmed African Americans' rights of citizenship, and an ongoing post–Civil War revival was energizing the newly independent black Baptist denomination in Virginia as free men and women withdrew from white-controlled churches to form their own institutions. The future seemed bright for the realization of the Christian and republican freedom that had so long eluded black Virginians. Indeed, the Shiloh Association agreed that its churches should no longer use the term *African* in their names, "as we are not Africans, but Americans." When the association's presiding elder called on the Cool Springs delegates to rise and proudly stated that Cool Springs "was located where Nat Turner first struck for freedom," there was "much shaking of hands and general felicitation."[1]

White commentators, however, took strong exception to this public rehabilitation of Turner's memory. Turner's "massacre was the most barbarous and brutal of all the human butcheries of this century," wrote one newspaper editor. Another asserted that the unkind feelings the rebellion provoked among whites had undermined rather than promoted

the cause of black freedom. For white Virginians, the specter of Nat
Turner and the reality of black freedom and independent religious activity conjured nightmarish visions of racial disorder that matched their
worst fears about Radical Reconstruction.[2]

From long experience, black Baptists had reason to be skeptical of
white efforts to define the appropriate methods and boundaries of freedom for them. Freed from the institutional controls of the white church,
they could assert their own interpretations of evangelicalism's meaning
and pursue their own spiritual, political, and social agendas. The fact
that seventeen new black Baptist churches had applied for membership
in the Shiloh Association between the end of the Civil War and that 1867
meeting suggests that the independent black evangelical world that had
spawned Turner and shaped the revolt itself was not only alive but flourishing.[3] These black Baptists' attempts to claim Turner's legacy as their
own contrasted profoundly not only with Reconstruction-era white attitudes but also with white attempts at the time of the rebellion to distance Baptists and other evangelicals from Turner. The Shiloh Association reversed the process that had defined Turner as a deluded wretch
and turned him into a Baptist prophet and hero. It is not clear that all of
their predecessors necessarily would have agreed with this assessment,
but they had as much right as any to claim and shape for themselves
their own usable Baptist past. In celebrating Nat Turner they were celebrating their own freedom.

The road that both black and white Baptists traveled to the formal separation that emerged in the wake of the Civil War was a long one, and the
years following the Turner rebellion were a crucial phase of that journey. Independent black worship continued to grow in this period, particularly in the black churches of Portsmouth, Norfolk, and Petersburg
but also among black congregants in rural, biracial churches of Isle of
Wight, Southampton, and Sussex counties. This independence became
a preoccupation of the white men who ran the Portsmouth Association.
In 1838 the black Gillfield Church in Petersburg requested that one of
its own members be permitted to represent the church as a delegate to
the association, as some black ministers and preachers in the eighteenth
century had done. This request demonstrated the increasing assertive-

ness of independently organized black Baptists in the antebellum era, but the response also indicated the decreasing willingness of whites to accept such independence. The association "*unanimously* rejected" the motion to permit such representation, and several years later it amended its constitution "to provide that '*White male members*' be the delegates to this body."[4]

The white delegates of the Portsmouth Association also frequently expressed concern about forming a plan "which will more efficiently secure the moral and religious instruction of our colored brethren and slaves generally."[5] The notion of lumping "our colored brethren" together with "slaves generally" suggests some of the transformations that had occurred over the previous half-century. From a white perspective, black Baptists were no longer individual members of a community of saints; instead they were a subset of "slaves generally," treated as a group to be managed and instructed but—as the association's refusal to accept a black delegate suggests—not engaged as individual believers. From a black perspective, this increasing, if generalized, concern also suggests the extent to which white Baptists no longer knew precisely what black Baptists were up to. The mutual suspicion created by the Turner rebellion had attenuated, if not severed, the links of fellowship between them. Much of black religious life disappears from the records of white-controlled churches in the 1830s and only becomes visible again as independent black institutions like Cool Spring Baptist Church emerge in the wake of the Civil War. This separation of black and white religious life was in part the result of racism and changing priorities on the part of whites, but it also reflected a defensive strategy on the part of black Baptists, who preserved a space to create their own interpretations of evangelical principles by taking advantage of their white brethren's neglect for their own purposes.

For their own part, the majority of white Baptists continued to work to bring evangelical and emergent white southern values into harmony with one another. One of the primary ways in which they did this was to continue to refine a notion of white masculinity that blended evangelical standards of piety and denominational engagement with southern emphases on mastery and household authority. In June 1837, for instance, the members of Raccoon Swamp noted the death of their longtime member and deacon William Peters:

With deep regret, the church at Racoonswamp Meetinghouse records the death of our belov'd Bro. Wm Peters, who departed this
life on Wednesday 10th of May 1837 (aged 68 years 2 months & 3
days) who became a member of this Church May 8th 1805 and was
chosen their deacon in Aug't 1806 which office he fill'd thro life with
credit; whose consiliating manners made him share largely in the
confidence and regards of acquaintance in general[.] In our dec'd
Bro we rejoice to mark the evidences of a truly pious man he was a
good husband; Neighbour; Master; & christian. He is gone to receive
the rewards of his labours of love; and left us to mourn our loss[.]
Blessed are the dead that die in the Lord

Oh! lit us be diligent to make our calling and election shure, that
at the last we may be found in peace with all the sons of God. Amen.[6]

This memorial served as both a celebration of Peters's life and a reminder
and example to other church members of the demands of the faith and
the glories of heaven. Central to this idea was Peters's status as a "good
husband; Neighbour; Master; & christian." These categories marked
the ultimate in white male Baptist piety, the proper fulfillment of those
roles in which God had placed him. The easy, self-assured blending
of these roles in the 1837 minute seems a far cry from the complaint
of the author of the 1772 "Address to the Anabaptists" that "Wives are
drawn from their Husbands, Children from their Parents, and Slaves
from the Obedience of their Masters" and that "the very Heartstrings
of those little Societies which form the greater are torn in sunder, and
all their Peace destroyed."[7] The categories of relationship and subordination that marked Baptists' unacceptability in 1772 became "the evidences of a truly pious man" to white Baptists in the antebellum era.

The language of Raccoon Swamp's minute also illustrates an important shift in emphasis. While the critic of the 1770s focused on the potential disorders that Baptist religion encouraged in wives, children, and
slaves, the Baptist memorialists of the 1830s focused on the uniquely
white and male form of piety encapsulated in the notion of a "good husband; Neighbour; Master; & christian." In the decades between these
two moments, Baptists and other southern evangelicals had moved from
the margins of southern social and cultural life to a space much closer to
its center. The shift toward emphasizing an orderly white male evangeli-

cal identity that corresponded with the key southern categories of subordination and social order was a crucial part of this transformation.

Like the increasing independence and segregation of black church members, this transformation was clearly under way even before the Nat Turner rebellion, but the uprising and the collapse of biracial fellowship it entailed hastened and intensified the process. By the 1840s the minutes of Baptist churches in Isle of Wight, Southampton, and Sussex counties focused almost exclusively on the concerns of white church members, and particularly on those of white men. Some aspects of white evangelical masculinity remained distinctive. Temperance societies, for instance, became extraordinarily popular in the churches during the antebellum era. Crusades against rampant drunkenness seem to have taken on some of the revitalizing functions that other forms of church discipline or the reforms of the 1750s and 1770s had served in the early Baptist churches in the region. Mission societies also gained popularity during this era, although not without controversy. The church at South Quay split over the issue, and the anti-mission group united with churches of similar mind in North Carolina, while the other group remained in the strongly pro-mission Portsmouth Association.[8] White Baptists in southeastern Virginia had not given up their outsider's stance toward worldly relations and behaviors, but they expressed their desires for reforms in ways that no longer seemed as threatening to the fundamental familial, gender, and racial order of the South.[9]

White orthodoxy in interpreting the meanings of evangelical fellowship for Virginia's social order was not unproblematically achieved at some particular point in time, however. It was actively maintained through an ongoing series of practices and encounters. These encounters always entailed a degree of risk, as meanings could be contested and reinterpreted in practice, but the powerful institutional and cultural resources that denominational leaders could bring to bear usually ensured an acceptable outcome. In 1844, for instance, William Cofer, of Tucker's Swamp, "stated that he had thought slavery was wrong and could not fellowship those who held slaves." Cofer attempted to revive conceptions of justice that had been persistent minority opinions among white members of the churches of Nat Turner's Virginia, and he adopted the language and processes of fellowship to gain a hearing in church. His fellow white church members, however, were "unwilling to receive his reasons as good & sufficient." Faced with the disapproval of his brethren, Cofer "acknowledged he was wrong, and . . . changed his mind on the subject."[10]

Similarly, Jonathan Lankford, excommunicated from Black Creek because of his refusal to commune with slaveholders, returned to his brethren in 1841, seeking restoration. The church agreed to hold a special conference to consider his request, noting "that a full attendance is requested." At the conference, Lankford "confessed that he was in error as regards slavery," but when the conference asked whether he could commune with the church if he were restored, Lankford answered "that he was not prepared to make that declaration at this time, but that he would wait without taking any other steps at the present and would make the matter a subject of prayer and wished the church to do the same."[11] It is unclear whether Lankford truly internalized this admission of error, however, because he never rejoined the church. As with Cofer, the practices of communion, fellowship, and discipline gave shape to a debate about the implications of evangelical ideals. It seems unlikely that either man thought that he could transform his church's position on slavery; instead, both used the rituals of the church to force the issue into public consideration. Unlike Cofer, however, Lankford ultimately refused the conformity sought by the church. While he acknowledged his error, he remained unable to unite with his brethren.

The institutional power of the churches was only one of the mechanisms through which the shaping of white Baptist orthodoxy took place. Print served as another important medium. As we have seen, beginning in the early nineteenth century, ministers like William Fristoe and Robert Semple began to craft denominational histories that organized and interpreted the meanings of Baptists' "rise and progress." The Revolutionary era and the achievement of religious liberty were important reference points for these works, serving to link the denomination's history to that of the emerging republican nation. In his 1859 edition of *Virginia Baptist Ministers*, James B. Taylor took this process a step further. Taylor's book memorialized the lives and work of the white men who had helped found and spread the denomination in the Old Dominion, including those who had shaped the movement in southeastern Virginia, from Shubael Stearns to John Meglamre to David Barrow. In glowing prose he described their devotion, talents, and energetic commitment to true religion in the face of hardship and persecution in ways that made the Baptist triumph seem both inevitable and eminently beneficial to society. Through the accumulation of biographical detail and conventional mid-nineteenth-century pieties, the work achieves a hagiographic fusion of national, southern, and evangelical identities.

In his brief biography of Barrow, Taylor eagerly recounted the minister's successful career, his talents as a scholar and a speaker, his contributions to religious liberty, and his Revolutionary service. Taylor even extensively quoted Barrow's 1798 *Circular Letter,* including his frank statements of his faith and of his republican principles. But Taylor carefully and thoroughly excised all references to slavery in the letter and made no reference at all to Barrow's anti-slavery beliefs or activities—a remarkable feat given the extent of those activities.[12] More than six decades after the effective defeat of the Baptist anti-slavery movement in Virginia, it still took a bold act of editorial will and selective memory to create a seemingly unproblematic, unified, usable Baptist past for white southerners.

This book traces the ways in which black and white Baptists sought to define the boundaries and mechanisms of fellowship within and around the churches of Isle of Wight, Southampton, and Sussex counties. The story of Nat Turner's Virginia is, to a great extent, the story of how the persistent tensions over these issues shaped relations between black and white Virginians and the larger discourses of race, slavery, household, and family that constituted Virginia society. The Turner rebellion itself must be understood as arising in large part out of these tensions. Just as importantly, these tensions shaped the diverse meanings that black and white Virginians gave to the uprising as they sought to understand what had happened and what it meant for their society. Understanding the Turner rebellion in this way provides a useful framework for understanding the rise and transformation of evangelical faith from its origins in colonial Virginia into the antebellum period, foregrounding the diversity and contestation that were central to its success. Even as Baptist churches increasingly asserted a white, paternalist orthodoxy, some members, even among the white congregation, continued to actively interpret and shape their faith in ways that did not conform to that orthodoxy. Evangelicalism did not come to dominate the South simply because it adapted itself to the language and institutions of the master class, although it certainly did that. It succeeded because it proved adaptable to the demands of that class while at the same time offering a powerful system of meaning and authority to those in positions of subordination or dissent, providing a perspective from which they could evaluate and criticize the conditions of their own subordination and the righteousness of their own society, in both spiritual and social terms. Even as the context of this dynamic and the processes of interpretation and contestation that it entailed shifted as part of larger political and cultural developments, it remained a central element of southern religious life not only through the antebellum period but also, as the Cool Springs Baptist Church demonstrates, into the late nineteenth century and beyond.

NOTES

Abbreviations

Burkitt   Lemuel Burkitt and Jesse Read. *A Concise History of the Kehukee Baptist Association from its Original Rise Down to 1803.* 1803. Edited by Henry L. Burkitt. 1850. Reprint, New York: Arno, 1980.

Confessions   *The Confessions of Nat Turner, the leader of the late insurrection in Southampton, Va. As fully and voluntarily made to Thomas R. Gray* (1831). In *The Confessions of Nat Turner and Related Documents,* edited by Kenneth S. Greenberg. Boston: Bedford Books of St. Martin's Press, 1996.

LVA   Library of Virginia, Richmond.

Semple   Robert B. Semple. *A History of the Rise and Progress of the Baptists in Virginia.* 1810. Revised and extended by Rev. G. W. Beale. Richmond: Pitt & Dickenson, 1894.

Tragle   Henry Irving Tragle, comp. *The Southampton Slave Revolt of 1831: A Compilation of Source Material.* Amherst: University of Massachusetts Press, 1971.

VBHS   Virginia Baptist Historical Society, University of Richmond.

Introduction

1. *Richmond Constitutional Whig,* 30 August 1831, in Tragle, 51.

2. Quoted in Peter H. Wood, "Nat Turner," 30.

3. James McDowell, speech to Virginia House of Delegates, 21 January 1832, in Robert, *Road from Monticello,* 104.

4. For accounts and contrasting interpretations of this debate, see Robert, *Road from Monticello;* and Alison Goodyear Freehling, *Drift toward Dissolution.*

5. On the complex issues of authorship and voice in the *Confessions*, see Greenberg, "*Confessions of Nat Turner:* Text and Context," 7–10. For an interpretation that emphasizes Gray's "framing remarks," see Gross and Bender, "History, Politics, and Literature." My own view follows the persuasive recent interpretation of Eric J. Sundquist, who finds Turner's voice and authorial intentions a pervasive presence in the *Confessions*. See Sundquist, *To Wake the Nations*, 27–83.

6. For examples, see the trial records transcribed in Tragle, 177–228.

7. *Richmond Enquirer*, 26 August 1831, in Tragle, 46.

8. *Richmond Constitutional Whig*, 29 August 1831, in Tragle, 51–52.

9. See John Floyd to James Hamilton Jr., 19 November 1831, in Tragle, 275–76.

10. See, e.g., *Richmond Constitutional Whig*, 29 August 1831, in Tragle, 53.

11. On the development of different theories of the revolt, see French, *Rebellious Slave*, 33–64; and Allmendinger, "Construction of *The Confessions of Nat Turner.*"

12. *Confessions*, 54.

13. *Richmond Constitutional Whig*, 26 September 1831, in Tragle, 91.

14. *Richmond Enquirer*, 25 November 1831, in Tragle, 144–45.

15. *Lynchburg Virginian*, 15 September 1831, in Tragle, 80.

16. "Minutes of the Virginia Portsmouth Baptist Association, Held at Otter Dams Church, Surry County, Virginia, May the 26th, 27th, and 28th, 1832" (1832), 9, 14, 25, VBHS.

17. Mill Swamp Baptist Church, Minute Book, 1812–1840, 31 August 1832, 6 April, 29 November 1833, LVA. For a full discussion of this case, see chapter 5; and Patrick H. Breen, "Contested Communion."

18. On eighteenth-century radicalism, see Isaac, *Transformation of Virginia;* Gewehr, *Great Awakening;* and Mathews, *Religion in the Old South*, 1–80. On antebellum proslavery conservatism, see Fox-Genovese and Genovese, *Mind of the Master Class;* idem, "Divine Sanction of Social Order"; Snay, *Gospel of Disunion;* and McCurry, *Masters of Small Worlds.*

19. The classic overview is Mathews, *Religion in the Old South.*

20. Ibid., 150.

21. Lindman, "Acting the Manly Christian"; Ambrose, "Of Stations and Relations"; Spangler, "Salvation Was Not Liberty"; idem, "Becoming Baptists."

22. Sewell, "Concept(s) of Culture," 44, 49–51.

23. Ibid., 51.

24. Sidbury, *Ploughshares into Swords*, esp. 1–3.

25. On geography and landscape, see Kirby, *Poquosin*, 3–4, 29, 95–103. On agricultural products, focusing on the later antebellum era, see Crofts, *Old Southampton*, 75–90. Production in all of these counties became increasingly market oriented after the construction of several rail lines through the area in the late antebellum period. Parramore, *Southampton County Virginia.*

26. James O'Kelly, quoted in Essig, *Bonds of Wickedness*, 83.

27. Studies focused on South Carolina have been particularly influential in shaping the understanding of proslavery evangelicalism. See McCurry, *Masters of Small*

Worlds; and Klein, *Unification of a Slave State.* On the Lower South, see Sparks, *On Jordan's Stormy Banks.* For a view of Virginia that emphasizes the proslavery aspects of evangelicalism, see Spangler, "Presbyterians, Baptists, and the Making of a Slave Society in Virginia."

1. Charming Liberty

1. See, e.g., Gewehr, *Great Awakening.*

2. Isaac, *Transformation of Virginia;* Upton, *Holy Things and Profane;* Parent, *Foul Means.*

3. See, e.g., Nelson, *Blessed Company;* Bond, "Anglican Theology and Devotion"; idem, *Damned Souls in a Tobacco Colony;* Gundersen, "Non-Institutional Church"; and idem, *Anglican Ministry in Virginia.*

4. Bonomi, *Under the Cope of Heaven,* 15–17; Bond, "Brief History," 14–24.

5. Beverley, *History and Present State of Virginia,* 264; Isaac, *Transformation of Virginia,* 143–47.

6. Bonomi, *Under the Cope of Heaven,* 43.

7. Upton, *Holy Things and Profane,* xiv. The actual number was probably significantly more.

8. Ibid., 164.

9. Ibid., 177–83.

10. Fithian, *Journal and Letters,* 29. See also Isaac, *Transformation of Virginia,* 60–61.

11. George Carrington Mason, "Colonial Churches of Isle of Wight and Southampton Counties"; idem, "Colonial Churches of Surry and Sussex Counties." John K. Nelson argues that the parish should be seen as an equal and complementary partner of the county as the fundamental unit of local governance in colonial Virginia. Nelson, *Blessed Company,* 4, 13–14.

12. Nelson, *Blessed Company,* 13–16.

13. Fithian, *Journal and Letters,* 100.

14. Samuel Davies to Thomas Sherlock, Bishop of London, 10 January 1752, reprinted in Foote, *Sketches of Virginia,* 195, 196. Davies's letter was never delivered to the bishop.

15. Bond, "Brief History," 35.

16. John Wesley, quoted in Nelson, *Blessed Company,* 190.

17. Richard Beale Davis, *Intellectual Life in the Colonial South, 1585–1763,* vol. 2 (Knoxville: University of Tennessee Press, 1978), 580, cited in Bond, "Anglican Theology and Devotion," 328.

18. Nelson, *Blessed Company,* 5.

19. Butterfield, "Puritans and Religious Strife in the Early Chesapeake"; Bond, "Brief History," 12–13. For the brief period of parliamentary rule in Virginia, from 1652 to 1660, the use of the Book of Common Prayer was technically outlawed, but the commissioners seem to have disregarded this rule. See Bond, "Brief History," 13; and McIlwaine, *Religious Toleration,* 19.

20. McIlwaine, *Religious Toleration*, 21–28; Worrall, *Friendly Virginians*, 19–66.

21. Quoted in Foote, *Sketches of Virginia*, 34–35. See also Bond, "Brief History," 29.

22. Much of my argument here follows Brown, *Good Wives, Nasty Wenches, and Anxious Patriarchs*, 141–44.

23. McIlwaine, *Religious Toleration*, 28–29.

24. Worrall, *Friendly Virginians*, 91–121; McIlwaine, *Religious Toleration*, 32–34.

25. See, e.g., Clark, "Gangreen of Quakerism." The foundation of the Society for Promoting Christian Knowledge (SPCK) and the Society for the Propagation of the Gospel (SPG) and their efforts to take advantage of the Keithian schism in Pennsylvania were part of this renewed Anglican activism in the colonies. See Levy, *Quakers and the American Family*, 172–87.

26. James Blair, *Our Savior's Divine Sermon on the Mount* (1722), in Bond, *Spreading the Gospel*, 104–5.

27. John Page, *A Deed of Gift to My Dear Son* (1687), in ibid., 97.

28. See Barbour, *Quakers in Puritan England*, 234–56; Horle, *Quakers and the English Legal System;* and Reay, *Quakers and the English Revolution*, 107–11.

29. *Baptist* and *Anabaptist* were labels that were applied to a wide variety of Protestant sects in Europe and America who rejected the idea of infant baptism, so it is not possible to treat all Baptists as members of a single coherent movement, much less a denomination, for the early modern period. Instead, we must specify particular traditions emerging from particular historical and theological contexts. Among English groups, the major division was between the predestinarian Particular Baptists and the universalist General Baptists.

30. On the strong affinity between the Quaker and General Baptist movements in seventeenth-century England, see McGregor, "Baptists."

31. Worrall, *Friendly Virginians*, 107; Lumpkin, *History of the Portsmouth Baptist Association*, 1.

32. Thomas White, a minister who accompanied Norden, died at sea. Lumpkin, *History of the Portsmouth Baptist Association*, 1. The exact location of this first church has not been determined, but most recent historians prefer Prince George County over the other option, Isle of Wight County, where another early church was founded. The question is even more confusing because some writers refer to this first church as Burleigh Baptist Church, while others refer to the Isle of Wight church as Burleigh. Robert G. Gardner places the Burleigh church in Isle of Wight County, with a foundation date of 1727, and lists a distinct church in Prince George County, founded in 1714, as the first Baptist church in Virginia. See Gardner, *Baptists of Early America*, 254, 272. On this confusion, see Semple, 444–46.

33. Worrall, *Friendly Virginians*, 107. Worrall suggests that Norden's willingness "to 'take the oaths required' by the Toleration Act" may have "dismayed" his Quaker hosts, who were opposed to oath-taking, forcing him to find a new meeting place.

34. This account of the Hanover activities draws on Davies, *State of Religion Among the Protestant Dissenters;* "Origin of Presbyterianism in Virginia"; Bond, "Brief History," 36–40; Gewehr, *Great Awakening,* 40–105; and Payne, "New Light in Hanover County."

35. Davies, *State of Religion Among the Protestant Dissenters,* 10.

36. On the importance of preexisting models of revivalism in spreading revivals, see Lambert, *Inventing the "Great Awakening,"* 22. Rodger M. Payne points out the particular influence of Scottish Presbyterianism in Hanover in "New Light in Hanover County," 687–91.

37. Davies, *State of Religion Among the Protestant Dissenters,* 11.

38. See Bonomi, *Under the Cope of Heaven,* 139–49.

39. Davies, *State of Religion Among the Protestant Dissenters,* 17.

40. Patrick Henry to William Dawson, 13 February 1744/5, in Henry et al., "Letters," 263.

41. Ibid., 265.

42. Davies, *State of Religion Among the Protestant Dissenters,* 13.

43. Foote, *Sketches of Virginia,* 137–38.

44. Davies, *State of Religion Among the Protestant Dissenters,* 15.

45. Foote, *Sketches of Virginia,* 137.

46. Ibid., 135–36.

47. Governor William Gooch, quoted in Hockman, "Hellish and Malicious Incendiaries," 161.

48. Hockman, "Hellish and Malicious Incendiaries," 166.

49. Henry to Dawson, 8 June 1747, in Henry et al., "Letters," 273.

50. Foote, *Sketches of Virginia,* 165.

51. Davies, *State of Religion Among the Protestant Dissenters,* 21.

52. Foote, *Sketches of Virginia,* 177.

53. Ibid., 178.

54. Davies, *State of Religion Among the Protestant Dissenters,* 44.

55. Foote, *Sketches of Virginia,* 186.

56. Davies, *State of Religion Among the Protestant Dissenters,* 6.

57. Ibid.; Foote, *Sketches of Virginia,* 190.

58. Davies, *State of Religion Among the Protestant Dissenters,* 7.

59. Ibid., 23.

60. Foote, *Sketches of Virginia,* 285. George William Pilcher cites "Old Documents," 540, for the same letter that appears in Foote and identifies Robert Crutenden as the recipient. Pilcher, "Samuel Davies," 293.

61. Pilcher, "Samuel Davies," 294–98.

62. Frey and Wood, *Come Shouting to Zion,* 96–97.

63. See Jerome W. Jones, "Established Virginia Church," 17–23; Frey and Wood, *Come Shouting to Zion,* esp. 63–79; and Butler, *Awash in a Sea of Faith,* 129–63.

64. See Berlin, *Many Thousands Gone,* 41–42.

65. See Jordan, *White Over Black,* 91–98; Edmund S. Morgan, *American*

Slavery, American Freedom, 331–33; Brown, *Good Wives, Nasty Wenches, and Anxious Patriarchs,* 135–36; and Billings, "Cases of Fernando and Elizabeth Key."

66. Frey and Wood, *Come Shouting to Zion,* 69–70; Edmund S. Morgan, *American Slavery, American Freedom,* 332 (quotation).

67. Berlin, *Many Thousands Gone,* 110–13, 120–23.

68. See Frey and Wood, *Come Shouting to Zion,* 35–62. See also Sobel, *Trabelin' On,* 41–46.

69. "A Draught of a Bill For Converting the Negroes in Plantations," ca. 1713, Lambeth Palace Papers, Lambeth Palace Library, London, quoted in Parent, *Foul Means,* 243.

70. Parent, *Foul Means,* 197–235, 249–53; Frey and Wood, *Come Shouting to Zion,* 68–69. On slavery and patriarchy in the colony, see also Brown, *Good Wives, Nasty Wenches, and Anxious Patriarchs,* 319–61.

71. Parent, *Foul Means,* 253–58.

72. Ibid., 262.

73. Frey and Wood, *Come Shouting to Zion,* 69–70.

74. Ibid., 70.

75. Philip D. Morgan, *Slave Counterpoint,* 61, 81.

76. Dunn, "Black Society in the Chesapeake," 54; Philip D. Morgan, *Slave Counterpoint,* 98.

77. Philip D. Morgan, *Slave Counterpoint,* 420–37.

78. For a compelling analysis of these dimensions of evangelical experience, see Isaac, *Transformation of Virginia.*

79. See Frey and Wood, *Come Shouting to Zion,* 100–101; and Sobel, *Trabelin' On,* 90–91, 100–101.

80. Frey and Wood, *Come Shouting to Zion,* 101.

81. Foote, *Sketches of Virginia,* 285.

82. Davies, *Religion and Patriotism,* 19.

83. Davies, *State of Religion Among the Protestant Dissenters,* 23.

84. Foote, *Sketches of Virginia,* 285.

85. Davies, *Letters,* 31.

86. "Old Documents," 544.

87. Foote, *Sketches of Virginia,* 291.

88. Davies, "Family Religion," 203.

89. Ibid., 205, 222.

90. "Old Documents," 548.

91. Ibid., 544.

92. Ibid., 546.

93. Davies, *Letters,* 30–31. This discussion draws on the insightful analysis of the same material in Calhoon, *Evangelicals and Conservatives,* 14–16, and Frey and Wood, *Come Shouting to Zion,* 97–99.

94. See Raboteau, *Slave Religion,* 318. For a useful overview of perspectives on the psychology of slave conversion, including Raboteau's, see Schweiger, "Max Weber in Mount Airy," 40–44. Schweiger in particular highlights the "strangely

irreducible" nature of slave Christianity and the "poverty of any analysis that would force a false choice between accommodation and resistance as the only two possibilities for understanding the meaning of Christianity for slaves" (44).

95. Frey and Wood, *Come Shouting to Zion,* 98. See also Calhoon, *Evangelicals and Conservatives,* 14–15.

96. Davies, *Letters,* 30–31.

97. Calhoon, *Evangelicals and Conservatives,* 15–16.

98. Davies, *Letters,* 31.

99. Ibid., 29.

100. Lambert, *Inventing the "Great Awakening,"* 185–250.

2. Little Societies

1. Mill Swamp Baptist Church, Minute Book, 1777–1790, membership list at beginning of book and entry for 13 June 1777, LVA; Burkitt, 268–70, 271.

2. James B. Taylor, *Virginia Baptist Ministers,* 164.

3. Burkitt, 268–69 (quotations); James B. Taylor, *Virginia Baptist Ministers,* 164.

4. See Semple, 31–40, 382–83. See also Heyrman, *Southern Cross,* 15–18; and Gewehr, *Great Awakening,* 115, 119–28.

5. Semple, 20.

6. Williams, "John Williams' Journal," 798; Morgan Edwards, "Materials Towards a History of the Baptists in the Province of Virginia," 31 (75–76) (hereafter cited as Edwards, "Virginia Materials," with typescript page number followed in parentheses by manuscript page number); Isaac, *Transformation of Virginia,* 162–63; Heyrman, *Southern Cross,* 85.

7. James B. Taylor, *Virginia Baptist Ministers,* 113. Baker escaped that particular fate, but he continued to face harassment and intimidation. Burkitt, 284–85.

8. Edwards, "Virginia Materials," 8–9 (29–30). There are numerous accounts of these and other persecutions and violent or nearly violent confrontations recorded in Edwards, "Virginia Materials,"; James B. Taylor, *Virginia Baptist Ministers;* Semple; and individual journals or published lives, e.g., *The Life of the Rev. James Ireland* and *The Writings of the Late Elder John Leland.*

9. Rhys Isaac's evocative descriptions of this process remain indispensable to any understanding of evangelicalism in Revolutionary Virginia. See Isaac, "Evangelical Revolt"; and idem, *Transformation of Virginia,* 161–77.

10. In most places, Calvinist Baptists were referred to as Particular Baptists because of their endorsement of limited atonement in contrast to the General Baptists' belief in general atonement. In Virginia and North Carolina, however, groups linked to the Philadelphia Baptist Association came to be called Regular Baptists to distinguish them from the Separate Baptists, who represented a similar theological tradition but had their ecclesiastical origins in the schisms of New England revivalism rather than in the Middle Colonies. For the sake of simplicity and consistency, I employ the term *Regular* rather than *Particular.*

11. Lumpkin, *History of the Portsmouth Baptist Association*, 1–2; Gardner, *Baptists of Early America*, 248–82, 287–309; Edwards, "Materials Towards a History of the Baptists in the Province of North-Carolina," 369n2 (hereafter cited as Edwards, "North Carolina Materials"); Edwards, "Virginia Materials," 1 (21–22); Semple, 444–47; Burkitt, 31–32.

12. Gardner, *Baptists of Early America*, 101.

13. Ibid., 277; Edwards, "North Carolina Materials," 372; idem, "Virginia Materials," 1 (21).

14. Gardner, *Baptists of Early America*, 107; Lumpkin, *History of the Portsmouth Baptist Association*, 3. For estimates of the extinction dates of the early Virginia churches, see Gardner, *Baptists of Early America*, 254, 272, 277.

15. Edwards, "North Carolina Materials," 370.

16. Burkitt, 32.

17. Ibid., 33.

18. Edwards, "North Carolina Materials," 370; Burkitt, 31–37; Semple, 446–49; Lumpkin, *History of the Portsmouth Baptist Association*, 3–4.

19. Edwards, "North Carolina Materials," 372–73; Burkitt, 31–32.

20. Edwards, "North Carolina Materials," 370.

21. Burkitt, 33.

22. Edwards, "Virginia Materials," 1–2 (21–22).

23. Gardner, *Baptists of Early America*, 254.

24. Semple, 11–14; Edwards, "North Carolina Materials," 384–87.

25. Semple, 15.

26. John Gano, quoted in ibid., 66.

27. Ketocton Association letter, quoted in ibid., 68.

28. Semple, 67.

29. Ibid., 450–51.

30. James B. Taylor, *Virginia Baptist Ministers*, 163.

31. Burkitt, 41–43; Semple, 450–51.

32. Burkitt, 32.

33. Ibid., xx.

34. Ibid., xx–xxiv.

35. Another Regular group linked to the Philadelphia Association expanded in the northwestern section of the colony, representing a third hearth of early Baptist religious culture in Virginia. Details of this movement can be found in Fristoe, *Ketocton Baptist Association*. See also Gardner, "Ketocton and Philadelphia Associations in the Eighteenth Century, Part I"; and idem, "Ketocton and Philadelphia Associations in the Eighteenth Century, Part II."

36. See Edwards, "North Carolina Materials," 373–74; James B. Taylor, *Virginia Baptist Ministers*, 63–63; and Burkitt, 278–79.

37. Burkitt, 60–63 (quotations on 61); James B. Taylor, *Virginia Baptist Ministers*, 172–73.

38. Burkitt, 286–87.

39. Ibid., 278–79. Baptist church naming practices were very informal during this period, so churches were often referred to by their location, the nearest body of water, the pastor's name, or the name of the person who built or donated land for the meetinghouse. Raccoon Swamp, for example, was often called "the church on Raccoon Swamp" or "Brother Meglamre's church in Sussex County." For the sake of consistency, I have adopted the more formal designations upon which most churches eventually settled during the period of this study. Raccoon Swamp officially changed its name to Antioch Baptist Church in 1853, and many of its records are catalogued under that name.

40. Ibid., 286–87. Bell died in 1778, and for several years the church had to rely on Raccoon Swamp for ministerial oversight. See Raccoon Swamp [Antioch] Baptist Church, Minute Book, 1772–1837, 9 August 1782, LVA. Unfortunately, no records for Sappony survive for the period of this study. After Bell's death the church struggled along without a regular pastor for many years before becoming more active in the nineteenth century.

41. Garnett Ryland, quoted in Lumpkin, *History of the Portsmouth Baptist Association*, 6. The Mill Swamp church was initially called Isle of Wight, but it adopted the name Mill Swamp Baptist Church in 1791. Mill Swamp Baptist Church, Minute Book, 1791–1811, 16 September 1791. The surnames that repeat are Mintz, Jones, Mangum, Cofer, and Jordan. The only full name that repeats is Thomas Cofer/ Copper. Thomas Cofer signed the 1756 letter, and two Thomas Coppers appear at Mill Swamp, Thomas Copper Jr. and Thomas Copper Sr. It seems probable that one of these two (probably Thomas Sr.) was the same as the 1756 signer. Mill Swamp Baptist Church, Minute Book, 1777–1790, membership lists at beginning and end of book.

42. South Quay was in a section of Nansemond that became part of Southampton County after an adjustment of the county boundaries in 1786. In 1835 the church split over the issues of missionary and Sunday-school societies. The antimission group took control of the meetinghouse in Southampton County, while the pro-mission group moved across the Blackwater River into Nansemond County. The Nansemond group was recognized as the true South Quay church by the Portsmouth Association, and the Southampton group united with other anti-mission Baptists in North Carolina. Thus, for the period of this study the South Quay church began and ended in Nansemond County but for most the time was located in Southampton County. Nansemond County became part of the independent city of Suffolk in 1974.

43. Mill Swamp Baptist Church, Minute Book, 1777–1790, 16 September 1774, 13 June 1777, 19 March 1779; Raccoon Swamp [Antioch] Baptist Church, Minute Book, 1772–1837, 8 May, 17 July, 11 September 1773, 5 May 1776, 7 May 1779. For information on individual churches in southeastern Virginia during this period, see Burkitt, 255–88; Semple, 444–68; Gardner, *Baptists of Early America*, 248–82; and Lumpkin, *History of the Portsmouth Baptist Association*, 5–10. Reuben Jones, *History of the Virginia Portsmouth Baptist Association*, also contains a great deal of

useful information and oral history, particularly regarding the nineteenth-century history of the churches in the association, but has many factual errors regarding dates and locations.

44. Burkitt, 41; Semple, 450; James B. Taylor, *Virginia Baptist Ministers*, 162–63; Lumpkin, *History of the Portsmouth Baptist Association*, 6–7; Raccoon Swamp [Antioch] Baptist Church, Minute Book, 1772–1837, 25 December 1773.

45. Burkitt, 42.

46. The 1773 minute is difficult to read, so there is a slight possibility that it originally read "may not" but that the "not" has become obscured. The minute book for this period is a transcription, so it is also possible that the minute was mistranscribed. But if the minute is correct, it seems that the church reversed its position on the question in a matter of months.

47. On discipline and revivalism, see Wills, *Democratic Religion*, 33–36.

48. Burkitt, 44–45.

49. Semple, 450–51.

50. Burkitt, 48–54 (quotations on 53, 54).

51. Ibid., 55. This query was referred to the association by the members of Barrow's church at Mill Swamp. See Mill Swamp Baptist Church, Minute Book, 1777–1790, 13 June 1777.

52. See Burkitt, 56–94.

53. Accounts of the division can be found in ibid., 108–10; Semple, 453–54; and Lumpkin, *History of the Portsmouth Baptist Association*, 7–10.

54. Semple, 101.

55. Burkitt, 98.

56. Thomas, *Virginian Baptist*, 12.

57. Ibid., 13.

58. Ibid., 9.

59. Ibid., 10.

60. Ireland, *Life*, 73–75.

61. Fristoe, *Ketocton Baptist Association*, 28.

62. Ibid.

63. Ireland, *Life*, 122.

64. Thomas, *Virginian Baptist*, 13–14.

65. The issue of individualism versus communalism in southern evangelical religion has been the subject of debate among some of its foremost historians. Boles, *Great Revival*, argues that "in practically every aspect, the fundamental emphasis of the popular churches in the South was individualistic" (125). See also idem, "Evangelical Protestantism in the Old South." Donald G. Mathews, on the other hand, emphasizes the communal dimension, arguing that "the polarity of 'community' and 'individual' simply did not exist for Evangelicals" and that the main opposition was between "true believers, who were united in bonds of love, and worldlings, who were 'senseless' to divine things and 'careless' for their own lives." See Mathews, *Religion in the Old South*, 40. Rhys Isaac emphasizes the tensions between the two poles of "radical individualization" that converts experienced in the process of conviction and

conversion and "the comfort of close fellowship" they found in church membership. Isaac, *Transformation of Virginia*, 171. Isaac suggests that evangelicals' ambivalence was part of a larger ambivalence about the rise of individualism in other cultural realms. My own view lies somewhere between Mathews's and Isaac's. While both individual and communal experience were essential to evangelical life, most often there was no contradiction between the two. They were not mutually exclusive. The conversion experience and a direct relationship to God gave individual believers status and authority within the community and allowed them to exercise leadership or develop their own interpretations of their faith, but this leadership and these interpretations were still enacted and articulated in terms of what the Christian community was and should be.

66. Fristoe, *Ketocton Baptist Association*, 28; Burkitt, xviii.

67. Burkitt, xix.

68. Fristoe, *Ketocton Baptist Association*, 27.

69. Ibid., 29.

70. Spangler, "Becoming Baptists," 247 (quotation), 253–58.

71. Mill Swamp Baptist Church, Minute Book, 1777–1790, 2 July 1774.

72. Lumpkin, "Early Virginia Baptist Church Covenants," 773, 775.

73. Mill Swamp Baptist Church, Minute Book, 1777–1790, 2 July 1774; South Quay Baptist Church, Minute Book, 1775–1827, "The Baptist Church Covenant," LVA; Black Creek Baptist Church, Minute Book, 1776–1804, 27 May 1786, LVA. See also Lumpkin, "Early Virginia Baptist Church Covenants," 779–80.

74. Burkitt, 34–35.

75. Raccoon Swamp [Antioch] Baptist Church, Minute Book, 1837–1892, beginning of book, LVA.

76. See Black Creek Baptist Church, Minute Book, 1776–1804, 27 May 1786 ("state of nature"); South Quay's covenant contains the same phrase, and the beginning of Mill Swamp's covenant is missing, but given the similarity of the rest of the covenant, it most likely did as well. Burkitt, 34 ("marvellous light," which also appears in the Raccoon Swamp covenant).

77. The Mill Swamp, South Quay, and Black Creek covenants all refer directly to the Philadelphia Association's adoption of the London Confession of Faith, but the Kehukee / Raccoon Swamp version does not, nor do the later, nineteenth-century covenants at other churches in the region.

78. All the covenants contain some version of this language. The quotation given in the text is from Black Creek Baptist Church, Minute Book, 1776–1804, 27 May 1786. The Mill Swamp, South Quay, and Black Creek covenants cite 2 Cor. 8:5 as the source of this concept: "And this they did, not as we hoped, but first gave their own selves to the Lord, and unto us by the will of God."

79. Mill Swamp Baptist Church, Minute Book, 1777–1790, 2 July 1774.

80. See, e.g., Raccoon Swamp [Antioch] Baptist Church, Minute Book, 1772–1837, 7 November 1772, 8, 31 May, 17 July, 15 November 1773; Mill Swamp Baptist Church, Minute Book, 1777–1790, 16 September 1774, 19 March 1779; and South Quay Baptist Church, Minute Book, 1775–1827, 10 February 1776.

81. The most complete recent discussion of church discipline in itself is Wills, *Democratic Religion*. Other examinations of church discipline in the South include Mathews, *Religion in the Old South*, 42–46; Heyrman, *Southern Cross*, esp. 249–52; Isaac, *Transformation of Virginia*, 168–70; McCurry, *Masters of Small Worlds*, 171–207; Sparks, *On Jordan's Stormy Banks*, 146–73; Lindman, "World of Baptists," 204–35; Friedman, *Enclosed Garden*, 11–20; Betty Wood, "For Their Satisfaction or Redress"; and Cortland Victor Smith, "Church Organization," 131–205. Also useful is Susan Juster's exploration of church discipline among Baptists in New England, *Disorderly Women*, esp. 75–107, 145–79.

82. Mathews, *Religion in the Old South*, 45–46.

83. Isaac, *Transformation of Virginia*, 168–71; Mathews, *Religion in the Old South*, 42–45; Spangler, "Becoming Baptists," 281–85.

84. Spangler, "Becoming Baptists"; Beeman, *Evolution of the Southern Backcountry*; Payne, "New Light in Hanover County."

85. For example, nearly all disciplinary charges at Raccoon Swamp from 1772 to 1776 were recorded as "disorderly walking." Raccoon Swamp [Antioch] Baptist Church, Minute Book, 1772–1837.

86. Black Creek Baptist Church, Minute Book, 1776–1804, 22 August, 10, 25 October 1783, 4, 20 February, 24 May, 21 August 1784.

87. South Quay Baptist Church, Minute Book, 1775–1827, 3 January, February 1783; Raccoon Swamp [Antioch] Baptist Church, Minute Book, 1772–1837, 5 April 1777.

88. Raccoon Swamp [Antioch] Baptist Church, Minute Book, 1772–1837, 3 August 1778.

89. Ibid., 5 May 1776.

90. For a quantitative discussion of discipline, see chapter 4.

91. Mill Swamp Baptist Church, Minute Book, 1777–1790, 18 January, 14 March 1777.

92. Black Creek Baptist Church, Minute Book, 1776–1804, 23 May, 20 September 1776, 20 November 1778, 26 February 1779.

93. Ibid., 20 November 1778, 26 February 1779; Mill Swamp Baptist Church, Minute Book, 1777–1790, 17 September 1779.

94. Mill Swamp Baptist Church, Minute Book, 1777–1790, 18 January 1777.

95. Leland, *True Account*, 2–6.

96. Ibid., 7–8.

97. Semple, 30.

98. *Virginia Gazette* (Purdie & Dixon), 20 February 1772.

99. Ireland, *Life*, 84.

100. For an excellent discussion of this dimension of evangelicals' reception in the south, see Heyrman, *Southern Cross*, 28–76.

101. *Virginia Gazette* (Purdie & Dixon), 20 February 1772.

102. "A petition of sundry inhabitants of the county of Cumberland," 21 May 1777 (transcribed from the *Journal of the House of Delegates*), Virginia General Assembly, Religious Petitions, 1774–1802, LVA (hereafter cited as "Religious Petitions").

103. Thomas, *Virginian Baptist,* 57–58.

104. Ibid., 58–59.

105. This is particularly significant given that Thomas was willing to concede other points. In response to an objection to the noise and physical exercises of Baptist congregations, he claimed that his own preaching had never had that effect but admitted that it did occur and that he could "find no account of it in the word of GOD." Ibid., 63. For a contemporary's view of Thomas, see Edwards, "Morgan Edwards' 1772 Virginia Notebook," 865–66, 871n66.

106. James B. Taylor, *Virginia Baptist Ministers,* 164.

107. Burkitt, 269–70. The long-term success of this transformation of Barrow and Mintz's dunking into an emblem of Baptist triumph is indicated by the inclusion of a 1990 painting of the incident by Sidney King in the 1998 Library of Congress exhibition Religion and the Founding of the American Republic. The images and text of this exhibition are available online at http://www.loc.gov/exhibits/religion/. The painting itself is held by the Virginia Baptist Historical Society. It can be viewed online as part of the Library of Congress exhibition at http://www.loc.gov/exhibits/religion/f0509s.jpg.

108. Leland, "Events in the Life of John Leland; Written by Himself," in *Writings,* 20.

109. Burkitt, 59–60. See also Mathews, *Religion in the Old South,* 103.

110. Mill Swamp Baptist Church, Minute Book, 1777–1790, 18 September, 17 December 1784. For an example in the Tidewater (Lancaster County), see Morattico Baptist Church, Minutes, 1778–1787, 1792–1844, 13 January 1781, Van Pelt Library; for an example in the Piedmont, see Albemarle [Buck Mountain, Chestnut Grove] Baptist Church, Minutes, 1773–1779, 1792–1811, November 1799, Van Pelt Library.

111. Mill Swamp Baptist Church, Minute Book, 1777–1790, 13 March 1778; South Quay Baptist Church, Minute Book, 1775–1827, 3 April 1778; Shoulder's Hill Baptist Church, Minute Book, 1783–1923, 3 December 1784, VBHS. No such call was recorded at Black Creek, but the 1776–1804 minute book includes an extensive list of children and their dates of birth that seems to have been carefully kept up to date well into the 1810s.

112. Burkitt, 99.

113. On the Anglican "monopoly" and a general description of Virginia marriage practices, see Nelson, *Blessed Company,* 222–25.

114. Ibid., 222.

115. See, e.g., the petition of 20 June 1776 from Baptists in Prince William County and the record in the *Journal of the House of Delegates* of a petition of 25 October 1779 that does not survive from the "Baptist Association." Religious Petitions. Illegal performance of marriages was also among the many complaints the Reverend Patrick Henry lodged against Samuel Davies, while Davies argued that his rights as a licensed dissenting minister should include "the Priviledge of marrying" if he forwarded the relevant fees to the appropriate parish officials. See Davies, letter of 3 February 1749/50, and Henry to Dawson, 22 August 1751, in Henry et al., "Letters," 273–76.

116. Raccoon Swamp [Antioch] Baptist Church, Minute Book, 1772–1837, 2 February 1778.

117. Mill Swamp Baptist Church, Minute Book, 1777–1790, 18 January 1777.

118. Shoulder's Hill Baptist Church, Minute Book, 1783–1923, 19 December 1783, 3 December 1784.

119. Albemarle [Buck Mountain, Chestnut Grove] Baptist Church, Minutes, 1773–1779, 1792–1811, October, December 1778, Van Pelt Library.

120. Raccoon Swamp [Antioch] Baptist Church, Minute Book, 1772–1837, 3 September 1774. This conciliatory approach seems to have paid off in this case. In 1783, nearly a decade later, Henry Tuder was received into the church. Ibid., 7 February 1783. Henry Tuder is the only head of household with that surname in the Sussex County tax list for 1782. U.S. Bureau of the Census, *Heads of Families at the first census of the United States*, 44–45.

121. Burkitt, 73.

122. Mill Swamp Baptist Church, Minute Book, 1777–1790, 14 March 1777.

123. Black Creek Baptist Church, Minute Book, 1776–1804, 22 November 1776.

124. Burkitt, 73–74.

125. On the concept of mastery and its Christian incarnations, see McCurry, *Masters of Small Worlds*, 130–207; and Heyrman, *Southern Cross*, 206–52. On eighteenth-century Virginian notions of household and family order, see Brown, *Good Wives, Nasty Wenches, and Anxious Patriarchs*, pt. 3.

126. South Quay Baptist Church, Minute Book, 1775–1827, July 1785. This page of the minute book is badly torn, so no answer to the query is legible.

127. Burkitt, 172.

128. Raccoon Swamp [Antioch] Baptist Church, Minute Book, 1772–1837, membership list at the beginning of the book. This may even undercount the actual proportion, because the list has a number of tears and holes, so that some white surnames are likely missing from the count if they do not appear elsewhere in the early church minutes. Church records usually only mention owners' surnames, from which information there is often no way to tell precisely who the owner was.

129. South Quay Baptist Church, Minute Book, 1775–1827, membership list near the front of the book.

130. Burkitt, 58. For more discussion of this issue, see chapter 4.

131. *Virginia Gazette* (Purdie & Dixon), 8 October 1767.

132. *Virginia Gazette* (Purdie & Co.), May 1766.

133. Dozier, "Richard Dozier's Historical Notes," 1402, 1414.

134. Ibid., 1416–17.

135. South Quay Baptist Church, Minute Book, 1775–1827, 2 April, 31 December 1779.

136. Several historians mention the initial confrontation between Nero and John Lawrence as evidence of evangelicalism's racial inclusiveness and egalitarianism and its evenhandedness in church discipline. See Daniel, "Virginia Baptists and the Negro," 63; Sobel, *World They Made Together*, 196–97; and Philip D. Morgan, *Slave Counterpoint*, 431. None of these authors examines any of the other conflicts

between Nero and Lawrence, however, and the ongoing nature of their relationship, particularly its final outcome, delivers a more ambivalent message than these authors suggest. All of these authors also state, slightly misleadingly, that Lawrence was "expelled" from the church. Censure was not necessarily the same as expulsion and could involve such intermediate punishments as being barred from communion until reconciled with the church without officially separating from the church. Daniel and Sobel make no mention of the fact that Nero's initial charge against Lawrence was a response to Lawrence's charges against him.

137. South Quay Baptist Church, Minute Book, 1775–1827, 30 June, October 1780, January 1781.

138. Ibid., 4 January, 5 April, 5 July 1782.

139. Ibid., 5 May, 3 June, 1 July 1786.

140. Black Creek Baptist Church, Minute Book, 1776–1804, 25 August 1786; Mill Swamp Baptist Church, Minute Book, 1791–1811, 25 March 1802.

141. South Quay Baptist Church, Minute Book, 1775–1827, 2, 3 April 1791.

142. Black Creek Baptist Church, Minute Book, 1776–1804, 20 February, 22 May 1778.

143. Mathews, "Christianizing the South," 87.

144. See Sidbury, "Reading, Revelation, and Rebellion," 120 and n3. Sidbury uses Brian Stock's notion of "textual communities" to focus attention on literate slaves' ability to interpret the Bible and exercise religious leadership in local communities. I would extend this idea to interpretations of religious practices such as baptism and communion, particularly ones as distinctive and laden with meaning as the Baptists', which could be "texts" in their own right.

3. Sacred Regard to the Rights of Mankind

1. Allen, "David Barrow's *Circular Letter*," 444. Allen reproduces the full text of Barrow's letter and provides a useful introduction. Other accounts of Barrow's decision can be found in Essig, *Bonds of Wickedness*, 77–78; Bailey, *Shadow on the Church*, 33–35; and Freeberg, "Why David Barrow Moved to Kentucky," 1617–27.

2. Allen, "David Barrow's *Circular Letter*," 445; Southampton County, Deed Book 6 (1782–1787), 11 March 1784, LVA.

3. Allen, "David Barrow's *Circular Letter*," 445.

4. See Fischer and Kelly, *Bound Away*, 138–40, 152–68, 323n9, 324. On the character and magnitude of the settlement of Kentucky, see also Aron, *How the West Was Lost;* Perkins, *Border Life;* and Friend, *Buzzel about Kentuck.*

5. Bailey, *Shadow on the Church*, 27.

6. Semple, 226. In general see Bailey, *Shadow on the Church;* Spencer, *History of Kentucky Baptists;* Crimson, "Virginia Baptist Ministers"; and idem, "Virginia's Contribution to Kentucky Baptists."

7. Daniel, "Virginia Baptists and the Negro," 66–67.

8. McColley, *Slavery and Jeffersonian Virginia*, 159–62.

9. Schmidt and Wilhelm, "Early Proslavery Petitions in Virginia."

10. Butler, *Awash in a Sea of Faith*, 215–24.

11. Heyrman, *Southern Cross*, esp. 227–30, 241–47. See also Lindman, "Acting the Manly Christian."

12. See Frey, *Water from the Rock.*

13. The account of the events of the Revolution in Virginia in this and the following paragraphs is drawn from Selby, *Revolution in Virginia;* Eller, *Chesapeake Bay in the American Revolution;* Holton, *Forced Founders;* and Frey, *Water from the Rock.*

14. Holton, *Forced Founders*, 140–43.

15. Deposition of Dr. William Pasteur, quoted in Frey, *Water from the Rock*, 55; Holton, *Forced Founders*, 143–45.

16. Holton, *Forced Founders*, 146.

17. Selby, *Revolution in Virginia*, 62–63.

18. Dunmore's proclamation, quoted in ibid., 66.

19. Selby, *Revolution in Virginia*, 64–68; Frey, *Water from the Rock*, 63–74.

20. Selby, *Revolution in Virginia*, 67; Holton, *Forced Founders*, 156.

21. Pybus, "Jefferson's Faulty Math," 249–50.

22. See Fallaw and Stoer, "Old Dominion under Fire."

23. Pybus, "Jefferson's Faulty Math," 251–52.

24. See Goldenberg, "Virginia Ports in the American Revolution," 320–23.

25. Fallaw and Stoer, "Old Dominion under Fire," 447.

26. Ibid.; see also Parker, "Old South Quay in Southampton County," 169–70.

27. Inspection Rolls of Negro Emigrants, 23–27 April, 29–31 July, 22 September–19 November 1783, Miscellaneous Papers of the Continental Congress, 1774–1789, M332, reel 7, David Library of the American Revolution.

28. Southampton County Court Minutes, 7 September 1831, in Tragle, 202.

29. Black Creek Baptist Church, Minute Book, 1776–1804; Raccoon Swamp [Antioch] Baptist Church, Minute Book, 1772–1837; Mill Swamp Baptist Church, Minute Book, 1777–1790; Burkitt, 65–66.

30. Semple, 465. See also Spencer, *History of Kentucky Baptists*, 1:194.

31. Allen, "David Barrow's *Circular Letter*," 450. For Barrow's, Sarah Gilliam's, and Hinchea Gilliam's membership at Raccoon Swamp, see Raccoon Swamp [Antioch] Baptist Church, Minute Book, 1772–1837, membership list near beginning of book and entry for 1 May 1774. For the exact date of Mill Swamp's constitution, see Mill Swamp Baptist Church, Minute Book, 1777–1790, copy of constitution on first page. For other biographical details, see James B. Taylor, *Virginia Baptist Ministers*, 161–62; Spencer, *History of Kentucky Baptists*, 1:192–97; and Semple, 464–66.

32. Semple, 465.

33. Mathews, *Religion in the Old South*, xvii.

34. See, e.g., Burkitt, 66, 76, 78–79, 80, 100, 101, 106; and Minutes of the Virginia Portsmouth Baptist Association, 1791–96, VBHS. The Portsmouth Association was formed in 1791 by the Virginia churches that had formerly belonged to the Kehukee Association. See also Semple, 453; and James B. Taylor, *Virginia Baptist*

Ministers, 164–65. For Kentucky, see "Minutes of the Elkhorn Baptist Association," 479, 481, 483, 487–89, 493–96, 502, 506–7; and North District Association Minutes, 1802–1804, in "Transcript of the Minutes," University of Kentucky Library.

35. "Minutes of the Elkhorn Baptist Association," 486–90, 494 (quotation on 489); North District Association Minutes, 1802, in "Transcript of the Minutes"; John Taylor, *Baptists on the American Frontier,* 245–46.

36. See Southampton County Court, Minute Book, 1786–1790, LVA.

37. In 1782, before he freed his slaves, Barrow owned 270 acres of land valued at £40.10, two slaves, two horses, and ten head of cattle. Southampton County Land Tax List and Southampton County Personal Property Tax List, both 1782, LVA.

38. Fristoe, *Ketocton Baptist Association,* 148.

39. Excerpt from *Journal of the House of Delegates,* 16 August 1775, Religious Petitions.

40. "Petition of Baptist Church at Occaquon," 20 June 1776, Religious Petitions.

41. In many ways these efforts by Virginia Baptists echoed those of Baptists in the North, who similarly consciously chose to support and shape the patriot cause. And as with the Virginia Baptists, this strategy had unintended consequences that conservative leaders of the denomination sought to restrain and control. See Juster, *Disorderly Women.* For more general overviews of the challenges and opportunities presented by the Revolution, see Butler, *Awash in a Sea of Faith,* 194–224; and Bonomi, *Under the Cope of Heaven,* 161–216.

42. On the issues of religious toleration and religious liberty, see the following by Thomas E. Buckley, S.J.: *Church and State;* "Evangelicals Triumphant"; "After Disestablishment"; and "Use and Abuse of Jefferson's Statute." See also Isaac, *Transformation of Virginia;* and the essays in Peterson and Vaughan, *Virginia Statute for Religious Freedom.*

43. *Virginia Gazette* (Dixon & Hunter), 11 October 1776. Thomas's poem is quoted and briefly discussed in Terman, "American Revolution and the Baptist and Presbyterian Clergy," 57. It is also reproduced, with several extra lines, in James B. Taylor, *Virginia Baptist Ministers,* 48. A brief discussion of part of this poem, excluding the opening link to Henry's famous speech, appears in Buckley, *Church and State,* 22–23.

44. Isaac, *Transformation of Virginia,* 266–67. See also Cohen, "'Liberty or Death' Speech."

45. The dating of Ireland's poem comes from James B. Taylor, *Virginia Baptist Ministers,* 124. Ireland died in 1806, and the poem was published in the posthumous *Life of the Rev. James Ireland,* 222–24, along with other examples of his poetry.

46. Details of the cheese story appear in Dreisbach, "Thomas Jefferson," 65–69. Leland remains his own best biographer. See Leland, *Writings.*

47. Leland, "The Virginia Chronicle" (1790), in *Writings,* 118.

48. Ibid., 122–23.

49. Ibid., 123.

50. Ibid., 95–96.

51. For differing but not entirely opposed views of the significance of the General Committee's adoption of this resolution, see Spangler, "Salvation Was Not Liberty," 226–27; and Daniel, "Virginia Baptists and the Negro," 65–66.

52. Leland, "Letter of Valediction on Leaving Virginia, in 1791," in *Writings*, 174.

53. Burkitt, 79.

54. Mill Swamp Baptist Church, Minute Book, 1777–1790, 17 June 1785.

55. Black Creek Baptist Church, Minute Book, 1776–1804, 20 May 1785.

56. David Barrow to Isaac Backus, 27 January 1797, VBHS.

57. James B. Taylor, *Virginia Baptist Ministers*, 163.

58. Southampton County, Virginia, Deed Book 6 (1782–1787), 11 March 1784.

59. Compiled from Southampton County Deed Books 6–11 (1782–1787 through 1805–1809) and Isle of Wight County Deed Books 15–20 (1782–1786 through 1805–1808). Of 188 manumissions, 133 (70.74%) made some combined statement of natural rights and religious justifications; 31 (16.49%) made no ideological statement of any kind; 20 (10.64%) made only a natural-rights statement; and only 1 (0.53%) made a religious statement alone. This pattern differs significantly from that found by Eva Sheppard in her study of manumission in Virginia, suggesting the importance of the influence of Quakers and anti-slavery Baptists in the particular case of Southampton and Isle of Wight counties. See Sheppard, "Question of Emancipation in Virginia." For overviews of Quaker anti-slavery, see Soderlund, *Quakers and Slavery;* David Brion Davis, *Problem of Slavery in the Age of Revolution,* 213–54; Aptheker, "Quakers and Negro Slavery"; and Weeks, *Southern Quakers and Slavery.*

60. From 1782 to 1806 at least 67 of 188 manumitters (36%), and possibly as many as 80 (43%), in Southampton and Isle of Wight were Quakers. More importantly, in 1782, the critical first year of the act, Quakers were responsible for 27 of 30 manumissions (90%). Calculated from Southampton County Deed Books 6–11 (1782–1787 through 1805–1809) and Isle of Wight County Deed Books 15–20 (1782–1786 through 1805–1808). Quakers were identified primarily by the use of numerical rather than standard "pagan" month and day names. The lower estimate was obtained by counting only those who clearly used this terminology, while the higher estimate included those whose deeds used both Quaker and standard language and those who had clear ties to prominent Quaker families but did not use Quaker terminology. This method, while rough, is sufficient to provide a general impression of the profile of manumitters in Southampton and Isle of Wight counties. The 1688 reference is based on a document presented to the Quarterly Meeting at Philadelphia, quoted in Aptheker, "Quakers and Negro Slavery," 335–36.

61. Black Creek Baptist Church, Minute Book, 1776–1804, 22 August 1788, membership list at end of book.

62. Southampton County, Deed Book 6 (1782–1787), 8 September 1785. There are several John Johnsons on the Southampton County Personal Property Tax Lists for 1782 and 1787. The Black Creek John Johnson was most likely the one who lived near Barrow in the neighborhood of the church. If so, Milly was the only slave he owned. (This information can be gleaned from the original order of the tax lists,

which generally proceed from household to household within particular neighborhoods.)

63. Black Creek Baptist Church, Minute Book, 1776–1804, 24 February, 26 May, 25 August, 24 November 1786, 23 February, July 1787.

64. Hughes, "Slaves for Hire," 260–61. For evidence that Isle of Wight, Southampton, and Sussex counties fit this general economic profile, see Kirby, *Poquosin*, 3–4, 29, 95–103; and Crofts, *Old Southampton*, 75–90.

65. These figures were arrived at by cross-referencing church membership data from the minute book with the Southampton County Personal Property Tax List, 1787. It is difficult to obtain reliable concrete figures because of names missing from or duplicated on tax lists, but general conclusions can be reached by calculating a maximum and minimum range of both slaveholding and holding size within the church based on names that can tentatively be identified.

66. Southampton County, Deed Book 7 (1787–1793), 14 February 1788. Both men had written the deeds several months earlier, in December 1787.

67. A Benjamin Beal was a member of Black Creek at the time, but there were two men of that name on the Southampton County Personal Property Tax Lists for 1782 and 1787, and it is not clear that Benjamin Beal Jr., who manumitted Mingo, is the same man who belonged to Black Creek. On the 1787 list one Benjamin Beale was listed as "son of Richard," so he was probably not Benjamin Beal Jr. The other Benjamin Beale, listed as a cooper, was a neighbor of Barrow's and was most likely the Black Creek member, although he was not listed as a junior Benjamin Beale. Although Benjamin Beal Jr., the manumitter, used the standard natural-rights and golden-rule formula in freeing Mingo, he did not use Barrow's specific language. I think it is more likely than not that Benjamin Beal Jr. was the Black Creek Benjamin Beal, but it is far from certain.

68. Black Creek Baptist Church, Minute Book, 1776–1804, 17 October 1801; Black Creek Baptist Church, Minute Book, 1804–1818, membership list at end of book, VBHS.

69. Black Creek Baptist Church, Minute Book, 1776–1804, 27 January 1776, 22 August 1783, 28 July 1787, 22 May 1789, 21 August 1790, 26 November 1802.

70. See Spangler, "Salvation Was Not Liberty," 226–27; and Daniel, "Virginia Baptists and the Negro," 65–66.

71. Daniel, "Virginia Baptists and the Negro," 66–67.

72. Black Creek Baptist Church, Minute Book, 1776–1804, 24 June, 26 August 1791, 20 August 1793, 21 February 1794, 22 February, 21 June, 23 August 1799, 26 February, 26 March 1802.

73. Isle of Wight County, Deed Book 17 (1791–1796), 5 September 1791, 6 July 1795, 6 February 1797.

74. The *Circular Letter* was originally published for Barrow in Norfolk by Willett & O'Connor in 1798 and is reprinted in full in Allen, "David Barrow's *Circular Letter*." The most complete statement of Barrow's views is his *Involuntary, Perpetual, Absolute, Hereditary Slavery, Examined*. Also useful is "Rev. David Barrow's Journal & some notes," in the Lyman C. Draper Manuscript Collection.

75. Barrow, *Involuntary Perpetual, Absolute, Hereditary Slavery, Examined,* 41.

76. For discussions of Barrow's thought, see Essig, *Bonds of Wickedness,* 74–78; and Allen, "David Barrow's *Circular Letter,*" 440–42.

77. Essig, *Bonds of Wickedness,* 75–77.

78. Barrow, *Involuntary Perpetual, Absolute, Hereditary Slavery, Examined,* 26.

79. "Rev. David Barrow's Journal," 17 May 1795.

80. Black Creek Baptist Church, Minute Book, 1818–1862, December 1825–September 1827, VBHS.

81. Ibid., September 1827.

82. Petition of the inhabitants of Lunenburg County, in Schmidt and Wilhelm, "Early Proslavery Petitions in Virginia," 141.

83. Petition of the inhabitants of Brunswick County, in ibid., 143.

84. Petition of the inhabitants of Lunenburg County, in ibid.

85. "Minutes of the Virginia Portsmouth Baptist Association, Holden at London Bridge Meeting House, Princess Anne County" (1796), 5, VBHS.

86. Ibid.

87. David Barrow to Isaac Backus, 27 January 1797.

88. North District Association Minutes, 1805–1807, in "Transcript of the Minutes," 45–61 (quotations on 45, 54, 49, 46). See also Najar, "Meddling with Emancipation."

89. In fact, the initial complaint against Barrow that led to his expulsion from the North District Association had come from the Bracken Association, which Barrow had attended as messenger. See North District Association Minutes, 1804–1805, in "Transcript of the Minutes." As noted above, Barrow was a frequent messenger between associations.

90. Allen, "David Barrow's *Circular Letter,*" 449, 450.

91. See "Resolutions" of the Baptised Church of Christ, Friends of Humanity, in Grigg, *Remarks and Selections,* 60–64. For more on the wider context of these developments, see Najar, "Meddling with Emancipation," 180–86; and White, "History of the Baptized Licking-Locust Association."

92. Spencer, *History of Kentucky Baptists,* 1:197. Spencer did not entirely approve of Barrow's chosen life's work: "How sad that fourteen years of the life of such a man should have been wasted in so hopeless an enterprise" (ibid.).

93. Ibid. Spencer seems to have based this information on an interview with "an aged son of Mr. Barrow, recently living in Montgomery County" (ibid.).

94. Pybus, "Jefferson's Faulty Math," 258–59.

95. Luther P. Jackson, "Religious Development," 177.

96. Berlin, *Many Thousands Gone,* 278. On the contradictions and equivocations of this era, see also McColley, *Slavery and Jeffersonian Virginia;* and Wolf, *Race and Liberty in the New Nation.*

97. Berlin, *Many Thousands Gone,* 266–68.

98. Ibid., 277–85.

99. Frey, *Water from the Rock,* 284–97.

100. Semple, 170; Sobel, *Trabelin' On,* 192–93.

101. See chapter 4 for a full discussion of the effects of rising black membership within the churches.

102. Frey, *Water from the Rock,* 284–87; Luther P. Jackson, "Religious Development," 188–96.

103. Semple, 148. The date 1781 comes from Asplund, *Universal Register . . . for the Years 1790, 1791, 1792, 1793, and part of 1794,* 50. See also Luther P. Jackson, "Religious Development," 189.

104. Burkitt, 264. See also Sidbury, *Ploughshares into Swords,* 37. Semple suggests that Bishop served as pastor to the whole church, and some historians have followed him, but as Luther P. Jackson points out, this point is not entirely clear. Semple, 458; Frey, *Water from the Rock,* 269; Sobel, *Trabelin' On,* 192; Jackson, "Religious Development," 177 and n26b.

105. Burkitt, 264–65.

106. "Minutes of the Virginia Portsmouth Baptist Association, Holden at Malone's Meeting-House, Mecklenburg County, Saturday, May 26, 1798" (1798), 2, VBHS.

107. Sidbury, "Reading, Revelation, and Rebellion," 131.

108. Sidbury, "Saint Domingue in Virginia," 538–44. See also idem, *Ploughshares into Swords,* 41–48.

109. This account of Gabriel's Rebellion draws on Sidbury, *Ploughshares into Swords;* Frey, *Water from the Rock,* 256–57, 320–21; and Egerton, *Gabriel's Rebellion.*

110. Egerton, *Gabriel's Rebellion,* 109.

111. Ibid., 35–49.

112. Postconspiracy trial records, Executive Communications to the Legislature, box 24, LVA, quoted in Sidbury, *Ploughshares into Swords,* 97.

113. Sidbury, *Ploughshares into Swords,* 74–75; Frey, *Water from the Rock,* 320–21.

114. Debate between Ben Woolfork and Martin reported in Woolfork's confession, Executive Communications to the Legislature, box 24, LVA, quoted in Sidbury, *Ploughshares into Swords,* 76–78. See also idem, "Reading, Revelation, and Rebellion," 119–23.

115. Sidbury, "Reading, Revelation, and Rebellion," 120, 132–33.

116. Egerton, *Gabriel's Rebellion,* 163–68.

117. Sobel, *Trabelin' On,* 190, 192.

118. Fristoe, *Ketocton Baptist Association,* 157–62.

119. Semple, 465–66.

120. Ibid., 148.

121. Ibid., 170.

122. Ibid., 458.

4. SOMEWHAT LIBERATED

1. South Quay Baptist Church, Minute Book, 1775–1827, 4 October 1788.

2. Tom (Porter's) is listed on both Mill Swamp's and South Quay's first mem-

bership lists, covering the periods 1777–90 and 1775–1827, respectively. Internal evidence in the lists suggests that he became a member of Mill Swamp before 1777. In 1785 Tom was dismissed from Mill Swamp along with other members to constitute South Quay as a separate church. Abraham Porter was the only white male church member of that surname, and several enslaved members are listed on the membership list as "Porter's" and in the disciplinary records as "Bro. Porter's," suggesting that they belonged to a fellow church member.

3. South Quay Baptist Church, Minute Book, 1775–1827, November 1788.

4. See Juster, *Disorderly Women;* see also Lindman, "World of Baptists."

5. Edwards, "Virginia Materials"; see also idem, "Morgan Edwards' 1772 Virginia Notebook."

6. This view builds on Mathews, "Christianizing the South."

7. South Quay Baptist Church, Minute Book, 1775–1827, 5 March 1791, 4 December 1802. On the nature and meanings of church discipline, see Wills, *Democratic Religion.*

8. In her excellent study of female preaching Catherine A. Brekus briefly discusses female preaching and exhorting in the South, but in general the South occupies a marginal place in her account. Besides the Separate use of deaconesses and "eldresses," there is no indication that female preaching ever had a formal status comparable to male licensed preaching. See Brekus, *Strangers and Pilgrims,* esp. 61–67, 128–31, 248–49. For examples of how the licensing process worked in the churches of southeastern Virginia, see Raccoon Swamp [Antioch] Baptist Church, Minute Book, 1772–1837, 1 May 1774, 22 May, 3 August 1778; Black Creek Baptist Church, Minute Book, 1776–1804, 25 February 1785, 28 July 1787; Mill Swamp Baptist Church, Minute Book, 1777–1790, 13 June 1782; and High Hills [of Nottoway] Baptist Church, Minute Book, 1787–1845, 14 February 1824, 18 February 1826, LVA.

9. The division is discussed and explained in Burkitt, 108–10. See also Lumpkin, *History of the Portsmouth Baptist Association,* 1–21.

10. The remarkable exception is Sappony, the Separate Baptist church founded in the same revival that spawned Raccoon Swamp, which declined rapidly after the early death of its influential first pastor, James Bell, a justice of the peace and sheriff in Sussex County, in 1778 at the age of forty-three. Burkitt, 60–63.

11. See, e.g., South Quay Baptist Church, Minute Book, 1775–1827, 3 September 1785, 2 April 1786, 6 October 1787.

12. Black Creek Baptist Church, Minute Book, 1776–1804, membership list at end of book; Southampton County, Deed Book 6 (1782–1787), 8 September 1785.

13. Essig, "A Very Wintry Season." See also Mathews, *Religion in the Old South,* 66–80.

14. The 1772–83 Raccoon Swamp membership list is damaged, so the totals in table 4 do not include the approximately forty-eight names that are missing or illegible, but even accounting for the missing names (assuming they were distributed similarly to the legible ones), the total number of black members over the entire

period 1772–83 would be about twenty-four, while in 1789 alone there were fifty-six black members.

15. Spangler, "Salvation Was Not Liberty."

16. Conclusions were reached by cross-referencing church membership with the 1787 tax lists and on U.S. Bureau of the Census, Federal Manuscript Censuses of 1810 and 1830 for Isle of Wight, Southampton, and Sussex Counties, National Archives and Records Administration Research Center, Philadelphia, PA. Exact figures are impossible to obtain because of duplicate or missing names in the records. General conclusions are possible, however, and show that at Raccoon Swamp, Mill Swamp, South Quay, High Hills, Seacock, and Smithfield churches slaveholders formed the majority of white male members in 1787, 1810, and 1830. Black Creek Baptist Church appears to have had a small majority of non-slaveholders throughout the period. Tucker's Swamp Baptist Church probably had a small majority of non-slaveholders in 1810 (the first year for which data are available for that church), but by 1830 slaveholders formed the majority. Beaver Dam Baptist Church had a majority of non-slaveholders in 1830, just after its 1828 split from Black Creek.

17. On the development of racial ideology and slave society in Virginia, see Brown, *Good Wives, Nasty Wenches, and Anxious Patriarchs;* Kulikoff, *Tobacco and Slaves;* and Edmund S. Morgan, *American Slavery, American Freedom.*

18. Mill Swamp Baptist Church, Minute Book, 1779–1790, 13 June 1777.

19. South Quay Baptist Church, Minute Book, 1775–1827, 2 October 1778, July 1785.

20. Ibid., July 1785.

21. Burkitt, 80.

22. Black Creek Baptist Church, Minute Book, 1776–1804, 24 June 1791; Black Creek Baptist Church, Minute Book, 1818–1862, June 1825.

23. High Hills [of Nottoway] Baptist Church, Minute Book, 1787–1845, "Decorum," near beginning of book.

24. Mill Swamp Baptist Church, Minute Book, 1777–1790, 19 September 1777.

25. See South Quay Baptist Church, Minute Book, 1775–1827, 1 October 1791; High Hills [of Nottoway] Baptist Church, Minute Book, 1787–1845, 1802[?]; Burkitt, 66–67 (rules adopted at meeting of 27 May 1782); Black Creek Baptist Church, Minute Book, 1776–1804, 22 February 1793.

26. "Minutes of the Virginia Portsmouth Baptist Association Holden at Black-Water Meeting-House, Princess Anne County, May 24th, 25th, & 26th, 1794" (1794), 6, VBHS.

27. See, e.g., Black Creek Baptist Church, Minute Book, 1776–1804, 26 November 1790, 25 November 1791, 23 March 1792, 26 August, 24 December 1796, 20 January 1797.

28. Mill Swamp Baptist Church, Minute Book, 1791–1811, 14 September 1799. Among the free blacks who joined during this period was a man named Peter who had been freed by Mill Swamp's assistant clerk and deacon, James Gwaltney, in

1797. Despite his freedom, the church continued to refer to him as "Gwaltney's." See, e.g., the minutes for August 1799.

29. Ibid., 14 March 1800.

30. Ibid.

31. "Minutes of the Virginia Portsmouth Baptist Association Holden at Shoulder's Hill Meeting House, Nansemond County, May 24, 1800" (1800), 6, VBHS.

32. See Spangler, "Becoming Baptists"; idem, "Salvation Was Not Liberty"; idem, "Presbyterians, Baptists, and the Making of Slave Society in Virginia"; Lindman, "Acting the Manly Christian"; and Eslinger, "Beginnings of Afro-American Christianity."

33. Eslinger, "Beginnings of Afro-American Christianity," esp. 197–202, 207–10 (quotation on 202).

34. See chapter 2 for a background discussion of discipline and its meanings.

35. Black Creek Baptist Church, Minute Book, 1776–1804, 20 February 1789, 7 December 1792, 21 February 1800.

36. Burkitt, 58.

37. "Minutes of the Virginia Portsmouth Baptist Association Holden at Meherrin Meeting House, Southampton County, May 26, 1792" (1792), 2–3, VBHS.

38. "Minutes of the Virginia Portsmouth Baptist Association Holden at Black-Creek Meeting-House, Southampton County, May 25 &c., 1793" (1793), 4, VBHS.

39. "Minutes of the Virginia Portsmouth Baptist Association Holden at Black-Water Meeting-House, Princess Anne County, May 24, 25, and 26, 1794" (1794), 5–6, VBHS.

40. See, e.g., South Quay Baptist Church, Minute Book, 1775–1827, 4 June 1813, 30 July 1814; South Quay Baptist Church, Minute Book, 1827–1899, 4 December 1829, LVA; Mill Swamp Baptist Church, Minute Book, 1812–1840, 3 September 1830; Black Creek Baptist Church, Minute Book, 1804–1818, June 1812.

41. Mill Swamp Baptist Church, Minute Book, 1791–1811, 15 September 1797, 16 March 1798, 20 April 1799.

42. U.S. Bureau of the Census, Federal Manuscript Census of 1810 for Southampton County. The average slaveholding in Southampton in 1810 was 4.78, putting Gardner's 13 slaves well above the average for the county as a whole.

43. "Minutes of the Virginia Portsmouth Baptist Association, Holden at Rackoon Swamp Meeting House, Sussex County, Virginia, May 24th, 25th, and 26th, 1806" (1806), 4, VBHS; South Quay Baptist Church, Minute Book, 1775–1827, September, 2 October 1813.

44. South Quay Baptist Church Minute Book, 1775–1827, 31 August 1811.

45. See Isaac, *Transformation of Virginia;* and idem, "Evangelical Revolt."

46. South Quay Baptist Church, Minute Book, 1775–1827, 30 November 1808.

47. On the goals of discipline and the importance of acknowledgment and repentance, see Mathews, *Religion in the Old South,* 46. See also Wills, *Democratic Religion.*

48. South Quay Baptist Church, Minute Book, 1775–1827, 30 November 1808, 30 August 1812.

49. Ibid., 4 March 1814, 2 June, 1 December 1815, 6 April, 31 May, 30 August 1816.

50. Mill Swamp Baptist Church, Minute Book, 1791–1811, 14 September 1792, 19 April, 17 May, 14 June 1793.

51. Mill Swamp Baptist Church, Minute Book, 1777–1790, 16 March 1787.

52. Mill Swamp Baptist Church, Minute Book, 1791–1811, 4 March, 3 June 1808.

53. South Quay Baptist Church, Minute Book, 1775–1827, 4 March, 1 April 1809.

54. Ibid., April 1805.

55. Ibid., 3 March, 2, 30 June, 1 July 1810.

56. Ibid., 1 September, 1 December 1810, 2 March, 31 August, 30 November 1811, 29 February 1812.

57. Ibid., 30 May, September 1817, 4 June, 3 September, 3 December 1819.

58. Black Creek Baptist Church, Minute Book, 1776–1804, membership list, 22 August 1788.

59. Ibid., 23 August, 22 November, 21 December 1799, 25 December 1800, 20 February, 26 June, 21 August 1801, 18 November 1803, 23 March 1804.

60. Black Creek Baptist Church, Minute Book, 1804–1818, 22 November 1805, 22 February 1806, November, 26 December 1807.

61. Ibid., June, September 1812.

62. Black Creek Baptist Church, Minute Book, 1776–1804, February 1792.

63. South Quay Baptist Church, Minute Book, 1775–1827, "The Baptist Church Covenant."

64. The predominance of drunkenness and other social offenses among white men and that of sexual offenses among white women in the final decade of the study is somewhat masked by a marked increase in religious offenses for both groups because of a major controversy over missions at South Quay that resulted in a division of the church in 1835. Drunkenness accounted for 65 percent of all charges of social offenses for white men from 1821 to 1840, up from only 41 percent over the preceding four decades.

65. This argument is consistent with Lindman, "Acting the Manly Christian."

66. Mathews, *Religion in the Old South,* 45.

67. Blair Pogue points out the importance of understanding this dimension of church discipline and fellowship in "I Cannot Believe the Gospel That Is So Much Preached."

68. The quotations are from the King James Version of the Bible.

69. See Ahlstrom, *Religious History of the American People,* 70–83.

70. "Minutes of the Virginia Portsmouth Baptist Association Held at the Meeting-House Near Cut-Banks of Nottoway, Dinwiddie County, May 23, 1801" (1801), 13, VBHS.

71. See Ahlstrom, *Religious History of the American People,* 70–83.

72. *Oxford English Dictionary,* s.v. "Liberty," http://www.oed.library.upenn.edu (accessed 24 February 1999). One recent commentator discusses *liberation* and *salvation* as essentially synonymous terms in religious discourse. See Surin, "Liberation." Surin's definition of *liberation* as "the name of a desire . . . to overcome,

circumvent, or ameliorate an unacceptable condition of being, whether individual or transindividual or both," highlights the ways in which the spiritual and the social inevitably overlap in the religious language of liberty.

73. Donald Mathews noted the importance of liberty as theme in antebellum southern religion in his field-shaping work *Religion in the Old South*, 237–50.

74. Southampton County, Deed Book 7 (1787–1793), 14 February 1788; Black Creek Baptist Church, Minute Book, 1776–1804, membership list located at end of book; Black Creek Baptist Church, Minute Book, 1804–1818, membership list located at end of book.

75. Burkitt, 67; Raccoon Swamp [Antioch] Baptist Church, Minute Book, 1772–1837, 10 May 1835.

76. Mill Swamp Baptist Church, Minute Book, 1791–1811, 14 March 1800; Black Creek Baptist Church, Minute Book, 1804–1818, June 1808; Burkitt, 74.

77. John Williams Journal, 10 May 1771, VBHS, quoted in Isaac, *Transformation of Virginia*, 163.

78. Williams, "John Williams' Journal,"

79. Black Creek Baptist Church, Minute Book, 1818–1862, covenant at beginning of book.

80. South Quay Baptist Church, Minute Book, 1775–1827.

81. Mill Swamp Baptist Church, Minute Book, 1812–1840, 31 August 1827. For similar language, see Black Creek Baptist Church, Minute Book, 1776–1804, 20 February 1789, 21 August 1790.

82. South Quay Baptist Church, Minute Book, 1775–1827, 3 March 1810.

83. Ibid., December 1812, 4 December 1813, February, 4 March 1814.

84. Tom of Battle apparently remained in the church until his death. Abram of Maney is listed on the membership list as "gone to TN" sometime between 1814 and 1827. There is no other record of Aaron of Blackledge or any other Aaron.

85. Black Creek Baptist Church, Minute Book, 1804–1818, March, September 1812.

86. "Minutes of the Virginia Portsmouth Baptist Association Held at Otterdam Meeting-House, Surry County, Virginia, May 26, 27, & 28, 1810" (1810), 5, VBHS.

87. Mill Swamp Baptist Church, Minute Book, 1812–1840, 31 August 1821.

88. Semple, 148.

89. South Quay Baptist Church, Minute Book, 1775–1827, 30 November 1822, 1 March 1823.

90. Ibid., 6 December 1823, 23 April, 4 September 1824; South Quay Baptist Church, Minute Book, 1827–1899, 2 January 1828, September 1829.

91. South Quay Baptist Church, Minute Book, 1775–1827, 24 July 1824.

92. Ibid., October 1791, March 1813.

93. See, e.g., Beaver Dam Baptist Church, Minute Book, 1828–1894, March 1831, LVA.

94. Black Creek Baptist Church, Minute Book, 1818–1862, membership list near the beginning of the book; Black Creek Baptist Church, Minute Book, 1804–1818, membership list at the end of the book.

95. Black Creek Baptist Church, Minute Book, 1804–1818, June 1813.

96. South Quay Baptist Church, Minute Book, 1775–1827, 4 June 1813.

97. See, e.g., ibid., 30 May, 30 November 1817, 22 February 1818, 3 September 1819, 26 August 1821; Black Creek Baptist Church, Minute Book, 1818–1862, 20 December 1822, June 1829; Tucker's Swamp Baptist Church, Minute Book, 1818–1830, 10 September 1825, 17 May 1829, February, 16 May, 15 August, November 1830, VBHS.

98. Raccoon Swamp [Antioch] Baptist Church, Minute Book, 1772–1837, 7 October 1826.

99. Eslinger, "Beginnings of Afro-American Christianity," esp. 198, 206–11.

100. South Quay Baptist Church, Minute Book, 1775–1827, 4 June 1813.

101. Ibid., August, 30 November 1817.

102. Black Creek Baptist Church, Minute Book, 1818–1862, December 1825.

103. Ibid., March, June 1826.

104. Ibid., September 1827.

105. See Wills, *Democratic Religion,* 11–37; and Mathews, *Religion in the Old South,* 43–44.

106. Black Creek Baptist Church, Minute Book, 1818–1862, September 1827.

107. Ibid., emphasis in the original.

108. Ibid.

109. South Quay Baptist Church, Minute Book, 1775–1827, 25 September 1825, LVA.

110. South Quay Baptist Church, Minute Book, 1827–1899, February 1829, 3 September, October, November 1830.

111. Black Creek Baptist Church, Minute Book, 1818–1862, March 1823.

112. South Quay Baptist Church, Minute Book, 1827–1899, January 1831.

5. REBELLIOUS AND UNGOVERNABLE

1. *Confessions,* 44–45.

2. Ibid., 46.

3. Ibid.; Sobel, *Trabelin' On,* 162–65.

4. *Confessions,* 46–47.

5. Ibid., 47–48. On the eclipse and its effects, see Masur, *1831,* 3–10.

6. This account is based largely on the chronology given in Tragle, xv–xviii.

7. See McCurry, "Two Faces of Republicanism"; and idem, *Masters of Small Worlds.* Other important aspects of this vision are described in Genovese, *Roll, Jordan, Roll;* Fox-Genovese, *Within the Plantation Household;* Klein, *Unification of a Slave State,* esp. chap. 9; Faust, "Evangelicalism and the Proslavery Argument"; idem, "Proslavery Argument in History"; Fox-Genovese and Genovese, "Divine Sanction of Social Order"; and Mathews, *Religion in the Old South,* 136–84.

8. On Turner's subversive use of Christian and Revolutionary traditions, see Sundquist, *To Wake the Nations,* 27–82.

9. Robert, *Road from Monticello;* Alison Goodyear Freehling, *Drift toward Dis-*

solution. The classic statement of the proslavery position in Virginia that emerged from the legislative debates is Dew, *Review of the Debate in the Virginia Legislature of 1831 and 1832*, an extended version of his article "Abolition of Negro Slavery."

10. On white arguments that Christianization promoted harmony, see Butler, *Awash in a Sea of Faith,* 129–63; Ambrose, "Of Stations and Relations," esp. 56; and Frey and Wood, *Come Shouting to Zion.*

11. Gross and Bender, "History, Politics, and Literature," 493–94.

12. Tragle, 16–17.

13. Drewry, *Southampton Insurrection,* 81.

14. *Richmond Constitutional Whig,* 29 August 1831, in Tragle, 52.

15. Quoted in Peter H. Wood, "Nat Turner," 30.

16. *Richmond Compiler,* 24 August 1831, in Tragle, 38.

17. *Petersburg Intelligencer,* 26 August 1831, in Tragle, 38; *Richmond Constitutional Whig,* 29 and 23 August 1831, in Tragle, 51 and 36.

18. *Richmond Constitutional Whig,* 23 August 1831, in Tragle, 35; *Richmond Compiler,* 24 August 1831, in Tragle, 36; *Petersburg Intelligencer,* 26 August 1831, in Tragle, 38.

19. *Richmond Constitutional Whig,* 30 August 1831, in Tragle, 51.

20. *Richmond Enquirer,* 30 August 1831, in Tragle, 44.

21. See the works cited in n. 7, above.

22. McDowell, speech to Virginia House of Delegates, 21 January 1832, in Robert, *Road from Monticello,* 104.

23. The operative meaning of *wretch* in this case is "a vile, sorry, or despicable person; one of opprobrious or reprehensible character; a mean or contemptible creature." *Oxford English Dictionary,* 2nd ed.

24. *Richmond Constitutional Whig,* 23 August 1831, in Tragle, 36; *Richmond Compiler,* 24 August 1831, in Tragle, 37; *Petersburg Intelligencer,* 26 August 1831, in Tragle, 38; *Norfolk American Beacon,* 26 August 1831, in Tragle, 42.

25. *Richmond Enquirer,* 30 August 1831, in Tragle, 43–44.

26. There were no reports of rape or other "outrages" committed by the rebels, and several newspaper reports note their absence. William Sidney Drewry, a white southerner writing at the height of Jim Crow, flatly refused to believe that no sexual assaults had occurred. "Women were insulted," he insisted, "and it is said that Nat offered protection to one beautiful girl if she would consent to be his wife, but death was to this noble woman a blessing in comparison with such a prospect." Drewry, *Southampton Insurrection,* 117. In the controversy surrounding William Styron's novel *The Confessions of Nat Turner,* published in 1967, Styron and many of his defenders revealed a similar insistence on the centrality of racialized psychosexual issues to the revolt that probably owed more to Drewry's era than to Nat Turner's.

27. *Richmond Compiler,* 27 August 1831, in Tragle, 48.

28. See, e.g., ibid., 24 August 1831, in Tragle, 37.

29. *Petersburg Intelligencer,* 26 August 1831, in Tragle, 39.

30. *Richmond Constitutional Whig,* 29 August 1831, in Tragle, 55.

31. Peter H. Wood, "Nat Turner," 33.

32. *Norfolk American Beacon*, 1 September 1831, in Tragle, 57.

33. *Richmond Constitutional Whig*, 6 September 1831, in Tragle, 72–73, emphasis in the original.

34. Ibid., 3 September 1831, in Tragle, 71.

35. Ibid., 26 September 1831, in Tragle, 89–90.

36. *Lynchburg Virginian*, 15 September 1831, in Tragle, 80.

37. See *Richmond Enquirer*, 30 August 1831, in Tragle, 45; *Richmond Compiler*, 3 September 1831, in Tragle, 60–61; *Richmond Constitutional Whig*, 3 and 26 September 1831, in Tragle, 67–68 and 96.

38. *Richmond Constitutional Whig*, 3 September 1831, in Tragle, 67.

39. *Richmond Enquirer*, 30 August 1831, in Tragle, 45.

40. *Confessions*, 52–53.

41. *Richmond Enquirer*, 27 September 1831, in Tragle, 100.

42. Floyd to Lt. Col. W. J. Worth, 2 September 1831, in Tragle, 271.

43. *Richmond Constitutional Whig*, 26 September 1831, in Tragle, 99.

44. Dew, "Abolition of Negro Slavery," 28.

45. "Message of Governor Floyd to the Virginia Legislature," 6 December 1831, in Tragle, 432.

46. On Floyd's "hidden polemic" against Garrison and Walker, among others, see Mary Kemp Davis, *Nat Turner before the Bar of Judgment*, 15–41, esp. 23–34. On the more general relationship between the Turner rebellion and the textual antislavery tradition, see Sundquist, *To Wake the Nations*, 64–67.

47. *Confessions*, 48.

48. For a discussion of the possible meanings of this date, see Sundquist, *To Wake the Nations*, 65–66.

49. *Norfolk Herald*, 4 November 1831, in Tragle, 135.

50. *Liberator*, 1 October 1831, in Tragle, 115.

51. Southampton County Court Minutes, 7 September 1831, in Tragle, 202.

52. *Richmond Compiler*, 27 August 1831, in Tragle, 48; *Norfolk American Beacon*, 29 August 1831, in Tragle, 49.

53. *Richmond Compiler*, 27 August 1831, in Tragle, 49.

54. *Richmond Enquirer*, 30 August 1831, in Tragle, 44–45.

55. *Richmond Constitutional Whig*, 29 August 1831, in Tragle, 53.

56. Gross and Bender, "History, Politics, and Literature," 493–94. This article is also deeply problematic, however, since many of its perceptive points are made in the context of a larger argument defending William Styron from criticism for his controversial novel *The Confessions of Nat Turner*. Thus, while the authors rightly call attention to the significance of Gray's intentions and "framing" of the 1831 *Confessions*, they are overly dismissive of the religious aspects of Turner's motivations because they want to defend Styron's imaginative license to re-create those motivations as psychosexual pathology.

57. Sundquist, *To Wake the Nations*, 36–56 (quotations on 49–50).

58. Ibid., 61.

59. *Confessions*, 54.

60. *Richmond Enquirer,* 26 August 1831, in Tragle, 46.

61. *Richmond Constitutional Whig,* 29 August 1831, in Tragle, 51–52.

62. See Oates, *Fires of Jubilee,* 13–14.

63. Sidbury, *Ploughshares into Swords;* Egerton, *He Shall Go Out Free.*

64. Floyd to Hamilton, 19 November 1831, in Tragle, 275–76.

65. *Richmond Enquirer,* 2 September 1831, in Tragle, 59.

66. Ibid., 20 September 1831, in Tragle, 85.

67. Ibid., 27 September 1831, in Tragle, 99–100. Solomon Parker is not listed as a member of any of the churches in the counties, but many enslaved Baptists are listed as "Parker's," and several white female Parkers were members of the churches.

68. Ibid., 27 September 1831, in Tragle, 100.

69. See Raccoon Swamp [Antioch] Baptist Church, Minute Book, 1772–1837, 20 October 1831.

70. French, *Rebellious Slave,* 37–41.

71. *Liberator,* 1 October 1831, in Tragle, 114.

72. *Richmond Constitutional Whig,* 26 September 1831, in Tragle, 91–92.

73. Ibid., in Tragle, 91.

74. *Confessions,* 42–48. Stephen B. Oates crafts a narrative of the rebellion based in part on a similar view of Nat's frustrated ambitions; see Oates, *Fires of Jubilee.* On Travis, Francis, and Porter, see Parramore, "Covenant in Jerusalem," 58, 262n1.

75. *Richmond Enquirer,* 25 November 1831, in Tragle, 144–45.

76. *Lynchburg Virginian,* 15 September 1831, in Tragle, 80.

77. "Minutes of the Virginia Portsmouth Baptist Association . . . 1832," 45, VBHS.

78. *Lynchburg Virginian,* 15 September 1831, in Tragle 80.

79. Black Creek Baptist Church, Minute Book, 1818–1862, September 1831.

80. Mill Swamp Baptist Church, Minute Book, 1812–1840, October 1831; Raccoon Swamp [Antioch] Baptist Church, Minute Book, 1772–1837, 20 October 1831.

81. Mill Swamp Baptist Church, Minute Book, 1812–1840, 31 August 1832.

82. Ibid., 31 August, 30 November 1832, 6 April, 29 November 1833.

83. "Minutes of the Virginia Portsmouth Baptist Association . . . 1832," 45; see also ibid., 9, 14, 25. The association's language in its letter directly echoes phrases from the reports of Raccoon Swamp and Mill Swamp, also recorded in the minutes.

84. Ibid., 26.

85. Tucker's Swamp Baptist Church, Minute Book, 1818–1857, 7 January 1832, VBHS. For other examples, see Raccoon Swamp [Antioch] Baptist Church, Minute Book, 1772–1837, 12 November 1831, 25 March, 22 April, 25 November 1832; and Black Creek Baptist Church, Minute Book, 1818–1862, December 1831, January, March, April 1832.

86. "Minutes of the Virginia Portsmouth Baptist Association . . . 1832," 27. On the actions of the state legislature, see Alison Goodyear Freehling, *Drift toward Dissolution,* 188–89.

87. Raccoon Swamp [Antioch] Baptist Church, Minute Book, 1772–1837, 9 June 1832; South Quay Baptist Church, Minute Book, 1827–1899, March 1833; Black Creek Baptist Church, Minute Book, 1818–1862, 1841.

88. Smithfield Baptist Church, Minute Book, 1830–1894, 11 August 1833, VBHS. Raccoon Swamp apparently began requiring masters' permissions in 1833.

89. South Quay Baptist Church, Minute Book, 1827–1899, February 1841.

90. High Hills [of Nottoway] Baptist Church, Minute Book, 1787–1845, 18 August 1838. See also Raccoon Swamp [Antioch] Baptist Church, Minute Book, 1837–1892, 8 June 1839. These are the first explicit mentions of segregated seating, indicating that it had become more of a priority for white church members and was being purposely inscribed in the architecture of the churches. W. Harrison Daniel finds the earliest evidence of segregated seating in Virginia at the First Baptist Church in Alexandria in 1811 and Wicomico Baptist Church in 1812. See Daniel, "Virginia Baptists and the Negro," 60.

91. Seacock [Elam] Baptist Church, Minute Book, 1832–1889, 13 March 1842, VBHS. See also, South Quay Baptist Church, Minute Book, 1827–1899, March 1842; Tucker's Swamp Baptist Church, Minute Book, 1818–1857, 11 March 1842. This change in the Portsmouth Association's constitution was specifically prompted by an ongoing conflict with black churches in Petersburg and Norfolk over whether they could be represented in the association by one of their own members or had to appoint a white minister as their representative. White members of rural churches eagerly embraced the change in the constitution, suggesting that they felt a degree of investment in the codification of white male privilege above the specific controversy. Indeed, the association requested a change only in the first article of its constitution, so Elam's more sweeping idea that *white* should precede *male members* in every instance is suggestive. See Minutes of the Virginia Portsmouth Baptist Association, 1838–42, VBHS. See also Raboteau, *Slave Religion,* 188–89.

92. Tucker's Swamp Baptist Church, Minute Book, 1818–1857, 7 June 1844, 24 August 1853.

93. Cornelia Carney, interview, n.d., in Perdue, Barden, and Phillips, *Weevils in the Wheat,* 67.

94. "Minutes of the Portsmouth Baptist Association . . . 1832," 25.

95. Allen Crawford, interview, 25 June 1937, in Perdue, Barden, and Phillips, *Weevils in the Wheat,* 76. See also French, *Rebellious Slave,* 205–6. On the lack of female participation in the rebellion, see Greenberg, "*Confessions of Nat Turner:* Text and Context," 12–13.

96. South Quay Baptist Church, Minute Book, 1775–1827, 4 March 1814.

97. See, e.g., Snay, *Gospel of Disunion;* and Ambrose, "Of Stations and Relations." See also the works cited in n. 7, above.

EPILOGUE

1. Crofts, *Old Southampton,* 243–44.

2. Ibid.

3. Ibid., 243.

4. See "Minutes of the Forty-Eighth Session of the Virginia Portsmouth Baptist Association held with the Newville Church, Sussex County, Va., May 23rd, 24th,

25th and 26th 1838" (1838), VBHS; and "Minutes of the Fifty-Second Session of the Virginia Portsmouth Baptist Association held at the Market Street Church, Petersburg May 28th, 29th, 30th, and 31st, 1842" (1842), 6, VBHS. See also Raboteau, *Slave Religion*, 188–89.

5. "Minutes of the Forty-Ninth Session of the Virginia Portsmouth Baptist Association held at Sycamore Hill Meeting House, Norfolk County, May 22nd, 23rd, 24th, and 25th 1839" (1839), 8, VBHS.

6. Raccoon Swamp [Antioch] Baptist Church, Minute Book, 1837–1892, 11 June 1837.

7. *Virginia Gazette* (Purdie & Dixon), 20 February 1772.

8. See South Quay Baptist Church, Minute Book, 1827–1899, minutes for 1835–37; and "Minutes of the Forty-Sixth Session of the Virginia Portsmouth Baptist Association, held at Pungo Church, Princess Anne County, Virginia, May 21st, 22nd, 23rd, 1836" (1836), 4, 7–8, 14, VBHS.

9. See Loveland, *Southern Evangelicals and the Social Order.*

10. Tucker's Swamp Baptist Church, Minute Book, 1818–1857, 6 September 1844.

11. Black Creek Baptist Church, Minute Book, 1818–1862, June, July 1841.

12. James B. Taylor, *Virginia Baptist Ministers,* 161–71. Carlos R. Allen also points out Taylor's omissions in his introduction to Barrow's circular letter. Allen, "David Barrow's *Circular Letter,*" 442.

BIBLIOGRAPHY

Archival Sources

David Library of the American Revolution, Washington Crossing, PA.
Barrow, David. "Rev. David Barrow's Journal & some notes." Copy in hand of John D.
    Shane (1812–64). Lyman C. Draper Manuscripts, series CC, Kentucky Papers.
    12CC 164–85. Microfilm.
Barrow, William. "Memorial of William Barrow." Lyman C. Draper Manuscripts,
    series CC, Kentucky Papers. 12CC 190–91, 210–12. Microfilm.
Miscellaneous Papers of the Continental Congress, 1774–1789. M332. Microfilm.

Kentucky Historical Society, Frankfort.
Bryan's Station Baptist Church, Minute Book, 1786–1901. Microfilm.

Library of Virginia, Richmond.
Church Records
Albemarle Parish Register, 1717–1778, 1781–1782, 1787.
Barrett's Christian Church, Minute Book, 1832–1839.
Beaver Dam Baptist Church, Minute Book, 1828–1894.
Black Creek Baptist Church, Minute Book, 1776–1804.
High Hills [of Nottoway] Baptist Church, Minute Book, 1787–1845.
Mill Creek Baptist Church, Minute Book, 1789–1847.
Mill Swamp Baptist Church, Minute Book, 1777–1790.
Mill Swamp Baptist Church, Minute Book, 1791–1811.
Mill Swamp Baptist Church, Minute Book, 1812–1840.
Raccoon Swamp [Antioch] Baptist Church, Minute Book, 1772–1837.
Raccoon Swamp [Antioch] Baptist Church, Minute Book, 1837–1892.
Smith's Creek Baptist Church, Minute Book, 1779–1805.

South Quay Baptist Church, Minute Book, 1775–1827. Microfilm.

South Quay Baptist Church, Minute Book, 1827–1899. Microfilm.

County Court Records

Isle of Wight County, Deed Books 15–20, 1782–1808. Microfilm.

Isle of Wight County Court, Order Book, 1772–1780. Microfilm.

Southampton County, Committee of Safety Proceedings, 1775–1776. Microfilm.

Southampton County, Deed Books 5–11, 1773–1809. Microfilm.

Southampton County Court, Minute Book, 1775–1778. Microfilm.

Southampton County Court, Minute Book, 1786–1790. Microfilm.

Sussex County, Deed Books F–K, 1779–1812. Microfilm.

Tax Records

Isle of Wight County Personal Property Tax Lists, 1782, 1815, 1840. Microfilm.

Southampton County Land Tax List, 1782. Microfilm.

Southampton County Personal Property Tax Lists, 1782, 1815, 1840. Microfilm.

Sussex County Personal Property Tax Lists, 1782, 1815, 1840. Microfilm.

Other Sources

Virginia General Assembly, Religious Petitions, 1774–1802. Microfilm.

NATIONAL ARCHIVES AND RECORDS ADMINISTRATION RESEARCH CENTER, PHILADELPHIA, PA.

U.S. Bureau of the Census, Federal Manuscript Censuses of 1810 and 1830 for Isle of Wight, Southampton, and Sussex Counties. Microfilm.

UNIVERSITY OF KENTUCKY LIBRARY, SPECIAL COLLECTIONS, LEXINGTON.

David's Fork Baptist Church, Records, 1802–1937. Microfilm.

Lulbegrud Baptist Church, Minutes, 1793–1804, 1818–1820, 1835–1903. Clark County Records, M-235, reel 51. Microfilm.

Marble Creek [East Hickman] Baptist Church, Minute Book, 1787–1842. Typescript.

"Transcript of the Minutes of the South Kentucky Association of Baptists from 1787 to 1803 and the Minutes of the North District Association of Baptists from 1803 to 1823." Typescript.

VAN PELT LIBRARY, UNIVERSITY OF PENNSYLVANIA, PHILADELPHIA.

Church Records

Albemarle [Buck Mountain, Chestnut Grove] Baptist Church, Minutes, 1773–1779, 1792–1811. Minute Books of Baptist Congregations in Eighteenth-Century Virginia. Microfilm.

Broad Run Baptist Church, Minutes, 1762–1873. Minute Books of Baptist Congregations in Eighteenth-Century Virginia. Microfilm.

Chesterfield Baptist Church, Minutes, 1773–1788. Minute Books of Baptist Congregations in Eighteenth-Century Virginia. Microfilm.

Hartwood-Potomac Baptist Church, Minutes, 1771–1859. Minute Books of Baptist Congregations in Eighteenth-Century Virginia. Microfilm.

Meherrin Baptist Church, Minutes, 1771–1837. Minute Books of Baptist Congregations in Eighteenth-Century Virginia. Microfilm.

Morattico Baptist Church, Minutes, 1778–1787, 1792–1844. Minute Books of Baptist Congregations in Eighteenth-Century Virginia. Microfilm.

Tussekiah Baptist Church, Minutes, 1784–1833. Minute Books of Baptist Congregations in Eighteenth-Century Virginia. Microfilm.

Other Sources

Cobb, Daniel William. Diary, 1842–1872. Records of Antebellum Southern Plantations. Series M, section 3, reel 5. Mss5:1C6334:1–25. Microfilm.

———. Student Notebook, 1825. Records of Antebellum Southern Plantations. Series M, section 3, reel 5. Mss5:4C6334:1. Microfilm.

Edwards, Morgan. "Materials Towards A History of the Baptists in the Province of Virginia." 1772. Typed from the original manuscript, in the possession of Mr. Alester G. Furman, of Greenville, SC. Microfilm.

Story, Elliott Lemuel. Diary, 1838–1876. Records of Antebellum Southern Plantations. Series M, section 3, reel 33. Mss5:1St762:1–6. Microfilm.

Virginia Baptist Historical Society, University of Richmond.

Church Records

Black Creek Baptist Church, Minute Book, 1804–1818.

Black Creek Baptist Church, Minute Book, 1818–1862.

Buck Marsh Baptist Church, Minute Book, 1785–1803.

Seacock [Elam] Baptist Church, Minute Book, 1819–1839.

Seacock [Elam] Baptist Church, Minute Book, 1832–1889.

Shoulder's Hill Baptist Church, Minute Book, 1783–1923. Typescript.

Smithfield Baptist Church, Minute Book, 1830–1894.

Tucker's Swamp Baptist Church, Minute Book, 1818–1830.

Tucker's Swamp Baptist Church, Minute Book, 1818–1857.

Upper King and Queen Baptist Church, Minute Book, 1774–1816.

Upper King and Queen Baptist Church, Minute Book, 1816–1836.

Other Sources

Barrow, David, to Isaac Backus. 27 January 1797.

Minutes of the Virginia Portsmouth Baptist Association. 1791–1846.

"United Baptist Association formerly Kehukee Association, Meeting at Davis's Meeting House, Halifax County, North Carolina, October 10–11, 1790." Typescript.

Virginia Historical Society, Richmond.

Baptist, Edward. Diary, 1790–1861. Typescript.

Collins, Christopher. Journal, 1803–1804. Hammond Family Papers, 1796–1836. Mss2 H1858b.

———. Memorandum Book, 1796–1804. Hammond Family Papers, 1796–1836. Mss2 H1858b.

Gwathmey, William. Diary, 1833–1834. Gwathmey Family Papers, 1790–1982. Box 2. Mss1 G9957 c FA2.

Madison, James, to John Leland. 23 August 1781. Mss2 M26538.
Todd Family Papers. 1825–1865. Mss1 T5662.
Wellford, Robert. Diary, 1814. Mss1 W4599 a6.

NEWSPAPERS

Virginia Chronicle and Norfolk and Portsmouth General Advertiser. 1792–93.
Virginia Gazette. 1750–80.

PUBLISHED SOURCES

"After Nat Turner: A Letter from the North." Edited by Ira Berlin. *Journal of Negro History* 55 (1970): 144–51.

Ahlstrom, Sydney E. *A Religious History of the American People.* New Haven, CT: Yale University Press, 1972.

Allen, Carlos R., Jr. "David Barrow's *Circular Letter* of 1798." *William and Mary Quarterly,* 3rd ser., 20 (1963): 440–51.

Allmendinger, David F., Jr. "The Construction of *The Confessions of Nat Turner.*" In Greenberg, *Nat Turner: A Slave Rebellion in History and Memory,* 24–42.

Ambrose, Douglas. "Of Stations and Relations: Proslavery Christianity in Early National Virginia." In McKivigan and Snay, *Religion and the Antebellum Debate over Slavery,* 35–67.

Andrews, Dee E. *The Methodists in Revolutionary America, 1760–1800.* Princeton, NJ: Princeton University Press, 2000.

Aptheker, Herbert. *American Negro Slave Revolts.* 1943. Fiftieth Anniversary Edition. New York: International Publishers, 1993.

———. "The Quakers and Negro Slavery." *Journal of Negro History* 25 (1940): 331–62.

Aron, Stephen. *How the West Was Lost: The Transformation of Kentucky from Daniel Boone to Henry Clay.* Baltimore: Johns Hopkins University Press, 1996.

Asplund, John. *The Universal Register of the Baptist Denomination in North America, For the Years 1790, 1791, 1792, 1793, and part of 1794.* 1794. Reprint, New York: Arno, 1980.

———. *The Universal Annual Register of the Baptist Denomination in North America; for the Years 1794 and 1795.* Hanover, NH: Dunham & True, 1796.

Ayers, Edward. *Vengeance and Justice: Crime and Punishment in the 19th-Century American South.* New York: Oxford University Press, 1984.

Backus, Isaac. *The Diary of Isaac Backus.* Edited by William G. McLoughlin. Vol. 3, *1786–1806.* Providence, RI: Brown University Press, 1979.

Bailey, David T. *Shadow on the Church: Southwestern Evangelical Religion and the Issue of Slavery, 1783–1860.* Ithaca, NY: Cornell University Press, 1985.

Balfour, Daniel T. *Southampton County and Franklin: A Pictorial History.* Norfolk, VA: Donning, 1989.

Barbour, Hugh. *Quakers in Puritan England.* New Haven, CT: Yale University Press, 1964.

Barrow, Asa. "David Barrow and his Lulbegrud School." *Filson Club Historical Quarterly* 7 (1933): 88–93.

Barrow, David. *Involuntary, Unmerited, Perpetual, Absolute, Hereditary Slavery, Examined; On the Principles of Nature, Reason, Justice, Policy, and Scripture.* Lexington, KY: D. & C. Bradford, 1808.

Beeman, Richard R. *The Evolution of the Southern Backcountry: A Case Study of Lunenburg County, Virginia, 1746–1832.* Philadelphia: University of Pennsylvania Press, 1984.

———. "Social Change and Cultural Conflict in Virginia: Lunenburg County, 1746–1774." *William and Mary Quarterly,* 3rd ser., 35 (1978): 455–76.

Beeman, Richard R., and Rhys Isaac. "Cultural Conflict and Social Change in the Revolutionary South: Lunenburg County, Virginia." *Journal of Southern History* 46 (1980): 525–50.

Berlin, Ira. *Many Thousands Gone: The First Two Centuries of Slavery in North America.* Cambridge, MA: Harvard University Press, Belknap Press, 1998.

Berlin, Ira, and Ronald Hoffman, eds. *Slavery and Freedom in the Age of the American Revolution.* Charlottesville: University Press of Virginia, 1983; Urbana: University of Illinois Press, 1986.

Beverley, Robert. *The History and Present State of Virginia.* Edited by Louis B. Wright. Chapel Hill: University of North Carolina Press, 1947.

"Bible of Rev. David Barrow." Transcript by Leon A. Pounds of genealogical information in the Barrow family bible. *Kentucky Ancestors* 17 (1982): 167–68.

Billings, Warren M. "The Cases of Fernando and Elizabeth Key: A Note on the Status of Blacks in Seventeenth-Century Virginia." *William and Mary Quarterly,* 3rd ser., 30 (1973): 467–74.

Bloch, Ruth H. "The Gendered Meanings of Virtue in Revolutionary America." *Signs* 13 (1987): 37–58.

Boles, John B. "Evangelical Protestantism in the Old South: From Religious Dissent to Cultural Dominance." In *Religion in the South,* edited by Charles Reagan Wilson, 13–34. Jackson: University Press of Mississippi, 1985.

———. *The Great Revival, 1787–1805.* Lexington: University Press of Kentucky, 1972.

———, ed. *Masters and Slaves in the House of the Lord: Race and Religion in the American South, 1740–1870.* Lexington: University Press of Kentucky, 1988.

———. *Religion in Antebellum Kentucky.* Lexington: University Press of Kentucky, 1976.

———. "Slaves in Biracial Protestant Churches." In Hill, *Varieties of Southern Religious Experience,* 95–114.

Boles, John B., and Evelyn Thomas Nolen, eds. *Interpreting Southern History: Historiographical Essays in Honor of Sanford W. Higginbotham.* Baton Rogue, LA: Louisiana State University Press, 1987.

Bolton, Charles C. *Poor Whites of the Antebellum South: Tenants and Laborers in Central North Carolina and Northeast Mississippi*. Durham, NC: Duke University Press, 1994.

Bond, Edward L. "Anglican Theology and Devotion in James Blair's Virginia, 1685–1743: Private Piety in the Public Church." *Virginia Magazine of History and Biography* 104 (1996): 313–40.

———. "A Brief History of Religion in Colonial Virginia." Introduction to Bond, *Spreading the Gospel in Colonial Virginia*, 3–71.

———. *Damned Souls in a Tobacco Colony: Religion in Seventeenth-Century Virginia*. Macon, GA: Mercer University Press, 2000.

———, ed. *Spreading the Gospel in Colonial Virginia: Preaching, Religion, and Community, with Selected Sermons and Other Primary Documents*. Lanham, MD: Lexington Books for the Colonial Williamsburg Foundation, 2005.

Bonomi, Patricia U. *Under the Cope of Heaven: Religion, Society, and Politics in Colonial America*. New York: Oxford University Press, 1986.

Breen, Patrick H. "Contested Communion: The Limits of White Solidarity in Nat Turner's Virginia." *Journal of the Early Republic* 27 (2007): 685–703.

———. "A Prophet in His Own Land: Support for Nat Turner and His Rebellion within Southampton's Black Community." In Greenberg, *Nat Turner: A Slave Rebellion in History and Memory*, 103–18.

Breen, T. H. "Horses and Gentlemen: The Cultural Significance of Gambling among the Gentry of Virginia." *William and Mary Quarterly*, 3rd ser., 34 (1977): 239–57.

———. *Tobacco Culture: The Mentality of the Great Tidewater Planters on the Eve of Revolution*. Princeton, NJ: Princeton University Press, 1985.

Brekus, Catherine A. *Strangers and Pilgrims: Female Preaching in America, 1740–1845*. Chapel Hill: University of North Carolina Press, 1998.

Brown, Kathleen M. *Good Wives, Nasty Wenches, and Anxious Patriarchs: Gender, Race, and Power in Colonial Virginia*. Chapel Hill: University of North Carolina Press, 1996.

Bruce, Dickson D. *And They All Sang Hallelujah: Plain-Folk Camp-Meeting Religion, 1800–1845*. Knoxville: University of Tennessee Press, 1974.

———. "Religion, Society and Culture in the Old South: A Comparative View." *American Quarterly* 26 (1974): 399–416.

Buckley, Thomas E., SJ. "After Disestablishment: Thomas Jefferson's Wall of Separation in Antebellum Virginia." *Journal of Southern History* 61 (1995): 445–80.

———. *Church and State in Revolutionary Virginia, 1776–1787*. Charlottesville: University Press of Virginia, 1977.

———. "Evangelicals Triumphant: The Baptists' Assault on the Virginia Glebes, 1786–1801." *William and Mary Quarterly*, 3rd ser., 45 (1988): 33–69.

———. "The Use and Abuse of Jefferson's Statute: Separating Church and State in Nineteenth-Century Virginia." In Hutson, *Religion and the New Republic*, 41–63.

Burkitt, Lemuel, and Jesse Read. *A Concise History of the Kehukee Baptist Associa-

tion from its Original Rise Down to 1803. 1803. Edited by Henry L. Burkitt. 1850. Reprint, New York: Arno, 1980.

Butler, Jon. *Awash in a Sea of Faith: Christianizing the American People.* Cambridge, MA: Harvard University Press, 1990.

———. "Enlarging the Bonds of Christ: Slavery, Evangelicalism, and the Christianization of the White South, 1690–1790." In Sweet, *Evangelical Tradition in America.*

Butterfield, Kevin. "Puritans and Religious Strife in the Early Chesapeake." *Virginia Magazine of History and Biography* 109 (2001): 5–36.

Bynum, Victoria E. *Unruly Women: The Politics of Social and Sexual Control in the Old South.* Chapel Hill: University of North Carolina Press, 1992.

Calendar of Virginia State Papers and Other Manuscripts from August 11, 1792, to December 31, 1793 Preserved in the Capitol at Richmond. Edited by Sherwin McRae. Vol. 6. 1886. Reprint, New York: Kraus Reprints, 1968.

Calhoon, Robert M. *Evangelicals and Conservatives in the Early South, 1740–1861.* Columbia: University of South Carolina Press, 1988.

Carr, Lois Green, and Lorena S. Walsh. "The Planter's Wife: The Experience of White Women in Seventeenth-Century Maryland." *William and Mary Quarterly*, 3rd ser., 34 (1977): 542–71.

Clark, Richard. "'The Gangreen of Quakerism': An Anti-Quaker Anglican Offensive in England after the Glorious Revolution." *Journal of Religious History* 11 (1981): 404–29.

Clayton, Bruce, and John Salmond, eds. *Varieties of Southern History: New Essays on a Region and Its People.* Westport, CT: Greenwood, 1996.

Clinton, Catherine, and Michele Gillespie, eds. *The Devil's Lane: Sex and Race in the Early South.* New York: Oxford University Press, 1997.

Cohen, Charles L. "The 'Liberty or Death' Speech: A Note on Religion and Revolutionary Rhetoric." *William and Mary Quarterly*, 3rd ser., 38 (1981): 702–17.

Crimson, Leo T. "Virginia Baptist Ministers Who Migrated to Kentucky before 1800." *Virginia Baptist Register* 16 (1977): 757–71.

———. "Virginia's Contribution to Kentucky Baptists." *Virginia Baptist Register* 17 (1978): 832–40.

Crofts, Daniel W. *Old Southampton: Politics and Society in a Virginia County, 1834–1869.* Charlottesville: University Press of Virginia, 1992.

Cromwell, John W. "The Aftermath of Nat Turner's Insurrection." *Journal of Negro History* 5 (1920): 208–34.

Crow, Jeffrey J. "Slave Rebelliousness and Social Conflict in North Carolina, 1775 to 1802." *William and Mary Quarterly*, 3rd ser., 37 (1980): 79–102.

Crowther, Edward R. "Holy Honor: Sacred and Secular in the Old South." *Journal of Southern History* 58 (1992): 619–36.

Daniel, W. Harrison. "Virginia Baptists and the Negro in the Early Republic." *Virginia Magazine of History and Biography* 80 (1972): 60–69.

Davies, Samuel. *Letters from the Rev. Samuel Davies &c., Shewing the State of Reli-*

gion in Virginia, particularly among the Negroes. Likewise an Extract of a Letter from a Gentleman in London to his Friend in the Country Containing Some Observations on the Same. London: R. Pardon, 1757.

———. "The Necessity and Excellence of Family Religion." In *Sermons on Important Subjects, by the Late Reverend and Pious Samuel Davies, A.M., Sometime President of the College in New-Jersey in Three Volumes. The Fifth Edition, to Which are Now Added Three Occasional Sermons Not Included in the Former Edition; Memoirs and Character of the Author; and Two Sermons on Occasion of His Death, by the Rev. Drs. Gibbons and Finley,* edited by Thomas Gibbons, vol. 2. New York: T. Allen, 1792.

———. *Religion and Patriotism the Constituents of a Good Soldier.* Philadelphia: James Chatten, 1755.

———. *The State of Religion Among the Protestant Dissenters in Virginia, in a letter to the Rev. Mr. Joseph Bellamy.* Boston: S. Kneeland, 1751.

Davis, David Brion. *The Problem of Slavery in the Age of Revolution, 1770–1823.* 1975. Reprint, New York: Oxford University Press, 1999.

Davis, Mary Kemp. *Nat Turner before the Bar of Judgment: Fictional Treatments of the Southampton Slave Insurrection.* Baton Rouge: Louisiana State University Press, 1999.

Dew, Thomas R. "Abolition of Negro Slavery." In Faust, *Ideology of Slavery,* 21–77.

———. *Review of the Debate in the Virginia Legislature of 1831 and 1832.* Richmond: T. W. White, 1832.

Dozier, Richard. "Richard Dozier's Historical Notes, 1771–1818." Edited by John S. Moore. *Virginia Baptist Register* 28 (1989): 1387–1442.

Dreisbach, Daniel L. "Thomas Jefferson, a Mammoth Cheese, and the 'Wall of Separation Between Church and State.'" In Hutson, *Religion and the New Republic,* 65–114.

Drewry, William Sidney. *The Southampton Insurrection.* Washington, DC: Neale, 1900.

Duff, John B., and Peter Mitchell, eds. *The Nat Turner Rebellion: The Historical Event and the Modern Controversy.* New York: Harper & Row, 1971.

Dunn, Richard S. "Black Society in the Chesapeake, 1776–1810." In Berlin and Hoffman, *Slavery and Freedom in the Age of the American Revolution.*

Edwards, Morgan. "Materials Towards a History of the Baptists in the Province of North-Carolina." Edited with an introduction by G. W. Paschal. *North Carolina Historical Review* 7 (1930): 365–99.

———. "Morgan Edwards' 1772 Virginia Notebook, Edited with Notes and Comments." Edited by John S. Moore. *Virginia Baptist Register* 18 (1979): 845–71.

Egerton, Douglas R. *Gabriel's Rebellion: The Virginia Slave Conspiracies of 1800 and 1802.* Chapel Hill: University of North Carolina Press, 1993.

———. *He Shall Go Out Free: The Lives of Denmark Vesey.* Madison, Wis.: Madison House, 1999.

———. "Nat Turner in Hemispheric Perspective." In Greenberg, *Nat Turner: A Slave Rebellion in History and Memory,* 134–47.

Eller, Ernest McNeill, ed. *Chesapeake Bay in the American Revolution*. Centreville, MD: Tidewater, 1981.

———. "Chesapeake Bay in the American Revolution." In Eller, *Chesapeake Bay in the American Revolution*, 3–54.

Escott, Paul D., and Jeffrey J. Crow. "The Social Order and Violent Disorder: An Analysis of North Carolina in the Revolution and the Civil War." *Journal of Southern History* 52 (1986): 373–402.

Eslinger, Ellen. "The Beginnings of Afro-American Christianity among Kentucky Baptists." In Friend, *Buzzel about Kentuck*, 196–215.

———. *Citizens of Zion: The Social Origins of Camp Meeting Revivalism*. Knoxville: University of Tennessee Press, 1999.

Essig, James David. *The Bonds of Wickedness: American Evangelicals against Slavery, 1770–1808*. Philadelphia: Temple University Press, 1982.

———. "'A Very Wintry Season': Virginia Baptists and Slavery, 1785–1797." *Virginia Magazine of History and Biography* 88 (1980): 170–85.

Fallaw, Robert, and Marion West Stoer. "The Old Dominion under Fire: The Chesapeake Invasions, 1779–1781." In Eller, *Chesapeake Bay in the American Revolution*, 432–73.

Faust, Drew Gilpin. "Evangelicalism and the Proslavery Argument: The Reverend Thornton Stringfellow of Virginia." In *Southern Stories: Slaveholders in Peace and War*. Columbia: University of Missouri Press, 1992. First published in *Virginia Magazine of History and Biography* 85 (1977): 3–17.

———, ed. *The Ideology of Slavery: Proslavery Thought in the Antebellum South, 1830–1860*. Baton Rouge: Louisiana State University Press, 1981.

———. *James Henry Hammond and the Old South: A Design for Mastery*. Baton Rouge: Louisiana State University Press, 1982.

———. "The Proslavery Argument in History." Introduction to Faust, *Ideology of Slavery*.

Fischer, David Hackett, and James C. Kelly. *Bound Away: Virginia and the Westward Movement*. Charlottesville: University Press of Virginia, 2000.

Fithian, Philip Vickers. *Journal and Letters of Philip Vickers Fithian, a Plantation Tutor of the Old Dominion, 1773–1774*. Edited by Hunter Dickson Farish. 1957. Reprint, Charlottesville: University Press of Virginia, Dominion Books, 1968.

Foner, Eric. *Nat Turner*. Englewood Cliffs, NJ: Prentice Hall, 1971.

Foote, William Henry. *Sketches of Virginia, Historical and Biographical*. 1st ser., 1850. Reprint, Richmond, VA: John Knox, 1966.

Foster, Gaines. "Guilt over Slavery: A Historiographical Analysis." *Journal of Southern History* 56 (1990): 665–94.

Fox-Genovese, Elizabeth. *Within the Plantation Household: Black and White Women of the Old South*. Chapel Hill: University of North Carolina Press, 1988.

Fox-Genovese, Elizabeth, and Eugene D. Genovese. "The Divine Sanction of Social Order: Religious Foundations of the Southern Slaveholders' World View." *Journal of the American Academy of Religion* 55 (1987): 211–33.

———. *The Mind of the Master Class: History and Faith in the Southern Slave-holders' Worldview*. New York: Cambridge University Press, 2005.

Freeberg, Ernest A., III. "Why David Barrow Moved to Kentucky." *Virginia Baptist Register* 32 (1993): 1617–27.

Freehling, Alison Goodyear. *Drift toward Dissolution: The Virginia Slavery Debate of 1831–1832*. Baton Rouge: Louisiana State University Press, 1982.

Freehling, William W. "Defective Paternalism: James Henry Thornwell's Mysterious Antislavery Movement." In *The Reintegration of American History: Slavery and the Civil War*. New York: Oxford University Press, 1994.

French, Scot. *The Rebellious Slave: Nat Turner in American Memory*. Boston: Houghton Mifflin, 2004.

Frey, Sylvia R. *Water from the Rock: Black Resistance in a Revolutionary Age*. Princeton, NJ: Princeton University Press, 1991.

Frey, Sylvia R., and Betty Wood. *Come Shouting to Zion: African American Protestantism in the American South and British Caribbean to 1830*. Chapel Hill: University of North Carolina Press, 1998.

Friedman, Jean E. *The Enclosed Garden: Women and Community in the Evangelical South, 1830–1900*. Chapel Hill: University of North Carolina Press, 1985.

Friend, Craig T., ed. *The Buzzel about Kentuck: Settling the Promised Land*. Lexington: University Press of Kentucky, 1999.

Fristoe, William. *A Concise History of the Ketocton Baptist Association*. Staunton, VA: William Gilman Lyford, 1808.

Gardner, Robert G. *Baptists of Early America: A Statistical History, 1639–1790*. Atlanta: Georgia Baptist Historical Society, 1983.

———. "The Ketocton and Philadelphia Associations in the Eighteenth Century, Part I." *Virginia Baptist Register* 27 (1988): 1365–82.

———. "The Ketocton and Philadelphia Associations in the Eighteenth Century, Part II." *Virginia Baptist Register* 29 (1990): 1482–1500.

———. "Virginia Baptists and Slavery, 1759–1790, Part I." *Virginia Baptist Register* 24 (1985): 212–20.

———. "Virginia Baptists and Slavery, 1759–1790, Part II." *Virginia Baptist Register* 25 (1986): 1257–74.

Garmon, Connie D. "The Role of Women in Georgia Baptist Life, 1733–1840." *Viewpoints: Georgia Baptist History* 12 (1990): 11–21.

Genovese, Eugene D. *Roll, Jordan, Roll: The World the Slaves Made*. New York: Random House, 1974.

Gewehr, Wesley M. *The Great Awakening in Virginia, 1740–1790*. Durham, NC: Duke University Press, 1930.

Goen, Clarence C. *Broken Churches, Broken Nation: Denominational Schisms and the Coming of the American Civil War*. Macon, GA: Mercer University Press, 1985.

———. "Scenario for Secession: Denominational Schisms and the Coming of the Civil War." In Hill, *Varieties of Southern Religious Experience*, 11–23.

Goldenberg, Joseph A. "Virginia Ports in the American Revolution." In Eller, *Chesapeake Bay in the American Revolution*, 310–40.

Greenberg, Kenneth S. *"The Confessions of Nat Turner:* Text and Context." Introduction to Greenberg, *Confessions of Nat Turner and Related Documents*.

———, ed. *The Confessions of Nat Turner and Related Documents*. Boston: Bedford Books of St. Martin's Press, 1996.

———. *Honor & Slavery: Lies, Duels, Noses, Masks, Dressing as a Woman, Gifts, Strangers, Humanitarianism, Death, Slave Rebellions, the Proslavery Argument, Baseball, Hunting, and Gambling in the Old South*. Princeton, NJ: Princeton University Press, 1996.

———, ed. *Nat Turner: A Slave Rebellion in History and Memory*. New York: Oxford University Press, 2003.

Grigg, Jacob. *Remarks and Selections on Some of the Most Important Subjects Lately in Dispute between the Christians, called Presbyterians, Baptists, and Methodists on the one hand, and those called New-Lights or Martialites on the Other. Together with a short account of a New Sect among the Baptists in Kentucky*. Lebanon, OH: John M'Clean, 1807.

Gross, Seymour L., and Eileen Bender. "History, Politics, and Literature: The Myth of Nat Turner." *American Quarterly* 23 (1971): 487–518.

Gundersen, Joan R. *The Anglican Ministry in Virginia, 1723–1766: A Study of a Social Class*. New York: Garland, 1989.

———. "The Non-Institutional Church: The Religious Role of Women in Eighteenth-Century Virginia." *Historical Magazine of the Protestant Episcopal Church* 51 (1982): 347–57.

Hatch, Nathan O. *The Democratization of American Christianity*. New Haven, CT: Yale University Press, 1989.

Henry, Patrick, Sr., Samuel Davies, James Maury, Edwin Conway, and George Trask. "Letters of Patrick Henry, Sr., Samuel Davies, James Maury, Edwin Conway and George Trask." *William and Mary Quarterly*, 2nd ser., 1 (1921): 261–81.

Heyrman, Christine Leigh. *Southern Cross: The Beginnings of the Bible Belt*. New York: Alfred A. Knopf, 1997.

Hickman, William. *A Short Account of my Life and Travels. For more than fifty years; A Professed Servant of Jesus Christ. To which is added a narrative of the rise and progress of religion in the early settlement of Kentucky*. 1828. Published by the Kentucky Baptist Historical Commission and the Kentucky Baptist Historical Society, 1969.

Higginbotham, Evelyn Brooks. "African-American Women's History and the Metalanguage of Race." *Signs* 17 (1992): 251–74.

———. *Righteous Discontent: The Women's Movement in the Black Baptist Church, 1880–1920*. Cambridge, MA: Harvard University Press, 1993.

Hill, Samuel S. *The South and the North in American Religion*. Athens: University of Georgia Press, 1980.

———, ed. *Varieties of Southern Religious Experience*. Baton Rouge: Louisiana State University Press, 1988.

Hockman, Dan M. "'Hellish and Malicious Incendiaries': Commissary William Dawson and Dissent in Colonial Virginia, 1743–1752." *Anglican and Episcopal History* 59 (1990): 150–80.

Hoffman, Ronald, and Peter J. Albert, eds. *Religion in a Revolutionary Age.* Charlottesville: University Press of Virginia, 1994.

Holton, Woody. *Forced Founders: Indians, Debtors, Slaves, and the Making of the American Revolution in Virginia.* Chapel Hill: University of North Carolina Press, 1999.

Horle, Craig W. *The Quakers and the English Legal System, 1660–1688.* Philadelphia: University of Pennsylvania Press, 1988.

Horwitz, Tony. "Untrue Confessions: Is most of what we know about the rebel slave Nat Turner wrong?" *New Yorker,* 13 December 1999, 80–89.

Hughes, Sarah. "Slaves for Hire: The Allocation of Black Labor in Elizabeth City County, Virginia, 1782 to 1810." *William and Mary Quarterly,* 3rd ser., 35 (1978): 260–86.

Hutson, James H., ed. *Religion and the New Republic: Faith in the Founding of America.* Lanham, MD: Rowman & Littlefield, 2000.

Ireland, James. *The Life of the Rev. James Ireland.* Winchester, VA: J. Foster, 1819.

Irons, Charles F. "The Spiritual Fruits of Revolution: Disestablishment and the Rise of the Virginia Baptists." *Virginia Magazine of History and Biography* 109 (2001): 159–86.

Isaac, Rhys. "Dramatizing the Ideology of the Revolution: Popular Mobilization in Virginia, 1774 to 1776." *William and Mary Quarterly,* 3rd ser., 33 (1976): 357–85.

———. "Evangelical Revolt: The Nature of the Baptists' Challenge to the Traditional Order in Virginia, 1765 to 1775." *William and Mary Quarterly,* 3rd ser., 31 (1974): 345–68.

———. "Preachers and Patriots: Popular Culture and the Revolution in Virginia." In *The American Revolution: Explorations in the History of American Radicalism,* edited by Alfred Young. DeKalb: Northern Illinois University Press, 1976.

———. "Religion and Authority: Problems of the Anglican Establishment in Virginia in the Era of the Great Awakening and the Parsons' Cause." *William and Mary Quarterly,* 3rd ser., 30 (1973): 3–36.

———. "Stories of Enslavement: A Person-Centered Ethnography from an Eighteenth-Century Virginia Plantation." In Clayton and Salmond, *Varieties of Southern History.*

———. *The Transformation of Virginia, 1740–1790.* 1982. Reprint, New York: W. W. Norton, 1988.

Jackson, Harvey H. "Hugh Bryan and the Evangelical Movement in Colonial South Carolina." *William and Mary Quarterly,* 3rd ser., 46 (1986): 594–614.

Jackson, Luther P. "Manumission in Certain Virginia Cities." *Journal of Negro History* 15 (1930): 278–314.

———. "Religious Development of the Negro in Virginia from 1760 to 1860." *Journal of Negro History* 16 (1931): 168–239.

Jarrett, Devereux. *The Life of the Reverend Devereux Jarrett.* 1806. Reprint, with a foreword by David L. Holmes, Cleveland, OH: Pilgrim Press, 1995.

Jones, Jerome W. "The Established Virginia Church and the Conversion of Negroes and Indians, 1620–1760." *Journal of Negro History* 46 (1961): 12–23.

Jones, Reuben. *A History of the Virginia Portsmouth Baptist Association, together with Historical Sketches of the Churches Composing the Body; Biographical Sketches of Deceased Ministers and Prominent Laymen, Moderators, Clerks, Assistant Clerks and Treasurers; List of Ministers Raised up in the Association; Also Interesting Statistical Tables.* Raleigh, NC: Edwards, Broughton, 1881.

Jordan, Winthrop D. *White Over Black: American Attitudes toward the Negro, 1550–1812.* Chapel Hill: University of North Carolina Press, 1968.

Joyner, Charles. *Down by the Riverside: A South Carolina Slave Community.* Urbana: University of Illinois Press, 1984.

———. "Texts, Texture, and Context: Toward an Ethnographic History of Slave Resistance." In Clayton and Salmond, *Varieties of Southern History,* 21–40.

Juster, Susan. *Disorderly Women: Sexual Politics and Evangelicalism in Revolutionary New England.* Ithaca, NY: Cornell University Press, 1994.

Kierner, Cynthia A. *Beyond the Household: Women's Place in the Early South, 1700–1835.* Ithaca, NY: Cornell University Press, 1998.

Kirby, Jack Temple. *Poquosin: A Study of Rural Landscape and Society.* Chapel Hill: University of North Carolina Press, 1995.

Klein, Rachel N. *Unification of a Slave State: The Rise of the Planter Class in the South Carolina Backcountry, 1760–1808.* Chapel Hill: University of North Carolina Press, 1990.

Kroll-Smith, J. Stephen. "Transmitting a Revival Culture: The Organizational Dynamic of the Baptist Movement in Colonial Virginia, 1760–1777." *Journal of Southern History* 50 (1984): 551–68.

Kulikoff, Allan. *Tobacco and Slaves: The Development of Southern Cultures in the Chesapeake, 1680–1800.* Chapel Hill: University of North Carolina Press, 1986.

Lambert, Frank. *Inventing the "Great Awakening."* Princeton, NJ: Princeton University Press, 1999.

———. "'I Saw the Book Talk': Slave Readings of the First Great Awakening." *Journal of Negro History* 77 (1992): 185–98.

Lee, Jesse. *A Short Account of the Life and Death of the Rev. John Lee, a Methodist Minister in the United States of America.* Baltimore: John West Butler, 1805.

———. *A Short History of the Methodists, in the United States of America; Beginning in 1766, and continuing till 1809.* Baltimore: Magill & Clime, 1810.

Leland, John. *A True Account of How Matthew Womble murdered his wife, who was pregnant and his four Sons, on June the 19th 1784. He lived in Isle of Wight County (in Virginia).* 7th ed. Worcester, MA: Daniel Greenleaf for Richard Lee, 1801.

———. *The Writings of the Late Elder John Leland, Including Some Events in His Life, Written by Himself, with Additional Sketches, &c.* Edited by L. F. Greene. 1845. Reprint, New York: Arno, 1969.

Levy, Barry. *Quakers and the American Family: British Settlement in the Delaware Valley.* New York: Oxford University Press, 1988.

Lewis, Jan. *The Pursuit of Happiness: Family and Values in Jefferson's Virginia.* New York: Cambridge University Press, 1983.

Lindman, Janet Moore. "Acting the Manly Christian: White Evangelical Masculinity in Revolutionary Virginia." *William and Mary Quarterly,* 3rd ser., 57 (2000): 393–416.

———. "A World of Baptists: Gender, Race, and Religious Community in Pennsylvania and Virginia, 1689–1825." PhD diss., University of Minnesota, 1994.

Loveland, Anne C. *Southern Evangelicals and the Social Order, 1800–1860.* Baton Rouge: Louisiana State University Press, 1980.

Lumpkin, William L. "Early Virginia Baptist Church Covenants." *Virginia Baptist Register* 16 (1977): 772–88.

———. *A History of the Portsmouth Baptist Association, 1791–1991.* Lawrenceville, VA: Edmonds, 1991.

———. "The Role of Women in 18th Century Virginia Baptist Life." *Baptist History and Heritage* 8 (1973): 158–67.

Magee, Rosemary. "Recent Trends in the Study of Southern Religion." *Religious Studies Review* 6 (1980): 35–39.

Main, Jackson T. "Sections and Politics in Virginia, 1781–1787." *William and Mary Quarterly,* 3rd ser., 12 (1955): 96–112.

Mason, George Carrington. "The Colonial Churches of Isle of Wight and Southampton Counties, Virginia." *William and Mary Quarterly,* 2nd ser., 23 (1943): 41–63.

———. "The Colonial Churches of Prince George and Dinwiddie Counties, Virginia." *William and Mary Quarterly,* 2nd ser., 23 (1943): 249–71.

———. "The Colonial Churches of Surry and Sussex Counties, Virginia." *William and Mary Quarterly,* 2nd ser., 20 (1940): 285–305.

Mason, Keith. "Localism, Evangelicalism, and Loyalism: The Sources of Discontent in the Revolutionary Chesapeake." *Journal of Southern History* 56 (1990): 23–54.

Masur, Louis P. *1831: Year of Eclipse.* New York: Hill & Wang, 2001.

Mathews, Donald G. "'Christianizing the South': Sketching a Synthesis." In *New Directions in American Religious History,* edited by Harry S. Stout and D. G. Hart, 84–115. New York: Oxford University Press, 1997.

———. *Religion in the Old South.* Chicago: University of Chicago Press, 1977.

———. "Religion in the Old South: Speculation on Methodology." *South Atlantic Quarterly* 73 (1974): 34–52.

———. *Slavery and Methodism: A Chapter in American Morality, 1780–1845.* Princeton, NJ: Princeton University Press, 1965.

McColley, Robert. *Slavery and Jeffersonian Virginia.* Urbana: University of Illinois Press, 1964.

McCurry, Stephanie. *Masters of Small Worlds: Yeoman Households, Gender Relations, and the Political Culture of the Antebellum South Carolina Low Country.* New York: Oxford University Press, 1995.

———. "The Two Faces of Republicanism: Gender and Proslavery in Antebellum South Carolina." *Journal of American History* 78 (1992): 1245–64.

McGregor, J. F. "The Baptists: Fount of All Heresy." In *Radical Religion in the English Revolution*, ed. J. F. McGregor and Barry Reay, 23–62. New York: Oxford University Press, 1986.

McIlwaine, Henry Read. *The Struggle of Protestant Dissenters for Religious Toleration in Virginia*. 1894. Reprint, New York: Johnson Reprints, 1973.

McKivigan, John R., and Mitchell Snay, eds. *Religion and the Antebellum Debate over Slavery*. Athens: University of Georgia Press, 1998.

"Minutes of the Elkhorn Baptist Association, Kentucky, 1785–1805." In *Religion on the American Frontier: The Baptists, 1783–1830; A Collection of Source Material*, edited by William W. Sweet, 417–509. New York: Henry Holt, 1931.

Montgomery County, Kentucky, County Clerk Tax Assessment Records, 1801, 1802, 1803, 1804, 1805. Transcr. Thelma M. Willoughby Dunn. N.p., 1996.

Montgomery County, Kentucky, County Clerk Tax Assessment Records, 1806, 1807, 1808, 1809, 1810, and the 1810 U.S. Census Record. Transcr. Thelma M. Willoughby Dunn. N.p., 1996.

Montgomery County, Kentucky Tax Records, 1797, 1799, 1800. Transcr. Thelma M. Willoughby Dunn. N.p., 1996.

Moore, John S. "Virginia Baptist Petitions for Religious Liberty, 1770–1798." *Virginia Baptist Register* 25 (1986): 1225–39.

———. "Writers of Early Baptist History: (1) Morgan Edwards." *Virginia Baptist Register* 11 (1972): 519–26.

Morgan, Edmund S. *American Slavery, American Freedom: The Ordeal of Colonial Virginia*. New York: W. W. Norton, 1975.

———. *Virginians at Home: Family Life in the Eighteenth Century*. 1952. Reprint, Charlottesville: University Press of Virginia, 1968.

Morgan, Philip D. *Slave Counterpoint: Black Culture in the Eighteenth-Century Chesapeake and Lowcountry*. Chapel Hill: University of North Carolina Press, 1998.

Morris, Brian. *Anthropological Studies of Religion: An Introductory Text*. Cambridge: Cambridge University Press, 1987.

Najar, Monica. "Citizens of the Church: Baptist Churches and the Construction of Civil Order in the Upper South." *American Baptist Quarterly* 16 (1997): 206–18.

———. "'Meddling with Emancipation': Baptists, Authority, and the Rift over Slavery in the Upper South." *Journal of the Early Republic* 25 (2005): 157–86.

Nelson, John K. *A Blessed Company: Parishes, Parsons, and Parishioners in Anglican Virginia, 1690–1776*. Chapel Hill: University of North Carolina Press, 2001.

Nichols, Michael. "Passing Through This Troublesome World: Free Blacks in the Early Southside." *Virginia Magazine of History and Biography* 92 (1984): 50–70.

Norton, Mary Beth. "The Evolution of White Women's Experience in Early America." *American Historical Review* 89 (1984): 593–619.

———. "Gender and Defamation in Seventeenth-Century Maryland." *William and Mary Quarterly*, 3rd ser., 44 (1987): 3–39.

Oakes, James. *The Ruling Race: A History of American Slaveholders*. New York: Alfred A. Knopf, 1982.

———. *Slavery and Freedom: An Interpretation of the Old South*. New York: W. W. Norton, 1990.

Oates, Stephen B. *The Fires of Jubilee: Nat Turner's Fierce Rebellion*. New York: Harper & Row, 1975.

"Old Documents." *Virginia Evangelical and Literary Magazine* 4 (1821): 538–52.

"Origin of Presbyterianism in Virginia." *Virginia Evangelical and Literary Magazine* 2 (1819): 345–53.

Ownby, Ted. *Subduing Satan: Religion, Recreation, and Manhood in the Rural South, 1865–1920*. Chapel Hill: University of North Carolina Press, 1990.

Parent, Anthony S., Jr. *Foul Means: The Formation of a Slave Society in Virginia, 1660–1740*. Chapel Hill: University of North Carolina Press, 2003.

Parker, John Crump. "Old South Quay in Southampton County: Its Location, Early Ownership, and History." *Virginia Magazine of History and Biography* 83 (1975): 160–72.

Parramore, Thomas C. "Covenant in Jerusalem." In Greenberg, *Nat Turner: A Slave Rebellion in History and Memory*.

———. *Southampton County Virginia*. Charlottesville: University Press of Virginia for the Southampton County Historical Society, 1978.

Payne, Rodger M. "New Light in Hanover County: Evangelical Dissent in Piedmont Virginia, 1740–1755." *Journal of Southern History* 61 (1995): 665–94.

Perdue, Charles L., Jr., Thomas E. Barden, and Robert K. Phillips, eds. *Weevils in the Wheat: Interviews with Virginia Ex-Slaves*. Charlottesville: University Press of Virginia, 1976.

Perkins, Elizabeth A. *Border Life: Experience and Memory in the Revolutionary Ohio Valley*. Chapel Hill: University of North Carolina Press, 1998.

The Personal Property Tax Lists for the Year 1787 for Isle of Wight County, Virginia. Transcr. Netti Schreiner-Yantis and Florene Speakman Love. Springfield, VA: Genealogical Books in Print, 1987.

The Personal Property Tax Lists for the Year 1787 for Southampton County, Virginia. Transcr. Netti Schreiner-Yantis and Florene Speakman Love. Springfield, VA: Genealogical Books in Print, 1987.

The Personal Property Tax Lists for the Year 1787 for Sussex County, Virginia. Transcr. Netti Schreiner-Yantis and Florene Speakman Love. Springfield, VA: Genealogical Books in Print, 1987.

Peterson, Merrill D., and Robert C. Vaughan, eds. *The Virginia Statute for Religious Freedom: Its Evolution and Consequences in American History*. Cambridge: Cambridge University Press, 1988.

Pilcher, George William. "Samuel Davies and the Instruction of Negroes in Virginia." *Virginia Magazine of History and Biography* 64 (1966): 293–300.

Pogue, Blair. "'I Cannot Believe the Gospel That Is So Much Preached': Gender,

Belief, and Discipline in Baptist Religious Culture." In Friend, *Buzzel about Kentuck,* 217–41.

Pybus, Cassandra. "Jefferson's Faulty Math: The Question of Slave Defections in the American Revolution," *William and Mary Quarterly,* 3rd ser., 62 (2005): 243–64.

Raboteau, Albert J. *Slave Religion: The "Invisible Institution" in the Antebellum South.* New York: Oxford University Press, 1978.

Reay, Barry. *The Quakers and the English Revolution.* New York: Palgrave MacMillan, 1985.

Robert, Joseph Clark. "Excommunication, Virginia Style." *South Atlantic Quarterly* 40 (1941): 243–58.

———. *The Road from Monticello: A Study of the Virginia Slavery Debate of 1832.* 1941. Reprint, New York: AMS Press, 1970.

Robson, David W. "'An Important Question Answered': William Graham's Defense of Slavery in Post-Revolutionary Virginia." *William and Mary Quarterly,* 3rd ser., 37 (1980): 644–52.

Ruether, Rosemary Radford, and Rosemary Skinner Keller, eds. *Women and Religion in America.* Vol. 2, *The Colonial and Revolutionary Periods.* New York: Harper & Row, 1983.

Sandlund, Vivien. "'A Devilish and Unnatural Usurpation': Baptist Evangelical Ministers and Antislavery in the Early Nineteenth Century; A Study of the Ideas and Activism of David Barrow." *American Baptist Quarterly* 13 (1994): 262–77.

Scherr, Arthur. "Governor James Monroe and the Southampton Slave Resistance of 1799." *Historian* 61 (1999): 557–78.

Schmidt, Fredrika Teute, and Barbara Ripel Wilhelm, eds. "Early Proslavery Petitions in Virginia." *William and Mary Quarterly,* 3rd ser., 30 (1973): 133–46.

Schneider, A. Gregory. *The Way of the Cross Leads Home: The Domestication of American Methodism.* Bloomington: Indiana University Press, 1993.

Schweiger, Beth Barton. *The Gospel Working Up: Progress and the Pulpit in Nineteenth-Century Virginia.* New York: Oxford University Press, 2000.

———. "Max Weber in Mount Airy, Or, Revivals and Social Theory in the Early South." In Schweiger and Mathews, *Religion in the American South,* 31–66.

Schweiger, Beth Barton, and Donald G. Mathews, eds. *Religion in the American South: Protestants and Others in History and Culture.* Chapel Hill: University of North Carolina Press, 2004.

Scott, Joan W. "Gender: A Useful Category of Historical Analysis." *American Historical Review* 91 (1986): 1053–75.

Scully, Randolph Ferguson. "A Gospel Fellowship: Evangelicalism, Republicanism, and Southern Culture in Southeastern Virginia, 1750–1840." PhD diss., University of Pennsylvania, 2002.

———. "I Come Here Before You Did and I Will Not Go Away: Race, Gender, and Evangelical Community on the Eve of the Nat Turner Rebellion." *Journal of the Early Republic* 27 (Winter 2007): 661–84.

———. "Somewhat Liberated: Baptist Discourses of Race and Slavery in Nat Turner's Virginia, 1770–1840." *Explorations in Early American Culture* 5 (2001): 328–71.

Selby, John E. *The Revolution in Virginia, 1775–1783.* Charlottesville: University Press of Virginia for the Colonial Williamsburg Foundation, 1988.

Semple, Robert B. *A History of the Rise and Progress of the Baptists in Virginia.* 1810. Revised and extended by Rev. G. W. Beale. Richmond: Pitt & Dickinson, 1894.

Sensbach, Jon F. *A Separate Canaan: The Making of an Afro-Moravian World in North Carolina, 1763–1840.* Chapel Hill: University of North Carolina Press, 1998.

Sewell, William H., Jr. "The Concept(s) of Culture." In *Beyond the Cultural Turn: New Directions in the Study of Society and Culture,* edited by Victoria E. Bonnell and Lynn Hunt, 35–61. Berkeley and Los Angeles: University of California Press, 1999.

Shade, William G. "Society and Politics in Antebellum Virginia's Southside." *Journal of Southern History* 53 (1987): 163–93.

Shammas, Carole. "Black Women's Work and the Evolution of Plantation Society in Virginia." *Labor History* 26 (1985): 5–28.

———. *A History of Household Government in America.* Charlottesville: University of Virginia Press, 2002.

Sheppard, Eva. "The Question of Emancipation in Virginia from the Revolution to the Slavery Debate of 1832." PhD diss., Harvard University, 2000.

Sidbury, James. *Ploughshares into Swords: Race, Rebellion, and Identity in Gabriel's Virginia, 1730–1810.* Cambridge: Cambridge University Press, 1997.

———. "Reading, Revelation, and Rebellion: The Textual Communities of Gabriel, Denmark Vesey, and Nat Turner." In Greenberg, *Nat Turner: A Slave Rebellion in History and Memory.*

———. "Saint Domingue in Virginia: Ideology, Local Meanings, and Resistance to Slavery, 1790–1800." *Journal of Southern History* 63 (1997): 531–52.

———. "Thomas Jefferson in Gabriel's Virginia." In *The Revolution of 1800: Democracy, Race, and the New Republic,* edited by James Horn, Jan Ellen Lewis, and Peter S. Onuf. Charlottesville: University of Virginia Press, 2002.

Smith, Cortland Victor. "Church Organization as an Agency of Social Control: Church Discipline in North Carolina, 1800–1860." PhD diss., University of North Carolina, Chapel Hill, 1966.

Smith, Daniel Blake. *Inside the Great House: Planter Family Life in Eighteenth-Century Chesapeake Society.* Ithaca, NY: Cornell University Press, 1980.

Snay, Mitchell. *Gospel of Disunion: Religion and Separatism in the Antebellum South.* Cambridge: Cambridge University Press, 1993.

Sobel, Mechal. *Trabelin' On: The Slave Journey to an Afro-Baptist Faith.* Westport, CT: Greenwood, 1979. Abr. paperback ed., Princeton, NJ: Princeton University Press, 1988.

———. *The World They Made Together: Black and White Values in Eighteenth-Century Virginia.* Princeton, NJ: Princeton University Press, 1987.

Soderlund, Jean. *Quakers and Slavery: A Divided Spirit.* Princeton, NJ: Princeton University Press, 1985.

Spangler, Jewel L. "Becoming Baptists: Conversion in Colonial and Early National Virginia." *Journal of Southern History* 67 (2001): 243–86.

———. "Presbyterians, Baptists, and the Making of a Slave Society in Virginia, 1740–1820." PhD diss., University of California, San Diego, 1996.

———. "Salvation Was Not Liberty: Baptists and Slavery in Revolutionary Virginia." *American Baptist Quarterly* 13 (1994): 221–36.

Sparks, Randy J. *On Jordan's Stormy Banks: Evangelicalism in Mississippi, 1773–1876.* Athens: University of Georgia Press, 1994.

Spencer, J. H. *A History of Kentucky Baptists from 1769 to 1885.* 2 vols. 1885. Reprint, Dayton, OH: Church History Research and Archives, 1984.

Spruill, Julia Cherry. *Women's Life and Work in the Southern Colonies.* Chapel Hill: University of North Carolina Press, 1938.

The Statutes at Large; being a collection of all the Laws of Virginia, from the first session of the legislature, in the year 1619. Edited by William Waller Hening. Vol. 11. Richmond, VA: George Cochran, 1823.

Stevenson, Brenda E. *Life in Black and White: Family and Community in the Slave South.* New York: Oxford University Press, 1996.

Stone, Albert E. *The Return of Nat Turner: History, Literature, and Cultural Politics in Sixties America.* Athens: University of Georgia Press, 1992.

Stowe, Stephen M. *Intimacy and Power in the Old South: Ritual in the Lives of the Planters.* Baltimore: Johns Hopkins University Press, 1987.

Sundquist, Eric J. *To Wake the Nations: Race in the Making of American Literature.* Cambridge, MA: Harvard University Press, Belknap Press, 1993.

Surin, Kenneth. "Liberation." In *Critical Terms for Religious Studies,* edited by Mark C. Taylor, 173–85. Chicago: University of Chicago Press, 1998.

Sweet, Leonard I. "The Evangelical Tradition in America." In Sweet, *Evangelical Tradition in America.*

———, ed. *The Evangelical Tradition in America.* Macon, GA: Mercer University Press, 1984.

Sydnor, Charles. *American Revolutionaries in the Making: Political Practices in Washington's Virginia.* New York: Free Press, 1965. Originally published as *Gentlemen Freeholders* (Chapel Hill: University of North Carolina Press, 1952).

Tarleton, Banastre. *A History of the Campaigns of 1780 and 1781, in the Southern Provinces of North America.* 1787. Reprint, North Stratford, NH: Ayer, 1999.

Tarrant, Carter. *The Substance of a Discourse Delivered in the Town of Versailles, Woodford County, State of Kentucky, April 20, 1806. With Some Additions and Miscellaneous Thoughts Connected With the Subject.* Lexington: Daniel Bradford, 1806.

Taylor, James B. *Virginia Baptist Ministers*. 3rd ed. Philadelphia: J. B. Lippincott, 1859.

Taylor, John. *Baptists on the American Frontier: A History of Ten Baptist Churches Of Which the Author Has Been Alternately a Member*. 1823. 3rd ed. Edited with an introduction by Chester Raymond Young. Macon, GA: Mercer University Press, 1995.

Terman, William Jennings, Jr. "The American Revolution and the Baptist and Presbyterian Clergy of Virginia: A Study in Dissenter Opinion and Action." PhD diss., Michigan State University, 1974.

Thomas, David. *The Virginian Baptist: or A View and Defence of the Christian Religion as it is Professed By the Baptists of Virginia In These Parts; Containing a True and Faithful Account I. of their Principles. II. Of their Order as a Church. III. Of the principle Objections made against them, especially in this colony, With a serious answer to each of them*. Baltimore: Enoch Story, 1774.

Tragle, Henry Irving. Introduction to Tragle, *Southampton Slave Revolt of 1831*.

———, comp. *The Southampton Slave Revolt of 1831: A Compilation of Source Material*. Amherst: University of Massachusetts Press, 1971.

Turner, Nat. *The Confessions of Nat Turner, the leader of the late insurrection in Southampton, Va. As fully and voluntarily made to Thomas R. Gray*. In Greenberg, *Confessions of Nat Turner and Related Documents*.

Upton, Dell. *Holy Things and Profane: Anglican Parish Churches in Colonial Virginia*. Cambridge: Architectural History Foundation and Massachusetts Institute of Technology, 1986. Paperback ed., New Haven, CT: Yale University Press, 1997.

U.S. Bureau of the Census. *Heads of Families at the first census of the United States taken in the Year 1790: Records of the State Enumerations; 1782 to 1785, Virginia*. Washington, DC: GPO, 1908.

U.S. Census Office. *Return of the Whole Number of Persons Within the Several Districts of the United States* [First Census, 1790]. 1802. Reprint, New York: Arno, 1976.

———. *Return of the Whole Number of Persons Within the Several Districts of the United States* [Second Census, 1800]. 1802. Reprint, New York: Arno, 1976.

———. *Urban Statistical Surveys: Aggregate Amount of Each Description of Persons Within the United States of America and the Territories in the Year 1810* [Third Census, 1810]. 1811. Reprint, New York: Arno, 1976.

———. *Census for 1820* [Fourth Census, 1820]. 1821. Reprint, New York: Arno, 1976.

———. *Abstract of the Returns of the Fifth Census* [1830]. 1832. Reprint, New York: Arno, 1976.

———. *Compendium of the Enumeration of the Inhabitants and Statistics of the United States as obtained from the Returns of the Sixth Census* [1840]. 1841. Reprint, New York: Arno, 1976.

Varon, Elizabeth R. *We Mean to Be Counted: White Women and Politics in Antebellum Virginia*. Chapel Hill: University of North Carolina Press, 1998.

Virginia Writers' Project. *Sussex County: A Tale of Three Centuries*. Richmond: Whittet & Shepperson, 1942.

Weeks, Stephen B. *Southern Quakers and Slavery: A Study in Institutional History*. Baltimore: Johns Hopkins Press, 1896.

White, Linda M. "A History of the Baptized Licking-Locust Association, Friends of Humanity." *Filson Club Historical Quarterly* 63 (1989): 453–68.

Williams, John. "John Williams' Journal, Edited with Comments." Edited by John S. Moore. *Virginia Baptist Register* 17 (1978): 795–813.

Wills, Gregory A. *Democratic Religion: Freedom, Authority, and Church Discipline in the Baptist South, 1785–1900*. New York: Oxford University Press, 1997.

Wolf, Eva Sheppard. *Race and Liberty in the New Nation: Emancipation in Virginia from the Revolution to Nat Turner's Rebellion*. Baton Rouge: Louisiana State University Press, 2006.

Wood, Betty. "'For Their Satisfaction or Redress': African Americans and Church Discipline in the Early South." In Clinton and Gillespie, *Devil's Lane*, 109–23.

Wood, Peter H. "'Jesus Christ Has Got Thee at Last': Afro-American Conversion as a Forgotten Chapter in Eighteenth-Century Southern Intellectual History." *Bulletin of the Center for the Study of Southern Culture and Religion* 3 (1979): 1–7.

———. "Nat Turner: The Unknown Slave as Visionary Leader." In *Black Leaders of the Nineteenth Century*, edited by Leon Litwack and August Meier, 21–42. Urbana: University of Illinois Press, 1988.

Worrall, Jay, Jr. *The Friendly Virginians: America's First Quakers*. Athens, GA: Iberian, 1994.

Wyatt-Brown, Bertram. "God and Honor in the Old South." *Southern Review* 25 (1989): 283–96.

———. *Southern Honor: Ethics and Behavior in the Old South*. New York: Oxford University Press, 1982.

INDEX